The Sociology of Food

The Sociology of Food

Eating and the Place of Food in Society

JEAN-PIERRE POULAIN

TRANSLATED BY AUGUSTA DÖRR

Bloomsbury Academic
An Imprint of Bloomsbury Publishing Plc

B L O O M S B U R Y
LONDON · OXFORD · NEW YORK · NEW DELHI · SYDNEY

Bloomsbury Academic

An imprint of Bloomsbury Publishing Plc

50 Bedford Square	1385 Broadway
London	New York
WC1B 3DP	NY 10018
UK	USA

www.bloomsbury.com

BLOOMSBURY and the Diana logo are trademarks of Bloomsbury Publishing Plc

First published in French in 2002

© Jean-Pierre Poulain, 2002, 2011, 2013 and 2017
English language translation © Augusta Dörr, 2017

Jean-Pierre Poulain has asserted his right under the Copyright, Designs and Patents Act, 1988, to be identified as Author of this work.

British Library Cataloguing-in-Publication Data
A catalogue record for this book is available from the British Library.

ISBN: HB: 978-1-4725-8620-9
PB: 978-1-4725-8621-6
ePDF: 978-1-4725-8623-0
ePub: 978-1-4725-8622-3

Library of Congress Cataloging-in-Publication Data
A catalog record for this book is available from the Library of Congress.

Cover design by Sutchinda Thompson

Typeset by Deanta Global Publishing Services, Chennai, India

Translation with the aid of Université Toulouse Jean Jaurès—Toulouse School of Tourism Hospitality Management and Food Studies (ISHTIA), Research Center on Work, Organizations and Policies (CERTOP) UMR-CNRS 5044 and Taylor's Toulouse University Center (Malaysia)

Contents

List of figures and tables

Figures

Tables

Preface

Over the last twenty years, the status of food and diet in the media has undergone a change. The endless succession of crises, the rise in obesity and in noncommunicable diseases, together with the food riots that took place in the spring of 2008, have all brought the subject of food to the forefront of public attention. Today, in addition to the benign articles discussing gastronomy, or nutrition and diet, there are pages devoted to food-related public policies and international relations. Food has now made headline news on a countless number of occasions. Following a process of epidemiological transition, degenerative disorders, cancer and heart disease have replaced epidemics as the principal causes of death. As lifestyle plays a part in the onset of these pathologies, the treatment of food and diet are viewed under the umbrella of preventive measures.

In a reaction to globalization, regional food cultures have been endowed with "heritage" status. The domain of fine cuisine, which had long kept regional food cultures at a distance, has now begun to view them as a fresh source of inspiration. In 2010, at the culmination of a lengthy process, UNESCO added the "gastronomic meal of the French" and "traditional Mexican cuisine" to its Representative List of the Intangible Cultural Heritage of Humanity, followed by the Mediterranean diet in 2013. In this way, table traditions and culinary styles have officially become examples of a cultural legacy.

The controversies accompanying the application of biotechnology and genetic engineering to food crops, and the production of biofuels from plant biomass in potential competition with that of food, have become the subjects of political debates. "Citizens' conferences" have witnessed public calls for moratoriums on the marketing of certain products and for the introduction of organic foods into school canteen menus. In various countries, the ministries of health and agriculture (sometimes in competition) have launched national initiatives relating to nutrition and diet.

The food riots brought the old question "How can we feed the world?" back into the spotlight. Thomas Malthus had previously expressed this problem in the form of two growth curves developing at different rates: one, representing food production, grew at an arithmetic rate, while the other, representing population increase, developed in a geometric progression.

In the event of the latter catching up with the former, the ensuing situation would be characterized by famines and wars. Many have already sounded the alarm, among them Josué de Castro, René Dumont, and Jean Ziegler, attempting to disassociate the problem of hunger from the domain of charity and to establish it as part of the international political agenda. To some extent they have succeeded and their gloomy prognoses regarding food availability have not come to pass—for the time being. Technological developments have brought about a considerable improvement in productive capacity, and this, coupled with a drop in birth rate that has occurred during the transitional process, is pushing this fateful moment ever further into the future. The famines currently being experienced are due more to problems of accessibility than of availability.

In this way, food and diet have become political, environmental, heritage, cultural, and public health issues. All these different domains represent various frameworks within which to investigate our modern world, and provide the social sciences with "food for thought." The topical nature of these themes in the 1990s and 2000s, both as a social issue and as a news item, contributed to a change in the academic status of food and dietary practices. Indeed, during the crises relating to "mad cow disease", the media called for comments from sociologists, who had been working on this theme for some time in an environment of relative indifference. Their discourse was heard; it played a part in identifying the symbolic, political, and scientific issues involved in the questions that could not be answered easily using the traditional knowledge accumulated through biological research, and which those responsible for managing the crisis interpreted in terms of irrational consumer behavior. Noted by press and public alike, the sociologists' comments confirmed the fact that eating involved far more than simply providing the body with nutrients. They were also noted by researchers in the human and social sciences, who discovered the potential interest presented by a sociology *through* food, in addition to a sociology *of* food.

This change in its social and media status has contributed to the scientific thematization of food and food practices.

However, some work was necessary in order to eliminate certain epistemological obstacles and to establish this subject within the domain of sociology and the social sciences. The French sociological tradition is characterized by the tension between a disciplinary approach based on the Durkheimian principle of the "social fact," and the Maussian concept of the "total social fact." The former adheres more or less scrupulously to the notion of the social fact as autonomous, while the latter is established within the tradition inaugurated by Marcel Mauss, as part of the concept of the "techniques of the body," according to which the disciplinary boundaries between psychology and biology are characterized by a certain fluidity. From the Maussian perspective, therefore, it is necessary to establish a pluridisiplinary dialogue. Once the boundaries are removed, this dual dynamic adapts itself perfectly to every aspect of the subject, allowing it to become established within the social space. In this way, human eating practices may be presented as a "social fact" (Émile Durkheim), a "total social fact" (Marcel Mauss), and as a "total human fact" (Edgar Morin). These three definitions all share the same principle—that the act of eating amounts to much more than the biological infrastructure on which it is based. Moreover, each of the definitions, from the first to the third and with ever-increasing emphasis, highlights the vital importance of implementing an interdisciplinary dialogue. The "food social fact" will therefore constitute the subject of this book.

The way in which humankind experiences the fulfillment of its dietary needs cannot be reduced to purely biological, technical, or even utilitarian considerations. That concept of fulfillment occupies a prominent position within the culture of each social group. Eating is a "social act"—indeed, a "social event"—an equally central aspect of both family and public life. The meal lies at the heart of the socialization process in the two senses of the word: it is a site of apprenticeship, where the life rules governing a group are learned, and a place of sociality, of sharing and conviviality. It would appear that obesity and other troubles related to dietary behavior represent the price to be paid by societies that tend to overlook this.

Man needs nutrients: carbohydrates, lipids, proteins, mineral salts, vitamins, water, and so on, elements which he finds in the natural products forming part of his environment. However, he can only ingest and absorb these in the form of food, more particularly, in the form of cooked dishes—in other words, natural products that have been developed within a culture, and are transformed and consumed in accordance with highly socialized conventional practices. Eating is, therefore, both a natural and a cultural act, through which these two focal points, so often presented in Western thought as opposite extremes, interlock and merge, and the social practices that it maintains likewise contribute to its organization.

As a physical manifestation of a culture's fundamental values, culinary activity and table manners provide us with an ideal domain within which to observe social representations at work. From the production, distribution, preparation, and consumption of food, the act of eating structures the organization of the human group, establishing itself as a vital subject for socio-anthropological research. Food cultures demonstrate the specific character of the bio-anthropological connection between a human group and its biotope. Although this has been recognized by a certain number of researchers, ethnologists, sociologists, anthropologists, historians, and geographers, it has nonetheless proved somewhat difficult to establish the subject as a legitimate domain within the human and social sciences.

The complex interweaving of its social and cultural dimensions with its biological and corporal aspects, together with its ubiquitous presence in social life, whether in a personal, everyday context, or on festive public occasions, has, arguably, cloaked the "food social fact" in a type of paradoxical invisibility with regard to science. France, the land that witnessed the birth of gastronomy, was perhaps more affected by this paradox than other nations, and experienced particular difficulty in accepting food as a subject for serious scientific study. And yet there was Roland Barthes, who left us all too soon, with his famous article "Toward a Psychosociology of Contemporary Food Consumption," as well as his superb introduction to the new edition of Brillat-Savarin's *La Physiologie du goût*. There was also Claude Lévi-Strauss, who, with *Le cru et le cuit* and *L'origine des manières de table*, attained the highest rankings based on bibliometric indicators, although for a considerable period of time that section of his work was relegated to the domain of theoretical curiosities and simply "written off" as examples of structuralist criticism. It was not until the late 1970s that the social sciences turned their attention to food, beginning with history and sociology. The next twenty years or so witnessed the emergence of numerous works on the subject, produced in a relatively clandestine fashion. This amounted to the construction of a scientific legacy, which was to come to light during the crises of 1990 and 2000. Historians, sociologists, anthropologists, and psychologists then found themselves required both to describe the phenomena most frequently interpreted by those responsible for managing the situation as "irrational consumer behavior," and to highlight the issues involved. It became apparent that cracks had emerged in the globalized productivist model based on the upstream processing of food products, although it had previously functioned successfully and had enabled the West to emerge from a period of atavistic malnutrition following the Second World War.

The aim behind this book, which was published in France in 2002 (but written between 1999 and 2001), was to reveal the richness of the studies exploring the social and cultural dimensions of food and eating.

Its standpoint is encapsulated in the use of the plural form, *Sociologies de l'alimentation*. The intention was to emphasize the fact that, through its complexity and the status of eating as a universal social activity, the study of food involves all the various paradigms and perspectives of the social sciences, thus underlining the need to establish a dialogue with neighboring disciplines. With hindsight, this use of the plural form has nothing to do with any suggestion of the relative immaturity of this domain pending the creation of a sociology of food, as I might previously have believed. Instead, it confirms the benefit of adopting a multiparadigmatic epistemological approach, especially with regard to this particular subject.

The second aspect of this book, which I would like to highlight, is the section devoted to gastronomy, which is presented both as one of the characteristic features of French culture and, at the same time, as an epistemological obstacle. It is characteristic in the sense that the attitude toward it is not confined solely to the affluent classes, but is shared by society as a whole, for reasons based on various sociohistorical considerations. It is an epistemological obstacle because the subject has been the focus of a tension within the French sociological domain, between a critical stance based on defending the autonomy of popular tastes (in certain cases succumbing to a naïve populism), and the theory of distinction, whereby gastronomy was left in the shadow cast by the process of social differentiation.

Finally, works previously published in French and not widely known to the English-speaking world will be brought to its attention through the translation of this book, which is both a theoretical essay and an introductory guide.

Since it first appeared, there have been considerable developments in this field in the English and French-speaking worlds alike. However, they have followed somewhat different scientific routes. Food studies was mainly developed and institutionalized in the United States. At the same time, France and the United Kingdom continued their commitment to certain disciplinary bases, albeit from different perspectives: socio-anthropology in the case of France and cultural sociology in the United Kingdom. For this reason, we have decided to add a new chapter, with a view to identifying the issues arising from this dual trajectory.

As a way of completing and extending this work, we invite those readers undeterred by the French language to explore the dictionary of food cultures edited by us with the support of a ten-member international scientific committee.

In addition to its function as an inventory of the different disciplines concerned with the food social fact, this book forms part of a longer-term perspective. We are surely on the threshold, if not of a revolution, at least of a profound change in our conceptions of nutrition. The rapid developments that have taken place in nutrigenetics, nutrigenomics, and particularly in epigenetics, are remodeling the current view of food and diet by opening new areas of research and above all, of dialogue, between the social sciences and nutrition studies. The knowledge acquired in relation to food consumption models and the food social fact will therefore serve a dual purpose with regard to research and food education.

We are currently facing a challenge; this entails ceaselessly connecting and reconnecting the "nutritional" social fact with the food social fact.

As knowledge develops in the former domain through the identification of personal risk factors, this will inevitably emphasize the individualization of our relationship with food. The food social fact, for its part, serves as a reminder that eating is an act of sharing, a social, meaningful act established within cultural frameworks. The nutritional social fact and the food social fact constitute two aspects that contribute to the well-being and health of the human eater.

Jean-Pierre Poulain
Kuala Lumpur, March 2016

By the same author

Le tourisme dans les DOM-TOM, with G. Fontaine, Éditions Lanore-Dela-grave, 2004.

Penser l'alimentation, with J.-P. Corbeau, Éditions Privat, 2002.

Manger aujourd'hui. Attitudes, normes et pratiques, Éditions Privat, 2001.

Histoire de la cuisine et des cuisiniers. Techniques culinaires et pratiques de table en France du Moyen Âge à nos jours, with E. Neirinck, Éditions Lanore, 1987, 5th ed., extended, 2004, Japanese translation published by Dohosha, 1993, 1998, and 2005, Portuguese translation published by Colares, 1999, Spanish translation published by Zendrera Zariquiey, 2001.

Les jeunes seniors et leur alimentation, Cahiers de l'OCHA, no. 9, 1998.

Pratiques alimentaires et identités culturelles, Éditions The Goï, "Les Études vietnamiennes," 1997.

Abrégé d'ingénierie hôtelière et touristique, with G. Larosse, Éditions Lanore, 1997.

Traité d'ingénierie hôtelière, Conception et organisation des hôtels, restaurants et collectivités, with G. Larrose, Éditions Lanore, 1986, 3rd ed., extended, 1995.

La cuisine d'assemblage, Éditions BPI, 1992.

Vins et cuisine de terroir en Languedoc, with J. Clavel, Éditions Privat, 1989, 2nd ed.,1990, out of print.

Histoire et recettes de l'Alsace gourmande, with J.-P.- Drischel and J.-M. Truchelut, Éditions Privat, 1988, out of print.

Histoire et recettes de la Provence et du Comté de Nice, with J.-L. Rouyer, Éditions Privat, 1987, out of print.

Le Limousin gourmand, Éditions Privat, 1984, to be republished.

Le pot-au-feu, convivial, familial: histoire d'un mythe, co-author, Éditions Autrement, 1999.

Cultures. Nourriture, co-author, Éditions Actes Sud, "Babel," no. 245, 1997.

L'histoire du vin; une histoire de rites, co-author, Office international de la vigne et du vin, 1997.

Acknowledgments

This book would not have been possible without the research I conducted with colleagues and without long conversations with other researchers engaged with food. Among the sociologists involved are:

- Edgar Morin, who supervised my thesis in the 1980s, when the theme was not especially in vogue.

- Georges Condominas, to whom I am indebted for his theories, for Vietnam, his energy, and that meal at the Hue citadel . . .

- Claude Fischler, for our shared debt to Edgar Morin, for fresh territories revealed in France and abroad, and for all our reciprocal and friendly assistance.

- Jean-Pierre Corbeau, a friend and colleague at the "Sociology and Anthropology of Food" Research Committee, AISLF.

- Françoise Paul-Lévy, a friend whose radical approach and rigorous attitude to theory helped me to construct or reconstruct my positions during our long conversations.

  - Annie Hubert, for her solidarity, her knowledge of the technology of cuisine – both academic, as the heir to André Haudricourt, but also practical and gastronomic – for South-East Asia, Reunion Island and the smoked meats . . .

    - Jean-Louis Lambert; our encounters through various Ministry of Agriculture research programs were always fruitful and friendly.

    - Claude Rivière, for his encouragements and highly stimulating comments, and our shared interest in Guinea-Conakry.

    - Jean-Michel Berthelot, who guided me on a career change, and whose advice was a powerful motivator.

    - Christiane Rondi, an organizer at the AISLF, who always paid close attention to the work of the CR17.

    - Dominique Desjeux, as an editor who offered me his trust, and as the anthropologist whose works inspired me.

I am indebted to many in the medical world, to all those who fought to ensure that sociologists have a voice in nutrition sciences. Pierre Barbe and Jean-Pierre Louvet, who gave me a platform at the first colloquiums. Monique Romon, Bernard Guy-Grand, Arnaud Basdevant, and Luc Méjan, my advocates at the editorial committee of the *Cahiers de nutrition et de diététique*. INSERM's expertise on child obesity gave me both the opportunity to conduct sociological studies on obesity and to observe nutrition sciences at work. My utmost gratitude goes to: Gérard Ailhaud, Bernard Beck, Pierre-François Bougnères, Marie-Aline Charles, Marie-Laure Frelut, Marina Martinosky, Marie- Françoise Rolland-Cachera, Daniel Rivière, Daniel Ricquier, Christian Waisse, Olivier Ziegler and Jeanne Étiemble.

In the domain of agronomical research, Jean-Claude Flamand, Georges Borie, Jean-Marie Guilloux, Valérie Péan and the team on the agrobioscience project at INRA created a fascinating dialogue between the supposedly hard sciences and the social sciences.

In the marketing sector, Mohamed Merdji and Geneviève Cazes-Valette were keen to create a link between our disciplines, and became our friends.

In a domain such as the sociology of food, research activities can only be developed through partnerships with that of economics. The studies conducted with and for the CIDIL under the direction of Yves Boutonnat and Mijo Vernay, the Compass group, with Patrick Bénard, Christophe Mériot, Roger Genty and Pierre Auberger, and Nestlé France with Simone Prigent, provided the opportunity to collect the empirical data vital to scientific work.

I also owe much to the members of the scientific committee of the *Observatoire CIDIL de l'Harmonie Alimentaire* (*OCHA*): Marian Apfelbaum, Claude Fischler, Matty Chiva, Jean-Louis Flandrin, Marie-Christine and Didier Clément, Francès Huffer, and Maggy Bieulac, the tireless organizer.

Finally, I am very grateful to the members of the CRITHA team: Jacinthe Bessière, Jean-Marie Delorme, Muriel Gineste, Sandrine Jeanneau, Cyrille Laporte, Frédéric Zancanaro, Paul-Emmanuel Pichon, Jean-Marc Vanhoutte, Jean Zammit, and, of course, last but not least, Laurence Tibère, are all fully associated with this work.

List of abbreviations

AFSSA	*Agence Française de Sécurité Sanitaire des Aliments*
AFERO	*Association Française d'Étude et de Recherche sur l'Obésité*
AISLF	*Association Internationale des Sociologues de Langue Française*
ALFEDIAM	*Association de Langue Française pour l'Étude du Diabète et des Maladies Métaboliques*
ANAES	*Agence Nationale d'Accréditation et d'Évaluation en Santé*
AOC	*Appellation d'origine contrôlée*
BMI	*Body Mass Index*
BSE	*Bovine Spongiform Encephalopathy*
CNAC	*Conseil National des Arts Culinaires*
CNOUS	*Centre National des Oeuvres Universitaires et Scolaires*
CNRS	*Centre National de la Recherche Scientifique*
CREDOC	*Centre de Recherche et d'Étude*
ESRC	*Economic and Social Research Council*
FAO	*Food and Agriculture Organization*
GATT	*General Agreement on Tariff and Trade*
GIRA	*Gordon Institute Research Associates*
GMO	*Genetically Modified Organism*
HACCP	*Hazard Analysis and Critical Control Points*
IDC	*International Classification of Diseases*
INSEE	*Institut National de la Statistique et des Études Économiques*
INSERM	*Institut National de la Santé et de la Recherche Médicale*
IOTF	*International Obesity Task Force*

ISO	*International Organization for Standardization*
NAAFA	*National Association to Advance Fat Acceptance*
NIH	*National Institute of Health*
RHF	*(Restauration Hors Foyer) Non-Domestic Catering*
SNDLF	*Société de Nutrition et de Diététique de Langue Française*
UNESCO	*United Nations Educational, Scientific, and Cultural Organization*
WHO	*World Health Organization*
WTO	*World Trade Organization*

Introduction

Man needs nutrients: carbohydrates, lipids, proteins, mineral salts, vitamins, water and so on, which he finds in the natural products that form part of his environment. However, he can only ingest and absorb these in the form of food—in other words, natural products that have been culturally constructed and developed and transformed and consumed in accordance with highly socialized conventional practices. Cooking and the observance of table manners are social activities carried out within a space free of the material restrictions of an ecological, technological, and biological nature. Human beings' conception of the fulfillment of their nutritional needs cannot be reduced to strictly utilitarian or technological considerations. Food plays a structuring role in the social organization of a human community. Whether the focus is on production, distribution, preparation or consumption, it is a vital area of socio-anthropological scholarship and has been recognized as such by a large number of researchers in social and human sciences: ethnologists, sociologists, anthropologists, geographers, historians and psychologists. However, it has proved somewhat difficult to present the subject of "food" as a distinct category within these disciplines.

In the field of sociology, food practices initially appear to be a commonplace, almost standard theme, and one to which various schools of thought have applied their "explanatory paradigms." At the same time, however, they are also the subject of a theoretical paradox. These practices are almost invariably the focus of sociological scrutiny. Perhaps most particularly in the case of France, they serve as identity markers and as a means of developing a coding system to differentiate between social groups—and yet they have had difficulty in being accepted as a genuine subject for sociological study.

Today's sociologists are called on by colleagues who specialize in neighboring scientific disciplines—nutritionists, food science and food safety specialists, economists, administrators and political analysts—to attempt to elucidate what they term the "irrational" behavior of eaters or consumers in the context of a "food crisis." Food has long been confined within the categories of "health," "gastronomy" and "cookery," and is seen as one of those perennial, constantly recurring themes in articles of the "Want to shed those excess kilos before your holiday?" variety. In today's media, it occupies the prominent position reserved for major social issues or even worse, for scandals. Now it makes headlines in the main daily papers and is the focus of features on TV magazine programs or in the written press.

Still reeling from the shock of having to manage the "contaminated blood scandal," politicians in France have called on experts to attempt to identify the scientific and social issues underlying this crisis. A food safety agency, AFSSA (*Agence Française de Sécurité Sanitaire des Aliments*), has been established, and "citizen conferences" on food have been held. These public consultations are presented as a system for democratic risk management and a new tool for governance.

For over twenty years now, the signs of new scientific interest and activity are becoming evident. These come in response to an intense social demand from the general public as well as from public and private institutions, which are in a position to finance research into the social and human sciences.[1] There have been theses, scientific books and articles, commissions from institutions for research and studies, and more insistent questions from the public and the press. Ultimately, these could lead to a new definition of the theoretical status of this subject.

This work is intended to form an appraisal of the sociology of food and eating, or more precisely, the "sociologies," the plural form being more apposite at this point. Our study will be divided into two stages. The initial focus will be on contemporary food practices, the changes they are undergoing, and the permanent features that have become apparent. What are the impacts of globalization? Between "McDonaldization" and the re-invention of traditional local cuisine, what has become of food consumption models? What effects—described by some as disintegration—have transformations in the structure of our everyday lives had on our eating habits? What lies behind this feeling of crisis, of aggravated risk in relation to modern eating practices? Our aim is to see how sociology can contribute to our understanding of this phenomenon and to identify the social issues that underlie them. We will take the case of obesity and its development in the Western world as a means of analyzing transformations in attitudes to food. The medicalization of our daily eating habits will serve as our starting point with regard to the dialogue between the social sciences and human nutritional sciences.

In the second section, we will turn to the history of sociology to see how the chief schools of thought within this discipline have considered the subject of food while studying issues deemed more important. We will then examine the gradual shift that has taken place, from a general sociological interest in food practices to the attempts to establish a "sociology of food and eating." Indeed, from the 1970s onward, this subject was central to the work of certain sociologists and anthropologists: Igor de Garine, Claude Fischler, Annie Hubert,

Claude Grignon, Nicolas Herpin, Jean-Pierre Corbeau, Jean-Louis Lambert, and Jean-Pierre Poulain.

However, there are many possible avenues of study; these may form an extension to the sociology of consumption, or to studies of "body techniques" (the ways in which the body is used in different societies), to the sociology of culture, or to the sociology of the imaginary. It is actually more accurate to speak of sociological approaches toward food rather than a sociology of food.

Our interest, therefore, lies in the epistemological status of food within the domain of sociology and, more broadly, within French culture. In France, the history of sociology as a discipline and of its establishment in the university system, in competition with other disciplines, has had a significant bearing on the definition of its subject: social phenomena. This has created a sensitive situation with regard to the study of complex topics in which sociological, biological, and psychological dimensions all come into play. There have been all too few sociological studies devoted to the socio-historical phenomenon of gastronomy, that prime marker of French identity. Until its extreme complexity and the social functions it fulfills have been clarified, the development of sociological reflections on eating and food will be impeded. Finally, using the concept of the "food social space," developed in the work of Georges Condominas (1980), we will seek to discover the circumstances under which the sociological gaze falls on food and eating practices.

PART ONE

Permanent and changing aspects in modern eating practices

At the end of the Second World War, while hardship and shortages were still fresh in the collective memory, a productivity pact was formed between the farming sector and the French nation. The challenge quite simply involved feeding the entire population. Both cherished and cursed by the political world, French farmers, backed by agronomic research, accomplished a true technological revolution in less than two generations. This was to enable them not only to meet that commitment, despite their steadily decreasing numbers, but also to ensure the development of the agri-industrial sector, which spearheads the nation's exports today.

The history of food consumption in the Western world is marked by a fundamental break that occurred in the latter half of the twentieth century, when man lost his connection to his environment. Following centuries of atavistic malnutrition, everyone can now eat their fill; there are distinctive social practices, of course, but at least food is finally available to all (Aron 1987). A lasting impression of abundance—soon to become overabundance—was established.

These structural transformations in the food sector were accompanied by a change in collective thought. The early 1980s witnessed the emergence of a "new poverty," with people struggling to feed themselves just as European Community fridges were being piled high with thousands of tonnes of beef and butter taken off the market in order to maintain prices. Artists, singers and musicians then joined forces in support of the charitably founded "restaurants du cœur" (literally "restaurants of the heart") chanting the refrain: "No-one should be allowed to be cold or hungry today!" Underlying this generosity of spirit was a fundamental change in the value systems of Western society: eating had ceased to be the primary aim of the social group and had become an entitlement. No longer associated with "charity," which was rooted in religious sentiment or in the socially oriented political thought that had long prevailed, it now entered the domain of human rights. The right to eat was elevated to a fundamental value, just as the rights to healthcare and leisure time were established in the 1930s.

The year 1996 witnessed the eruption of the crisis related to "mad cow disease" followed a few months later by the row on genetically modified foods (GMO). The headline in *Libération* proclaimed: "Après la vache folle, le soja fou . . ." ("First mad cows, and now mad soya beans"). Food became a focus of intense media interest, with listeriosis and food poisoning in general making front-page news. It was discovered that our cows' fodder included bone meal made from slaughterhouse waste; this caused immense shock, which was symbolic in its nature. Here were herbivores being made to eat animal products and, worse still, products from their own species—when they were not being fed human placenta instead. Some newspapers ventured to run the headline: "From Mad Cows to Cannibal Cows."

The nightmare goes on. We have been informed that sewage sludge and used oil have been put into chicken feed. The slightest details regarding animal fodder, the conditions in which livestock are reared, and food processing methods are all out in the open. This world, hitherto unknown to urban consumers, is now brought to them directly by the TV news, just as they are eating their family meal. This is a world of increasingly sophisticated technology, manipulated by "sorcerers' apprentices" ready to sacrifice the laws of nature on the altar of productivity and profit. We are becoming appreciably more anxious about what we are putting into our bodies. "We no longer know what we are eating," and, if that is the case, "we cannot know what we will become" (Fischler 1990). The expression *"La mal bouffe"*[1]—known in English as "Frankenfood"—now serves to accentuate a perverted form of modernity. We gradually veer from crisis to scandal, toward the unthinkable.

Manufacturers would like to teach us how to "manage" the risks involved in eating, to reassure consumers, as they put it. However, entrenched in a techno-scientific culture of quality, they have difficulty in grasping the reactions of contemporary consumers, viewed as too irrational and accused of giving way to hysteria. They have equal trouble in understanding the insistence of the press on reporting the slightest incident, condemning this as irresponsible. For, ever since the mad cow saga, food, particularly of the *mal bouffe* variety, has become a regular feature in the media, and one that requires constant refueling.

Politicians have had their fingers burned by the contaminated blood scandal and are taking steps to cover themselves. Suspect products are withdrawn from the market in the name of caution, sometimes too hastily, and with no thought for the disastrous effects this will have on certain production sectors. Advisory committees are called on to present us with the facts. However, current knowledge is insufficient (and at times even contradictory), particularly with regard to new issues such as prion diseases. The situation requires caution, and conclusions are being expressed in a probabilistic manner characteristic of the scientific domain. This does not exactly serve to reassure the public or the media, who are seeking a simple yes or no answer to the simple question: "Is this dangerous?" This has led to a permanent feeling of crisis, and the proliferation of seminars and conferences devoted to food safety has done more to aggravate the situation than to alleviate it.

As troubles never come alone, so France, which has previously had a good record regarding obesity, with its astonishingly low prevalence rate in adults (barely 6 percent), now seems to have been affected by this problem. Indeed, child obesity is developing at such a rate that in twenty years' time it could have reached the same level as that of the United States (INSERM 2000). French specialists in obesity, following in the footsteps of their American colleagues, have spoken of an epidemic, with some even venturing to use the term "pandemic." Changes in our eating practices have been singled out for blame—notably the "Americanization" of our habits. This has had an effect on our national pride; we have been deluded by nutritional discourses such as the "French paradox"[2] and "Mediterranean diets," which are more or less imaginary in nature (Hubert 1998).

A challenge to globalization arose in the very heart of the Aveyron department, on the Plateau du Larzac. That iconic site had previously played a central role in the resistance to Promethean modernity that had witnessed the participation of the "'68 generation." A protest movement was organized, and a McDonald's restaurant under construction in Millau was destroyed—or rather, dismantled. José Bové, the leader of the *Confédération Paysanne*

(Farmers' Confederation), who was arrested and subsequently imprisoned, was the key figure in the fight against globalization. Armed with a few kilos of Roquefort cheese, he took part in a counterevent during the World Trade Organization summit in Seattle. Within a few days, the *Confédération Paysanne* had changed from being a somewhat backward-looking group to an organization that championed victims of globalization. In the early summer of 2000, the Bové trial brought the little town of Millau out of its provincial lethargy, transforming it into a world capital in the fight against *la mal bouffe.* French news weekly *Marianne* ran the headline: "Should we canonize José Bové?" Pierre Bourdieu even traveled to Millau to address an audience with the possibly unsolicited promise: "Sociologists will help you to get organized and lead the resistance!" This book is much more modest in its ambitions. We will simply endeavor to show how the sociology of food and eating practices may help us to understand the changes now in progress and to shed light on the issues underlying the current food crisis.

1

The globalization of the food supply: Delocalization and relocalization

1 Food becomes internationalized—through regional specialties

Never before in history have consumers enjoyed access to such diverse types of food as in the Western world today. The developments made by the agribusiness sector regarding preservation methods, packaging, and transport have considerably reduced the pressure on the ecological niche. Markets no longer operate at national level, as transnational agrifood companies distribute products on a world-wide scale: frozen meats and fish, tinned foods, cheeses, Coca-Cola, ketchup, hamburgers, pizzas and so on. Foods are moved from one country to another and travel considerable distances in the course of their lives, as they develop from seeds in the case of vegetables, and from birth in the case of animals, to become cooked meals. There are green beans from Senegal and cherries from Chile on the shelves in the middle of December, for those who can afford them. Juice, squeezed from oranges in California, arrives in Europe as a fresh product packed in cartons. Modern food has been delocalized, in other words, disconnected from its geographical origins and the climatic constraints traditionally associated with them.

In France, for example, a number of products that were still unfamiliar thirty years ago, such as avocados, kiwi fruit and pineapples, have become part of our everyday diets. Mass-market retailers have developed their exotic food sections and the number of products is constantly increasing. Soy sauce, nuoc mam, guacamole, tacos and taramasalata are all to be found in supermarkets. Prepared foods such as couscous, paella, tabouleh, spring rolls, stuffed crab, steamed Asian dishes, and moussaka, formerly regarded as exotic, now feature in our daily menus. There is even a trade fair named Ethnic Foods, which is entirely devoted to exotic products.

However, the negative aspect of the globalization and industrialization of the food sector is that products have become standardized and homogenized. The hygiene regulations and quality policies put in place by the industrial sector are intended to guarantee the stability of the organoleptic and microbiological characteristics of the products for the whole duration of their existence. It is open season on microorganisms. Taste often gets written off in the course of these agri-industrial advances. Fruits and vegetables are calibrated, and certain varieties developed through agronomic research have become a dominant presence on account of their high yield and the fact that they are easy to preserve. At the same time, we lament the disappearance of several dozen varieties of apples and pears.

McDonald's has become the world's foremost restaurateur. It is the leading restaurateur in France, that land of gastronomy, where its first outlets were greeted with knowing smiles and disdain when it opened in 1974. Today, McDonald's occupies a paradoxical place in the French social imaginary; it is both a symbol of *mal bouffe* and industrialized food production, and at the same time the formula it offers has now been completely integrated into the practices of a growing number of our contemporaries. To draw applause from an audience by criticizing McDonald's has become child's play, and yet with over 800 of its restaurants established in France in the year 2000 alone, there must surely be some French people who frequent the famous fast-food outlet and eat the allegedly *mal bouffe*—some of them may even be found among the cheering audience.

It would certainly be a mistake, however, to believe that national and regional specialties could disappear so quickly. They still enjoy a very prominent status, and transnational food companies are obliged to take them into consideration. McDonald's itself, which might be seen as a caricatural example of homogenization, has had to implement microlevel diversification strategies in order to adapt to the tastes of local markets. The initial approach applied by the fast-food restaurant chain had been based on the notion of "marketing the offer." McDonald's saw that offer—that is, its product range, which was developed through a highly sophisticated organizational structure—as an unchangeable entity. Its goal was therefore to remove any obstacles to the acceptance of its product by means of effective communication. However, faced with resistance from the markets, various alterations to its formula have gradually been introduced, in order to adapt to local customs—a true Copernican Revolution for the marketing men. For instance, beer is served in French branches of McDonald's restaurants, while in the United States, only nonalcoholic beverages are available. And in France again, as well as in Belgium and Holland, McDonald's fries are served with mayonnaise on the side, while in the United States ketchup reigns supreme (Lupton 1996, 94). The most surprising adaptation must surely be the creation of a hamburger named the *"Royale"* for the French market; this land of revolution harbors some strange nostalgic hankerings. In Québec, the fries are covered in brown sauce and cheese so that they resemble *poutine*—and Canadian lobsters are regularly transformed into "McLobsters" in the blink of an eye. In addition to these minor adaptations, which effectively customize their products, McDonald's restaurants serve halal beef in areas where strict religious culinary regulations prevail. Coffee provides a further interesting example of these microlevel adaptations. When McDonald's restaurants were first established, their coffee machines produced a mild, American-type coffee from concentrate, whereas technology has now been adapted so that the coffee on offer suits local tastes. On the same theme, Nestlé, the world leader in freeze-dried coffee, makes several hundred different blends to reflect the tastes of the different markets it serves. The coffee drunk by Italians is completely different from the beverage drunk by Danes bearing the same name.

Those who worry about "McDonaldization" might be reminded that specific national features are still a very strong presence. Although the Italians, Spanish, German, and French may well occasionally eat hamburgers from McDonald's or Quick, or a pizza from Pizza Hut, they are very far from sharing the same eating practices. The Spanish continue to have their meals at times that the French or English consider too late, and savor their *pata negra* ham, the secret of which is known to them alone. The notion of what constitutes a meal varies considerably throughout Europe; the German definition, for instance, differs markedly from the French (Pfirsch 1997).

2 Local food cultures as champions of identity

During the 1993 debate over Europe, the status of unpasteurized Camembert cheese was elevated, as it was transformed into a symbol of the French nation. McDonald's restaurants were now the target of grievances. There were unruly scenes of the type routinely associated with GATT agricultural trade negotiations and, subsequently, with those of the WTO; these included displays of public behavior, such as attacks on fast-food outlets and the burning of American flags, which were thought to have died out in our Western culture. Underlying these economic and social phenomena there are signs, and sometimes symptoms, of an identity crisis that has crystallized in the domain of food adversely affected by industrial processes. As food markets have become globalized, so local products have become more enticing. This process began in the late 1960s, which saw the emergence of a phenomenon that ran counter to continued growth and unbridled progressivism, and was described by Edgar Morin as the "neo-archaic" mentality. This functions "by means of a return to the values of nature that is characterized by two aspects". . . . "Nature . . . is celebrated as a contrast to the artificial world of cities, and the notion of 'Arche' (meaning origin, or root), which had been rejected through the former vogue for modernity as being commonplace and retrograde, has now become a principle [on which to connect with] the authentic sources of existence." It involves

> partially overturning the gastronomic hierarchy in favor of rustic and "natural" dishes. In this way, hotpots, country breads and large slabs of butter have suddenly appeared on middle-class dining tables, along with roast potatoes, various meats grilled on wood fires, and "natural" vegetables. Food lovers seek out wines, oils, cooked meats from the *charcuterie* and farm produce, rather than manufactured products. All this reflects the new appreciation for rustic simplicity and natural quality, no longer despised in comparison with the pursuit of quintessential perfection and the complex art of fine gastronomy. The previous opposition, between high gastronomy and rustic foods, has now been replaced by that of high gastronomy and rustic gastronomy versus processed food. (Morin 1975)

In the early 1980s, when the style then known as "nouvelle cuisine" was at the height of its popularity, the movement developed and took on a regional aspect. Inspired by restaurant guides such as *Gault et Millau*, which awarded points to restaurants based on the quality of their local dishes, or the *Guide Champérard*, to which we owe the expression "local nouvelle cuisine," renowned professional chefs enthusiastically embraced the regional theme. Shrewd cookery book writers adopted a markedly regional approach (Bras 1992; Vanel 1992).

Certain traditional publishers specializing in the human sciences have ventured into the domain of indigenous cuisines. As we wrote in 1984, in a work forming part of a collection published by Privat that was characteristic of this trend:

> If ever there was an urgent task to undertake now that tastes in food are becoming increasingly standardized, it is to catalogue the gastronomic heritage of the French provinces. We need to re-establish traditional culinary practices within their primary cultural context: the customs, beliefs and regional attitudes from which they originated. The recipes should be

reproduced in simple, modern language so that they are easy to follow: these are the aims behind the '*Itinéraires Gourmands*' collection.

These works were divided into two sections. The first part examined culinary traditions within the context of their heritage, explaining how recipes and eating habits became established in the course of the history of the region; the second section presented the great contemporary chefs whose "practices were revitalized by traditional regional cuisines" (Bourrec 1983; Poulain 1984; Poulain and Rouyer 1987; Drishel, Poulain and Truchelut 1988; Clavel et al. 1990).

In the "home-cooking" version of this trend, every region nowadays boasts its book of authentic dishes, from those of *Tante Toinette* to the "secret recipes from our farms in the Périgord Noir." Include a touch of the local dialect, a dozen or so sepia prints, and a few anecdotes about festive evening gatherings and carnivals, and the recipe will be a sure-fire success. In 1989, the Logis de France hotel chain launched a regional cuisine competition among its members; the best recipes were later published.

Having originated from gourmet restaurants, the movement has spread throughout the whole of the food sector. Local cuisine represents a new line of promotion for the artisan foods sector and for small and medium agrifood and winemaking businesses. It is of particular interest as a strategic resource in view of the development of green tourism (Poulain 1997a). Indeed, a great many institutional structures linked to the tourist industry, such as regional or departmental committees for tourism, visitor information centers, tourist offices and chambers of commerce, play a role in promoting this theme, together with local restaurants and food-related businesses.

The notion that you eat well in the French regions is not only due to the fact that in a regional location they are closer to the origins of their food, but it also reflects the city dwellers' image of local inhabitants as the custodians of a gastronomic heritage, perhaps even a wisdom, in which meaning and tastes are closely interlinked. Contemporary interest in local regional cuisines is part of the nostalgia for a "social space" where one might eat untroubled by anxiety, sheltered by a clearly identifiable, and identifying, culinary culture.

In a circular causal relationship, the food crisis is linked to an identity crisis; this has been reinforced within the context of building the European Community and the risk of France becoming diluted into a larger entity. As a result, the culinary domain has become a site for a number of issues that transcend the subject of food. In the turbulent atmosphere of the world farming crisis, McDonald's represents the lowest level of gastronomic culture, the antithesis of French food, of "real" food. At a time when the constitution of the European Union was being developed, unpasteurized cheese emerged as a symbol of identity.

In 1990, the French Ministries of Agriculture and Culture launched a vast inventory of the country's gastronomic heritage. Their urgency recalled the rush to produce ethnographic registers of vanishing cultures that had occurred during the 1960s. This mission was entrusted to the Conseil National des Arts Culinaires (CNAC), and the resulting work was published by Albin Michel Editions in a series entitled *Inventaire du patrimoine culinaire de la France* (Inventory of the French culinary heritage).

This was a curious turnaround! Here was the world of fine cuisine now paying attention to regional food traditions. During the *Ancien Régime*, the gastronomic practices of the aristocracy were characterized by its distance from necessity and want. The nobility confirmed its social status by consuming expensive products from far-flung lands (such as spices) and in so doing it emphasized the contrast between its own eating practices and those of the general populace, who were more subject to the restrictions of the ecological niche. French gastronomy was founded on the repression of regional, popular practices, due to the country's centralized political structure, and the establishment of the Court at Versailles, which drew much of the provincial aristocracy toward the capital. At best, any culinary reference to a region merely indicated the origins of the product in question. The regions were of no interest apart from the products they offered. This is reflected in the words of Alexandre Balthazar Grimod de la Reynière: "The most amiable compliment that provincials can pay them [Parisians] unquestionably comes in the form of a basket of oysters, carriage paid" (1802 [1978], 231). For in the early nineteenth century, good cuisine was only to be had in Paris.

Although middle-class cuisine may appear to have been more influenced by its regional origins, it was heavily dependent on the aristocratic model, which it continued to copy. This attitude first became apparent in cookery books dating from the late seventeenth century. The provincial bourgeoisie were fixated on imitating aristocratic Parisian practices. Only peasant cuisine, more dependent on the relationship with necessity, had a regional character (Poulain 1997a). In 1790, during the Revolution, the provinces of the *Ancien Régime* were dissolved, to be replaced by the newly established *départements*. The first movement involving regional cuisine then emerged. Food traditions, through their emblematic nature, became a site of cultural resistance. Subsequently, the Félibrige association, and various other movements devoted to traditional ways of life, viewed them as fundamental markers of regional identity, akin to language or sartorial customs. What could be more telling than the fact that when the pioneers of the Félibrige movement (who included Mistral, Roumanille and Aubanel) launched Occitania's great militant journal, they chose as its title the name of an iconic Provençal dish: *Aïoli*?

However, in the spontaneous discourse of consumers, and also in restaurant and tourist industry parlance, the countryside and its local cuisines are frequently presented as a traditional world in the simplistic sense of the term. That is to say, they are stable, having been founded on enduring tradition, in contrast to the changes, cycles, and trends that occur in the market economy. They are also authentic, in contrast to the artificial world of urbanized environments where man-made objects override natural phenomena (Warnier 1994; Cuisenier 1995). In this "authentic space," products and practices are based on use-value, rather than on a rationale of distinction. Consumer demand has given rise to an Edenic vision of the rural world and a sense of otherness, elevating it to the rank of an anthropological universe where human beings are in harmony with themselves and with nature: a utopian ideal of a happy rural existence.

A sociological, historical, and anthropological approach to regional cuisines completely destroys this naïve, folkloric notion. For the most part, the great, iconic dishes of our so-called "regional cuisines" contain products from the New World that were introduced into techno-culinary niches (preparation methods and consumption systems created around indigenous products) that had already been established before their arrival. This is the case with the *cassoulet toulousian* (Poulain 1996), the *millas* from Languedoc, the *ratatouille provençale* (Poulain and Rouyer 1987), the *gaude* from Franche-Comté, the *gratin dauphinoise*, and the *farcedures* from Limousin (Poulain 1984).

This myth of a lost culinary paradise calls for the involvement of the sociologist and the anthropologist from a dual perspective. The first question centers on the way in which researchers in the human sciences might participate in the reconstruction of these examples of heritage. The answer clearly lies in subverting this expectation, in order to uncover its meanings and social functions, and to reveal the so-called "traditional" cultures from a less mythologizing angle, through knowledge acquired by studying the ethnology of France (Cuisenier and Segalen 1986) and of Europe (Cuisenier 1995).

With regard to essential research, the emergence of the topical themes of tourism (Corbin 1995; Amirou 2000) and of eating practices as independent anthropological subjects offers genuine opportunities to develop our knowledge. Furthermore, the phenomenon of viewing food as part of our heritage has established itself as an ideal domain for interpreting social changes. These involve a transformation in the representations associated with the food social space. Food products (whether processed or otherwise), the objects and skills used in their production, transformation, preservation, and consumption, as well as social codes and cooking methods and the customs associated with eating and drinking—known in the West as table manners—are presented as cultural phenomena, which play a part in conveying the history and identity of the social group. They should therefore be preserved as reflections of cultural identity in a changing world. The idea that skills, techniques, and products may be objects that should be protected and preserved suggests that we feel, or at least fear, that they are about to vanish. The fact that food and gastronomy are classed as examples of our heritage, arose from changes to our eating practices that are viewed as a form of deterioration and, more broadly, as a threat to our identity. The history of food practices has shown us that whenever local identity is in jeopardy, cooking and table traditions are the favored areas of resistance. The cuisine of Alsace is an exemplary case in this regard. Whenever this province was under French dominion, gastronomic characteristics from the Rhineland were much in evidence, whereas under German rule, meals became "Frenchified" (Drishel, Poulain and Truchelut 1988). The current presentation of food as part of our heritage is one aspect of the vast movement that has shifted the notion of heritage from the private to the public sphere, from the domain of economics to that of culture (Fabre-Vassas 1993; Paul-Lévy 1997). Yet it is also the sign of other transformations in social representations. First, it extends the notion of heritage from the tangible to the intangible; popular, everyday practices are certainly a modest example of intangible phenomena, far removed from the prestigious works described as high art from the realms of music, painting or indeed poetry (Condominas 1997a,b). Contemporary sociology, reconnecting with Simmel's intuitions (1910), has taken possession of that social space, long regarded with derision and condescension in the domain of academic sociology (Maffesoli 1979; Schütz 1987; de Certeau 1980; Giard 1980). The most astonishing trend, however, is the transsocial movement that locates practices originating from working-class, middle-class, and aristocratic social spaces within the sphere of shared heritage, although some of these constitute an explicit aspect of the rationale of social differentiation. Gastronomy in the aristocratic or bourgeois sense of the term now appears to be the common possession of the French population as a whole. At the same time, local food cultures have been categorized as "gastronomy" and we now refer to the "regional gastronomic heritage" (Poulain 1997b, 2000; Bessière, 2000).

3 From our rediscovered regions to the realm of the exotic

In the late 1990s, when the first mad cow crisis was nearing its end, and was yet to be replaced by the GMO food row, a debate arose in French gastronomic circles. This saw the champions of traditional French cuisine (including gastronomic and regional traditions) pitted against the proponents of an international culinary approach that was open to fusion and intermixing, which was described by some as "world cuisine." The former presented themselves as defenders of the French culinary art, allegedly under attack by the agrifood industry, controlled by major international firms based in America, and reproached the latter for "selling off" both regional and classic French cuisine. Behind the globalization of food practices lurked the fear of American neocolonialism. The latter reminded them that French cuisine was based on a large number of different influences and has continually borrowed products or techniques throughout its history, without ever losing its identity in the process.

The taste for exotic cuisines and culinary intermixing shared by our great chefs is rooted in the same movement that led them to regional cuisines. Indeed, after fairly turbulent beginnings marked by the desire to break with the canons of classic nineteenth-century gastronomy, French nouvelle cuisine came to accept both learned tradition and regional, popular cuisine as sources of inspiration (Poulain and Neirinck 2000).

It was with this concept in mind that the great chefs of France traveled the world during the 1980s. They were invited to promote French cuisine, or in the case of the most illustrious among them, to act as consultants for international hotel chains or major industrial agrifood groups. Roger Vergé and Georges Blanc went to Bangkok, Joël Robuchon, Pierre Gagnaire, Bernard Loiseau and Michel Bras to Japan, and Michel Guérard to the United States. Paul Bocuse traveled more or less everywhere, his role now filled by Alain Ducasse. The major hospitality schools of Europe, North America, and Asia welcomed the most eminent ambassadors of French cuisine. The winners of the "Best Craftsmen in France" awards and the happy recipients of the fabled three Michelin stars all spread the good news of French nouvelle cuisine, now drawing fresh inspiration from regional traditions.

Interest in foreign cuisines is by no means a completely new phenomenon in French gastronomic history. Urbain Dubois, one of the great nineteenth-century masters, produced a work entitled *La cuisine de tous les pays* (1868). However, his perspective was somewhat colonialist, and, to say the least, frankly ethnocentric. He did not hesitate to alter those cuisines deemed "lacking in gastronomic qualities," adapting them according to the rules of the true cuisine: that of France.

What differentiates today's French chefs from their predecessors is that they have ceased to view other culinary traditions as subcultures in need of civilizing, and see them instead as new sources of inspiration. First and foremost, these encounters with other food cultures contributed to the development of skillfully created cuisines of local inspiration. They also facilitated the birth of nouvelle cuisine in Québec, Japan, Australia, California, Germany, and so on, now maintained, with true panache, by a number of young chefs.

These were to have a reciprocal influence on French cuisine itself, leading to the emergence of a nouvelle cuisine featuring a mixture of international influences, enriched by the use of exotic products and techniques. This influence was most apparent with regard to decoration. Contemporary dishes owe much to the Asian art of embellishment, particularly Japanese.[3] From a culinary viewpoint, it is important to note the way in which the range of spices in use has extended, following a number of changes. Initially added in tiny amounts, they now play a much greater role, and are sometimes elevated to the ranks of actual ingredients. The use of Asian steamer baskets has likewise expanded our range of food steaming techniques (Poulain and Neirinck 2000).

The appeal of regional cuisine has become internationalized, and there is now evident interest in local gastronomic heritage in the West as a whole. In 1996, with the backing of the European Community, the Gastronomic Heritage Inventory Programme was extended to the whole of Europe. With the expansion of international tourism, the gastronomic traditions of host regions are now seen by those involved in the tourist industry as a cultural legacy to promote and as an effective contribution to local development (Poulain 1997a; Tibère 1997; Bessière 2000). The world cuisine debate should be reestablished in the context of modern eating practices. The overpromotion of popular tradition, the regions and their authentic products, counters anxieties linked to the increasing industrialization of the food supply and to the potential dissolution of local and national identities through globalization or within an expanded area such as Europe.

4 From massification to intermixing

The notion that modern eating practices are the result of a "massification" process that has crushed national and regional characteristics is generally widespread, and is shared by certain sociologists interested in food practices. Stephen Mennell sees two possible interpretations of the phenomenon. According to the first, which might be described as conservative, "The threat came 'from below': the rising power of the masses jeopardised culturally creative élites." With regard to contemporary eating practices, from this perspective, the predilection shown by the masses for convenience and other types of junk food is responsible for "the deskilling of the honest artisan cook," and of all those involved in the catering professions (Mennell 1985, 318).

The second interpretation, which forms part of the extended work of the Frankfurt School, emphasizes the fact that the consumer's "very tastes, wants and needs could be manipulated" by a "profit-seeking capitalist mass media," which uses every available marketing and media resource to further this aim. Its advocates therefore consider that "the threat . . . comes not from below but from above" and that blame lies with "the capitalist 'culture industry'" (Mennell 1985, 318).

Mennell, however, rejects both arguments and turns to the works of Theodor Adorno in relation to the effects of mass culture on music as a means of understanding the underlying characteristics of modern eating practices. He sees two mechanisms as relevant and, above all, transferable to the domain of food: "fetishism" and the "regression of listening."

Fetishism is used to describe a phenomenon whereby the emergence of a "pantheon of best-sellers" tends to reduce the range of works that receive attention. Nowadays this characteristic trend is encapsulated in the expression "the best of . . ."

> The programmes shrink, and the shrinking process not only removes the moderately good, but the accepted classics themselves undergo a selection that has nothing to do with quality. In America, Beethoven's Fourth Symphony is among the rarities. This selection reproduces itself in a fatal circle: the most familiar is the most successful and is therefore played again and again and made still more familiar. (Adorno 1938, 276, quoted by Mennell, 319)

There is no denying that the "best-of" approach has continued to develop in the musical domain since Adorno's analysis of the subject, and it extends to the variety artists performing today.

With regard to food, fetishization tends to lead to "the standardization of a limited repertoire of dishes." Underlying its apparent diversity, the haute cuisine of today is characterized by a relative decrease in its range, despite the fact that certain classic dishes may be revisited. What has become of the 7,000 dishes comprising the late nineteenth- and early twentieth-century classic cuisines of Marie-Antoine Carême and Auguste Escoffier? Even in the few luxury restaurants that explicitly advertise themselves as classic, the range of interpreted works has been reduced to a few dozen best-sellers (Poulain and Neirinck 2000). This development is echoed in the domain of everyday food and company canteens, and is likewise evident in McDonald's restaurants, which offer customers their "best-of" selection of popular items.

According to Adorno, the *regression* of listening is the second characteristic of modern musical culture. This phenomenon is not the result of a psychological process of individual regression, but of the regression of listening itself, "'arrested at the infantile stage' . . . in which the listener was docile and afraid of anything new" (Mennell 1985, 320). Fast food might be seen as the prime example of regression in eating practices. It is a regression of tastes, involving a small number of more or less "gadgetized" foods, a few fetishized products and a regression in table manners, with the elimination of table settings, knives, and forks. In the context of Norbert Elias's "civilizing process," eating with one's fingers and without plates in Western societies represents a significant relapse. This infantilization of taste might also be related to the decline in the consumption of foods with traditionally masculine associations, particularly offal and charcuterie products (Moulin 1974, 1988), while at the same time fresh dairy products (yogurts and milky desserts), seen as feminine or infantile, are rising in popularity.

The critical conception of the consumer society inherited from the Frankfurt School (Horkheimer, Marcuse and Adorno), involves a rejection of the liberal notion of individual taste; from this perspective, these phenomena are the result of the manipulation carried out on individuals, at the deepest level, by the agrifood industry and its "right arm," advertising. The theory of large-scale manipulation has recently been revisited, developed and extended to society as a whole, by George Ritzer in the United States (1995). As he sees it, McDonaldization is not confined to the domain of food alone, but affects the whole of society. It describes both a trend toward gadgetizing consumption and the growing influence of the neo-Taylorian organizational model applied in well-known fast-food companies. Philippe Ariès has become the spokesman for this theory in France (1997a,b).

Yet Mennell argues that the reality of modern food practices cannot be described in terms of *fetishism* and *regression* alone. For, although it may be evident that food has become more homogenized, he also draws attention to an increase in diversity regarding habits and tastes, a phenomenon that he summarizes as "*diminishing contrasts* and *increasing varieties*. . . . One trend, not two: for in spite of the apparent contradiction between diminishing contrasts and increasing varieties, these are both facets of the same processes, as will become clear if we look at each in turn" (1985, 322).

Claude Fischler reprises the analysis of massification on the basis of Edgar Morin's studies of mass culture with regard to the culture industry (Morin 1975). His much more optimistic interpretation leads him to perceive a process of intermixing operations in modern food practices: "It would be a mistake to believe that the industrialization of the food supply, developments in transportation and the advent of mass distribution will inevitably result in the disintegration and suppression of local and regional characteristics." He suggests that a mass food culture has emerged, characterized by a dual tendency involving "integration-disintegration, which produces a type of universal syncretic mosaic" (Fischler 1990, 190). There is disintegration, as the influence of food consumption models and their particular characteristics has certainly declined, and there is also integration, through the creation of a social space shared by a considerably greater number of individuals. This process of intermixing takes many forms, which have been analyzed by Jean-Pierre Corbeau, and may be imposed, involuntary, or, conversely, chosen (1994b, 1997c).

We propose to extend the interpretations put forward by Fischler and Corbeau in our own analysis, with the suggestion that the globalization of the markets has generated a threefold movement. This involves the disappearance of certain specific characteristics, the emergence of new foods resulting from the process of intermixing, and the spread of certain food products and practices at the transcultural level. These three processes should not be seen solely as a destructive influence on food cultures, but also as factors that contribute to their reconstruction. In order to identify the movements that operate in modern times, we will revisit the history of food practices, in particular the period that followed the discovery of the New World. The reception of the new foods, conditioned by the techno-culinary structures then in place, differed considerably from one location to the next.

The potato, for example, was accepted in some areas, yet rejected in others. This was not only due to certain irrational aspects of local food cultures, but also depended on whether the new item could be successfully incorporated into their recipes and socially valued customs. According to the food consumption model most favored in seventeenth-century France, bread was the central element of a meal: cheeses and cooked meats were simply accompaniments, rather than the reverse. It was also the principal feature of the soup course, being dipped into the bowls. The importance of bread is rooted in Christian symbolism. In regions where the soil was rich enough to produce cereals that could be made into bread, this dietary model dominated on a massive scale.

When the potato was introduced, attempts were therefore made to adapt it in such a way that it might be integrated into the bread-making process. These, however, proved a failure. The resulting product could not be preserved and this caused food poisoning. For several centuries, therefore, potatoes were used as pig fodder. In regions where the soil was too poor to cultivate sufficient amounts of wheat or rye, culinary techniques applicable to cereals that were not used for bread-making, such as buckwheat, oats, and millet, had been retained as part of the food consumption model. In these areas, the potato was rapidly incorporated into local diets, thanks to its successful use in cooking methods for making galettes and broths (Poulain 1984). Our regional cuisines owe their specific characters largely to the original ways in which they integrated the new products—tomatoes, beans, corn, and so on—into their repertoire. Rather than disappearing due to the effects of the new products and cultivation techniques, quite the reverse happened, as differences in local cuisines became more marked.

Returning to the present day, the globalization of markets and the intermingling of population groups (through migration and the development of international tourism) are conducive to the exchange of products and culinary techniques, fostering diversity by contributing to a widespread intermixing of food consumption models. A Vietnamese restaurant in Paris must surely be more confusing to a Vietnamese visitor than to our fellow citizens (Poulain 1997b). The food served there undoubtedly bears some resemblance to what is eaten in Vietnam, and chopsticks are certainly in evidence—but what transformations would have been required in order to make it acceptable in terms of the French food consumption model! Although we are sure to experience an impression of exoticism, there is nothing to shock us; dishes are served as individual portions and menus are structured in the same way as our own, with appetizers, first courses, main dishes, and desserts. The meal is served according to our own table traditions, with each individual having their own portion and their own dishes to themselves. In a setting such as this, the newly arrived Asian visitor will likewise find himself in an exotic world, perhaps more so than the Westerner. Of course, there is the décor, with images of the isles and waters of Ha Long Bay much in evidence, and the dishes naturally bear some similarity to what one would find in Vietnam. "But that's not how the Vietnamese actually eat!" In changing its cultural environment, Vietnamese cuisine has undergone profound transformations. Now, instead of being a central element, rice has become a peripheral part of the meal: a mere garnish, an accompaniment. At the same time, the dishes that are communal in Vietnam, intended to be shared by all the diners, have become principal elements and individual meals. Accompanying items (*non an*), which have an intermediary status between rice and a dish, and serve as a variation to the taste of rice, have been eliminated, just like the vegetable and rice broths (*canh*), which in France have become simple soups served as a first course. Also gone are the dishes of local vegetables, although they are available in France: water bindweed (*rau muong*), mustard leaves (*cai cay*), and sweet potatoes (*khoai lang*), not forgetting pickled vegetables (*muoi*) such as aubergines, carrots, and turnips (Krowolski 1993).

Table traditions are a clear manifestation of a culture's fundamental values. In the West, the focus is on individualism, and the table setting is structured around the individual diner, who constitutes the base unit of the meal. In Asia, communality takes precedence over individuality, and this principle of sharing is evident throughout the eating process. In Vietnamese meals, the rice bowl serves as a plate, and diners help themselves to a series of dishes placed in the center of the table for everyone to share. Although there are certainly some rules regarding the succession of dishes presented, they are mainly served simultaneously. In the language of Claude Lévi-Strauss, many observers have drawn attention to the synchronic character of this system, as opposed to the diachronic nature of French meals.

In this way, the encounter between two food cultures, French and Vietnamese, has given rise to a new, original form of eating. It will no doubt outrage purists, who forget that what they consider to be an authentic Vietnamese meal is already the result of multiple influences that are not as unified as one might believe (Poulain 1997b; Nguyen Tung 1997). Yet Vietnamese restaurants in the West—to continue with this example, although our argument could be developed using other forms of exoticism—are also places of initiation. They represent a gateway, the initial step toward an eventual, more authentic discovery of the food culture in question. International tourism plays a leading role in this regard. Although globalization does iron out certain differences, it also acts as the driving force in a dual process of diversification and integration. It involves both the establishment of new differences, resulting from original ways of appropriating new products and techniques, and the development of shared spaces serving as a link between food consumption models. From this viewpoint, hamburger and pizza restaurants appear in the role of shared intermediary spaces, as transcultural products.

The study of different forms of intermixing in areas that stand at the crossroads of major food cultures is one of the most promising themes of the sociology of food. Reunion Island, where European, African, Indian, and Oriental influences all coexist, is a case in point. Understanding how the different communities establish a shared culinary space, how Reunion Islanders express Creole culture while preserving certain specific markers of their own indigenous heritage, noting what is retained or discarded with regard to products, methods, and table traditions, all provide us with new perspectives on the process of constructing identities (Cohen 1993, 2000; Tibère 2000). In contrast to the simplistic, naïve ideologies relating to the generalized intermixing rightly condemned by Bernard Chérubini (1992), the creolization of the Reunion Islands has been established as an advanced model for the analysis of what Roger Bastide (1958) termed "the intertwining of civilizations" and, more specifically, the complex nature of the mechanisms involved in the intermixing of food consumption models that accompany the globalization process. The linguistic concept of creolization (Chaudenson 1979) enables us both to include a dynamic dimension in our understanding of the intermixing process and to establish the resulting practices as an organized whole that constitutes a system in itself. It enables us to identify different food consumption spaces—reflecting both shared and opposing characteristics—that express the developments of a dual dialectic of integration and differentiation. The analysis of different forms of exchange, the acceptance or rejection of a practice according to a rationale of functional or symbolic equivalence, but also of restructuration, reopens a series of theoretical questions central to the American anthropological studies carried out in the first part of the twentieth century. These were somewhat rapidly abandoned with the critical theories of diffusionism. Such questions became lost in the theoretical conflict between functionalism, evolutionism, and structuralism that occurred during the 1960s. Structuralism emerged victorious and monopolized the human sciences in the 1970s (Lévi-Strauss 1958). Yet these issues appear crucial to the study of modern food practices. Thanks to its capacity to establish the results of intermixing as a fully organized new form, rather than the residue of a process of decomposition, the concept of creolization has replaced that of acculturation, to positive effect (Baré 1991; Poulain and Tibère 2000).

2

Between the domestic and the economic spheres: The ebb and flow of culinary activity

In order to understand the development of food practices, it is interesting to analyze how certain activities can swing to either side of a line dividing the interior and exterior of the household sphere. This perspective can be applied in an anthropological interpretation (Sigaut 1993, 73). In societies that practice itinerant agriculture on a shifting cultivation basis, "agriculture and harvesting form part of the culinary domain, just as this in turn forms part of agricultural activity. In fact, there is no distinction to be made between the two, because everything related to the growing of crops relates equally to household tasks, forming an indivisible whole."

This contrasts with industrial societies, where a large number of tasks have left the domestic sphere and have been taken over by the retail sector. The amount of productive activity taking place within the household has therefore been reduced. "This process has resulted in two extremes, in other words two endpoints, between which it is possible, in theory at least, to place every agricultural system on the planet" (Sigaut 1993, 73).

This dividing line between interior and exterior in relation to the domestic sphere enables us to perceive the ebb and flow of culinary activity that characterize the changes in modern eating practices. The industrialization of production and distribution systems has weakened the relationship between consumers and their foods. In a simultaneous development, certain traditional food supply channels, such as hunting and gardening, have now been established as leisure activities, and are required to fulfill new social roles. The out-of-home food sector is developing, using technical distribution systems—notably self-service outlets—that provide consumers with an increasingly wide array of products. These new technical structures are creating profound changes in decision-making systems relating to food practices.

1 The industrialization of the food supply

1.1 The industrialization of food production and new forms of self-production

Just as the food supply is being delocalized as a result of globalization, so industrialization is simultaneously severing the link between food and nature. By encroaching upon the social functions of cooking, it partially disconnects consumers from their biocultural environment. A distinction should be made between the two aspects involved in the industrialization of the food supply: production and processing. Livestock production is a particularly significant feature of modern eating practices in this respect. It was conceived along Taylorian lines; [Frederick Winslow Taylor's *Principles of Scientific Management* (1911) advocated the use of "true science" and "systematic management" to achieve maximum efficiency and productivity]. However, this model has been entirely rejected as a means of organizing human productive activity, and has contributed to an objectification of animals destined to become food. Reduced to the level of a raw material, meat has become divorced from its animal origins and its existence as a living entity. At the same time, in a paradoxically compensatory fashion, animals living in a natural state have become personified. They have taken leading roles from the movie stars,[1] and are now educating us on natural ethics, as in Jean-Jacques Annaud's *The Bear;* this is a far cry from the fables of La Fontaine, where animals are used to personify human characters. As a consequence of this personification, the household pet enjoys a unique status and has become the object of inordinate attention. The pet food market is booming (Nefussi 1989), and marketing specialists study the lifestyles of our dogs and cats with the utmost gravity.

At first sight, this objectification/personification phenomenon might appear to be an extension of the suppression of corporality and of the spectacle of dead flesh identified by Norbert Elias (1939) as the driving force of the civilizing process. Yet, more fundamentally, it is surely the sign of a desacralization of food and eating, and of the difficulties involved in managing the act of killing for food. Above all, it reflects a complete change in the perception of modern man's place within the natural world and in the order of the animal species, the contemporary mad cow crisis being just one indication of this.[2] Yet, it may also be more broadly interpreted as a crisis of confidence in the values of science, which presides over animal slaughter in secular societies.

At the same time, culinary processes are being industrialized. The change in the way household activities are viewed by society has led agrifood industries to extend into the domain of home cooking, representing self-produced food. By offering items increasingly close to the state where they are ready for consumption, the industry is encroaching on the social function of cooking, yet without managing to fulfill this role in its entirety. Consumers have come to perceive food made in this way as lacking both identity and symbolic significance; anonymous and soulless, produced in a nameless industrial environment, it has become, in a word, desocialized. The anxiety generated by the industrialization of the food supply might be expressed in terms borrowed from Kleinian psychoanalysis (Klein 1952), relating to the phantasy of introjecting the "bad object."

Incorporation is already a somewhat momentous act, as it reflects issues that are both vital and symbolic, and is accompanied, in the case of an anonymous industrial product, by a deep-seated anxiety (Fischler 1990). Sociologists and "ad men" have subsequently found themselves required to curb this phenomenon. For the most part, the answer involves implanting the product in the public's affections, or connecting it with a rural or cultural environment; traditional local and regional cuisines, in contrast to industrial products, are seen by consumers as "good objects." Typical examples are the over-sentimental images associated with the La Tartelière products, Bonne Maman jam or the William Saurin brand's Tree of Tradition, simultaneously rooted in the land and in French gastronomic culture. In the same way, Herta's the "taste of simple things" entices us with memories of our holidays, or even of childhoods spent in the countryside. All these products are presented in the context of one generation passing its values or skills on to the next.

At the same time, self-produced food, which was still on the wane by the 1980s and had become a specific domain within the farming sector, is beginning to expand once more after a sharp decline, being established as a quality product (Bages and Rieu 1988). With the development of dispersed urbanization, it has reached new sections of the population in the form of a leisure activity. The garden retail sector, which sells fruit trees and garden vegetables as well as ornamental plants, is thriving.

In a survey on eating habits among fifty to sixty-year-olds conducted in 1998 (Poulain 1998), 32 percent of the individuals in the sample studied had a vegetable garden, in addition to which, over 10 percent stated that they regularly received garden produce from friends or relatives. In the case of retired individuals, the number of people with a garden rose to 50 percent. Do-it-yourself (DIY) and gardening have become favored male domains. There is a considerable rise in home-grown food consumption following retirement.

This is far from being due to purely economic considerations, and is associated with increased leisure time and awareness of product quality. It transforms supply systems and, above all, it facilitates the establishment or maintenance of local interpersonal networks through the redistribution of surplus items.

1.2 *The industrialization of distribution*

In 1930, France witnessed a reversal of her urban/rural population ratio. In the course of a century and a half, from 1846 to 1990, a totally symmetrical inversion occurred. These huge, unprecedented sociological transformations changed ways of life and, above all, fundamentally altered the connections between consumers and their food. The production, transformation, and commercialization of food govern, structure, and regulate life in rural society. The clearly identifiable, valued food item is a visible presence, in evidence at different stages of the transformation process: from the wheat field to the baker's oven, from the meadows to the butcher's counter, from the garden or market to the kitchen, from the vine to the table. The landscape itself is transformed during the production cycles. By disconnecting a food from the world of its origins, the urbanization process establishes it as a piece of merchandize and partly obliterates its links to its natural provenance and its social functions.

Food is gradually becoming a simple commodity, as mass-market retailing has given rise to the eater-consumer. Hypermarkets appeared on the scene in the early 1960s, and in one generation they have established themselves in a dominant position. In 1969 they accounted for 10.4 percent of food purchases; in 1991, this had risen to 62.2 percent. Although farmers' markets resisted the trend (with purchases only dropping from 8.6 percent in 1961 to 6.2 percent in 1991), small retailers, especially grocery shops, have literally been ruined; in 1961, they accounted for 24 percent of food purchases, as opposed to 3.8 percent in 1991. As a consequence of the loss of contact with production channels, food has become a mere consumer item, controlled by product managers and marketing experts. There are now an enormous number of foods on offer, with over 18,000 different items on the shelves in our Mammouth, Carrefour, or Leclerc hypermarkets.

Yet, while we certainly have abundant supplies of food, it is becoming increasingly difficult to identify and recognize; above all, it is generating an increasing amount of anxiety. For food is no commonplace commodity, it is something we incorporate. It enters the body of the eater and becomes the eater himself, participating both physically and symbolically in maintaining him as a complete being and in the construction of his identity. Eating is also an act that connects humankind to nature, to reality. The cooking and table traditions adopted by a society constitute a specific manner of regulating the relationship between nature and culture. Industrialized food raises questions that can rapidly turn into feelings of anxiety. Where does it come from? What transformation has it undergone? Who has handled it?

2 Semi-prepared foods and cooking for pleasure

Women's entry into the workplace has likewise altered domestic practices. In 1950, a French housewife (not in paid employment) spent almost four hours a day on food-related tasks (shopping, preparing meals and washing up). In 1992, a woman in paid employment spent less than an hour on these activities. This decrease in the productive work carried out in a household—due neither entirely to the use of electrical appliances nor to a new approach to gender-based household roles—has provided the agrifood industry with one of its main areas of economic development. The purchase of food products, including those adapted for consumption outside the home, rose from 50 percent in 1960 to 83 percent in 1991. Cooking plays an ever-diminishing role in our daily eating practices; precooked meals and convenience foods, from crêpes stuffed with mushrooms and vegetable stir-fries to desserts, are bought ready-made or semi-prepared. The household cook is required at best to assemble and complete the dish, or even simply to heat the meals. Despite its many twists and turns, the history of food practices has basically involved the shifting of a set of tasks from the domestic to the economic sector. There has been a transfer of activity from one sector to another. Pasta is a significant example of this phenomenon. Nowadays it is seen as a store-cupboard staple, whereas barely a century ago, it was a product made at home with flour and eggs.

In a market with stagnating sales, the food industry achieves growth through the downstream approach, that is, by offering products with integrated added value. "Insofar as it is perceived as the ultimate household task, the preparation of food now seems to be assailed from all sides by companies from the external sector: the restaurant business, home delivery services, supermarkets and so on" (Sigaut 1993).

However, not all social groups are affected by this to the same degree, and the shift is inverted during the weekend or on certain occasions. Cooking then takes on a markedly symbolic significance. From the survey conducted on fifty to sixty-year-olds, cooking emerges as a domestic activity with strong implications and significant social dimensions. Cooking is an activity that primarily focuses on others (67 percent). To cook is to give; to *bring pleasure* and *to share*.

Yet, alongside this set of positive associations there are also more negative dimensions connected with the repetitive and restrictive aspects of this domestic task. These restrictions, involving obligation, necessity, and routine, emerge as secondary considerations both as regards the frequency with which they appear and, above all, the order in which they are listed by the respondents (51 percent). Only 18 percent of those questioned saw cooking in a decidedly negative light, as a chore, a waste of time, and a bore. Finally, the cost aspect was emphasized by just 5 percent. Paradoxically, the women questioned, who were much more likely to carry out this activity on a daily basis than men, associated it with far more positive and fewer negative values than male respondents, who only very rarely assumed the task. An analysis carried out on a regional basis shows a far more positive attitude to cooking in the Île de France than in other French regions.

A comparison with results obtained thirty years earlier reveals a few surprises. In 1966, there was evidence of a rejection of the culinary model provided by the mother. This attitude was shared by all the female respondents, and was more marked in the case of younger women; 65 percent of those in the under-thirty age group registered a "no" with regard to the maternal model, as opposed to 60 percent of fifty to sixty-year-olds. This rejection was not limited to the sphere of cooking but extended to women's lives within the home, to their role as housewives, and, to some extent, as nurturing mothers. That role was conflicting with images of the modern woman promoted by the feminist movement and widely reprised and adopted by the advertising discourse of the day. There was an emphasis on the need to reduce the time devoted to food and to speed up the cooking process; at the same time, there was an evident commitment to taking note of new nutritional requirements. As we have seen, both in the analysis of food-related aspirations and in the hierarchies of nutritional values relating to essential foods, changes were occurring with regard to the concept of what should be eaten, in both the quantitative and qualitative sense. This explained the break with the culinary model transmitted by the mother (Table 1).

TABLE 1 "Do you cook in the same way as your mother?"

	1966 Women under 30	1996 Women aged 50–60	1998 Women aged 50–60
Yes	35%	40%	53%
No	65%	60%	47%

Source: OCHA, Poulain 1998.

Today, in the case of the fifty to sixty-year-old age group, the attitude toward the mother as a culinary role model has been revised. This turnaround should be understood within the context of the industrialization of the food sector, which has brought with it a growing fear that the French art of eating well is under threat. In the qualitative approach, the people interviewed emphasized the need to preserve and transmit traditions, a set of skills described as the *family culinary heritage.*

3 The restaurant and catering sector

The restaurant and catering sector (known in France as *la restauration hors foyer*, or RHF), has played a decisive role in the shift of food and eating practices from the domestic to the economic sphere. This domain is composed of two distinct sectors. The institutional catering sector incorporates school, university and company canteens, as well as the extensive health sector, and serves a more or less captive clientele. The management of these restaurants is either undertaken by the institutions themselves, or contracted to institutional catering companies.

The commercial restaurant sector, on the other hand, incorporates every type of eating establishment open to the general public, from fast-food outlets to restaurants serving fine cuisine. Figures produced by the French statistics institute (INSEE) in relation to this sector are not always easy to interpret. Until 1970, for example, expenditure on "hotels, cafés, restaurants and canteens" was still viewed as a whole (Lambert 1992; Combris 1995). After that date, specific studies on "out-of-home eating" were carried out, but not, unfortunately, with any regularity. The restaurant and catering sector (including both institutional and commercial establishments) has experienced considerable growth over the past thirty years, with expenditure in this domain, in inflation-adjusted francs, rising by 30 percent between 1970 and 1990. The percentage of household food budgets spent on eating out rose from 15.3 percent in 1980 to 20.2 percent in 1991 (INSEE 1993). Growth in this area of expenditure slowed down between 1984 and 1998, even showing a downturn in 1995 and 1996, before exhibiting a marked improvement in 1999. This does not mean that fewer meals were eaten outside the home during the two years of decreased expenditure in this area—far from it. In fact, a number of contradictory trends underlie this phenomenon. The effects of an increase in the number of restaurant meals eaten in nonprofessional circumstances (in other words, excluding institutional eating establishments) are masked by a drop in the average expenditure on such meals resulting from the following factors:

1   A simplification in the structure of meals. The classic menu structure: starter, main dish and accompaniments, cheese and dessert (or simply dessert) is often discarded in favor of a simpler format based on two or even just one of these courses, either consisting of a starter, main dish and coffee, or a main dish and dessert—sometimes even just a main dish with accompaniments.

2   A fall in wine consumption.

3   A fall in meal prices.

The restaurants that benefited most from this development were those offering simplified formats at lower prices. An analysis of this sector should therefore also be carried out according to the number of meals served. On this point, the most reliable data is provided by specialist private research centers such as the GIRA research institute (Table 2).

The number of meals taken outside the home between 1985 and 1999 increased by over 16 percent. These figures conceal very different variations according to the sector involved. In the case of institutional catering, the work sector (company restaurants) is affected by economic cycles in the short term. Moreover, the new ways of structuring working time, such as the implementation of the 35-hour week, have tended to reduce the number of days employees spend at work, thus also reducing the number of meals consumed in this sector.

By contrast, the education and health sectors (the latter comprising hospitals and retirement homes) are showing strong growth. Within the health sector, the aging population and institutionalized end-of-life care amply offset reductions in the length of hospital stays. Within a few years, the school catering sector may well feel the effects of the drop in the school population. Growth is still robust for the time being, maintained by an increase in the number of meals eaten outside the home by this segment of the population, especially its youngest members (Michaud 1997), and by the longer duration of studies.

For its part, the commercial restaurant sector is highly sensitive to the effects of economic crisis or recovery. Analyses of personal aspiration through questions such as "If you had more money to spend on food, what changes would you make?" show that regulating restaurant visits is a typical way of responding to fluctuations in purchasing power. In 1998, 62 percent of those questioned stated that if their food budget increased, they would want to spend it on more trips to restaurants or on entertaining (Poulain 1998b). Conversely, if their spending power were reduced, restaurant trips would be the first focus of a reduction in expenditure.

TABLE 2 Growth in the restaurant and catering sector

	1985	1996	Annual growth 1996/1985	1999	2000 Forecasts	Annual growth 2000/1999	2005 Forecasts	Growth 1985/2005	Annual growth 2005/2000
Institutional catering sector	3,600	3,720	+0.3%	3,695	3,675	−0.50%	3,770	+4.7%	+0.50%
Commercial restaurant sector	2,400	3,000	+2.00%	3,240	3,327	+2.70%	3,630	+51%	+1.80%
Total restaurant and catering sector	6,000	6,720	+1.00%	6,935	7,002	+1.00%	7,400	+23%	+1.10%

In millions of meals served (main meals and breakfasts)

Source: GIRA.

4 The eater, the restaurant system, and choice

In contrast with the family domain, where decisions regarding food are generally made by the mistress of the house, diners in self-service restaurants construct their own chosen meals individually from a more or less open selection. Professionals in the catering sector have created multiple options to meet the needs of a diverse clientele: the self-service restaurant, the scramble system, the buffet, the food court, and so on. These all offer customers a wide range of choices.

Readers familiar with the history of gastronomy will know that the buffet service, which is increasingly widely used in the institutional catering sector and offers a very extensive selection, bears a similarity to aristocratic festive food practices. This was the case, for example, with the formal French-style service in practice from the late Middle Ages to the French Revolution (Poulain and Neirinck 2000). This system involved a series of dishes, sometimes several dozen, being presented to the guests all together as three separate courses. Everyone ate as they pleased, in varying quantities. With this type of service, diners nibble at various dishes, rather than eating all the food offered. Formal French-style service was a display of abundance; however, this involved only a very small section of French society.

With regard to everyday food, having a choice is a new historical phenomenon, and the situation whereby the public have direct access to restaurants offering them a wide array of possibilities is relatively recent. Originating in the United States, self-service distribution systems date from the 1970s, and were rapidly developed in the institutional catering sector, particularly in company canteens (Poulain and Larrose 1995). These systems played a part in the shift from the social group to the individual that occurred in relation to food choices. And yet the consumer never has absolute freedom of choice. The selection on offer is created on the basis of what those involved in the institutional catering sector see as client expectation, and its range and complexity serve to reflect their professionalism and the conception they have of their own professional role. To apply Kurt Lewin's terminology, eating in a company restaurant involves using another food supply channel, the "gatekeeper" of which is no longer the housewife, but the chef, or the manager of the establishment in question.

Various constraints influence the diner through the selection of food on offer. These result from a concrete system of actions governing the food provided within the institutional catering sector. In order to gain a clear understanding of these actions, the context needs to be studied in greater depth. The series of dishes put before clients in a company restaurant is, first and foremost, the result of a business negotiation between a consultative committee or a human resources (HR) department and a catering company. This negotiation is itself influenced by the social representations of the various participants in these decision-making processes.

The theoretical offer, that is, the amount and type of food that diners will find in the company restaurant, is decided by the members of the consultative committees or the HR staff responsible for such matters. They may either be directly involved in managing the restaurant or restaurants themselves, or they may sign a management contract with a company specializing in institutional catering. These decisions operate within a normative perspective, with those responsible producing specifications or making selections from the suggestions put forward by a contract catering company, choosing those items that they consider desirable for their firm's employees. These decisions are made on the basis of more or less explicit social representations regarding diners' needs: what they consider good for the consumer, but also what they believe the said consumer wants, their own image of company restaurant food, their own food norms and, finally, the culture of the firm to which they belong.

But these decision makers themselves also work under supervision. Specifically selected, in the case of consultative committees, or company employees in the case of the HR department, they are mindful of the consequences their decisions might entail. The canteen is always considered as a somewhat dangerous space, where problems within the firm are expressed and sometimes exacerbated (Maho and Pynson 1989). As a result, these advisors generally develop fairly traditional conceptions of institutional restaurants and food; the main thing, above all, is not to make waves! Let there be a quality service and modern installations by all means—but nothing radical when it comes to the food!

For its part, the contract catering company is represented at this stage by a head of sector or a sales representative. Their thought processes and actions are likewise governed by certain social representations relating to customer needs and to what they deem "good" for diners. These needs are defined with reference to conceptions that are influenced to a greater or lesser degree by economic, marketing and sociological cultures; the conception of the role of institutional catering establishments; the culture within the contract company and their own food norms.

These commercial interactions lead to the development of a contract, which defines a service—a theoretical offer—with varying degrees of detail. However, there are a certain amount of disparities between that offer and the actual offer experienced by the diner. For the theoretical offer is subject to a dual interpretation by the restaurant management team: a culinary interpretation (in the musical sense of creating a work, the success of which will depend

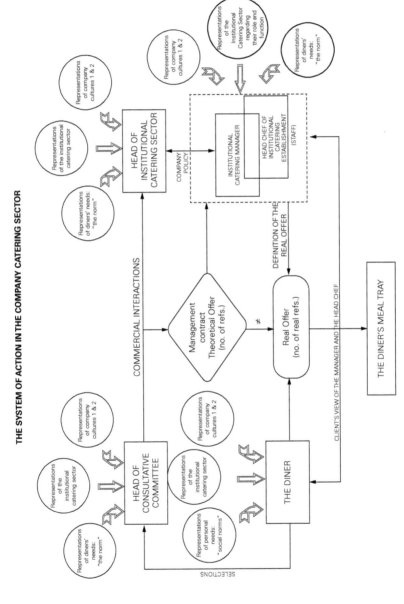

FIGURE 1 *The decision-making system in the contract catering sector.*

Source: J. P. Poulain, J. M. Delorme, M. Gineste, The Ministry of Agriculture, Compass, Cidil.

on the talents of the chef) and a commercial interpretation. The latter depends above all on how the manager and the chef perceive the consumer and their expectations. This translates for the most part into an increased number of references to the traditional meal structure (starter, main dish, accompaniments, dessert and so on). In going the extra mile, the restaurant manager or company restaurant chef feels that he has served his profession well, and the head of the consultative committee feels equally satisfied at receiving more than his due. The transformation from a theoretical to a real offer is also the result of a series of interactions based on representations. This is the case within the contract catering company regarding communications between the head of the sector, the manager, and the head chef (or manager chef). It also occurs in the restaurant itself, where diners encounter the chef on a daily basis through the selection offered in the self-service canteen. All these participants have representations relating to diners' needs, to their own professional roles and to the cultures of the firms to which they belong (Figure 1).

The situation regarding the diner in an institutional catering establishment is characterized by a greater degree of personal choice. Here, decisions regarding food are not subject to input from other family members, or from individuals who might eat with him or her, as the meals are individually paid for. This is accompanied by a difference in the range of foods on offer, which in this case is no longer defined by the eater or by his family environment, but by the head chef, working within the framework of a management contract that predetermines the service provided.

For, although the diner makes individual decisions regarding what he eats and how he composes his meal, he makes his choices from an array of products whose formation and range are determined by those running the restaurant. The choice on offer is much wider than he normally encounters at home, and the nature of the foods (both as regards their origins and the way in which they are cooked) is always somewhat different from what he usually eats in the domestic environment. Moreover, despite the fact that diners choose their own meals and payment methods, eating in an institutional catering establishment remains a socialized practice, with just 12.4 percent of diners eating alone. Making a choice has therefore become a spectacularized act indicative of an individual's social position.

5 Retirement, or the return to the domestic sphere

The importance of individualized choice with regard to decision making becomes clear when examining food practices following retirement. For a great many people, the end of working life also means an end to eating in company canteens; the midday meal, previously eaten outside the home, is therefore brought back to the domestic sphere. This affects between 200 and 250 meals per year. The first consequence of this shift is a notable increase in the amount of food bought for home consumption, but it also brings psychosociological consequences. In the company restaurant, the diner personally composes his or her own meal. With the return to the home, this strictly individual choice is then either delegated to the spouse, or becomes a matter for negotiation. Different male and female representations of the right things to eat then collide. Restrictions related to medical or slimming diets, as well as personal preferences, which are known to differ according to gender, need to be negotiated in purchase-related decision making, and give rise to new forms of interaction. For a couple, retirement often means learning to eat together once more (Poulain 1998).

Retirement is also an ideal time for observers to note a transformation in domestic roles. A comparison made after a gap of thirty years highlights profound changes in the food social space. The position of the mistress of the house is no longer as central and decisive as it was in the 1960s.

First, not everyone lives as part of a couple, and there has been an increase in both single-person and single-parent households. Secondly, food shopping is no longer exclusively a female domain, delegated to the housewife. Over 25 percent of men living as part of a couple state that they often do the shopping, while 38 percent do it from time to time. Moreover, in the case of couples in the fifty to sixty-year-old age bracket, the age gap between men and women means that retirement does not occur at the same time, the women usually being younger. There is thus a transitory phase when men re-inhabit the home before their wives; this marks a critical stage in the redistribution of domestic roles (Poulain 1998b).

Although cooking remains for the most part a female domain, men will certainly pull their weight, doing the shopping and laying the table while the meal is being prepared. For this section of the population in general, more free time means more shopping trips, with the market becoming a particularly popular destination for this activity.

Some men develop a taste for cooking as a leisure activity. This is mainly the case with those living in urbanized environments and belonging to social groups with greater cultural capital. They take over the responsibility on Sundays or on special occasions. For the most part, however, their contribution is limited to the most symbolic, high-profile activities, such as grilling on the barbecue or making the main dish, while women are left with secondary preparation work or washing and clearing away the kitchen utensils. Women, therefore, often have ambivalent feelings concerning this intervention. While it is recognized that men have assumed responsibility for a culinary task, thus relieving them of that charge and signaling a move toward a fairer division of household duties, it also marks an intrusion into their domain, their territory. This triggers territorial conflicts, the man being accused of taking over the prestigious and rewarding aspect of cooking, leaving his partner to tidy up the kitchen: "*Well yes, he does do the cooking sometimes, but it's me who's left with all the mess to clear up.*" For many women—particularly those in paid employment—this highlights a contradiction in roles, between that of the nurturing mother, responsible for all culinary activities, from deciding what to buy to clearing and washing up, and that of a busy, modern woman, who aspires to sharing domestic tasks (Chaudron, Sluys, and Zaidman 1990).

For the great majority of couples, however, it is the man who becomes the kitchen assistant, responsible for secondary tasks, especially after his retirement. For cooking, particularly of the everyday variety, remains a primarily female domain, and the transfer of duties to men mainly involves the least valued household tasks: laying and clearing the table, and washing up.

Food shopping is a separate area. If a question is put without specifying the priority attached to the task, such as "Do you ever do the food shopping?" men's role appears greater in this regard. Twenty percent of employed men frequently engage in this activity, a figure that rises to 38 percent in the case of those not in employment, with 25 percent of the male population as a whole undertaking the task. If one adds to this the number of men who claim to do the shopping on a frequent basis, or from time to time, the figures rise to 58 percent in the case of employed men and 76 percent for those not in employment.

Farmers, shopkeepers and artisans have the highest nonparticipation rates regarding food shopping: 57 percent in the case of farmers and 47 percent for the other two groups. A large number of executives and those working in the liberal professions claim to participate in this task, but not on a regular basis. Bernard Zarca (1990) distinguishes three separate sets of household tasks. There is a strictly female realm, entailing laundry-related work such as washing and ironing, a male realm, which involves washing the car and fetching wood, and a group of "negotiable" tasks, all structured around the preparation of meals; this last category is the focus of our interest.

For the fifty to sixty-year-old age bracket living in couples, male participation in these tasks, in decreasing order, involves laying the table, washing up, shopping, and lastly, to a lesser degree, cooking. At national level, an identical hierarchy of tasks is in force with regard to couples, but the declared participation rates are slightly higher among fifty to sixty-year-olds. The role played by retired men largely accounts for this difference. A cross-comparison of statements made by men and women reveals a discrepancy rising from 8 percent to 17 percent concerning the assumption of household responsibilities by men, and from 9 percent to 19 percent in the case of women. In this way, men's assessment of their participation is always greater than women's view of the same. Equally, men feel that women play a lesser role than they declare. At all events, if social roles are indeed changing, they are doing so gradually, and food-related domestic tasks remain a largely female sphere.

3

The evolution of eating practices

1 The theory of gastro-anomie and related debates

Fischler's article "Gastronomie-gastro-anomie" (1979) had considerable repercussions on the development of food practices as a sociological subject. He was motivated by two main objectives: to promote a pluri-disciplinary approach to the study of food, and to interpret the changes occurring in modern eating practices. The second point will be our focus of interest.

Very favorably received by journalists and the general public alike, surely due to the evocative force of the pun, the theory of "gastro-anomie" has been the subject of lively debate within the sociological field. Fischler coined the term as a way of describing the consequence of modern eating practices, which are themselves characterized by three concurrent phenomena.

1.1 An over abundant food supply

Economic development in Western societies, coupled with the progress made in food production, conservation, and transportation, have reduced the ecological constraints affecting food availability, establishing a lasting state of abundance and even of excess. This is perhaps not wholly unprecedented in anthropological history, Marshall Sahlins (1972), having demonstrated that certain hunter-gatherer societies could have been considered genuinely affluent. It is, however, a hitherto unknown phenomenon in the history of the Western world (Aron 1997).

1.2 *The relaxing of social constraints*

This development is accompanied by a series of transformations in our eating practices, such as the destructuring of meals and the rise of the grazing culture. These are the consequence of a relaxation of social constraints associated with eating and of a rise in individualism. Modern eating practices may therefore be identified as a process of destructuration. In France, the theme was quickly popularized, with references to the *système dé*: *de*-structuration, *de*-socialization, *de*-institutionalization, *de*-regularization, *de*-ritualization, and so forth. "This decade will have been marked by what we might call the "*système dé*, a general desire to dismantle ideas, institutions, and structures inherited from the past and ill-adapted to the present" (Mermet 1995, 13).[1] Basing his comments on American studies, Fischler writes:

> The structured, commensal meal is on its way to disappearing in the United States. Middle-class urban families might only find themselves around the dinner table together two or three times a week, and the meal will only last around twenty minutes. The same studies show that instances of food contact during the day average around twenty, and that the assumed system of three meals punctuating the day is now simply a relic of the past. Developments that may be similar in type, although they are occurring on a smaller scale, are now already apparent in Europe (1979).

Through this deregulation of eating practices, decisions previously taken by the group are being put back into the hands of the individual. Modern food practices have created an unprecedented situation that gives the eater a greater degree of autonomy. The all-important, obsessive question nowadays is: what shall I choose? "The modern eater must now make choices, food has become the subject of daily decision-making processes, and these decisions have fallen within the sphere of the individual" (1990, 204, 205).

1.3 *The multiple discourses on food practices and their contradictory aspects*

In the wake of Harvey Levenstein's study (1993), Fischler identifies the same cacophonous discourse on food practices occurring within France as the former had noted with regard to North American society (1980, 1993). "There are hardly any unequivocal, coherent criteria by which to make these choices. There is more of a mosaic, a cacophony of proposed criteria, often contradictory or dissonant" (1990, 204). There are discourses on diet, on morals, on identity. . . .

To summarize this situation regarding eating practices in our modern world, Fischler draws on Emile Durkheim's concept of *anomie*, coining a new term. Following the construction of the word "gastronomy" (*gastro*: the stomach and *nomos*: the rule, therefore by extension, rules governing food), his neologism "gastro-anomie" indicates loss by the presence of the *a*—the absence of rules by which to eat. Modern eaters, therefore, find themselves in a curious situation, whereby the decision-making space relating to food choices has extended, and at the same time, they have lost the security provided by a normative, socially-defined system.

"Autonomy is developing, yet anomie is also developing with it" (1990, 205). Gastro-anomie is associated with social deregulation.

> The gap created by anomie has generated multiple forms of pressure, all carrying contradictory messages that bear down on the modern eater. These include advertising, various suggestions and prohibitions, and above all, an ever-increasing number of health warnings. The freedom offered by anomie is also experienced as a sharp twinge of anxiety, and in turn, that anxiety over-determines the circumstances relating to aberrant eating practices. (Fischler 1979, 206)

According to Fischler's hypothesis, modern society is responsible for developing and exacerbating the fundamental anxiety connected with the act of eating that lies at the heart of the "omnivore's paradox." For, as he sees it, food is always a source of relative anxiety. The modern eater is now experiencing an easing of group pressure, which reduces the commensal aspect of eating; in other words, he is freed of the obligation to eat in company. At the same time, he is subject to a host of contradictory discourses, all of an exhortative nature. In this case, anomie is not solely linked to a crisis in the normative system, but also to an increase in contradictory injunctions regarding hygiene, identity, hedonism, aesthetics, and so on.

The notion of the balanced diet has developed in parallel with that of gastro-anomie, monopolizing both academic nutritional discourse and the preoccupations of the general public. In a study of spontaneous dietary discourse, Fischler concludes:

> On analysis, the discourse of mothers . . . suggests the following hypothesis: the omnipresent aspiration toward "balance" is perhaps quite simply the other side of this phenomenon (anomie), its inverted image: in short, it expresses the reaction to a void or to a symbolic state of disorder. This highly sought-after "balance" thus takes on a new, wider and more universal significance; it implies an end to symbolic disorder and to the anxiety it generates. (Fischler 1986)

In the 1980s, the theory of gastro-anomie received very wide media coverage; it was adopted by the world of marketing and by the research and development departments of major agrifood manufacturers. Changes in food practices were attributed to a set of socioeconomic phenomena as diverse as women's entry into the workplace, the practice of working through lunch, urban growth, the redefinition of gender roles, the industrialization of the agrifood sector, and the reduction in household food expenditure in favor of leisure activities.

The idea of a situation characterized by anomie was to be reprised and upheld by other sociologists, firstly by Jean-Pierre Corbeau (1991, 1995), and by Claude Rivière (1995) and Jean-Pierre Poulain (1996a, 1998b). Corbeau sees anomie "as a gap in the institutionalized system that disrupts unanimity, even solidarity, by preventing the actor from reproducing traditional norms. This gives rise to collective or individual creativity (certain forms of which were or are considered catastrophic or pathological) directed toward a potential experience for which the collective conscious has no regularizing concept" (1995).

2 The enduring class system

As a reaction to the theories of modern eating practices, all of which tend to uphold the notion that the class system is in decline, certain sociologists have been committed to demonstrating that social class remains a permanent influence. Nicolas Herpin has sought to construct different descriptors that might illustrate the process of "destructuration" at work in modern eating practices. Following a survey carried out among working-class groups in Northern France, he concluded that the phenomenon might not be as widespread as it might appear, but above all, that it did not significantly challenge the continued existence of social hierarchies (1988).

Claude Grignon attacks the theory of a declining class system in a more radical fashion, seeing it as a genuine myth. "In France," he writes, "the domain has now been taken over by a theory of 'modern eating practices,' which involves applying to the particular case of dietary behavior a general scenario of social change derived from the growth theories that accompanied the expansion and economic policies of the 1960s. . . . If mass production could give rise to the class system and the class struggle in the nineteenth-century, mass consumption combines and reunites them" (Aymard, Grignon and Sabban 1993, 25).

Grignon's argument is based on three criteria. The first is the absence of empirical material, or, more specifically, the use of data from the United States (it is somewhat doubtful that this could be legitimately transferred to the context of French society), and from market research companies, which, for reasons of confidentiality, do not publish their methodology. "Created by marketing companies in the early 1980s, and subsequently reprised and popularized by sociologists of modern eating practices, the micro-theory of de-structured meals is never supported by sources; in the absence of accessible data, it relies entirely on hearsay, on rumor" (1993, 30).

The second criterion emphasizes the extent to which agri-industrial interests have appropriated the theory of destructuration with regard to modern eating practices. Grignon sees these attacks on the traditional meal as a plot hatched by the agrifood industry.

> If the structured meal is now being sidelined, attacked in the name of modernity, condemned in the name of individual choice, challenged in the name of personal freedom and the rejection of authority, it is perhaps because the model currently used in France effectively forms an obstacle to the "extensive" and "continuous consumption" so keenly desired by the agrifood industry, or at least, by some of its branches, such as the biscuit, confectionary and chocolate sectors. (Aymard, Grignon and Sabban 1993, 31)

As he sees it, this "microtheory" is a shrewd way for the industry to package the more concrete, obviously self-serving notion of grazing. "The celebration of the grazing culture is an indirect way of denigrating the traditional meal as being just as uncool, staid, repressive, typically French and even harmful, as grazing is cool, relaxed, informal, unjustifiably restrained and good for the health." Grignon is referring here to a discourse presented in a marketing journal (Aymard, Grignon and Sabban 1993). "To tamper with these practices (the traditional meal), in the manner of these neoliberal attempts at 'modernization,' is to tamper with hidden, vital issues, the importance of which is sensed even when not consciously gauged" (Grignon 1993, 321).

Grignon's final censure is more fundamentally sociological in nature. He criticizes the theory of modern eating practices for grouping all social changes together, masking the social diversity involved in the process. He considers Fischler to have adopted an overly psychologizing approach; by placing himself on the same level as the eater, social differentiations seem to disappear. From a macrosociological viewpoint, choices and practices can always be associated with the class to which the individual belongs, as social differences have not been ironed out by the abundant food supply and the democratization of food products (Grignon 1980; Gomez 1992).

Mediating the debate on the destructuration of contemporary eating practices was a difficult enterprise; insufficient and above all contradictory empirical data made it impossible to settle the issue. Due to a lack of data extending over a long period, there was no possibility of "making a precise evaluation regarding the stability of the French food consumption model," explained Grignon in 1993. Paradoxically, this did not prevent him from arguing that the traditional French meal model remained secure. He supported his exposé with studies on the eating practices of French students, which will provide us with a topic for further discussion.

It therefore seemed necessary to stimulate the debate surrounding the theory of the destructuration of modern eating practices using empirical data. This was the aim behind the two research projects that we conducted within the framework of the "Food Tomorrow" program launched by the Ministry of Agriculture (Poulain et al. 1996, 1999). We now have two studies at our disposal enabling us to evaluate developments in eating practices; they were carried out two years apart (in 1995 and 1997), applying the same methodology and using similar samples. Since then, Grignon has had the opportunity to revisit his study on student eating practices, using the same research tools that he had applied in his previous analyses. Finally, the French research and survey organization, the Centre de Recherche pour l'Étude et l'Observation des Conditions de Vie (CREDOC), regularly conducts surveys of French eating habits; using these various analyses, we are able to make dynamic comparisons.

3 Changes in eating practices

Studies working on the basis of observed or reconstructed behavior reveal a simplification in the structure of meals and a rise in the habit of between-meal eating. They likewise highlight a discrepancy between social norms associated with meals and the practices actually in use. The former broadly echo the standard three-part meal (starter, main dish with accompaniments, and dessert), with snacking being frowned upon. This explains how these changes have largely escaped notice in surveys using only declarative methods and, above all, self-administered questionnaires.

Our methodology combines collecting behavioral data—obtained by noting both the contents of individual meal trays and the subject's food intake on the day preceding the observed meal[2]—with a questionnaire, administered by interview, focusing on representations. By cross-checking these different types of data we were able to assess the changes in eating habits now in progress, and the contradictory meanings that accompany them. These surveys are based on adults (18–65 years old), all of whom are in employment and have a canteen in their place of work. However, results concerning daily food consumption have a significance that extends well beyond individual cases, shedding light on eating practices in general.

3.1 The simplification of meal structures

Our two samples consisted of restaurants operating an all-inclusive system—in which the client pays a fixed price for a full meal, consisting of a starter, a main dish and accompaniments, cheese, and a dessert, with the possibility of making substitutions among the three courses peripheral to the main dish—and those operating on the à la carte system, with clients paying for each individual item they consume. After making readjustments with the associated sociological variables (gender and degree of urbanization) we were able to compare the composition of the meals trays from the two different payment systems—all-inclusive and à la carte. We noted an increase in meal trays showing a simplified composition.[3] There was a 5.1 percent shift away from the structured model toward the more simplified model in restaurants offering the à la carte option. This confirms that a simplification of meal structure is in progress (Table 3).

Correlation analysis provides us with a more precise picture of the population groups involved. The phenomenon of simplifying the midday meal is characteristic of the urban lifestyle (based on responses from those living in Paris and in the major provincial cities), and is more marked in cases of longer commutes to the workplace. The practice is more common among women than men, and among white-collar workers and executives in the third sector. However, neither age nor income is a significant factor here (Table 4).

TABLE 3 Composition of lunch 1995–97

Composition of meal trays	1995 % sample	1997 % sample	% variation
Starter, main and side dishes, cheese, dessert	10.1	7.8	−2.3
Starter, main and side dishes, dessert	40.8	38.0	−2.8
Subtotal, full meals	*50.9*	*45.8*	*−5.1*
Main and side dishes, dessert	36.1	38.9	+2.8
Starter, main and side dishes	5.2	5.2	0
Starter, dessert	5.9	7.0	+1.1
Other combinations	1.9	3.2	+1.3
Subtotal, simplified format	*49.1*	*54.2*	*+5.2*
Total	**100**	**100**	

Basic sample (N 95 = 1,027; N 97 = 877).

TABLE 4 Correlations between meal tray composition and independent variables

Variables	Related tendency
Place of residence	The practice of destructuring meals increases with the degree of urbanization
Gender	Women are more likely to destructure their meals than men
Profession and socioeconomic classification	White-collar workers and executives are more likely to destructure their meals
Total length of commute	Destructuration of meals increases with the length of the daily commute
Age	No connection
Income	No connection

The most astonishing finding was that diners eating in canteens offering an all-inclusive meal deal, whereby clients paid for a complete meal comprising five items, did not take all the dishes to which they were entitled. The theory of economic constraint is therefore not applicable here (Poulain 1998a).

3.2 Eating between meals

There has been an evident rise in the instances of food intake occurring during the day (i.e., meals plus between-meal snacks). This has been highlighted by a shift in the average daily number of such instances from 4.7 to 5.3 in the period between 1995 and 1997. An analysis based on three groups has enabled us to examine this development. The first category comprises individuals whose daily food intake is limited to the three traditional meals (some even forgo a meal, without compensating for this through additional intake). Eaters in the second category add one or two further instances of snacking to the three standard meals. The third category contains those eaters who consume food six times or more during the day; that is, they add at least three further instances of food intake to the three standard meals, rising to fifteen instances a day in some cases (Table 5). The profiles of the population groups showing increased instances of daily food intake is the same as that of the individuals simplifying the composition of their meals, the one exception being the distance of the commute to work (Table 6).

TABLE 5 Instances of food intake, comparison between 1995 and 1997

	1995	1997	Variation
<= 3 instances At least three traditional meals	22.80	18.90	−3.90
4 or 5 instances The three meals, plus one or two between- meal snacks	53.50	40.90	−12.60
6 or more instances (up to 15) The three meals plus three or more between- meal snacks	23.60	40.20	+16.60
Total	100.00	100.00	

TABLE 6 Correlation between food intake between meals and independent variables

Variables	Related tendency
Place of residence	Daily instances of food intake increase with degree of urbanization
Profession and socioeconomic classification	Daily instances of food intake are higher among executives and white-collar workers
Gender	Daily instances of food intake are higher among women
Age	No connection
Income	No connection
Total length of commute	No connection

Overall, out of 1,157 people studied, there were 6,144 instances of food intake (including both meals and consumption between meals). These were broken down into 3,266 meals, giving a consumption rate of 2.82 per person, and 2,875 instances of consumption between meals, corresponding to an intake rate of 2.48 per person. Three quarters of these represent liquid intakes (calorific drinks, fruit juices, beers, coffees, teas, and so on), and one quarter represents solid foods, such as cakes and fruit.

From a geographical viewpoint, the workplace is by far the main location for food consumption between meals. Types of intake are fairly clearly distributed

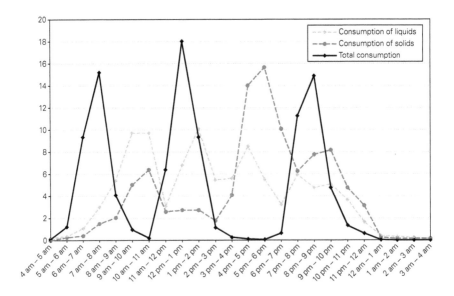

FIGURE 2 *Times of food intake occurring throughout the day.*

in relation to the time of day. The consumption of liquids generally takes place throughout the day, peaking at four points: morning, after lunch, midafternoon, and evening. The consumption of solid food is largely spread over the afternoon and evening, with a very high concentration evident in the afternoon (Figure 2).

3.3 The location of food consumption

The third characteristic of modern eating practices is the introduction of food consumption into the workplace. This does not refer to the company restaurant or cafeteria, but to the office itself, meeting rooms or staff lounges. This trend concerns lunch and consumption between meals. The practice of taking meals in one's office has increased more markedly in the third sector, affecting 26.25 percent of the sample studied in 1997, with around 10 percent of those questioned having over one meal a month in their offices. These figures represent general, declarative data that appear to underestimate the phenomenon, as from the analysis of the days preceding the survey, over 15 percent of the population concerned had eaten the previous day's lunch in their offices. The food had been brought from home or bought from takeaway establishments near their work, even in cases where the employees had access to a company restaurant. The lunchbox is making something of a comeback.

Contrary to what one might think, these new practices, which mainly concern female executives and employees, are not motivated by economic considerations (1.71 percent), nor even by a possible boredom with the company restaurant (3.77 percent). The first reason given relates to time management. You save time, extend meetings or work sessions, you avoid queueing and avoid wasting time moving around. This is therefore a way of regulating one's workload. The much higher proportion of women adopting this practice should be seen in relation to their schedules. For a woman with children, the working day is punctuated by two fixed points: time of arrival and time of departure. These are determined, to a greater or lesser degree, by bringing and collecting children to and from school or a childminder. In this context, any variations in the workload are partly regulated through meal duration. For men, with fewer exterior constraints of this type on their schedules, meal duration is more consistent. Their way of absorbing the workload consists of varying their hours of arrival and above all, of departure. In a more general context, however, this is a question of personal investment in the workplace; during meal times this becomes a matter of getting "a bit of space" to oneself. We should likewise note the high rate of nonresponses, which no doubt conceal some practices that deviate from company policy, such as more or less personal use of the telephone, the Minitel network or the internet.

The second way in which food consumption has been introduced to the workplace is through snacking between meals. Fifty-five percent of instances of consumption between meals take place in the working environment. This intake occurs in the form of drinks such as coffee, tea or fruit juice, or of biscuits, fruit, and so on. This type of consumption has a markedly socialized character, and forms part of the informal organization that operates within the professional domain. It provides occasions for social interaction, which, although unofficial, are not totally unconnected from the world of work. The image of the solitary, compulsive snacker has thus given way to an entirely different reality for the working population.

3.4 *Profiles of food days*

It is possible to construct various types of "food days" by examining ways in which people combine different main meals (breakfast, lunch, and dinner) with between-meal snacks, and the times of their consumption during the morning, afternoon or evening. These types can then be organized into groups in order to create profiles. A typological study of different food days has already been undertaken by Grignon in 1985, in an analysis of eating practices among students carried out for the Centre National des Œuvres Universitaires et Scolaires (Grignon 1987b, 1993).

It allows us to make two types of comparison. The first relates to the actual form of the typology, in other words, the choice of categories considered to be pertinent, and the second, in the case of shared categories, involves making comparisons between sample size and distribution.

In our study of 1997, the most frequently occurring type belonged to the "three meals a day" category, although it only accounted for 13.6 percent of cases. In second position came the category comprising "three meals a day with an afternoon snack" (8.58 percent), then in third place "three meals a day with a morning and afternoon snack" (8.41 percent). Finally, the fourth most common type of day featured "three meals a day plus a morning snack," accounting for 6.85 percent of the sample.

We have grouped these different types of food day into nine categories (Table 7). The modal profile comprises a daily intake of three traditional meals plus at least two further instances of consumption during the morning and afternoon. This profile accounts for 21.49 percent of the sample. The second most typical profile, accounting for 20.28 percent of the sample, represents individuals who skip one of the traditional meals and add one or more intakes between meals. The third-placed category represents those who consume nothing between meals (including instances of skipping a meal without replacing the intake). These account for just 14.64 percent of the sample.

If we compare these findings with Grignon's data, certain marked differences appear. "To eat normally," he writes, "also involves eating nothing,

TABLE 7 Profiles of food days

Categories	Frequency	%
3 meals + 1 intake in the morning + at least 1 intake in the afternoon	248	21.49
One of the 3 meals skipped + 1 or more intakes	234	20.28
3 meals or fewer	169	14.64
3 meals + at least 1 intake in the afternoon	149	12.91
3 meals +1 intake in the morning + afternoon + evening	124	10.75
3 meals + at least 1 intake in the morning	107	9.27
3 meals + at least 1 intake in the afternoon + at least 1 intake in the evening	58	5.03
3 meals + at least 1 intake in the morning + at least 1 intake in the evening	43	3.73
3 meals + at least 1 intake in the evening	22	1.91
Total	**1,154**	**100.00**

or as little as possible between meals. Over a third of the days studied (37.1%) feature only the three main meals; there are no increases in intermediary breaks (drinks, coffee breaks, aperitifs etc.), even on days when a meal is forgone" (Grignon 1993, 312).

In the case of the group studied (all of whom were in employment and had access to a company restaurant) we note that days comprising only the three traditional meals account for just 14.6 percent of the sample, as opposed to Grignon's statistic of 37.1 percent. They therefore do not (or no longer) represent the normal way of eating in the statistical sense. The data clearly shows an increased number of "intermediary breaks" (drinks, coffee breaks, aperitifs etc.), to use Grignon's words, including days when a meal is skipped, since 79.72 percent of the food days in the sample include intakes between meals. Days comprising at least three instances of consumption between meals, that is, the three traditional meals plus one intake in the morning, afternoon and evening respectively, accounted for just 1.7 percent in Grignon's survey, whereas in the present study they represent over 10 percent. It transpires that the normal form in the statistical sense, occurring in 21.49 percent of cases, features a combination of the three meals, plus one additional intake in the morning and afternoon respectively, whereas it accounted for just 5.6 percent of the samples in the survey on student eating practices.

How might such differences between the two pieces of research be explained? The first answer may lie in the groups selected for the survey; students in Grignon's case, and company employees who eat in their firm's restaurant in the case of the present study. Yet, considering the related variables, notably age (not related regarding meals and between-meal intakes, but related regarding profiles of food days) we might have expected the resulting differences to be quite the reverse. Grignon considers the student population to be a useful site of observation from which to identify possible changes. Indeed, he writes:

> Students are young people in a state of rupture (not established, not "fixed," allegedly prone to acts of contravention and protest, etc.), yet at the same time they are genuine trailblazers (insofar as they are likely to be future members of the dominant classes). As such, they are ideal subjects to observe regarding the practice of punctuating the day with food breaks, and the possible emergence of a new model. (Grignon 1993, 310)

The second explanation might take account of the time lapse between the two studies: the first dates from 1985, the second from 1997. The changes observed would therefore be the result of a series of shifts that had not been discerned in 1985. In this case, we would be dealing with an extremely rapid transformation. The third reason for these differences may lie in the methods implemented: the sampling and data collection techniques. The student survey centers on a nation-wide sample, structured according to discipline, cycle and year of studies, and the location of the universities in question. The data was collected by means of a self-administered questionnaire. Out of 4,530 questionnaires sent out, only 1,788 were genuinely usable, representing a response rate of 40 percent. Not all the students, therefore, took the time to fill in the questionnaire, which concerned their food intake for a whole week. We might equally argue that those students who accepted this task and thus filled in the questionnaire, were perhaps those least likely to be "in a state of rupture" ("not established, not 'fixed' . . .") and the least "prone to acts of contravention," to borrow the terms used by Claude Grignon. There would therefore have been a selection process at work in the sample, due to the method of collecting the data. In a face-to-face interview, we implement methods—such as those we have developed for this research—to enable interviewees to reconstruct their daily food intake. It frequently transpires that in the course of reconstructing their day, they remember instances of food consumption from the previous day that they had failed to recall. This phenomenon of forgetting, or of semantic reconstruction, whereby eating is associated solely with structured forms of meal consumption, seems all the more prevalent as there is a discrepancy between the normative system and the practices actually carried out (Poulain et al. 1996, 1998b).

4 The discrepancy between norms and practices

First, a distinction should be made between the "social norm" and the "dietary norm." The latter incorporates a series of recommendations supported by scientific knowledge of nutrition and disseminated by the medical community and its representatives. With a tendency to fluctuate according to scientific discoveries and the influences affecting the advisors, it defines, in both quantitative and qualitative terms, what constitutes a good, balanced meal. Furthermore, it explains[4] how food intake in general should be regulated in order to maintain the individual in a state of good health.

For its part, the social norm relates to a set of conventions regarding the structural composition of food intakes—both in the case of meals and between-meal consumption—and the circumstances and contexts of that consumption. Social and dietary norms exert a reciprocal influence on one another. In France, a meal regarded as the social norm is a unit composed of four categories: starter, main dish and accompaniments, cheese and dessert. A simpler version, comprising a starter, a main dish with accompaniments, and a dessert, is also acceptable. This format appears, for example, in school canteen menus, or in the contracts exchanged between an institutional catering company and a client firm or management. In defining the service to be provided for their clients, those responsible for drawing up such documents are clarifying the concept of a "normal" meal, shared by the particular group in question. It is also evident in the menu plans prepared by secondary school bursars, by dieticians in healthcare institutions, by nutrition and culinary consultants for women's magazines, and so on. At a personal level, the social norm may be identified through the definition of a proper meal given by the individual.

Commenting on American studies, Fischler highlights one of the essential difficulties involved in collecting food consumption data. "The number of food contacts in a day was around twenty. However, most of the respondents stated that they ate three meals a day. In this way, modern eaters always believe that they have three meals a day, a situation comparable to that of amputees who still feel their missing arm or leg, like a phantom limb" (1990).

The spontaneous response to the question "How many times did you eat yesterday?" reestablishes internalized social (individual) norms. A question of this type and its reply are certainly not devoid of interest, as they enable us to examine norms, attitudes and representations—but the data obtained cannot be seen in terms of objective behavior variables. It is therefore expedient to distinguish between actual practices that have been objectified—either directly through observation, or by the media, in relation to economic variables— and "reported practices" declared in interviews. The latter may be subject to transformation, semantic reconstruction, memory lapse or denial. In the distortion of behavior-related data during the communication process, in the possible discrepancy between declared and actual behavior, lies sociological material of prime importance that reveals the evolution of food practices. In cross-referencing data regarding behavior (what eaters actually do) with individual norms (what do you see as a proper meal?), a certain number of discrepancies emerge.

While around 62 percent of those questioned considered that a proper meal should comprise at least a starter, a main dish with accompaniments and a dessert, just 53 percent of them adhered to this norm at midday, and only 39 percent in the evening. The vast majority (80.8 percent) of the respondents considered that eating between meals "might cause problems"; 28.5 percent felt that the practice "should be examined," while 52.3 percent viewed it as "definitely bad." At the same time, 74.6 percent of these acknowledged that they did sometimes eat between meals. Only 22.8 percent adhered strictly to the principle of three meals a day, and 41.2 percent acknowledged that they had five instances of food intake or more during the day. In this way, a contradiction between internalized norms (social and/or dietetic) and actual practices has emerged.

An analysis of two midday meals viewed in relation to the individual norm brings to light different behavioral types, which can be plotted on a graph with two axes: traditional norm ⇐⇒ simplified norm, structured practices ⇐⇒ simplified practices. We can distinguish consistent behavior, whereby practices conform to the described norm. They represent 58.3 percent of the whole sample, but this consistency manifests itself in two ways:

- **Traditional consistency** (31.7 percent)
  In this case, the individuals describe a traditional norm (the complete meal) and adhere to it in their daily practices. The correlated variables are: place of residence (rural locations and middle-sized towns), professional category (blue-collar workers and middle-ranking professionals), and gender (predominantly male);

- **New consistency** (20.6 percent)
  In this case, the eaters refer to a simplified norm (a meal without a starter or dessert, or even just a single dish), and the meals consumed effectively take this form. This practice is predominantly characteristic of women, more common among employees and executives, and very strongly linked to urbanization (with a heavy emphasis on inhabitants of Paris and the Paris region). Lastly, it is generally more typical of young respondents.

The "new behavior", showing a consistency between practices and norms, is exhibited by social groups whose numbers are increasing (city dwellers, employees and executives in the third sector), while traditional behavior is linked to social groups whose numbers are in decline. A genuine process of change can therefore be identified here (Figure 3).

However, a significant number of individuals (47.7 percent) demonstrate a discrepancy between practices and declared norms. This difference increases with the level of urbanization, regardless of the norm. Two main forms may be identified:

- **Traditional norm, simplified practices** (17 percent)
  The norm is traditional, but the meals are incomplete, with varying degrees of consistency. While retaining traditional models as a reference, individuals have integrated changes of an adaptive nature into their practices. There is a slight male predominance here;

- **Simplified norm, traditional practices** (20.7 percent)
  The individual has internalized the notion of simplification, but continues to eat complete meals. The vast majority following this practice are women. This reflects the competing obligations of the female role in transmitting values expressed through meals, and the bodily aesthetic of slenderness, which imposes constraints on food intake.

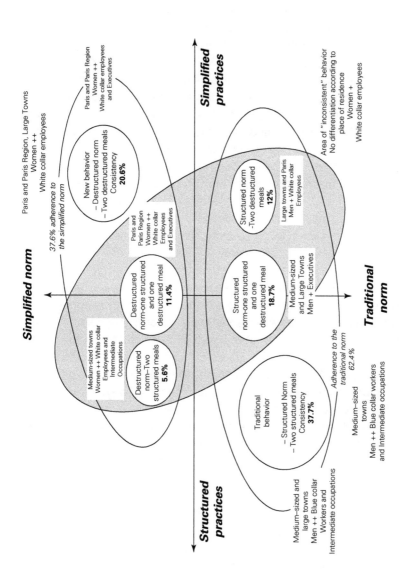

FIGURE 3 *Discrepancy between norms and practices.*

Source: J. P. Poulain, J. M. Delorme, M. Gineste, 1995, The Ministry of Agriculture, SHR.

The debate surrounding the destructuration of eating practices was unquestionably framed in excessively general terms, combining practices implemented at the concrete level, and, more broadly, the determining social factors. Are eating practices evolving? In a word—yes! Meals are becoming simpler in structure. Despite the use of self-administered questionnaires, which always have a fairly significant nonresponse rate, the most recent work carried out by Grignon (2000) and CREDOC, shows the same processes of simplification at work, even though they may be narrower in range.

Is eating between meals on the rise? Again, the answer is yes. The results of sociological studies and economic data can be used to support this argument. However, these changes are developing against a background of guilt. Faced with an uncertain situation that recalls the old problem of the half-full or half-empty glass, some tend to think that the traditional French-style meal is doing "quite alright." Comments from the press emphasize contradictions, the media coverage of the CREDOC report of 1997 being a perfect example of this. Page 145 of the report states that "the full meal, comprising a starter, main dish and dessert is taking something of a back seat nowadays, even in the evening"; it accounts for only 24.2 percent of cases in the survey. In its summary of the survey, CREDOC highlights the resistance of the traditional French meal, on the strength of which a number of daily papers ran the headlines: "Culinary traditions hold out against fast food."[5] This example shows how the issue of the destructuring process operating on modern eating practices, framed in excessively general, exaggerated terms, has been appropriated by the narrative based on fears of a threat to identity. It is quite true that not everything in France is "going to the dogs," and we are not being invaded by American habits; there are several signs to confirm the "resistance" of the French food consumption model. However, it should be recognized that our daily eating practices have undergone a transformation.

The model of three meals a day and of the three-course meal is a recent invention. An ethnological study of the eating practices of rural communities in different French regions reveals the existence of a system based on a dual structure. Five meals were eaten in summer and four in winter, in accordance with both the rhythm and nature of the work carried out and the length of the days (Poulain 1984; Poulain et al.1988). Jean-Paul Aron has highlighted the shift that occurred in the mid-nineteenth-century, when the *service à la française*—designating a meal organized into three successive services, the number of dishes being proportionate to the number of guests—was replaced by the *service à la russe*, or Russian style service, where everyone eats the same meal, and the dishes are presented sequentially (Aron 1976). In a detailed study on the times of meals between 1100 and 1808, Jean-Louis Flandrin shows that these have been subject to ceaseless changes throughout history (Flandrin 1993). A historical approach to the subject highlights the diversity of eating practices; on a social level, the rural peasantry did not eat in the same way as the middle class, laborers or craftsmen. In nineteenth-century rural eating practices, the timing and number of meals consumed varied according to season and was different, for instance, in summer and winter. "The new development" states François Sigaut, "is that there is now one sole norm, that of three meals a day, one eaten in the morning, one at midday and one in the evening, so that different forms of food days are now perceived as deviations from a shared norm rather than as different norms" (1993, 71).

At the symposium "Time for Eating: Food, Time and Social Patterns," Françoise Sabban examined a type of "culinary otherness" that was particularly enlightening with regard to understanding French eating habits. After describing the ritual surrounding Chinese meals, she explained:

> However, Chinese eating practices cannot be restricted to this meal system, which can seem fixed and constraining, although it is intended to contribute to food sufficiency. When economic and/or political conditions allow it, the time between meals is used for personalized consumption, which is not bound by rules. For centuries, the alleys and lanes have been lined with street food stalls and vendors offering specialty snacks that people eat whenever they like, quite informally, at any time of the day or night. (Sabban 1993)

There have been numerous anthropological studies showing systems of food consumption where highly institutionalized eating practices coexist with grazing habits.

5 From anomie to a crisis of legitimacy for the normative system

An analysis of discrepancies between norms and practices, and of the intensified attachment to the model of three structured meals, prompts a return to the theory of anomie. Philippe Besnard (1987) has shown how this notion owes its success partly to its polysemic nature. In the great era of classical sociology, the word became a marker of sociological discourse, a sign of recognition. Since then, it has experienced a period in the wilderness. This is due in no small part to the influence of Besnard's work, his self-appointed mission being to "do away with the somewhat magical concept of the golden age of sociology." Interest in anomie appears to have been revived in the domain of general sociology; its examination of norms occupies a significant place in current sociological studies. Aware both of the "limitations of the concept" and of the "notional void," Jean-Daniel Reynaud (1995) proposes abandoning an excessively broad definition, such as "absence of norms," in favor of a concept forming part of a theory of control. In this way, he reduces the notion of anomie to the loss of legitimacy of the normative system, with its rules and standards. In his view: ". . . the rule offers salvation, not because it is restrictive, but because its restrictions are accepted. Anomie is not defined by the 'objective' absence of rules, but by the weakening of legitimate control." In this way, the concept has regained its viability.

The situation in which modern eaters find themselves is not characterized by a lack of rules, but rather by a plethora of contradictory discourses of a didactic nature. Gastro-anomie is not only linked to a crisis in the normative system, but also to a proliferation of contradictory orders. These multiple discourses, based on well-being, aesthetics, identity, theoretical crises, and the trends that permeate them, all contribute to a dietetic "cacophony," formed of

1 Fluctuating and contradictory dietetic discourses

2 The reductionist nature of medical rhetoric with its focus on the body

3 A narrative centered on our inability to control the practices and methods of the agrifood industry, which from "Madrigal" cheese to mad cow disease, is tampering with man's position in the natural world and in the animal kingdom

4 A crisis in culinary aesthetics, aggravated by the opposition between international cuisine and dietary nationalism emphasized in the media

5 The obligation to attain the aesthetic physical ideal, which has established the emaciated body as the norm and stands in direct opposition to the principle of finding pleasure in eating

In this way, gastro-anomie refers to a surfeit of rules, rather than an absence, as a deluge of imperatives rains down upon the modern eater (Poulain 1998a). The most astonishing aspect is that, even though individuals express their attachment to the three-course meal, adhering to that norm is not generally thought to result in a balanced diet (fewer than 2 percent of those questioned thought it could do so, while the vast majority thought the norm should be respected). There is an anxious quest for new, legitimate rules, with science, the body, pleasure and moderation all being involved (Poulain 1998a). Certain best-selling diet books, presented as clear and simple digests, claim to combine various types of scientific expertise (along the lines of the Montignac Method). Their success can be ascribed to their function of conveying reassurance. They include both social norms and their "scientific" justification.

The perfect situation with books of this type occurs when tradition is reinforced by science, as is the case with the famous French Paradox. We may leave nutritionists with the task of discussing their scientific validity and of distinguishing between scientific discoveries and media blitz campaigns (Apfelbaum 1994). The sociologist, however, will undoubtedly note the apparent disregard for the contradiction between attachment to a traditional normative system and the appeal to scientific discourse in the quest for a balanced diet. As argued by Annie Hubert in an article devoted to the Mediterranean diet, which she has no hesitation in describing as a "bio-medical myth," there is not just *one* Mediterranean diet—there are *several*. From the Eastern to the Western Mediterranean, there are profound differences in food practices, as well as differences between various social categories within the same geographical area. "Are we not all engaged on a perpetual quest for the potion that will put an end to all our physical and psychological problems? Belief in an ideal, time-honored and unchangeable diet would at least have one beneficial effect: it would lessen our anxieties" (Hubert 1998, 159).

6 Overabundance and the new poverty

In identifying the consequences of a food surplus, it is important not to overlook the emergence of new forms of vulnerability, as not everyone is benefitting from the situation. The appearance of a new type of poverty amid plenty is the most striking and visible sign of this. It has mobilized charitable organizations and led to the establishment of social welfare programs for this "Fourth World," while certain associations such as the Restaurants du Cœur have been granted legal status as a recognized public utility. Social exclusion sociologists are trying to gain greater understanding of the different phases in the process of social disqualification, to identify the population groups involved and the trajectories that lead to exclusion (Paugam 1991, 1993). Yet the most visibly excluded groups, such as the homeless, are not alone in having less to eat than they would like. By studying people's aspirations we can identify the value systems underlying their needs and determine their prioritization. In a previously discussed study examining the food-related aspirations of the fifty to sixty-year-old age bracket, we asked the following question: "If you had more money to spend on food, what would you use it for?" This allowed us to compare the responses obtained by the Institut National de la Santé et de la Recherche Medicale (INSERM) in its survey of 1966 (Trémolières et al. 1966). It also gave us a deeper insight into the dynamics involved in contemporary food-related aspirations. All too often nowadays, the consumption experts analyzing these dynamics adopt a general, all-encompassing perspective,

TABLE 8 Food-related aspirations of 50–60 year olds

	1966	1998	1998
	In terms of % of responses		In terms of % of individuals
Improve quantity	38%	16%	19%
Improve quality	49%	27%	32%
Restaurants, entertaining	9%	51%	62%
Other	4%	7%	8%
	100%	100%	

Source: OCHA, Poulain 1998.

which leads them to describe food expenditure as "approaching saturation point" (Rochefort 1995, 237).

The shift in the aspiration to *improve quantity* from 38 percent in 1966 down to 16 percent in 1998, can certainly be explained by the increase in purchasing power that occurred between those years. However, the figure of 16 percent obtained from a sample of householders interviewed at home in 1998 confirms that there were still cases where not everyone had as much food as they would have liked, without necessarily going hungry (Table 8). The problems with modern-day eating practices are therefore not invariably related to an over abundant supply of food.

4

From food risks and food safety to anxiety management

Before the 1990s, the notion of food security encompassed a variety of measures implemented to fight the risk of famine threatening certain parts of the world. Economists, agronomists, anthropologists, and sociologists specializing in development engage in research and contribute their expertise to programs aimed at fighting hunger, backed by international sponsors and nongovernmental organizations (NGOs) (Olivier de Sardan 1995; Padilla et al. 1995). Recently, in developed societies where there is an abundance, even an over-abundance of food, the term "food security" has taken on a new meaning. However, in this instance, the notion of risk covers a series of dangers linked not to a lack or scarcity of food, but to its quality. These include poisoning from chemical or microbiological hazards, and in the long term, the consequences of new technological methods applied to food production and processing, in addition to newly discovered pathologies such as prion diseases. To differentiate between the two types of risk, experts suggest using "food safety" to designate those associated with food consumption.

The situation in the West is paradoxical, to say the least. While experts consider that the objective risks relating to food safety and hygiene in developed societies are at an all-time low, the general public feels them to be significantly greater (Apfelbaum 1998). The world is therefore now divided between those who lack or live in fear of lacking food, and those who are afraid of what they eat. In the Western press, reports on the famine in Somalia are juxtaposed, somewhat shamefully, with the real and imagined risks posed by the highly processed food known in France as *mal bouffe*. In a cartoon in French satirical weekly *Le Canard Enchaîné* entitled "Famine in the Horn of

Africa," Kerleroux highlights this modern-day contradiction, with his image of a Somalian asking for "Even a bit of *mal-bouffe*!"

In France, and more broadly in Europe, the feeling of anxiety has been exacerbated since the emergence of the second mad cow crisis, triggered by the development of bovine spongiform encephalopathy (BSE). The theme of a general phenomenon of madness has gripped society. Not only cows are mad—everyone seems to be similarly afflicted. That is the impression one gains from the discourse concerning the contemporary food crisis.

"Consumers have gone mad." "They want totally contradictory things." "This hysteria must end!" The same opinions may also be heard from beef industry professionals, politicians and experts, as well as from journalists. This diagnosis is hardly more cheering when given by a publicist, during one of the countless events connected with the subject of food risk, where consumers were quite simply described as "schizophrenic." There was an analyst, presenting definitions from a dictionary of psychiatry and talking of a "return to reality."

Yet, apparently the media was equally insane! Before the second mad cow crisis, certain politicians took to repeating: "It's not cows who are mad—it's the press!"

The accusation leveled at the press was widespread throughout the food industry, including the production and processing sectors, and even the scientific community. The media was criticized for being irresponsible, for "chasing headlines," or "looking for emotional reactions." "It's all about who's making the biggest fuss." "They're more interested in drama and sensationalism than serious investigation." Agribusiness industrialists were likewise accused of madness, with agricultural suppliers being singled out for particular blame. They were described as "drunk on profits," "capable of anything," of having "no respect for even the most basic laws of nature," and of being "ready to do anything for a bit of extra cash." Livestock animals had become "the dustbins of the industrial world": carcasses of diseased animals, sewage sludge, used oil, human placentas—all of these were transformed into fodder for livestock.

It was then time for the scientists to be accused of insanity. In late 1999, *Le Monde Diplomatique* ran the headline: "The mad scientists of agribusiness." Certain researchers were described in the article as being capable of anything in order to profit from the industry's largesse with the aim of supplementing their meager research funding, when they were not frankly "selling out to unscrupulous industrialists." Finally, for good measure, politicians were also portrayed as mad, oscillating confusedly between "scientism" and "psychologism" in their attempts to manage the crisis. "Sometimes they swear by the experts, other times it's all about pandering to public opinion and emotions"; "they're fixated on the polls."

The widespread use of vocabulary based on madness leads one to think of the crisis in psychopathological terms, whereby other parties have entirely lost their reason. This motivates the quest to reassure consumers, to help them regain their common sense, or at least their confidence. This attitude is common in the world of marketing, and plays a large part in company decision-making. It involves thinking of solutions to the crisis based on informing, communicating with, and sometimes educating the consumer.

A second way of approaching the critical situation caused by these outbreaks is rooted in the sociology of science. It involves studying the discrepancies between the notion of risk as defined by experts and the general public respectively. The view, according to this analysis, is that the latter's perception is far from irrational; on the contrary, it provides certain insights that scientists have excluded from their investigations. A dialogue based on the thoughts of scientists and the general public should therefore be established, in the interests not only of democracy, but of practicality. This communication would highlight the social issues underlying these crises. As a result, the public debate would be effectively controlled, facilitating crisis management.

The sociology of food provides a third perspective, in the view that food poisoning is a reality that has profoundly affected and shaped the collective imagination throughout history, and that anxiety has been a constant feature of human eating practices. It forms one of the bases of sociality, through the dual threats of shortage and poisoning respectively, and through the social relations involved in its control, from production to consumption. The problem is therefore not created by the risk as such, or even by the anxiety that accompanies it, but rather by the social changes affecting its management.

Anxiety related to eating lies at the heart of our relationship with food (Fischler 1990; Paul-Lévy 1997). It takes different guises according to social context and forms part of the ebb and flow of various trends. In this way, the current crisis may be interpreted as the result of the disintegration of regulatory systems. The objective of this perspective is to understand the functioning of systems designed to manage food-based anxiety, and to try to identify ways in which they might be reconstructed and updated.

While these three interpretive frameworks are not exclusive in character, they have different approaches to the various crisis-management tools, such as traceability, food labeling, and public conferences, as well as different expectations. In the case of the latter two perspectives, the loss of reason exhibited by other parties in the form of irrationality or madness is interpreted not as a lack of confidence, but as a crisis in the collective construction of the political, social and health-related choices underlying contemporary eating practices.

1 The misunderstanding of quality

A short-term view of history suggests that the food crisis began with the outbreak of mad cow disease. It is certainly true that this event marks a decisive moment, when risk took a new form, in both symbolic and actual terms. Yet an analysis reveals that history is positively overflowing with stories of food poisoning and food-related crises, the objective scale of which far exceeds the problem facing us today. Consequently, the situation calls for a study of the techno-social developments that preceded our modern-day crisis, to facilitate our understanding of its specific characteristics and the breadth of its impact.

In the 1970s, hormone-injected veal and chicken made the news. Chemical fertilizers, pesticides and plant growth regulators all reflected the obsessive, promethean ambitions of the agronomists. The environmental movement, which originated from the anti-establishment student uprising that erupted in France in May 1968, spurned this "industrial food" as categorically as it rejected the social structure that gave rise to it. The announcement that artificial "petroleum steaks" would be making an appearance in the near future was greeted with as much enthusiasm as the advent of genetically modified foods today.

During the 1980s, calm was regained on the food front. Consumers seemed to have confidence in industrial products. The agrifood sector no longer displayed its aggressive technology, and learned how to market its products, in other words, to care about what its clients thought. Its use of the four-color printing process for packaging confirmed the fact that this was proper food. Now the focus was on quality, an extension of the shift toward integrating the consumer's perspective into industrial management policies. Quality was now defined as "products adapted to consumer needs and uses."

In this way, individual consumers and the reasoning behind their choices have become the ultimate focus of quality monitoring systems. Dressed in their white coats, quality control specialists check raw material, manufacturing processes and final products. Attention is now centered on the International Organization for Standardization (ISO) standards, the Hazard Analysis and Critical Control Points (HACCP) method, self-testing and quality management.

This is a ubiquitous theme within companies, and is even becoming a major line of external communication. Although consumers do not always understand this discourse, the fact that it deals with quality means that they are certainly ready to take heed. Unfortunately, however, the word "quality" does not have exactly the same meaning for consumers and experts. The former see it in a simple and naïve light, as an indication of things that are good; this marks the beginning of a prodigious misunderstanding. They gradually discover a world of industry that is very different from the realm previously depicted in the packaging. They are now promised that bacteriological control systems are in place to reduce the risk of food poisoning. This leads them to conclude that the many precautions taken prove that eating is, in fact, a risky business, which is not something they had previously considered. They had simply thought that the very least they could expect when eating a product bought from a company, or a meal in a restaurant, was not to get food poisoning. They are reassured that raw materials are subject to quality control, when they had never even imagined that it could be otherwise, let alone that such materials might be of poor quality. In a curious boomerang effect, the more often firms or public authorities refer to safety and quality, the more anxious consumers become, the implicit reasoning behind this being: "if so many precautions are taken, then it must be really dangerous!"

This situation has prompted manufacturers and politicians to ask sociologists questions along the lines of: "how can we get consumers to understand all the efforts we are making?" The same effect is apparent with regard to product information. Although it is emphatically demanded by consumer associations, and seen by manufacturers as a way of showing they have absolutely nothing to hide, the information provided does not seem capable of allaying fears and reassuring consumers. Franck Cochoy (1999, 2000) has analyzed this paradox, showing that the dissemination of information has contributed to the development of "consumer expertise." The provision of such information reassures consumers, as it provides them with standards to govern their options, selections and direction when purchasing food; however, at the same time their knowledge makes them aware of new, previously unknown areas that have become sources of worry. With increased information now available to the consumer, the veil has been lifted on the previously little-known world of industrial kitchens, heralding the era of suspicion and its constant companion, the rhetoric of scandal: "They're not telling us everything! They're hiding something!"

2 Risk and modern societies

For the past few years, sociological studies in England, Germany and France have been identifying risk as one of the characteristics of modern society (Giddens 1993; Beck 1992; Le Breton 1991, 1995). These analyses do not focus explicitly on problems relating to food, but they may contribute to our understanding of some of the issues it involves. For Beck, the concept of risk emerges in modern societies when events that affect humankind "through destiny, the whims of the gods or nature" are no longer explained. He dates its appearance from the time of the great discoveries and the development of man's technological mastery over nature. The great expeditions and the rapid expansion of international maritime commerce both involved risk. People sought to control the future by calculating risks and producing risk-related statistics; this new framework of reference played a part in the transformation of the causal chain. Unfortunate events then appeared as the result of a series of misguided decisions. Destiny was thus supplanted by human responsibility. The notion of risk was associated with discovering the world, in both the geographical and the scientific sense. There was a shift away from revealed or traditional truth to a truth constructed within the experience of reality. "Risk emerges when nature and tradition lose their influence, and man must make decisions on his own initiative" (Beck 1999).

Victims were initially seen as responsible for their misfortunes, having made poor decisions.

A second phase followed, which involved seeking human accountability beyond that of the victims themselves. Those suffering an accident at work had previously been seen as victims of fate. They were subsequently considered to be responsible for what had befallen them. This responsibility was viewed in a moralizing light; they were thought of as culpable, the agents of their own misfortunes. Finally, looking further afield in the quest for accountability, the focus shifted to companies and their operating systems, with a view to possible compensation of a pecuniary nature. In this way, cause and responsibility in the case of accidents are dissociated from one another, as the latter becomes subject to a series of social norms and negotiations intended to establish the payment of damages.

These social systems both reflect and contribute to the process of judicialization that has been established in today's society. The emergence of huge transnational companies, both in the agribusiness and agrisupply sectors, has created conditions favorable for large-scale compensation payouts. At the same time, increasingly sensitive monitoring systems have been established, thanks to scientific progress in the identification and analysis of risk. Despite this, the rates at which knowledge and its attendant dark side are advancing have contributed to a growing feeling of insecurity. Yet, above all, they have facilitated the process of recognizing accountability and identifying guilty parties, which could in some cases lead to scapegoating (Champagne 2000, 279).

3 Risk: The experts' view, the public's view

The sociology of risk highlights the discrepancies between the methods of evaluating risk used by scientists and the general public respectively. The experts apply statistical tools, and their reasoning is based on probability. The public perception of risk is subject to the influence of certain social factors. In this way, the impression of risk is more keenly felt in social groups removed from centers of power and decision making (Douglas and Wildavsky 1982).

Familiarity with technology also plays a part (a new and hitherto unknown processing technique is deemed more dangerous than a traditional technological method; this is the case, for instance, with irradiated foods, which are seen as representing a greater risk than tinned items). The feeling of mastery and personal control is likewise a decisive factor; flying is viewed as more dangerous than driving a car oneself, although statistically the former is far safer (Slovic 1987, 1993).

Finally, it seems that women show more anxiety than men with regard to food, even in countries as diverse as France, Japan, Belgium, and Holland (Rozin et al. 1999).

Moreover, while scientific risk analysis focuses on evaluating the negative consequences of an act, the general public weighs up the possible advantages and risks using the cost-benefit principle.

As a result of these profound differences, the dialogue between quality control or safety specialists and consumers is often problematic, with the former viewing the latter as irrational and opposed to progress. In this type of situation, the experts are tempted either to take refuge in arguments based on their authoritative position, or to try and educate the "ordinary folk," enabling them to understand the scientific truth.

In order to find a way out of this impasse, we must consider the strategic conflicts that have developed around the theme of risk, viewing these discrepancies as a confrontation between different types of rationality (Beck 1999). Claire Marris emphasizes the qualitative dimension of risk analysis as evaluated by the public. While experts

focus on the probability of a harmful event occurring by assessing the consequences in quantitative terms, basing their conclusions almost exclusively on mortality . . . the general public incorporate more qualitative criteria into their definition of risk, being more interested in the nature of the consequences than in their probability. Moreover, they accord particular importance to the circumstances surrounding exposure to risks, and to the types of individuals concerned. (Marris 1999, 47)

Public perception is structured, perhaps quantified—according to the psycho-metric paradigm, for instance (Marris, Langford, and O'Riordan 1998)—and, to a certain extent, foreseeable. In this way, it is not irrational, but is more complex than that of the experts. Taking public perception into account is therefore a justifiable enterprise, as it can elucidate certain aspects of the problem that have not been clarified through scientific evaluation. Analyses based strictly on science exclude certain social dimensions of risk, such as identity issues and societal choices— precisely the factors that lie at the heart of social controversies and conflicts.

The psychometric model may at least be used to understand the intensified impression that we are experiencing a food crisis, although it may not explain why this has occurred so suddenly. The profound changes that have taken place within the food sector, its extension and its concentration in increasingly large-scale companies, are all distancing eaters from the natural origins of food products, disconnecting them from their traditional natural and social environment. In this way, the very nature of the food-related risk has been transformed. It has become immediate, as culinary activity has been partly taken over by industry. The concentration of food production into increasingly larger scale units makes it all the more likely that a considerable number of people will be affected by any problem. As a result of the extreme accuracy of evaluation tools, coupled with policies of observing and assessing hygiene risks, eating has been highlighted as the focus of new, immediate threats. These include food-borne disease outbreaks, or delayed illnesses such as those caused by the accumulative effects of heavy metal levels, or prion diseases. This transformation has reached its peak in the school canteen sector, where consumers represent the future of the nation but are seen as incapable of making choices.

Having worked on the risks presented by genetically modified organisms (GMOs), British researchers from the Economic and Social Research Council (ESRC) take the view that "the public is not stupid and ignorant in its approach to risks," and that it has a qualified understanding of the main issues. They conclude that it is vital to take public perception into account when evaluating risks, as it helps to clarify and question scientists' implicit knowledge and premises, as well as the reductionist perspective resulting from these (ESRC 1999). In this way, risk analysis restores dignity to public perception and a certain legitimacy to democratic debate.

Yet these analyses, which result mainly from studies carried out on environmental or nuclear-related risks, have not fully exhausted the subject of food safety. While sociologists of risk, following Ulrich Beck, have presented it as a characteristic of our modern era and are engaged in tracing the emergence of this notion, food sociologists and anthropologists see anxiety as an inevitable aspect of our relationship with food (Fischler 1990; Paul-Lévy 1997). Only its forms of expression have changed according to social context. Science historian Gaudillière (2001), has shown that at the beginning of the twentieth century, food-related anxiety intensified in the USA due to the industrialization of the food sector.

4 Risk as a constant aspect of human food consumption

From the perspective of the sociology of food, risks related to eating are presented in a unique manner, which is linked to the process of incorporation that accompanies consumption and contributes to the construction of social identities (Fischler 1998). In examining the forms of rationality and the levels of analysis applied by consumers, this approach completes our understanding of public perception. Eaters adopt a mode of intellectual functioning described by anthropologists as "magical thinking." Its laws are easy to formulate: the symbolic qualities of everything and everyone that come into contact with food, which may include tools, other products, natural or artificial, and packaging, as well as the individuals who produce, handle, cook and sell it, are all transmitted to the food itself through "symbolic contamination." American psychosociologist Paul Rozin has used experiments to demonstrate this phenomenon. It is enough to put a dead, disinfected—therefore bacteriologically safe—cockroach in a glass of milk and then remove it, to make the milk undrinkable, although from a strictly objective standpoint it is safe to consume. In a more extreme example, if individuals are asked to write the words "Danger, cyanide—beware" on a label and to attach it to a glass, then to fill the glass with some kind of beverage, a great many of them find it impossible to drink (Rozin 1994). In extending this problem to the context of food consumption today, we see that all technological interventions: handling, culinary transformations and marketing procedures, as well as all the professionals responsible for implementing them, have symbolic consequences on the identity of food. These must therefore be examined, so that we may attempt to control them. When we eat, we are incorporating an item of food that will become part of our personal physical existence. It crosses the barrier between us and the world. It reconstructs us and transforms, or may transform us. This is why eating gives us a certain sense of "control over our daily lives" (Ledrut et al. 1979b). We then have a better understanding of why fears and uncertainty over food exacerbate and echo uncertainties over the future of the eaters themselves.

4.1 The ambivalent nature of human food consumption

Rozin (1976), and later Fischler (1990), developed the idea that the opposing tendencies of "neophilia" and "neophobia" were the result of the contradiction between the biological necessity of eating a varied diet, and the cultural obligation of limiting one's diet to familiar foods, identified and valued by the social group. This dual constraint characterizing the situation of the human omnivore, which they named "the omnivore's paradox," would therefore constitute the source of the fundamental anxiety associated with human food consumption. Food-related anxiety is thus neither a new nor a temporary phenomenon; it is here to stay and requires constant management. According to Fischler, that management should be carried out by the "culinary system," that is to say, the set of rules defining which items may be classed as edible, and how they may be prepared and consumed. In this way, modern eating practices and the anxiety accompanying them are interpreted as a crisis in the regulatory functioning of culinary systems. The weakening of the social constraints weighing on the eater is associated on the one hand with the rise of individualism, and on the other hand with the industrialization of food production, processing, and marketing, which break the link between human beings and their food. This has resulted in a situation dominated by food-related anxiety. "If we don't know what we are eating, we don't know what we will become, but neither do we know what we are" (Fischler 1990, 70). The work of Alan Beardsworth (1990, 1995), of Françoise Paul-Lévy (1997) and of Saadi Lahlou (1999), as well as certain publications by Fischler himself (1997b, 1989b) prompt us to study the omnivore's paradox in greater depth. It seems possible to distinguish, with Beardsworth, different dimensions to the ambivalence surrounding human food consumption, each of which has its corresponding, specific form of anxiety.

The first type of ambivalence is that of *pleasure–displeasure*. It takes into account the fact that eating can be a source of sensuality, of gratification and intense sensory pleasure, yet that it can equally well give rise to a whole range of disagreeable sensations, from the merely unpleasant to revolted disgust leading to feelings of sickness or even vomiting. Anxiety in this case is associated with the senses and hedonism.

The second type of ambivalence is linked to the complexity of the connection between eating and *health or illness*. It is rooted in the fact that food is a source of energy, of vitality and health, yet at the same time it is a vector of poisoning, a potential cause of illness and disorders. The effects of these disorders may manifest themselves very rapidly. This is the case with food-borne diseases such as salmonella, botulism and listeria (Malvy et al. 1999), or poisoning from chemical toxins. However, the health problems may also become evident in the medium or even long term, as is the case with certain toxins (mycotoxins for instance), with insufficient or excessive nutrient intake, or with new infectious agents such as prions. Here, the anxiety accompanying food consumption is based on hygiene. It arises from the contradiction between the two principles connecting eating with health: Hippocrates' counsel *"let food be your medicine,"* and the adage *"a man digs his grave with his teeth."*

Françoise Paul-Lévy suggests that dread of food poisoning could equally originate from the fact that, for an omnivore, the risk is not only symbolic but also very real, even when one is consuming culturally identifiable items. She writes that the history of food is also "a long history of voluntary and involuntary poisoning" (Paul-Lévy 1997).

The third type of ambivalence is based on *connections with life and death*. It originates from the fact that although the act of eating is an absolute necessity, crucial for survival, in a great many cases it involves the death of animals considered to be edible. Some cultures correct this paradox by forbidding foods that necessitate the death of an animal, and promoting vegetarianism. In most cases, the killing of animals for food is surrounded by a set of protection rituals or social mechanisms, the purpose of which is to legitimize the slaughter. This type of anxiety is therefore the result of the moral conflict between the need to eat meat and the fact that it involves imposing suffering on animals and taking their lives.

Eating is therefore an act which necessitates choices and decisions, but also objective and symbolic risk-taking. These different categories of ambivalence give rise to three specific forms of anxiety, which food cultures endeavor to manage. The ambivalence relating to the *pleasure–displeasure* paradox is managed by culinary culture, in other words, by the set of social rules governing the ways in which food is prepared, cooked and seasoned. New foods are introduced into a culture through the use of strongly identifiable methods in their preparation, cooking and seasoning, which reassures eaters by giving these items a familiar taste. More generally, a recognizable method of preparation or seasoning has a reassuring effect, as it inserts the new item into normative food practices.

The management of the second type of ambivalence, connected to the health-illness opposition, is one of the most interesting questions relating to the anthropology of food. The ability of human societies to develop knowledge simply in order to avoid being poisoned and to ensure their survival is a genuine cognitive enigma. How, for example, were humans able to devise and implement the complex techniques of grating, then soaking cassava roots in order to rid them of the toxic cyanogenic glucosides naturally present in them? The empirical knowledge relating to the production, preparation and consumption of food that has been accumulated through the generations forms an immense body of expertise and techniques based on experience, in other words, on trial and error. This suggests that the origins of science may be found in food and diet, leading us to reexamine the history of scientific thought itself (Paul-Lévy 1997), and to revisit the question of ethnoscience, the relevance of which was demonstrated by Lévi-Strauss.

All cultures have a dietary system that has not been scientifically devised, but functions according to a set of categories classifying foods within a particular framework. It might be based on a binary system, such as the yin and yang principle of a macrobiotic diet, on the hot, cold, humid and dry categories applied in cultural spaces as diverse as Medieval Europe (Flandrin and Montanari 1996), fishing communities in the Malay Peninsula (C. Wilson

1981), indigenous peoples of Central America (Messer 1987), or certain ethnic groups in India (Mahias 1985; Pool 1987). The Chinese philosophy of the five elements of nature (Poulain 1997a) constitutes a further example of this type of system. Foods included within these categories are endowed with specific qualities justifying their consumption in certain contexts, or making them suitable in individual cases. Such nonscientific dietary systems enable us to explore the link between food and health.

The third type of ambivalence relates to *life and death*, presenting the question of the moral acceptability of killing animals, particularly those who, having a nervous system, are capable of feeling and showing pain. Different types of societies have developed various methods of regulating the practice in order to address this issue. In hunter-gatherer communities, there are numerous examples of rituals, prayers or apologies addressed to the soul or spirit of the animal (Frazer 1911; Kent 1989). Some, like the Chipewyan of Northern Canada, believe that the animal can only be killed if it consents to this (Sharp 1988, quoted by Beardsworth). In farming or livestock raising communities, it is very frequently the case that domestic animals are eaten following divine authorization. In the Judeo-Christian tradition, after "the Fall", permission was explicitly granted to mankind, at the beginning of Genesis, to eat animals: "Everything that lives and moves about will be food for you. Just as I gave you the green plants, I now give you everything. But you must not eat meat that has its lifeblood still in it" (Gen. 9:3, see Soler 1973). Judaism has a whole series of proscriptions in connection with this, such as the mixing of meat and milk—"Do not cook a young goat in its mother's milk" (Deut. 14:21)—and classifies animals as edible (clean), and inedible (unclean). The consumption of blood is likewise forbidden, as it is believed to carry the animal's soul. The slaughter of animals is carried out in a religious context, the process being supervised by a rabbi, who then pronounces the meat to be "kosher." Similar procedures are followed in the Islamic world, where meat cannot be classed as "halal" unless slaughter has been carried out according to a precise ritual and in the presence of an imam. The purpose of these rituals is to reassure eaters by making the killing of the animal morally acceptable. According to Christian belief, the sacrifice of the Son of God made man renders all other forms of sacrifice redundant, placing animal slaughter in the secular domain. The process is therefore carried out according to scientific principles and is supervised by veterinarians.

Examining these three forms of ambivalence provides us with a means of understanding the logical reasoning applied by humans in relation to food. The merit of this analysis lies in the fact that, by distinguishing different levels within each paradox, we are able to study the different forms of reasoning that are used. We can then also proceed to unravel the complexity of the socially constructed dimension of human food consumption.

4.2 Exacerbated risk and its corrosive effect on methods intended to manage the ambivalent nature of human food consumption

Today's food-related crises may be viewed as the result of a weakening in the systems designed to manage food-related anxiety (Beardsworth 1990, 1995; Fischler 1997). Now, with globalized markets, industrialized mass production, and the institutional catering sector's use of increasingly large-scale central kitchens capable of producing 10,000, 15,000 or even 30,000 meals a day (Poulain and Larrose 1995), the genetic taste markers characteristic of certain cultures have tended to decrease in number. Tastes have become homogenized. Consequently, distinctive culinary styles and the specific tastes they produce have lost something of their impact as cultural identifiers. Changes in daily eating practices, such as simplified meal structures, new approaches to eating between meals, and the shift of a series of decisions from the group to the individual, are often experienced as a form of erosion, a disintegration of the principles involved in eating well. As such, they reactivate the anxiety associated with type 1: pleasure–displeasure.

The links between food and health, and also between food and illness, are highlighted in modern medical discourse. Developments in methods of scientific analysis have led to an ever greater understanding of the origins of food poisoning and the chemical or microbial agents responsible (Pascal 1997; Borie 1999). Incidents of food contamination are publicized in the media, where they are presented as a new occurrence, although it is not actually known whether the phenomenon is becoming more widespread, or whether it is simply being better identified. This reawakens the anxiety associated with the second type of ambivalence. The long-term links between diseases and food practices are highlighted with increasing frequency in epidemiological studies (Hercberg 1991; Desjeux and Hercberg 1996). Examples of this are coronary disease and cancer, although in the latter case the data is inadequate, providing little more than the identification of a negative link between fruit and vegetable intake and cancer rates. The increasing medicalization of food consumption and the dissemination of scientific nutritional discourse have contributed to the decline of nonspecialist dietary systems, which are seen as fallacies. However, modern scientific dietetics are permeated with conflicting theories and are largely subject to the influence of passing trends, leaving the eater in a state of relative mistrust.

New illnesses have emerged, such as Creutzfeldt-Jakob disease, which appears to be transmitted to the human body via food, through the consumption of beef from cows suffering from BSE.

An assessment of the consequences of this phenomenon could reveal catastrophic results. The research carried out by some experts suggests that the possible number of victims may reach several tens of thousands. Today, advances in molecular biology have enabled us to conduct genetic programs using plants and animals, arousing both hopes and fears. These new food-related risks have contributed to exacerbating the anxiety associated with the second category of ambivalence (Apfelbaum 1998; Fischler 1997, 1998; Champagne 2000).

The mad cow crisis may also be analyzed in terms of a violation of boundaries. While people believed they were eating meat from a bullock, they came to realize that in a great many cases, it was actually from a cow. And while they thought these animals were herbivores, they discovered that they were being fed with animal products in the form of flour—moreover, with animals of the same species. In this way, the concept of the "cannibal cow" was established in the popular imagination (Kilani 1996; Lambert 1997; Cazes-Valette 1997). But equally, this crisis provided the public with a glimpse into the ways in which animal slaughter is managed. The news brought images of slaughterhouses into people's homes, showing cows' heads and carcasses lined up in the chilling rooms; this reminded urban inhabitants that in order to eat meat, one had to kill animals. Studies that had already been carried out some time ago had highlighted the particular methods of managing animal slaughter adopted by secular Western societies. These include removing abattoirs from public view by locating them on the outskirts of cities, and organizing the slaughter according to the Taylorian model, whereby responsibility for the act is diluted by separating the technical process into different phases (Vialles 1987; Méchin 1992; Kilani 1996).

The social imaginary with regard to the relationship between humans and animals has undergone a profound change over the last twenty years or so. Pets have become anthropomorphized (Digard 1999). As a result of developments in ethology and in the sciences of animal behavior, they are now presented as capable of feelings and intelligence, so that the boundaries between humans and animals are becoming increasingly blurred (Proust 1997; Poulain 1997; Fischler 1997). In this way, there have been calls for animals to be raised in more comfortable conditions (Burgat and Dantzer 1997; Burgat 1997). In some interviews, there have even been demands for the "humanization" of slaughter-houses (?) This is a curious choice of term, to say the least.

Perhaps the mad cow crisis may be interpreted as the result of a serious lack of confidence in scientific values, rather than the sign of a "decline of the concept of sacrifice" as suggested by Kilani (1996). The hygiene monitoring carried out by veterinarians has an objective purpose; it protects society from the risk of buying and consuming diseased animals. Yet it also has symbolic functions, by surrounding the slaughter of animals for food with the values and logical reasoning of science. The (temporary?) inability to understand and eliminate the BSE epidemic is damaging science's prestige. Consequently, the hygiene controls implemented by white-coated vets have lost their symbolic effectiveness. In unstructured interviews and discussions, mad cow disease is always associated with the "contaminated blood affair," which, to a certain extent, forms the background to the public's understanding of the issue (Champagne 2000). The crisis unleashed by that scandal had a devastating effect on the reputation of the medical community and weakened public confidence in the two authoritative bodies supposed to advise them: politicians and scientific experts. With science's prestige damaged, the symbolic functions of the vets regulating the process of slaughter and labeling the meat as edible were likewise affected. In the Anglo-Saxon world, this situation has contributed to the rise in vegetarianism (Beardsworth and Keil 1997); in France, however, the very marked attachment to meat, particularly beef, as an indicator of eating well, further emphasizes the anxiogenic dimension of this form of ambivalence. It brings to mind a survey on senior citizens carried out in 1998. When asked: "What, in your view, constitutes a good, traditional French meal?" Ninety-five percent of the respondents named a meat dish, and over fifty percent, a dish based on beef (Poulain 1998b).

In this way, the multiple backgrounds involved here show that risk evaluation cannot be limited to strictly hygiene-based objective dimensions. It also encompasses the notions of taste and symbolism. It is important to remember that, for the French, the taste of a food remains the primary criterion for choice, far more than any health benefits it may bring. Lastly, with regard to the symbolic aspects involved, assessments of this type take account of the ethical viewpoints originating from philosophical conceptions of man's place in nature, whether revealed or rationalist. Risk evaluation, and, more broadly speaking, the formation of a food-related decision, operate on the cost-benefit principle of calculation. This incorporates a series of criteria that may contain multiple forms of prioritization. However, these different levels within food-related thought processes are likewise based on multiple types of rationality. A strictly rationalist approach to risk, whereby the consequences of an act are considered according to the scientific, probabilistic model, is not the only form of reasoning. In the case of food practices, it coexists with value-based reasoning—in other words, a type of rationality in which respect for certain values is more important than the consequences of the decision itself. In order to be both respectable and respected, these values must be deemed legitimate, which involves drawing on domains as diverse as science, religion and symbolism. This clearly shows the benefits of engaging with the complex nature of food-related reasoning and risk evaluation.

Food consumption models may also be interpreted as systems that combine the multiple experiences of human communities in relation to their environment, created through trial and error. These are experiences in concentrated form, pivotal points between different aspects of eating and unique ways of prioritizing different criteria. Moreover, as food consumption models are central elements in the transmission of social codes and in the construction of social identities, every challenge to them is viewed as a threat to that identity. This explains why the issue of raw milk cheese, which caused such a stir within the European Community, cannot be reduced to a simple matter of food safety. International regulations, which are the result of mediated negotiations based on health and the principle of the free movement of goods, are deeply reductionist. They may lead to forms of ethnocide that are considered a genuine outrage. The violent reactions they arouse should therefore not be seen as pathological, but rather as defense mechanisms, in the positive sense of the term.

Food consumption models may also be studied from a scientific standpoint, just as ethnosciences study pharmacopeia or the medical practices of traditional ethnic groups. This is the perspective of ecological anthropologists, who aim to shed light on the advantages presented by certain empirical choices. Modern sciences and food consumption models are mutually enriching in this context, and their relationships may be envisaged on new terms. It is not for science to dictate what is good to eat simply on the basis of health. However, scientific knowledge can be used to uphold and improve a particular model, through the aim of reducing health risks while respecting the principles of taste and symbolic value. In simple terms, if there are risks involved in eating raw milk cheeses, rather than banning them outright, it would be preferable to study their composition in detail. The knowledge acquired in this way would either lead to improvements in production techniques, or would enable the population groups at risk to be identified. Policies designed to provide these groups with better information could then be implemented.

5 From democratic risk management to the social reconstruction of food

As nothing is ever entirely risk-free, and as scientific discoveries create new uncertainties even while they reduce others, we are obliged to negotiate the acceptable aspects of risk on a collective basis. Some experiments have already been attempted or are currently underway, in the form of citizen conferences, or forums in which experts, politicians and the public participate together. The first citizen conference was held in Denmark in 1987, its focus being "the use of gene technology in industry and agriculture." Since then, the experiment has been repeated there on several occasions, and was adopted by various Western countries from 1993. In France, the first event of this type was organized for the purpose of discussing genetically modified organisms (Boy et al. 1998; Joly 1999; Joly et al.1999, 2000; Marris and Joly 1999). The policy was extended through the establishment of food forums. These measures were intended to establish a dialogue between the different categories of social actors, and to debate the political choices involved in modern food practices, the aim being to build or rebuild consensus.

Pierre Lascoumes (1999) offers three interpretations of these mechanisms of risk management. The first, which is optimistic in nature, sees it as a form of progress in participatory democracy. By involving different categories of social actors, the mixed forums contribute to disseminating knowledge usually confined to a restricted circle. By exposing experts and politicians to public criticism, they play a part in repositioning issues related to techno-scientific progress within a political context, in the broadest sense of the term. In this way, they have established controversy as a method of managing society along democratic lines.

Equally, however, one might be concerned that they represent new forms of manipulation by modern states, in the guise of democratic discussion. From this perspective, citizen conferences appear as simulacra of genuine debates; chiefly designed as a publicity exercise, their true purpose would simply be to legitimize decisions that are "essentially always controlled by politico-administrative bodies" (Lascoumes 1999). The selection of nonspecialist participants raises questions concerning their function as representatives (for which social groups are they speaking?) and of their ability to fulfill that function (not simply their cognitive ability, but also the technical, media and political resources at their disposal). From this standpoint, these measures are merely a smokescreen intended to mask the real issues surrounding the decision, as well as its beneficiaries.

Between the first interpretation, with its sanguine claims of progress for democracy, and the more pessimistic second reading, based on large-scale manipulation or widespread conspiracy theories, there lies a middle ground. From this perspective, these tools form part of a conception of procedural democracy (Habermas). It is not always possible to build consensus on the issues at stake, and to agree on decisions. However, it is possible to reach agreement on methods of decision making and mediation between contradictory strategies within a social context. The advantage of measures intended to implement democratic risk management is that they enable us to stop seeing crises as social anomalies. They create conditions that facilitate a mutual learning process, where participants can share their respective reasoning processes. Problems associated with food and with the application of life science technologies to food production are the predominant topics in these discussions. They account for over 45 percent of public debates held in Western countries, as recorded by Claire Marris and Pierre-Benoît Joly[1] (Marris and Joly 1999).

More broadly still, the real theme underlying debates on or around food is that of the issues now facing society. For eating is a practice common to all individuals and it affects society as a whole. Consequently, a debate on food and eating is actually about much more: it is also a debate on the way in which society is organized, on civilization—a space where food is socially reconstructed.

5

Obesity and the medicalization of everyday food consumption

It is acknowledged nowadays that obesity is a multifaceted condition. However, given that its current rate of development conflicts somewhat with the hypothesis that genetics plays a major role, specialists in obesity consider that environmental and behavioral factors play a significant part in this process (Aimez et al. 1972; Basdevant et al. 1998; WHO 1998; Hill and Peters 1998).

The social dimensions of obesity have been the subject of intense research activity over the last thirty years or so, chiefly on the part of epidemiologists, but also, and to a lesser extent (especially in France), conducted by sociologists (Sobal 1991b, 1995; Poulain 2000).

The three main questions put to representatives of the social sciences are as follows:

1   Why is obesity unequally distributed along the social scale?

2   What transformations in the structure of the food industry sector or in eating practices might explain the rapid development of obesity in today's society?

3   How can we change eating habits?

The aim behind this last question is both the therapeutic treatment of obesity and, on a larger scale, its prevention.

The sociological study of obesity may operate from a dual standpoint. The first accepts the epistemological stance of epidemiology, and investigates the links between the development of this socially diversified pathology and certain social phenomena, such as the manner in which lifestyles have evolved, and transformations that have occurred in eating practices. It can also contribute to the identification and analysis of instances of stigmatization suffered by obese people in developed societies.

The second viewpoint focuses on medical discourse with regard to obesity and the public health policies of prevention and intervention arising from this. The aim in this case is to unravel the social issues that underlie and form the definition of obesity as an illness, leading certain specialists in this condition to think of its development in terms of an epidemic, or even a pandemic. And finally, researchers following this perspective are interested in the forms which policies of education and prevention might take.

In the English-speaking world, it is common practice in the domain of the sociology of health and illness to make a distinction between a sociology "in" and a sociology "of." In this way, Robert Straus speaks of the "sociology of medicine" and of "sociology in medicine" (Straus 1957), and Frederic Wolinsky refers to the "sociology of health" and "sociology in health" (Wolinsky 1980). The first perspective, that of sociology *in*, is unquestionably based on Émile Durkheim's seminal research on suicide, and focuses on the social causes of health or illness. It follows the tradition of Frédéric Le Play's monographic studies and the work carried out by the statistician Adolphe Quetelet. Adopting the empirical, positivist and determinist approach to research characteristic of epidemiology, it operates in collaboration with medical research, identifying the social dimensions associated with different forms of morbidity or mortality. This approach to research, sometimes labeled "social epidemiology," focuses on the social factors presented as causes, or as risk factors in an illness. It underwent a major development, particularly in North America, by concentrating on two principal themes of research: the effects of stress and the influence of social support, in other words, forms of social integration (Renaud 1987, 1991). Today, this theme has been revisited through the theory of social networks.

The second perspective, that of the sociology *of* centers on social roles and their transformation through the effects of illness, the social aspects of medical organizations, both official and unofficial, and their method of functioning. Additional areas of interest are accessibility to healthcare according to social group, and the influence of economic and public health policies (Herzlich and Pierret 1989; Drulhe 1996).

This distinction was also applied by Wm. Alex McIntosh and Jeffery Sobal in order to determine the focus of the sociology of food and nutrition. Sociology *in* nutrition forms part of social epidemiology, and is concerned with the study and analysis of the social causes of unsuitable eating habits (McIntosh 1996). In France, the work carried out by Annie Hubert on nasopharyngeal cancer is exemplary in this regard (Hubert 1990, 1995).

The study of nutritional status assessment methods carried out by Jean-Louis Lambert (1987), and the work of Igor de Garine on eating practices in Cameroon (1996) also correspond to this line of research. According to modern epidemiological studies, it appears that "there are practically no major areas of pathology in which the question of diet may not be suspected of playing a more or less direct role" (Hercberg 1991). This is therefore an immense field of research with a promising future.

According to the same authors, the sociology *of* nutrition is concerned with social relations within the sphere of nutrition, in other words, with the rationale behind the actions of nutritionists and dieticians, depending on the organizations for which they work; these include public hospitals, clinics, agrifood companies, and the restaurant business. It is equally concerned with the relationship between nutritionists and patients, and with the effects of economic policies on access to food and nutrition services. This approach has the advantage of providing sociology with a dual perspective:

- The internal sociological gaze—*in*—which accepts a certain number of presuppositions established by research into human nutrition, and can be applied to epidemiological questions, thereby contributing what nutritionists like to call "the sociologists' viewpoint."

- The external sociological gaze—*of*—which focuses on the action systems within which nutritionists exercise their profession.

In order to offer a complete picture, however, this perspective requires an additional dimension, as it omits the contributions that socio-anthropology could make to nutritional sciences. The first of these, which has been cultivated within the French tradition in particular, focuses on nutritional discourse, its development, its fluctuations, and its associations with social norms. Its critical perspective might be described as "the sociology of nutritional knowledge," or "the sociology of nutrition sciences."

We have already noted the influence of Durkheim's work on suicide as a foundation for epidemiological studies. In the second stage of the development of sociology, it gave rise to a very long series of investigations questioning the presuppositions and representations that affect both the process of constructing descriptors and, more broadly, the objectification of a social fact, revealing how these processes shape data. Variations in suicide rates, for instance, are influenced by the manner in which deaths are reported, and above all by their classification as suicide or death by natural causes, according to the level of condemnation suicide attracts in different social contexts. Therefore, differences in suicide rates are not only connected with concrete, actual facts, but also with a difference in presentation. In social spaces where Reformed religions are dominant, suicide is regarded with greater disapprobation, and there is a tendency to underreport such deaths (Beaudelot and Establet 1984).

It is therefore necessary to focus on nutritional knowledge itself, reestablishing it within a historical and cultural context, in order to understand how social concepts have influenced its construction. This perception has contributed to the development of an epistemological approach to nutrition pioneered by Jean-Paul Aron (1969). It falls within the scope of the sociology of knowledge, which, continuing in the tradition of Gaston Bachelard's work, has remained very much alive in French critical thought.

The second way in which social anthropology provides valuable input for food studies is through its contribution to our understanding of the act of eating itself. In a text that is, curiously, little known in the English-speaking world itself, Margaret Mead makes the point that in order to find ways of changing eating habits—an issue that nutritionists always put to representatives in the field of human sciences—it is first necessary to understand what eating means (Mead and Guthe 1945). There has been widespread interest in this question among contemporary French sociologists (Fischler 1979, 1990; Herpin 1988; Grignon and Grignon 1980; Corbeau 1995; Poulain 1985, 1997c; Paul-Lévy 1997; Lahlou 1998). It marks the preliminary stage of any communication and prevention strategy.

Finally, a further potential contribution from the sociology of knowledge is that it establishes the production of scientific knowledge as the result of a series of interactions between research environments and various political, economic and consumer pressure groups. Scientific knowledge is built on a system of actions involving competing researchers, who develop career strategies and mobilize resources from public and private funding bodies. These are administered and controlled by actors from the worlds of politics, economics and science, who are themselves subject to the influence of different pressure groups (lobbies) created for the promotion or defense of the production sector or of consumers, all being under the media spotlight (Callon and Latour 1991; Berthelot 1997). This is the complex system of action that Jean-Pierre Corbeau terms "the eating sector" (Corbeau 1998). This approach therefore presents scientific knowledge as a social construct. It demonstrates its relevance in the study of the fluctuations of nutritional discourse, by reestablishing these in the social contexts of their production and dissemination. This falls within the American constructivist perspective—from Peter Berger to Thomas Luckmann (1966) in general sociology, and from Joel Best (1989), Jeffery Sobal and Donna Maurer (1995), in the sociology of nutrition—according to which social problems are the result of interactions and representations. However, our position cannot be reduced to one of constructivism in the strict sense of the term, as we believe with Jean-Michel Berthelot that "facts used as a result of knowledge of social phenomena are both constructed and partially neutral as regards their explanatory value" (1990, 107). For this reason, in order to investigate the social dimensions of obesity, we propose to apply that dual perspective of a sociology *of* obesity and a sociology *on* obesity, extending this to a sociology of the knowledge of obesity.

The former will focus on the relationships between obesity and socioeconomic status with regard to adults, adolescents, and children, on changes in eating habits as factors influencing the development of obesity, and on the various forms of stigmatization suffered by obese people in modern societies.

The sociology on obesity will study the development of changes and perceptions associated with the overweight body. It will seek to deconstruct the implicit hypotheses and presuppositions underlying contemporary medical discourse, as well as attempts to intervene through public health policies.

1 Obesity and socioeconomic status

Despite the difficulties presented by the definition and, above all, the measurement of obesity, all the studies conducted by epidemiologists or sociologists highlight a relative variation in obesity rates based on socioeconomic status. Once the phenomenon has been objectivized, two distinct research axes emerge, based on whether socioeconomic status is seen as determining obesity, or whether it is a consequence of the condition.

As the first stance posits social status as a cause of obesity, its aim is to identify the influence of social positions and the lifestyles associated with them, regarding access to food, representations and eating habits, physical exercise or lack of it, and smoking.

According to the second interpretive framework, obesity itself partially determines socioeconomic status. It defines the way in which obese people are viewed, respected or discriminated against in a given society, then analyses the influence of obesity on social trajectories. However, before examining these approaches in greater depth, we will first study the nature of the links between obesity and socioeconomic status.

1.1 *The nature of the links*

Up until the 1960s, traditional analysis presented a negative relationship between obesity and economic status for women in developed countries, and a positive relationship in the case of men. In other words, at a macrosociological level, there were greater numbers of slim women in elevated social positions, while conversely, men occupying such positions were usually stouter: "The image of a successful middle-aged man in the middle and upper classes has been with a 'pouch', or 'bay-window'" (Powdermaker 1960). Since then, an increasing number of studies have taken the issue of obesity in relation to socioeconomic status as their chief or secondary object of examination. This enabled a sociologist and a specialist in medical obesity, Jeffery Sobal and Albert Stunkard (1990), to carry out a meta-analysis of 144 studies, providing information on connections between obesity and socioeconomic status and published in peer-reviewed scientific journals. The body of work collected in this way encompasses research on Western population groups (from North America, Europe and New Zealand) and on groups from developing countries. Their study enables the traditional approach to the social dimensions of obesity to be refined and developed.

This analysis confirms the markedly inverse relationship between obesity and socioeconomic status in the case of women. Indeed, in fifty-four studies containing collected data on women, this inverse relationship emerges on a very consistent basis (forty-six studies, as opposed to just one, show a direct link, while seven show no link). Female obesity is therefore more widespread among working-class social groups.

The situation is more complex in the case of men. An analysis of different studies reveals a bimodal distribution. Out of the sixty-five studies analyzed, twenty showed a direct relationship, thirty-four an inverse relationship, and eleven, no relationship. This means that a new form of male obesity has developed among poorer social groups over the last sixty years. Therefore, two types of male obesity coexist in Western societies today: "distinguished" and working-class.

In developing societies, the link is always positive regardless of gender; obese people, both men and women, all occupy the upper echelons of society. In the case of women, ten out of eleven studies showed a direct link, none showed an inverse relationship, and only one showed no relationship. In the case of men, twelve out of fourteen available studies showed a direct link, none showed an inverse relationship and two, no link (Table 9).

The situation with regard to children and adolescents in developing societies echoes that of adults, with obesity being evident only among the higher social classes. Thirteen out of fifteen studies concerning boys and fourteen studies out of fifteen focusing on girls, highlight a direct correlation, none show an inverse correlation, and only two show no link (Table 10).

Conversely, there is only a slight connection between social position and childhood and adolescent obesity in developed societies. Out of thirty-four studies on boys, nine showed direct links, (obesity among higher social classes), eleven showed inverse relationships (obesity at the lower end of the social scale), while there were fourteen instances of no link (no statistically significant correlation between obesity and socioeconomic status). In the

TABLE 9 Obesity and socioeconomic status in adults

	Relationships	Developed societies	Developing societies
Man	Direct	20	12
	Inverse	34	0
	None	11	2
Woman	Direct	1	10
	Inverse	46	0
	None	7	1

Source: After Sobal and Stunkard (1989).

case of girls, an analysis of the thirty-two available studies showed eight direct correlations (obesity in the upper social echelons), thirteen inverse relationships (obesity at the lower end of the social scale), and eleven cases of no statistical link between obesity and socioeconomic status. This meta-analysis therefore highlights an almost random distribution of obesity among social classes in the case of children and adolescents in developed societies. Recent studies confirm the lack of correlation between obesity and social class in children aged three to five, but show the emergence of a significant inverse relationship in the case of girls from twelve to fifteen years of age. In other words, there is an overrepresentation of adolescent girls suffering from obesity at the lower end of the social scale (de Spiegelaere et al. 1998a,b).

A few points relating to methodology should be clarified before we summarize these different results, and above all before we attempt to explain the transition that occurs in modern societies, from an almost random distribution of obesity among socioeconomic groups in the case of children, to a differentiated distribution among adults.

First, the nonhomogenous nature of the criteria used to define obesity in the 144 studies should be taken into account. Sometimes it is determined in relation to body mass index (BMI),[1] sometimes in relation to an ideal weight,[2] at other times by skin-fold measurements, and sometimes by a combination of these parameters. We should then note the extreme variation in the size of the samples featured in these different studies. This meta-analysis offers the advantage of encompassing a very wide range of studies, in relation to both size and methodology; however, it also presents the disadvantage of equating studies involving around a hundred individuals with others relating to several thousand. Although it demonstrates a high standard of proof, Sobal and Stunkard's work cannot, therefore, be seen as a randomized meta-analysis.

TABLE 10 Obesity and socioeconomic status in children and adolescents

	Relationships	Developed societies	Developing societies
Boy	Direct	9	13
	Inverse	11	0
	None	14	2
Girl	Direct	8	14
	Inverse	13	0
	None	11	2

Source: After Sobal and Stunkard (1989).

1.2 *Socioeconomic status as a determinant of obesity*

The absence of obesity among the working classes in developing societies may be explained by an insufficiency of available food, if not actual famine, coupled with a way of life that demands a considerable use of energy. The strong correlation between obesity and high socioeconomic status results from the fact that these social groups have much greater access to food, and is linked to the admiration accorded to larger bodies, which are seen as indicators of good health and affluence.

The rise in obesity in developed societies may be explained by lifestyles likely to determine certain factors that play a major part in causing weight gain, such as food practices or physical activity. The amount of energy expended by individuals in modern societies has decreased to a considerable degree. The causes of this are: heated and air-conditioned homes, advances in private and public transport, the mechanization of a large number of tasks in the primary and secondary sectors of the economy, and the development of office work. Concurrently with this reduction in energy expenditure, food intake has also decreased, but not to the same degree as food requirements themselves. Above all, this reduction is socially diversified in nature. On the basis of macroeconomic formulae, Lambert (1987), calculates this discrepancy at over two hundred calories a day, distributed among the middle, upper and working classes, the last category being the most affected.

This analysis could provide an initial explanation for the development of obesity in the lower echelons of society. However, the processing of large data sets, and the reconstruction of a diet likely to raise energy levels generates a whole series of problems regarding reliability (Fischler 1990; Poulain 1999b). For this reason, explanations of this type remain purely hypothetical.

Socially based differences in taste, reflected among working-class groups by an emphasis on energizing, robust, and hearty food (Chombart de Lauwe 1956; Bourdieu 1979; Grignon and Grignon 1980), could equally be used to account for this change. From a phenomenological perspective, Jean-Pierre Corbeau suggests interpreting this situation in terms of "social revenge." According to this theory, having been more affected by hunger than any other group throughout history, the poorer social class would collectively view the modern era of plenty as an opportunity for reprisal (Corbeau 1995).

Nutritional information could equally play a part in explaining the situation. It is received very differently according to both social status and gender, with women much more likely to be interested and responsive than men. However, as will become evident on examining the question in greater depth, the ready availability of extensive amounts of information concerning nutrition does not always translate into changes in behavior.

In developed societies, social status also has a bearing on exercise. Although there has been a considerable decrease in work-related physical activity, it has evolved very differently according to social group with regard to recreational pastimes. In the middle and upper classes men, and even more so women, pursue both sports and physical activities such as fitness exercises or jogging, with greater intensity than other social groups, being subject to the influence of the aesthetic ideal of a slim figure. The influence of social status, which affects girls from the age of twelve, may partly be explained by the fact that physical activity is practiced and regarded in markedly different ways according to social group (De Spiegelaere et al. 1998b).

1.3 *The stigmatization of the obese*

Studies that establish socioeconomic status as being determined by obesity are concerned with the social trajectories of individuals, based on whether or not they are obese. Their focus is on how obese individuals are considered in a given society, and on the different forms of approval or discrimination to which they are subject. In developed societies—with the exception of Sumo wrestlers in Japan—obese people are victims of stigmatization. This phenomenon has been described by Erving Goffman as a process that involves discrediting and excluding an individual deemed abnormal and deviant. In the course of social interaction, the label "deviant" is attached to an individual by other individuals, who are themselves assumed to be "normal." This label is then used to justify a series of socially discriminatory acts, even exclusion. Stigmatization becomes a true vicious circle when obese individuals accept the discriminatory treatment they receive and the prejudices they suffer, considering these to be normal. This subsequently gives rise to low self-esteem, leading in turn to a distorted self-image (Goffman 1963). Goffman conceptualized the notion of stigmatization when studying the social dimensions of mental illness and psychiatric organizations. Although he did not study the stigmatization of the obese himself, and, indeed, did not take it into consideration, his work *Stigma: Notes on the Management of Spoiled Identity* contains a fairly comprehensive account of different forms of victimization. However, the subject was highlighted and described in the late 1960s by another American sociologist, Werner J. Cahnman. He writes: "By stigmatization we mean the rejection and disgrace that are connected with what is viewed as physical deformity and behavioral aberration" (Cahnman 1968).

The obese individual is subject to numerous examples of discrimination and humiliation in contemporary developed societies. From the simple purchase of a seat in a plane or a cinema, to the pressure of a disapproval based on aesthetic ideals, the obese individual is devalued, marginalized, and exiled from society. Two types of sociological study have been carried out on this theme: those intended to describe and categorize the various ways of stigmatizing obesity, and those intended to reduce the significance of the discrimination suffered by obese individuals, by teaching them how to identify and protect themselves from such occurrences.

The widespread and premature development of obesity in the USA no doubt explains why studies describing the stigmatization of obesity have been carried out by American authors (Cahnman 1968; Allon 1981; Sobal 1984b, 1991a). They show how a certain number of negative attitudes to obese individuals can turn into genuine discrimination and affect their social trajectory. Statistically significant links have been highlighted at various levels. Obese people have a lower access rate to higher education (Canning and Mayer 1966). It is harder for them to find work (Matusewich 1983, Benson et al. 1980). Their level of income is significantly lower (McClean and Moon 1980). They are slower to gain promotion at work (Hinkle et al. 1968). Lastly, their domestic lives and access to community facilities are made considerably more complex (Karris 1977; Myers and Rosen 1999). Obesity can be viewed as a genuine social handicap in Western societies.

Children play a primary role in the phenomenon of stigmatization. Obese adults declare them to be the principal source of the discrimination they experience (Myers and Rosen 1999). Phebe Cramer and Tiffany Steinwert have shown that, from the age of three, children clearly display stigmatizing behavior toward overweight individuals, whether adults or children; this can take the form of mockery, avoidance and rejection (Cramer and Steinwert 1998).

Yet these negative attitudes are not solely confined to civil society; they may also be found at the very heart of the healthcare system. A number of studies underline the existence of negative attitudes toward obese individuals displayed by medical or paramedical personnel within healthcare institutions (Maddox et al. 1968; Price et al. 1987; Najman and Munro 1982; Myers and Rosen 1999), or by medical students (Blumberg and Mellis 1985). These studies highlight the receptiveness of health care professionals to dominant values (in this case, the ideal of a slim physique), and how these determine their conception of their roles.

As Goffman has already demonstrated in his work on mental illness, professionals in the health system play a major role as stigmatizers. Medical ideology helps to reinforce the justification for labeling individuals as deviant, and contributes to the devaluing of the obese. This discrimination is so extensive that it has sometimes galvanized legislative bodies into action, under pressure from associations established to defend or rather to support obese people, who have organized themselves to form genuine lobbies (Baker 1984). The largest such organization in the USA today is the National Association to Advance Fat Acceptance (NAAFA), which was founded in 1969. The movement also developed in Europe, although at a later date. The French advocacy group Allegro-Fortissimo, established in the late 1980s, set out its objectives in clear terms: "By founding this association, a few obese individuals have suddenly refused to live under the tyranny of the morphological ideal, and have taken charge of their own futures." The objectification of these phenomena of discriminating against the obese has enabled us to study the connections between obesity and socioeconomic status in greater depth, by analyzing the impact of stigmatization on social mobility. In this way, the shift from a random distribution of obesity among children to a markedly differentiated distribution in the case of adults, (particularly women), may be explained by the effects of obesity on social mobility.

The notion of social mobility takes account of an individual's movement within the social structure. An analysis of intragenerational mobility compares the social status of the same individual at two different times in their life (e.g., at the beginning and end of their career), whereas an intergenerational comparison looks at the respective social positions of a father and son, for instance. Mobility may be ascending/upward, descending/downward, or remain at the same level of the social scale (Cuin 1993).

A number of studies show that obesity has an effect on social mobility. It slows down intragenerational mobility (Canning and Mayer 1966; Hinkle et al. 1968) and increases the frequency of descending intergenerational mobility. The latter is influenced by three principal factors: level of education, professional activity and marriage, although their impact differs according to gender. In the case of men, education and professional life play a more significant role, with marriage being a considerably more decisive factor for women. In this way, slim women are more likely to "marry up"—in other words, to marry men of higher socioeconomic status than their own or their father's—whereas heavier women are more likely to "marry down," that is, to marry men whose socioeconomic status is lower than their own or their father's (Sobal 1984a; Garn, Sullivan and Hawthorne 1989). Under the pressure of an aesthetic ideal that values slender figures, marriage appears to serve as a shunting station, where lean women are directed to the higher end of society, and heavier ones, to the lower.

Obesity slows down social progress in the areas of education and professional career development, which appears to be held back in comparison with that of leaner individuals. Assessors, whether school or university examiners, or heads of department in the professional world—the "gate-keepers," to use Kurt Lewin's term (Lewin 1943)—are more likely to give negative evaluations to obese individuals (Canning and Mayer 1966; Hinkle et al. 1968). The phenomenon of stigmatizing obesity in developed societies may, therefore, explain the shift from an almost random distribution of obesity in children, to a distribution linked with inferior social standing in adult women, and with a new form of obesity among men in poorer social groups that has developed since the 1960s. From this perspective, obesity is seen as a factor influencing negative social differentiation, and challenging this stigmatization has become an immediate priority.

2 The development of obesity and modern eating practices

Whatever the methods used to measure obesity, specialists generally agree that it is developing at an accelerated pace, with the United States having the highest obesity rates. If obesity, particularly in the case of children, continues to develop at its current rate in France, we can expect to reach the same level as North America is experiencing today within around twenty years.

Common understanding and medical ideology point to modern eating practices as the chief reason for the development of obesity. This issue has been a focus of interest for French sociologists for over twenty years, and was a major issue when the sociology of food was inaugurated (Fischler 1979). Explanations of an evolutionist nature, based on a theory of long-term development, have been advanced. According to this premise, natural selection could have occurred in societies where food was scarce. A positive adaptive factor on which natural selection could have been based is the body's biological capacity to store energy in the form of adipose tissue, which differs considerably from one individual to another (Apfelbaum and Lepoutre 1978). Bernard Beck expresses this adaptive advantage in ironic fashion, explaining that in times of famine, whereas larger people will simply begin to get thinner, thin people are already dead. In developed societies where there is an abundance, or even a surplus of food, this capacity could have become counter-adaptive (Fischler 1979).

The speed at which obesity is developing suggests that we might trace its origins to social and economic changes. This is what we now propose to do as we attempt identify the roles played by food, taking the principle of epidemiologic transition as the basis for our study.

2.1 *The epidemiologic transition model*

This model constitutes an endeavor to explain the phenomenon of demographic transition, identified by demographers and historians of the subject, the most famous example of whom is undoubtedly Thomas McKeown (1976). Demographic transition refers to a structural transformation that occurs in populations in the course of demographic growth. More specifically, this involves a shift from very high mortality rates and low life expectancy, balanced by a high birth rate, to a second stage during which life expectancy increases considerably as the mortality rate drops. Developed countries are currently experiencing this second phase; although the birth rate has declined, the balance is largely positive and the population is growing. The so-called "transition" phase, which has given its name to the model, corresponds to the intermediary stage marking the shift from the first phase to the second. This demographic model considers phenomena that have occurred, in various ways and at slightly different times, in developed countries as a whole (Chesnais 1986).

In order to explain the causes of demographic transition, Abdel Omran suggests the model of epidemiologic transition, which analyses the transformation that has occurred with regard to the causes of mortality. There are three phases of epidemiologic transition, which correspond to the three stages in the model of demographic transition. In the first of these, known as "the age of pestilence and famine," the chief causes of death were infectious diseases, food shortages, and illnesses spread by parasites. Life expectancy was low and infant mortality rates very high. During the second stage, which marks the so-called "transition," these original causes of mortality declined; at the same time, degenerative diseases began to emerge, and life expectancy increased. Finally, during the third phase, known as "the age of degenerative and man-made diseases," death as a result of infectious illness was all but eradicated, while chronic disease became the chief cause of demise. Life expectancy rose higher still and the population increased, notably as a result of the greater longevity enjoyed by older sections of the population (Omran 1971).

Professor of Health Geography Henri Picheral has suggested completing this model with a fourth phase, which he names the "decline in chronic diseases as causes of death." It reflects the fact that these diseases have been tamed to a certain degree; societies have learned to live with them by disseminating information regarding prevention and through lifestyle changes, including hygiene practices, which would extend life expectancy (Picheral 1989).

In his turn, Marcel Drulhe suggests that the rise in deaths by suicide, together with the emergence of new diseases such as AIDS, certain characteristics of which are totally unfamiliar, prompt a review of the theory of epidemiologic transition by "extending it with a fifth phase: that of socio-pathological occurrences" (Drulhe 1996). Indeed, although HIV is a virus fairly similar to the epidemics of former times as experienced by its victims, "the mechanism of its propagation is operated through one of the driving forces of society: the sexual encounter." The author also classes as "sociopathological" occurrences of violent death; as an extension of Durkheim's work on suicide, he sees these as "the indication of a state of sociality, with its dual dimensions of integration and regulation." In other words, sociopathological occurrences are not new forms of morbidity, they have always existed. Syphilis, for example, is transmitted in quite a similar manner to AIDS. Yet, with other forms of morbidity under relative control, it appears to have greater impact. "When other causes of death are stabilized and reduced, the emergence of sociopathological occurrences is powerfully felt, as if the social aspect of health becomes more evident as the epidemiologic cycle progresses from one stage to another." This "fifth phase underlines the extent to which the dynamics of sociality may favor the emergence and development of deleterious processes" (Drulhe 1996, 25 and following).

2.2 *The roles played by food consumption in epidemiologic transition*

Epidemiologists and sociologists of health posit three causes of epidemiologic transition, all more or less based on McKeown's theory:

1 Developments in agriculture, cited by various authors as occurring during the seventeenth century in the case of Europe, would have ensured that both cities and rural areas possessed sufficient reserves of food.

2 The establishment of the food industry, due to developments in transport and commerce and the creation of new states, constituted a systematized endeavor to redistribute food supplies. It also helped to offset the effects of local food production problems (Drulhe 1996).

3   Lastly, the emergence and progress of experimental medicine and "the birth of the clinic" (Foucault 1963).

The first two causes are therefore explicitly related to food, to the extent that the notion of a "food transition" has been advanced. Adopting this framework of reference, we will take a closer look at the specific role played by food in the three phases of epidemiologic transition and in its two additional stages proposed by Picheral and Drulhe. We will examine how the different modes of social differentiation function within each of these phases.

First, however, we should focus on a debate instigated by certain food historians who have recently revisited the notion of a transition in food practices. They argue that there is evidence to suggest that the changes which occurred in seventeenth and eighteenth-century Europe brought about a deterioration in food supplies rather than an improvement (Livi Bacci 1987; Montanari 1995; Aymard 1997). Indeed, although the total quantity of available food increased considerably as a result of the crops introduced from the New World, coupled with improvements in agriculture, the concurrent population growth would have entailed a qualitative deterioration in food rations at individual level.

Transformations in methods of agricultural production, involving a shift from subsistence farming based on polyculture to a relatively monocultural system, altered the eating practices of less affluent classes. Monoculture led to monoconsumption, characterized by a gradual simplification in the range of available foods, as daily diets were once more based on a few staple products, chiefly cereals. These changes in production methods would have contributed to a reduction in dietary diversity and the qualitative deterioration of the food supply. This would cause illnesses associated with food shortage to resurface, as was the case with the pellagra epidemic in Italy, the result of a maize-based diet. Monoconsumption would also have increased dependence on the vagaries of the climate and agronomic yield, which sometimes triggered famines more deadly than those of former times. A typical case in point is that of the Irish potato blight and famine from 1845 to 1847. The mid-nineteenth century also saw a marked decrease in the consumption of animal protein, considered by these same historians as an indicator of the quality of food rations (Montanari 1995, 197). According to Massimo Livi Bacci, the author most categorically opposed to the epidemiologic transition theory, in considering the alleged link between food consumption and demographic development, we should therefore distinguish the short period during which this connection was relevant, from the longer period when there was no relation between the two. The relevance of the connection between food intake and population size would therefore be restricted to purely short-term phenomena, in other words to dramatic mortality crises. During periods of food scarcity, such crises were triggered either directly by famine, or more often by individual outbreaks or epidemics of infectious diseases, in a situation characterized by "the insanitary nature of the material environment." They would have had a significant impact on demographic development, particularly if they reoccurred within a short time frame. Yet in the medium and long term, food practices and demographic growth seem to regain their mutual independence (Livi Bacci 1987; Montanari 1995).

This standpoint itself is worth discussing, from a number of perspectives. The first of these involves methodology. The identification of the paradox created by the simultaneous occurrence of demographic growth and a qualitative deterioration in food rations is based on data that the authors themselves recognize to be unreliable. The statistics used focus above all on urban environments, and insufficient account is taken of both the rural and informal economies. Reconstructing food intake on the basis of statistics for production, slaughter and marketing is a very uncertain enterprise, even in contemporary societies where we have access to organizations that produce highly sophisticated statistical data (Lambert 1992; Poulain 1999b).

Despite the meticulous work and talent of these historians, the application of this type of data has proved to be an even more precarious endeavor. There is no instance of concrete proof; at most, there are indications to take into consideration in order to rework and refine the epidemiologic transition theory.

The second point that merits discussion relates to interpretation. The shift from a production mode combining polyculture and an economy based on gathering to a system tending toward monoculture could have brought about a certain reduction in the range of foods available, especially for city dwellers (Poulain 1984). However, it also increased the quantity of dietary energy produced from the same cultivated surface area, enabled more mouths to be fed, and favored the development of urbanization.

It is possible to escape this apparent paradox between demographic growth and the deterioration of food rations, not only by separating long- and short-term phenomena as proposed by Livi Bacci, but also by making a distinction between energy-based and qualitative nutritional requirements. Indeed, nutritional sciences have demonstrated the necessity of using a dual system of assessment with regard to food consumption, taking into account the fulfillment of both energy requirements and qualitative needs for macronutrients (Ziegler 2000a,b).[3] If we acknowledge the existence of a hierarchy in this case, and the priority of energy requirements over qualitative needs, we escape this contradiction. Cereal monoculture has increased the overall supply of dietary energy and facilitated demographic growth. It is certainly true that the reduction in food diversity may have maintained, and even in some cases increased, qualitative imbalances in the supply of macronutrients. Yet as the negative effects of this are only felt later, with the organism finding resources to redress the balance within itself, they would not have affected demographic growth.

Having now examined this question, we can return to the roles played by food in the epidemiologic transition model (Table 11). During the first phase, "the age of pestilence and famine," food availability was strongly influenced by biotopes, with soil characteristics and climatic impacts being decisive factors. In this situation, when food supplies were scarce and strongly localized, social differentiation was based on the visible abundance and overconsumption of products from faraway lands, such as spices, oranges, and lemons. The serving traditions of the aristocracy presented a display of abundance and reflected a tendency to favor items of nonlocal provenance; foods from distant lands had prestige. This was true of spices, but also of fats, with walnut oil being favored over locally produced olive oil at the court of Provence, due to the latter's undesirable associations with popular eating practices (Stouff 1970; Poulain and Rouyer 1987). In lower social groups, such plentiful displays of food were the order of the day on special occasions. In this context, a stouter figure was not seen as a positive attribute in the aristocratic world, where for women, beauty was equated with slenderness.

Phase 2 marked an increase in food availability. This was partly due to developments in agronomy regarding improvements in species and cultivation techniques (de Serres 1600), and later in the acclimatization and cultivation of New World crops such as maize, beans, potatoes, and tomatoes, which differed considerably according to geographical location.

The creation of states led to the introduction of official policies regarding food reserves and organized redistribution, which partly eradicated the effects of fluctuations in the climate and soil variability. In this context, social distinctions were established through a process of aestheticizing tastes, which became the basis for the development of French gastronomy (Poulain and Neirinck 2000).[4] The overweight figure became a mark of social status, a feature shared by the aristocrat and the bourgeois. The food practices of poorer classes were characterized by more marked differences than was the case in phase 1. These were linked to the very varied reception accorded to food products from the New World.

During phase 3, a situation of plentiful food reserves was established on an almost permanent basis, apart from the two periods of world conflict, which brought about severe food shortages. In this context of abundance, slenderness became a mark of social distinction. A new aesthetic of the body favoring long, lean figures then developed. Initially applied only to women, this standard subsequently extended to men (J. P. Aron 1997).

It is interesting to study the role played by food with regard to the suggested ways of developing this model. For Picheral's proposed fourth phase, which he names "the decline in chronic diseases," increased knowledge of nutrition and its dissemination could have contributed to the prevention of degenerative illnesses through improved awareness.

The case of osteoporosis is exemplary in this context. The circulation of knowledge regarding the role played by calcium and the preventive function of a food intake high in calcium, phosphorous and vitamin D, particularly for women, has contributed to "taming" this chronic disease (Poulain 1998a). The possible role played by fiber in helping to prevent colon cancer could likewise be cited. This knowledge, its promotion and dissemination, have played a part in the medicalization of our daily diet. The slim figure is now also associated with health.

Obesity could be classed among the sociopathological occurrences of the fifth phase proposed by Druhle. According to this interpretation, it could be the result of a series of transformations in food practices and in the social environment in which eating takes place. The development of obesity could be due to the phenomenon that Fischler termed "gastro-anomie" in 1979. This in fact refers to a weakening of the system of social norms surrounding food practices.

> For the ideal of slimness to be imposed in such a way that it influences and motivates individual dietary behavior to the exclusion of any other preoccupation, an additional circumstance is surely necessary; this has been overlooked in theories that link disordered eating solely to ideals promoted by mass culture. It surely also requires a weakening of the social framework on which dietary behavior is based. (Fischler 1990)

More broadly, eating disorders such as bulimia, anorexia, and compulsive eating, as well as the range of anxieties and fears triggered by food today (Apfelbaum 1998) may be included in the category of sociopathological occurrences.

This interpretation could, however, be criticized for only considering phenomena at the macrosociological level, and for a certain long-term approach to history that minimizes the processes of social differentiation. The emergence in the late twentieth century, an era of plentiful food supplies, of deficiency-related illnesses linked to both agri-industrial food processing (INSERM 1999) and to the advent of a new poverty, would be a good example of this (Chiva and Roux 1997; Poulain 1998).

2.3 Modern food practices: A risk factor?

There is general acknowledgment on the part of the medical world and the specialist press that changes in dietary behavior in developed industrial

TABLE 11 The roles played by food in epidemiologic transition

Stages	Causes of mortality	Life expectancy and mortality rates	Role played by food	Process of social differentiation
1 The age of pestilence and famine	Infectious diseases Shortages Parasitic diseases	Low life expectancy + - 40 years Very high infant mortality rates High adult mortality rates, population subject to epidemics	Food scarce and supplies unreliable Strong dependency on habitat	Display of abundance as indication of social distinction Delocalization as indication of social distinction
2 The transitory phase	Decline of: Infectious illnesses Food shortages Parasitic diseases Appearance of degenerative diseases	Increases in life expectancy + - 60 years Drop in infant mortality	Advances in agronomy increase food availability Organized redistribution	Aestheticization of taste Qualitative regional differentiation Large physiques a sign of high social status
3 The phase of establishment	Virtual elimination of death from infectious diseases Establishment of, and increase in mortality due to degenerative diseases	Increase in life expectancy + 70 years	Abundant food supplies	Slimness becomes a sign of social distinction
4 The decline in chronic diseases	Slowdown in chronic diseases between the ages of 45 and 54 and decline of chronic diseases between the ages of 55 and 75	Increase in life expectancy	Surplus food supplies, dissemination of nutritional knowledge	Development of the aesthetic ideal of bodily slimness. Slimness = Health
5 Sociopathological occurrences	Increase in suicide and violent death AIDS *Eating disorders* *Obesity*	Increase in life expectancy slows down	Surplus food supplies Anomie due to "deregulation"	Intensified pressure to conform to aesthetic model of bodily slimness Stigmatization of the obese

societies could be responsible for the rise in obesity. These transformations tend to be collectively referred to as "the destructuring of traditional eating practices," a term carrying strongly negative connotations. It is chiefly characterized by changes in meal composition, a rise in snacking habits, skipped meals, and increased consumption of sugary products and "junk food." The theory of modern eating practices has been the subject of lively debate among food sociologists and anthropologists. We have seen that much of the disagreement relates to the ways in which data is collected. Studies based on observed behavior clearly show a simplification in meal composition and a relatively strong emphasis on eating between meals (Poulain et al. 1996; Poulain 1997a,b, 1998b). These same studies identify a discrepancy between social norms (what in the individual's view constitutes a proper meal) and the practices actually carried out (Poulain 1998). This explains how such changes partly escape surveys relying solely on declarative methods, and the reason why this phenomenon is even more marked when questionnaires are self-administered. In this way, the core problem regarding epidemiological research into obesity has resurfaced in sociological surveys: subjects underreport their food intake. Indeed, obesity specialists have noted the apparent lack of connection between food consumption and weight in adults and children alike, even in situations where physical activity is monitored (Perusse et al. 1984; Rolland-Cachera and Bellisle 1986). The explanation for this situation may be based on methodology, with obese subjects underreporting their food intake, particularly in the case of between-meal snacks (Romon 1998). Research has been undertaken in order to improve data collection techniques (Suvimax, CREDOC, Lambert), but there is still much work to be done. Collaborative work carried out by nutritional epidemiologists, sociologists, anthropologists, and psychologists promises a fruitful outcome (Romon 1999).

In France, the process of simplifying meals has partly entailed the removal of elements peripheral to the main dish and its accompaniments. For the most part, this involves starters, so that the consumption of raw vegetables and fruit has effectively been reduced in favor of between-meal snacks. Nowadays the majority of between-meal snacks, produced by the modern agrifood sector, are based on biscuit-type products such as cereal bars and sugary items. Considering the consequences of these changes in qualitative terms, with regard to the nutritional value of such items, some nutritionists—or the media reporting their words—have been tempted to condemn such new food practices and to interpret them as the first sign of a general decline in food-related behavior. The discourse then develops into the theme of restoring good practices—three structured meals a day, with no between-meal snacking—and of the need to re-educate the modern eater. This approach overlooks the fact that meals (and, more broadly speaking, instances of food intake) are not simply a matter of individual decision, but also the result of a series of situations and social constraints.

The form that food consumption takes (the way in which meals are structured and the number of daily instances of food intake) is a tangible manifestation of social values. It varies considerably from culture to culture and, in previous times, there were differences in form within the same culture (Poulain and Neirinck 1988).

This theory finds an echo in the media and society, attentive to its message. Its social effectiveness lies in its function of alleviating fears. This hinges on its apparent minimizing of the contradiction between attachment to the traditional normative system on the one hand (a very large majority of those questioned believe that snacking is bad for the health and that a proper meal has three courses) and, on the other hand, disbelief regarding the ability of this system to create a balanced diet, concluding with the appeal to science to legitimize the quest for balance (Poulain 1998). This discourse responds to society's naïve desire, which might be paraphrased as: "Mr Nutritionist, do tell us that scientists are advising us to go back to traditional meals." In many cases, such recommendations are not based on sound scientific evidence; trials—when they are actually held—tend to be ethnocentric in approach and follow fixist conceptions of food history. Moreover, the popularity of these views, and their association with common sense, often obstructs the necessary scientific debate. Does the origin of a possible qualitative imbalance in modern French food consumption lie in simplified meal structures and regular instances of snacking, or in the nature of the foods consumed? We will only be able to investigate this question in greater depth through pluridisciplinary nutritional studies comparing food consumption cultures, both massed and distributed. An additional aspect of modern eating practices is the transformation that has taken place with regard to food-related decisions. The eater's decision-making space has extended through the development of institutional catering, which now presents multiple options, as with the self-service and "scramble" systems. This is the case in primary, junior and senior schools, universities, and company restaurants. A junior high school student at a self-service counter has to choose from a selection of starters, main dishes and desserts, not all of which have the same nutritional value. Institutional catering is not in itself a new phenomenon, and has grown relatively slowly; in contrast, systems offering multiple food options have developed extremely rapidly, in both the educational and professional domains. Many of those concerned—parents, beneficiaries, and administrators alike—see these changes as progress since they allow greater freedom of individual choice.

Within families, or in the older type of canteens, eaters made few decisions regarding food, especially in the case of men and children. The composition of the menus and the dishes offered were decided by wives or company restaurant managers. The choices made by the eater were confined to portion size, or, more rarely, to whether or not to eat. Now, even when families eat together, modern food practices include instances of personalized food consumption among certain social groups. It is not uncommon to find specific dishes for the mother, father, and children and so on, within the same shared meal.

Modern food habits are therefore characterized by a change in the social controls governing food intake, and a decrease in remotely controlled food decisions. Yet at the same time, the space established for individual choice has generated feelings of anxiety:

> The gap created by anomie has generated multiple forms of pressure, all carrying contradictory messages, that bear down on the modern eater. These include advertising, various suggestions and prohibitions and above all, an ever-increasing number of health warnings. The freedom offered by anomie is also experienced as a sharp twinge of anxiety, and in turn, that anxiety over-determines the circumstances relating to aberrant eating patterns. (Fischler 1979, 206)

We have seen that a rereading of the concept of anomie conceived by Reynaud (1995) in terms of a loss of legitimacy of social norms, has allowed us to reinterpret gastro-anomie. The modern eater is subject to multiple contradictory discourses, all of a didactic character. Modern eating practices may therefore be defined not only by a crisis in the normative system, but also by an excessive amount of contradictory recommendations. The plethora of discourses based on health, aesthetics, and identity, together with the trends that influence them, all contribute to what Fischler describes as a "dietary cacophony" (Fischler 1993, 1996b).

3 Is obesity a social construct?

From the perspective of the sociology of obesity, the condition constitutes a genuine problem, either because of the health threats it represents (morbidity and mortality) or on account of the social risk of stigmatization that it entails. The view within this discipline is that stigmatization results from the definition of obesity as abnormal. The question of whether there is actually an obesity problem is not asked; the focus of interest is on the process of change that has occurred in the social representation of the obese and on the various social interactions that have accompanied this, contributing to the labeling of obesity as deviant.

We have seen that not all cultures share the same attitude in this respect, and that even within Western cultures, very overweight bodies were more highly regarded in former times than they are today. A certain number of individuals in developed societies, therefore, had to persuade society as a whole that obesity represented a genuinely problematic situation in order to bring about the shift from a positive or relatively positive view, to one of condemnation (Germov and Williams 1996). From this perspective, the portrayal of obesity as abnormal and deviant in comparison with the norm is therefore a social construct, the phases of which require closer examination.

Obesity was initially presented as a moral problem. The obese individual was denounced as an antisocial glutton, incapable of mastering his appetites, gross not only in size but also in morals. The second stage in this process involved the gradual medicalization of obesity. In other words, the reasons why it was viewed as abnormal changed. Condemnation based on moral grounds gave way to the notion of fighting obesity due to the health risks it presented. This process of medicalization may be seen as an endeavor to remove obesity from the moralizing framework within which it was portrayed (Conrad and Schneider 1992). However, it is important to find a clear, scientific answer to the question asked in the title of a review article written by two major specialists some time ago: "Obesity: a State or an Illness?" (Van Itallie and Simopoulos 1982). If we fail to do so, there is a risk that the medicalization of obesity may contribute to legitimizing the phenomenon of stigmatization.

3.1 *The change in the social representations of obesity and fat*

"One of the most ancient sculpted representations of the human body in the Western world is female: the Venus of Lespugue. Is she obese or is she beautiful?" asked Annie Hubert (1997). We therefore need to understand how and why the values associated with the large body vary from culture to culture, and fluctuated within the same culture in former times. Large and slim bodies are viewed in different ways according to the cultural space concerned. From the Maoris of New Zealand to Mauritania, which has "fattening farms," where women are even employed to force-feed girls, there are several examples of cultures where young women are fattened before marriage (Chippaux 1990; de Garine 1996). An analysis conducted by Brown and Konner on a sample from the *Human Relation Area Files* (1987) reports that among the fifty-eight traditional cultures studied and on which data was available regarding values associated with body size, 81 percent considered that a characteristic we might define as plumpness represented the ideal of female beauty. The capacity to store fat in one's own body is seen as a sign of good health and vitality in a great many cultures, where individuals displaying a high level of adiposity attain social positions of power and prestige.

However, the way in which the larger body is regarded also varies in Western cultures and, in former times, it was accorded varying degrees of esteem within individual cultures. The huge excitement with which young Japanese women greet the arrival of a Sumo wrestler in the bars of the hip Tokyo districts of Ginza or Shibuya reflects the relative nature of the aesthetic ideal of slimness, even within developed societies. Slightly built, delicate and small-breasted bodies represented the ideal of female beauty for the aristocracy of Medieval Europe. The women painted by Lucas Cranach were typical examples of this aesthetic, although depictive conventions varied according to era (Hubert 1997; Elias 1939; Phan and Flandrin 1984). The concept of the ideal body underwent a transformation in the Renaissance, when beautiful women were defined by their more buxom figures. A large, portly, even obese body became a mark of wealth and success, reflecting a comfortable social position far removed from need (Nahoum-Grappe 1979). "In the 19th century, it behoved an entrepreneur, a figure of authority, to be physically large: a man whose word carried weight needed a weighty body" explained J.P. Aron (1987). In France, the first signs of a sea change became evident toward 1930. However, it was not until the 1950s that the ideal of a slim body was established as an imperative. There followed a dramatic shift from the notion of *good butter* to *bad fat* and an *embonpoint* suddenly became a *sore point*, to borrow Fischler's image (1990). The aesthetic ideal of slenderness emerged at a time when society was entering a permanent state of abundance. In a social environment where food is scarce, being large-bodied and heavily built were seen as positive qualities. The value accorded to a slim bodily aesthetic was concomitant with third-world awareness and a critical view of capitalism. Just as the capitalist accumulates wealth, the stout individual accumulates energy in the form of his own body fat. Traditional anti-capitalist images of the 1960s depict a pot-bellied boss, huge cigar in hand and banknotes spilling out of his top-hat, voraciously devouring his Lilliputian workers. Such images do not simply denounce the exploitation of workers, with returns on capital being accumulated (like fat) by effectively stealing from over-worked employees, whose small size indicates their distance from decision making. They also carry a symbolic content that transcends the class consciousness of the activists who use them. The image of the fat individual was used to denounce both the capitalist for exploiting his workers, and the over-fed Northern nations for "starving" Southern countries through the imposition of colonial or postcolonial economic structures. Excess weight is condemned not simply for being unsightly, but more particularly, for being immoral. The larger individual eats more than his fair share, and rejects the principle of redistribution. The obese person, like the glutton "does not play the game of reciprocity; he takes the gift without waiting, receives it without reciprocating, or reciprocates with less than he has received, seemingly without feeling any obligation" to follow with a counter-gift (Fischler 1987). From this perspective, obesity is "morally incorrect," as it represents selfishness and reflects a loss of self-control, while a slim body becomes an indication of moral integrity.

However, throughout history, even during eras when the dominant ideal tended toward a portly figure, social representations of obesity were marked by ambivalence. There has always been a barrier, a size beyond which the positive image of obesity undergoes a change, and the larger individual becomes someone who no longer respects social rules, and eats more than his fair share. "It is not strictly true to say that in the contemporary developed world we moved purely and simply from a pro-obese body ideal to an anti-obese one. In reality, the socially defined threshold of obesity became lower" (Fischler 1990).

3.2 *The Paradoxes of the medicalization of obesity*

However, as scientific knowledge in this domain is still uncertain, and levels of proof are fairly low, the separation of the moralizing and medical approaches to obesity so eagerly sought by medical obesity specialists, remains as yet very incomplete. If we adopt the viewpoint of sociologists *on* obesity, the first problem lies in the very definition of obesity itself. Some time ago, Sobal and Stunkard suggested that the excessively diverse methods used to measure obesity (proximity to an ideal weight, BMI, skinfold thickness, waist to hip ratio, weight in relation to a reference population, and so on) formed the main obstacle to carrying out a meta-analysis (Sobal and Stunkard 1990). There was therefore an urgent need to promote a single method to enable comparisons to be made. The decision recently made by an international committee of experts under the aegis of the World Health Organization (WHO) to adopt the BMI and the ninety-seventh centile as international descriptors of obesity, will certainly facilitate communication between researchers, (Rolland-Cachera, Deeheeger, and Bellisle 1999). However, it presents certain inconvenient aspects that should not be underestimated.

On a world-wide scale, not all human beings share the same body type. And, although in introductory reports obesity specialists frequently reiterate that the BMI is only valid for "Caucasians" (their expression), tendencies toward generalization often resurface. A number of studies apply this criterion, with its interpretive range, for population groups with different body types. The myth of the average being on which these applications are based, effectively eradicates anthropological variations, which themselves form the very foundations of anthropology (Hubert 1997). It is therefore important to examine the extent to which such data is valid, and the consequences of selecting this method.

The strongest scientific arguments supporting the medicalization of obesity are the statistical links between obesity and morbidity, and above all, between obesity and mortality, as highlighted in epidemiological studies. The latter connection forms a U-shaped curve in the case of women and a J-shaped curve in that of men (for a review of the question, see Charles 2000). That is to say, mortality increases both when the BMI is low (the thin body) and when it is high (the overweight body). In this way, there is a weight range that could be described as ideal from a medical viewpoint, which is generally understood to be a BMI between eighteen and twenty-five, values representing the lowest risks to health.

However, current knowledge does not yet enable us to take full account of what epidemiologists describe as "confounding variables." These are associated factors, such as smoking, alcohol consumption, or a sedentary lifestyle, which might act with, or perhaps replace, thinness or obesity as determining influences. The sociologist could add a further element: *insecurity*. It will be noticed that obesity affects a high percentage of women at the lower end of the social scale, and is rapidly increasing in men from the same groups.

These categories actually present the highest mortality rates of any social class, and sociologists of health have shown that this imbalance is partly due to huge differences in accessibility to healthcare (Drulhe 1996). What part does obesity itself play in these excessively high mortality rates, and to what extent are they determined by lack of care?

Moreover, although weight loss may have immediate, positive effects on certain illnesses associated with obesity, such as diabetes, there has been no information to date demonstrating that losing weight has an inverse effect on the probability of death.

Ultimately, the greatest difficulty lies in the fact that the different treatments intended to achieve weight loss, and above all the many and varied slimming diets (cognitive restriction) followed, have very limited short-term success, and frankly poor medium-term success rates (five years). As different trends and concepts have come and gone, successful long-term results of treatments for obesity remain "thin" on the ground, as it were, and disappointing (Ostermann 1997; Apfeldorfer 2000).

As the dividing line between the overweight and healthy body varies according to era and geographical location, the growing medicalization of obesity and its classification as an illness may be interpreted as a new form of social control, compensating for the loss of prestige affecting traditional moralistic institutions. It may equally be seen as the reincarnation of a process of differentiation, serving the interests of the elite groups, and founded on a rationale more or less akin to social distinction (Bourdieu 1979).

Basing their views on the rate at which obesity—particularly child obesity— has developed, some specialists have been tempted to see the early signs of a pandemic in this phenomenon. This argument is built on a line of reasoning that connects the overweight with the obese on the same continuum. Can we legitimately transfer acquired knowledge of severe obesity to members of the population who are simply overweight? Although current medical knowledge has shown that obesity is a risk factor in a certain number of illnesses, it does not always provide clear information with regard to subjects who are merely overweight. Is this transference a justifiable enterprise?

Although some studies show that cardiovascular mortality and BMI are linked by a J-shaped curve, it has not yet been proved beyond doubt that overweight individuals improve their life expectancy as a result of slimming. Moreover, even if this turned out to be the case, are these slimming methods sound? In a study on American eating habits in the twentieth century and the policies they generated, Harvey Levenstein (1996) showed that, in the light of current knowledge, it is fortunate that the programs launched met with no success. Is the knowledge we have acquired to date, both regarding the risks entailed by obesity and the methods used to change dietary habits, sufficiently well-established to justify interventionist policies?

There is a danger that a shift from the fight against obesity to a fight against the condition of being overweight will result in medical discourse legitimizing an obsessive quest for thinness. The motivations expressed by women concerning cognitive restriction, in other words, adherence to a diet intended to control their weight, are not based on health, but chiefly on aesthetic considerations, (McKie et al. 1993), on sex appeal (Charles and Kerr 1988), or, more generally, on the desire to feel better (Basdevant 1998). Voluntary calorie control is highly prevalent in France, accounting for 52 percent of women (Basdevant 1998). For many Western women, being on a diet, regardless of their actual weight, is part of the normal female condition, while adolescent girls often see calorie restriction as a positive sign of maturity. Not only is the failure rate of calorie-controlled intake (not to mention fad diets) actually very high, but cognitive restriction may create additional health problems for normal subjects, such as the "yo-yo" effect and compulsive eating. There is a danger that the over-medicalization of contemporary eating habits will justify such practices, apparently on scientific grounds. In a provocative article, Germov and Williams argue that any epidemic or pandemic that might exist would be more accurately described as an "epidemic of dieting women"; this could well play a part in the development of obesity.

Certain nutritionists even suggest that there could be still greater risk involved in promoting cognitive restriction and the weight cycling that generally accompanies it (Lester 1994; Basdevant 1998). In this way, the *New England Journal of Medicine* did not hesitate to publish an editorial stating that until better data emerged concerning the risks of excess weight and the advantages and disadvantages of losing weight, it should be borne in mind that the treatment of obesity could be more damaging than the problem itself (Stevens et al. 1998). Research should therefore be pursued in the fields of epidemiology and human nutrition, not only in order to scrutinize the links between obesity, morbidity, and mortality in greater detail, but also to verify, using experiments, that loss of weight does indeed invert these links. Until such results are forthcoming, caution is the best policy.

4 The dangers of a public health discourse on weight loss

Obesity and its associated complications have created a significant market. This is estimated by health economists as accounting for around 7 to 8 percent of health expenditure in the USA, and from 2 to 4 percent in the case of France. The launch of drugs with new active ingredients represents a potential annual turnover of several billion francs, even though such medication may not currently be covered by health insurance. With such sums at stake, it is in the interests of the manufacturers involved to develop the medicalization of obesity, and they show large-scale support for research, media coverage, and communication on the subject.

The medicalization of obesity may be qualified as scientific, in other words, it is controlled by a sophisticated system of procedures accompanying the creation, validation, and marketing of a particular drug. Underlying this process, however, there are other, still greater interests: the flourishing weight-loss industry, the promoters of various more or less faddish diets, sellers of "miracle" pills, and so forth. All of these are founded on obesity, and all benefit from its labeling as an illness.

In this way, weak levels of proof and of scientific argumentation mean that medicalized discourse on obesity is all too often characterized by a mixture of scientific knowledge and moralistic attitudes. The medical community must be aware that it risks playing the role of a major stigmatizer (Sobal 1995). The most serious problem generated by such medicalization is that it endows the stigmatization of obese individuals with a form of scientific legitimacy, confining them to a new ghetto created by a combination of dietetics and psychology. This has reached a point where some sociologists are explicitly campaigning for the demedicalization of obesity (Sobal 1995; Sobal and Maurer 1995; Germov and Williams 1996).

Should this demedicalization process actually be implemented? The true question is surely more complex, involving on the one hand, the separation of obesity and excess weight, and on the other, the medical and social dimensions of the obesity problem. Leading French researchers are starting to express themselves clearly on the first point. "Our aim," explained Bernard Guy-Grand, in an interview with *Quotidien du Médecin*, "is to convince people that this is a public health problem, rather than ceaselessly presenting the idea that it's all about shedding excess kilos. Indeed, with the focus solely on combatting kilos and the obsessive quest for slimness, the medical aspect of the problem has actually been obscured" (Guy-Grand and Gozlan 1998).

Arnaud Basdevant, the author of one the French recommendations on the subject, is even plainer in his language:

> Most of the people following treatments for obesity are not actually obese, while most of those who are morbidly obese are not receiving help. In this way, we have situations of over-medicalization and under-medicalization occurring at the same time, with cosmetic treatments on the one hand, and failure to assist on the other. In fact, the prevention of obesity should be de-medicalized. Prevention should be achieved through health promotion, civic initiatives, and educating young consumers. (Basdevant 1999)

In order to demedicalize the prevention of obesity, it is first necessary to deconstruct the implicit hypotheses on which nutritional initiatives are based. Campaigns designed to alter eating patterns are used to justify the question regularly put to specialists in food practices in the human and social sciences by members of the medical profession: "How can we change food habits?" This question is based on several premises, and may be reformulated in the following manner: "A given population has a fixed set of habits, some of which are bad, and we wish to transform these into a new, fixed set of practices that conform to the scientific principles of good nutrition." It rests on several assumptions that have not been fully verified:

- That the individuals concerned are more or less fixed in their erroneous practices

- That the social environment is more or less stable

- That nutritional knowledge is definitive

It is a classic example of a badly put question. Instead of: "How can we change food habits?" Our question should be: "What is the nature of nutritional behavior?" Only then can we ask a new question: "How can we develop food habits which have the requisite stability and flexibility appropriate for given individuals in a given society at a given time?" (Mead and Guthe 1945).

The conception implicit in what one might describe as a more or less psychoanalytical approach to diet, is that eaters are free in their choices and rational in their decisions. Yet we know that food-related decisions are neither individually made, nor based on a rationale. Although greater individualization in food-related decisions (or more specifically, a transformation in forms of socialized eating practices) has occurred within developed societies, eating is not a purely personal activity. Moreover, neither the accumulation, nor even the comprehension of nutritional knowledge necessarily changes individual dietary behavior (Duff 1990; Hollis et al. 1986; Poulain 1998a). It is advisable to exercise caution, in order to avoid sending out messages that might have undesirable consequences.

We might even point to that curious American paradox, whereby the highest obesity rates are to be found in the society where nutritional culture is also the most widely disseminated (Rozin et al. 1999). Would the best way to prevent obesity be to turn a deaf ear to advice from contemporary nutritionists? In the context of our current knowledge of the act of eating, Germov and Williams (1996) propose a moratorium on all types of intervention pending the results of certain interdisciplinary research programs intended to improve understanding of the processes involved in making food-related decisions. One such example is "The Nation's Diet," a program conducted in the UK by Anne Murcott (1998).

From a sociological standpoint, the vibrant cultural, and above all hedonic dimensions of French eating practices might be seen as the explanation for the astonishingly weak correlation between food consumption and morbidity conventionally known as the French paradox.

One way of combatting child obesity could therefore be to ensure that children receive a good food education. The word food is used here, rather than nutrition, because this is not a question of simply increasing their rational knowledge of the subject, but of creating conditions where they can learn to find pleasure in food.

To conclude, until progress is made in epidemiology, treatments for obesity and multidisciplinary research on human nutrition, our priority must be to challenge the stigmatization suffered by the obese. This is not only important as a question of fundamental human rights. It is also necessary in order to break the vicious cycle in which some obese people are trapped: stigmatization: loss of self-esteem: compensatory eating: maintenance or development of obesity.

Recognizing the socially constructed aspect of obesity should enable us to distinguish between the medical dimension and the stigmatization of the obese resulting from a transformation in the value system. From a methodological viewpoint, obesity demonstrates the contribution to be made by the various sociological interpretations that can be applied to the subject, and by connecting these perspectives. The question may be seen in relation to the domain of social epidemiology, so that both macro and micro sociological frameworks of reference would be used in order to further understanding of its origins. Yet, it also represents an excellent means of analyzing changes in social representations. The sociohistoric and anthropological interpretations show that the problem of obesity results partly from the transformation that occurred in the way society views the large body and fat-based products. The problematic aspect of obesity and its extension to daily dietary habits, and the condition of being overweight are social constructs. This contribution from sociology tempers the naturalizing discourse of the medical world. The act of eating and personal tastes are subject to very powerful social determinants, and there are many different cognitive approaches to forming choices: value-rational actions, rationally purposeful actions, symbolic representations, and so forth (Fischler 1993, 1996a; Lahlou 1997; Desjeux 1996; Rozin et al. 1999). A new area of research is opening at the interface between nutritional sciences and socio-anthropological food studies, the aim of which is to understand the complex nature of dietary decisions. Its challenge is to overcome the reductionist arguments, whether based on biology, dietetics, and psychology or sociology, which form epistemological obstacles to our understanding of this public health phenomenon characteristic of modern societies.

PART TWO

From sociological interest *in* food to sociologies *of* food

Ever since the founders of sociology first opened the window onto social realities, the subject has been "geographically" separated into distinct territories: work, religion, health, education, art, the working-class, rural communities, and so on. Each territory was then subdivided by a second series of demarcations; these new boundaries represented various epistemological perspectives, each offering different approaches to the study of a phenomenon, and different ways of explaining its occurrence. This dual set of boundary lines (subdividing territories into fields and paradigms, each with its respective explanations) has produced a certain Tower of Babel effect within the domain of sociology. Such a polymorphous discipline has left the layman feeling somewhat skeptical. Acquiring the culture of a particular field, and, often within that field, of a specific subject and methodology, is a lengthy and demanding process that makes communication between researchers a challenging enterprise.

The current status of the sociology of food has been assessed in a number of works by English-speaking authors: Jack Goody (1982), Anne Murcott (1988), Stephen Mennell, Anne Murcott and Anneke Van Otterloo (1992), Wm. Alex McIntosh (1996), and Alan Beardsworth and Teresa Keil (1997). Jack Goody launched this series by identifying three principal movements: functionalism, culturalism and structuralism. After a critical review of these interpretive frameworks, he emphasizes the advantages of applying a combination of the historical and comparative approaches. In his opinion, this would provide researchers with greater insight into the changes in food practices established as the result of transformations in technical systems of production and consumption. As he did not consider this to be a genuinely new paradigm, but simply an approach to research combining different points of view, he did not describe it as a fourth movement.

Mennell, Murcott, and Van Otterloo took the plunge, and named the perspective proposed by Goody "developmentalism," a movement in which they included their own work. From this perspective, the culturalist approach is seen as too general, and applicable to the concept of the common good; the sociology of food is therefore presented through three main movements: functionalism, structuralism, and developmentalism.

However, the originators of these classifications have all had certain difficulties regarding the contribution made by the French sociological tradition, with the exception of the English translations of Fischler's first articles. The ways in which this author has been presented provide a typical example of such difficulties. He is categorized by Goody and Mennell as a structuralist, whereas Beardsworth sees him as representative of the developmentalist approach. There is certainly something ironic about the pigeon-holing of a sociologist, and those who confine themselves to a single explanatory approach are few and far between, even when they are the promoters of a new paradigm. Yet these difficulties concerning the organization of knowledge are far from being as anecdotal as they might appear. They actually provide a characteristic picture of the status of food in the domain of the social sciences.

In order to assess the current state of affairs, we believe it is necessary to distinguish two major periods in the history of social thought with regard to food. During the first phase, which extends from the birth of the discipline to the mid-1960s, the subject was not, or only very rarely, the chief focus of the sociological gaze. It served as a reference point for the interpretation of other social phenomena.

The second phase was characterized by the desire to establish a territory based on the study of food. This enterprise was heralded by the works of Claude Lévi-Strauss (1964), clearly initiated by those of Léo Moulin (1967) and Jean-Paul Aron (1967, 1976), and extended by those of Igor de Garine (1978), Claude Fischler (1979), Claude Grignon (1980), Annie Hubert (1984),

Jean-Pierre Poulain (1985), Jean-Louis Lambert (1987), Nicolas Herpin (1988), and Jean-Pierre Corbeau (1991).

We therefore see a dividing line in the history of this discipline, between a period when food practices were a potential area of interest within traditional sociology, and a second period that witnessed initiatives to establish a sociology of food. An analysis in terms of paradigms has proved to be a pertinent method of summarizing the first period.

We propose to study the history of the ways in which the major trends of socioanthropological thought have treated the subject of food. We will then complete this approach with an analysis based on the major sociological domains. There too, we will see that the themes of food and eating practices were very much in evidence. A true "sociology of food," however, was yet to be established.

In the case of the second period, two distinct movements may be identified in the emergence of food practices as a sociological subject. The first, adhering to the traditional sociological perspective of the autonomy of the social domain, is based on the study of types of food consumption or on the diverse nature of tastes. The second establishes the act of eating as a "total social fact," and adopts an open sociological position to the study of interfaces with biology and physiology. Centered on the social characteristics of the human eater, its studies emphasize aspects specific to the act of eating, and the way in which sociocultural factors shape its physiological and psychological dimensions.

A sociological program based on the analysis of cooking and table manners as the enactment and portrayal of a culture's values, and consequently as a site for the study of cultural identity, already presents a certain interest. However, it is not sufficient in itself as a foundation on which to base a sociology or anthropology of food. For, in the final analysis, food-related phenomena provide a lens through which to study culture itself, its modes of expression, and transmission. From this viewpoint—as Jean-Michel Berthelot suggests in an article seeking the epistemological foundations for a sociology of the body—socioanthropological food studies would be more appropriately described as "a set of interests rather than a real area of investigation" (1982, 63). In this way, the subject becomes dissolved in a sociology of culture or in cultural anthropology. It is from this perspective that a work such as Pierre Bourdieu's *La distinction* is rightly identified as belonging to the domain of the sociology of culture. It is likewise from this perspective that *Les mythologiques* by Lévi-Strauss is read only as an anthropological reflection on the functioning of human thought. It is primarily remembered for its objective of identifying invariables such as binary oppositions and the interplay of permutations and substitutions, while the nature of the empirical material on which he was working is totally forgotten. Although this approach is not without interest, it does not appear to do full justice to the rich domain of food; indeed, this is far from being the case.

We must firstly, however, attempt to identify and remove the epistemological obstacles that prevented the study of food from becoming an independent sociological discipline. We will revisit the circumstances in which sociology was founded in order to assess the consequences of Durkheim's definition of the social fact and of the premise of the autonomous social domain. We will then evaluate the importance of the social phenomenon that is French gastronomy.

Once we have removed these obstacles, we will endeavor to demonstrate how the socio-anthropology of food may usefully adopt and implement the concept of social space proposed by Georges Condominas (1980), in order to overcome the oppositions between culturalist and materialist theoretical perspectives. While the former is more or less governed by value monism, the latter considers production systems to be the foundation of the cultural domain.

Rather than defining a new movement, our aim is to investigate how the focus of the sociology and anthropology of food might be reformulated in such a way that existing frameworks of reference could be connected. As these themes do not yet constitute a fully established field of study, they are not currently included in the power issues underlying the strategies involved in obtaining posts or resources that characterize the world of university research. Although this situation is somewhat inconvenient from an institutional standpoint, it does free the subject from influences that could lead to its fragmentation. Food and eating have subsequently emerged as a favored area for expressing interpretive theories.

6

The major socio-anthropological movements and their encounters with the "food social fact"

The first ethnologists and sociologists approached human food consumption from the perspectives of sacrifice, totemism, and the prohibitions associated with them. Presented in connection with religious belief, this standpoint prevailed up to the first quarter of the twentieth century. Areas of interest included food offerings made to the dead and to divinities (Smith 1889; Frazer 1911), and particular attention was accorded to cannibalistic practices. These were used to indicate degrees of development, and served the evolutionist concepts that characterized the discipline in its early days. In *The Elementary Forms of the Religious Life*, Émile Durkheim notes:

> Now in a multitude of societies, meals taken in common are believed to create a bond of artificial kinship between those who assist at them. In fact, relatives are people who are naturally made of the same flesh and blood. But food is constantly remaking the substance of the organism. So a common food may produce the same effects as a common origin.

Commenting on the work carried out by Smith, he extends it by showing that the sacrificial meal cannot be reduced to a communal act and the bonds that it forges. In eating, the participants incorporate the qualities of the animal consumed: "So they [the eaters] communicate with the sacred principle residing in it [the animal] and they assimilate it" (Durkheim 2008, 337). However, the analysis remains limited to so-called "primitive" societies.

In 1930, in a review entitled *État social des peuples sauvages*, Paul Descamps shows evidence of a new interest in techniques used to acquire food, such as fishing, hunting and agriculture, yet still focuses primarily on the themes of sacrifice and forbidden items. Not a word is devoted to how the food was eaten, to serving rituals or culinary traditions (methods used in preparation and cooking). The forms they take are not mentioned, either as descriptors of a social condition, or as indicators of development—and this from a book still strongly influenced by evolutionism.

1 The functionalist perspective

In France, the extreme care taken by Durkheim, in *The Rules of Sociological Method*, to distinguish social facts from the fields of both biology and psychology, had the effect of confining the study of food and eating to the field of physical and medical anthropology, or of subordinating it to more weighty sociological issues. With regard to the first tendency, mention should be made of the work of Léon Pales,[1] a French anthropologist and doctor who led the anthropological expedition to French West Africa from 1945 to 1950. During this period he conducted an extremely large-scale, exemplary study of the food and nutrition of African peoples (Pales and Tassin de Saint Pierre 1954). Today, the fate that has befallen this work within the anthropological domain is surprising. How could a study of this nature be so totally overlooked? Why does it not feature in any bibliographies? The hermetic perspective of French culture with regard to this type of research is an enigma that surely warrants in-depth analysis.

In the case of the second tendency, food practices are reduced to those aspects that are easier to "sociologize." In this way, they become an extension and an illustrative example of weightier subjects, such as the sociology of poverty, which is largely dominated by the functionalist perspective, or the analysis of gift exchange, the underlying theories of which were conceptualized by Marcel Mauss. In this way, Maurice Halbwachs, in a markedly Durkheimian interpretation, establishes the meal as an "institution," playing a fundamental role in the processes of socialization and the transmission of norms. "The most important aspect of family life certainly appears to be the meal shared with one's wife and children . . . the working-class man is well aware that the organization of the meals, the habit of consuming certain foods and the value attributed to each of them are social institutions in themselves" (Halbwachs 1912).

Chombart de Lauwe reflects a similar approach in his study of the everyday life of working-class families, noting that "good food" must above all be "nourishing," that is to say "abundant" and "satisfying" (1956).

Equally, exchanges of food form an extremely important part of the principles governing the giving of gifts and counter-gifts that underlie the tradition of "potlatch" practiced by the Nookta Indians of the Northwestern United States. The custom was studied by Franz Boas, and provided Marcel Mauss with a major subject for discussion in his essay *The Gift* (1925). Significantly, the essential meaning of "potlatch" is "to nourish," or "to consume" (1966, 153).

The development in England of an ethnological approach based on empirical data and favoring field studies, resulted in the first real insights into food consumption as an activity generating sociality. Alfred Radcliffe-Brown noted that "by far the most important social activity is the getting of food" (1922, 227). Bronislaw Malinowski's notion of "derived need," emphasizes the social elements of the context in which the satisfaction of a need is expressed and fulfilled. He states:

> If we were to study its diffusion or any other historical adventures, we would have here to make the absurd assumption that a fork can be used under conditions which make its use completely inadequate, that is, non-related to any needs, individual or collective, or else we would conclude reasonably that its historical destinies can be scientifically subsumed under the formula: the fork goes where it is needed and is transformed in form and function according to new needs and new local co-determinants of culture. (Malinowski 1944, 118)

However, it is Audrey Richards who stands out as a truly pioneering figure in the anthropology of food practices. She was a student of Malinowski, who wrote in the preface to her first book, *Hunger and Work in a Savage Tribe: A Functional Study of Nutrition Among the Southern Bantu* (1932): "The author presents us with the first collection of facts on the cultural aspects of food and eating"; he went on to describe her work as "the foundations for a sociological theory of nutrition" (1932, XIX, XX). In a particularly groundbreaking manner, Richards does not hesitate to state: "Nutrition as a biological process is more fundamental than sex. . . . The individual man can exist without sexual gratification, but he must inevitably die without food" (Richards 1932, 2). In subsequent studies, she focused her attention on the cultural determinants of food and eating, and considered that these works contributed to the proof that hunger constituted the principal determining factor in human relationships, starting within the family and extending outward to other social groups, such as village communities, age-groups or political states (Richards 1939).

This marked a major shift in perspective, as eating was established as an activity that gave structure and organization to social life. Trained in the sciences, Richards was one of the first ethnologists to seek "the possibilities of co-operation between anthropologists and nutrition experts in the study of native diet" (Richards 1937, 3), and participated in several multidisciplinary research projects in Africa. Yet, although she certainly pioneered a sociology of eating, she did not found a school of thought. Her work was to fall victim to the critique of functionalism and remained almost totally overlooked[2] until the early 1980s, and has Jack Goody to thank for its recent rediscovery (1982).

2 The perspective of the anthropology of techniques

At the end of the Second World War, André Leroi-Gourhan introduced a completely different approach to the problem by studying food in terms of "techniques of consumption." Following a system of classification in the great tradition of Carl Linnaeus, he created a general overview of the different techniques that have enabled humankind to manage its relationship with matter. Basing his work on an extremely rich variety of material, he identifies techniques used in culinary preparation, from shelling, filtering, cutting and grating, to cooking techniques, then turns to methods of preserving: drying, smoking, wet salting, canning, and so on. His next focus of interest is the foods themselves, which are grouped into major "families": animals, vegetables, minerals, seasonings, beverages, and stimulants, and he concludes the categorization with actual techniques of consumption and the materials associated with them, such as dishes, plates, spoons, and ladles (Leroi-Gourhan 1943, 1945).

The theoretical content of the work, which is limited to a fairly short reflection "on invention and borrowing and on the problems of the origin and dissemination" of techniques is somewhat dated. Nevertheless, this classification marks a decisive stage in the emergence of "economic anthropology and comparative technology" in the eyes of its author himself (Leroi-Gourhan 1945), and remains a basis of these disciplines.[3] Developing well beyond the domain of economic anthropology, for the first time in France, food and eating became a fully established part of material culture, in an extension of the categories proposed by Mauss.

After the Second World War, they were included as a standard feature in ethnological descriptions of societies. In this way, Jeanne Cuisinier devotes no fewer than thirty-four pages to the subject in her work on the Muong people of Vietnam, this time with a set of specific descriptors. Among the chapter titles we find: "Meals: frequency, abundance, composition. Food resources. Ordinary and ceremonial meals. Culinary methods: the preparatory treatment of rice; cooking; the pots. Equipment used for consumption. Hospitality. Beverages. Annual periods of scarcity, exceptional periods of scarcity. Feeding children. Dietary taboos" (Cuisinier 1948). In *Ethnology of the French Union,* a two-volume reference work published just before the Union in question was shattered in the Dien Bien Phu valley, André Leroi-Gourhan, Jean Poirier, André-Georges Haudricourt, and Georges Condominas include food and eating as a category in ethnological descriptions (1953). Since then, food practices have always featured under the general classification "material life," together with agriculture, techniques of acquiring food, livestock farming, clothing, and habitation. Contents are usually divided into three sections: material culture, social organization, and intellectual and spiritual life (beliefs, arts, and oral or written literature). Paul Raybaut improved methods of data collection and created a "study guide for the anthropology of food and eating" (1977). This perspective resulted in the establishment of an ethnology of cooking practices, Condominas being one of its first advocates. This discipline favored fieldwork (Asemi 1978), and generated research such as the thesis by Annie Hubert, presented in 1980, on *Eating Practices in a Yao Village in Northern Thailand: from the Hereafter to Ready Meals* (1985), and by Marie-Claude Mahias: *Deliverance and Conviviality: the Culinary System of the Jains* (1985).

3 The culturalist perspective

Cultural anthropology was to focus its attention on the extreme variability of the forms and techniques of eating practices. In *An Introduction to Cultural Anthropology* the author, Robert H. Lowie, devotes a chapter to the subject. Entitled "Fire, Cooking, and Meals," it is much wider in scope than the heading would suggest, as it deals not only with culinary traditions and a multiplicity of different cooking techniques, but also with meals and etiquette. In this way, he shows that "the time and nature of meals differ greatly even in civilized countries," while "primitive peoples," in fact, "differ still more in their customs" (Lowie 1934, 64). In *Sex and Temperament in Three Primitive Societies* and *Coming of Age in Samoa,* Margaret Mead shows how parental attitudes regarding the distribution of food to children, which is more or less frustrating in character, participate in the construction of what Ralph Linton was later to term the "basic personality" type (Mead 1928).

Mead unquestionably devoted more time to the subject of eating practices than any other anthropologist. From 1942 and over a number of years, she served as executive secretary of the Committee on Food Habits at the US Academy of Sciences,[4] and even temporarily left her post at the National Museum in order to settle in Washington and carry out this function. The Committee on Food Habits was founded in December 1940,[5] and formed part of the policies established in preparation for war. The aim was to improve information on dietary habits in order to optimize the efforts which the country needed to accept "if our freedom and democratic way of life was to be preserved" explains M. L. Wilson, chief of the Nutrition and Food Conservation Branch at the War Food Administration, in the preface to the Committee's first publication. In collaboration with Carl E. Guthe, Mead published a *Manual for the Study of Food Habits*. The definition of food habits put forward in this work takes account of the culturalist conception: it is "the way in which individuals or groups of individuals, in response to social and cultural pressures, select, consume, and utilize portions of the available food supply" (Mead and Guthe 1945, 13). It is therefore culture, or the cultural system, which determines the original character of eating practices. This perspective was to be extended by the neo-Freudian school of the basic personality structure, under the direction of Abram Kardiner and Ralph Linton (1945) and Ruth Benedict (1946), the aim of which was to show the importance of food and eating in the construction of personality and of what Igor de Garine proposed calling the "ethnic style" of food (de Garine 1996, 25). Working on ethnological material, in which food practices occupied a dominant place, Marshall Sahlins developed the theory according to which human cultures are not "formulated out of practical activity," such as production techniques for example, and do not stem from "utilitarian interest," but rather from a process of reasoning rooted in "a definite symbolic scheme" (Sahlins 1976, vii–viii). The interest presented by these perspectives lies in its emphasis on cultural influence and its arbitrary nature, although its weak point is that it does not take full account of the interactions between biological and cultural constraints.

Léo Moulin was to extend this approach in Europe (Moulin 1967, 1974). Observing the problems involved in constructing a European domain devoted to the subject, he drew on differences in food habits and tastes with a view to understanding both the problem of constructing identities and of their transformation. Highly erudite in the domain of gastronomy, he favored a sociolinguistic approach.

> We do not eat with our teeth and we do not digest with our stomachs; we eat with our minds, we taste according to the cultural norms linked to the system of reciprocal exchanges that forms the basis of all social life. This is why each community is defined by its food practices and table manners, just as clearly and surely as by its language, beliefs or sexual practices. (Moulin 1974)

4 The structuralist perspective

Structuralism very rapidly found fertile ground for research in this theme. There is a tendency to believe that Claude Lévi-Strauss's interest in food practices began with the very famous article "The Culinary Triangle," published in the review *L'Arc* in 1965. However, his preoccupation with the subject is already very much in evidence in 1947, in the publication that contributed most to endowing his work with scientific legitimacy, *The Elementary Structures of Kinship,* where he frequently draws on Richards's work. Chapters devoted to "The Universe of Rules" and the "Principle of Reciprocity" explain the conventions that govern the giving of gifts and counter-gifts, and the ways in which these practices are transgressed. In the course of an apposite digression, Lévi-Strauss deciphers the rites of exchange and politeness accompanying the meals eaten daily in the more inexpensive restaurants of Southern France:

> In the small restaurants where wine is included in the price of the meal, each customer finds in front of his plate a modest bottle of wine, more often than not very bad. This bottle is similar to his neighbor's bottle, as are the portions of meat and vegetables which a waitress passes around. Nevertheless, a remarkable difference in attitude towards the wine and the food is immediately manifested. Food serves the body's needs and wine its taste for luxury, the first serving to nourish, the second, to honor. . . . wine is a social commodity, while the *plat du jour* is a personal commodity. The little bottle may contain exactly one glassful, yet the contents will be poured out, not into the owner's glass, but into his neighbor's. And his neighbor will immediately make a corresponding gesture of reciprocity. What has happened? The two bottles are identical in volume, and their contents similar in quality. Each person in this revealing scene has, in the final analysis, received no more than if he had consumed his own wine. From an economic viewpoint, no one has gained and no one has lost. But the point is that there is much more in the exchange itself than in the things exchanged. (Lévi-Strauss 1969, 58, 59)

Through this example, Lévi-Strauss shows the difference between economics, which is interested in exchanges based on monetary value, and sociology, which takes account of exchanges that take place outside the system of economic calculation, and likewise play a part in forging social links.

In considering that rules of kinship serve to ensure the circulation of women within a society, Lévi-Strauss launched a genuine "Copernican" revolution that involved interpreting society as a whole, based on a theory of communication (Haudricourt and Granai 1955). From then on, the structuralists saw linguistics as an ideal science for the analysis of social facts within all the human sciences. "In the study of kinship problems, the anthropologist finds himself in a situation which formally resembles that of the structural linguist. Like phonemes, kinship terms are elements of meaning; like phonemes, they acquire meaning only if they are integrated into systems" (Lévi-Strauss

1963, 34).[6] Without reducing a society or a culture to its language: "This endeavor is possible on three levels, since the rules of kinship and marriage serve to insure the circulation of women between groups, just as economic rules serve to insure the circulation of goods and services, and linguistic rules the circulation of messages" (Lévi-Strauss 1963, 83).

To illustrate this general idea, Lévi-Strauss introduces the term *gusteme*, a concept reflecting those of *phoneme* and *mytheme*, and initiates a structural analysis of food systems, starting with a comparison between French and English culinary traditions.[7]

> Like language, it seems to me, the cuisine of a society may be analyzed into constituent elements, which in this case we might call "gustemes," and which may be organized according to certain structures of opposition and correlation. We might then distinguish English cooking from French cooking by means of three oppositions: *endogenous / exogenous* (that is, national versus exotic ingredients); *central / peripheral* (staple food versus its accompaniments); *marked / not marked* (that is, savory or bland). (Lévi-Strauss 1963, 86)

Having set himself the aim of interpreting society as a whole, based on a theory of communication, Lévi-Strauss proceeds to decipher the unconscious structures that form culinary systems, just as he had done with kinship a few years earlier (1964, 1966, 1968). Man is a "cooking animal," and culture finds its origins in the fire used for this purpose: "cooking . . . , it has never been sufficiently emphasized, is with language a truly universal form of human activity: if there is no society without a language, nor is there any which does not cook in some manner at least some of its food" (Lévi-Strauss 2008, 36). Later, he states: "the cooking of a society is a language in which it unconsciously translates its structure—or else resigns itself, still unconsciously, to revealing its contradictions" (Lévi-Strauss 2008, 43).

Little by little, dietary practices, food, and above all cooking, came to be just as fundamental an element of Lévi-Strauss's perspective as the analysis of institutions that surround and shape human sexuality, such as incest, marriage, and kinship. The sociological, or, to be more precise, the anthropological status of food studies was further consolidated by the material on which the author's work is based. This remained essentially exotic in nature, although he took pleasure in showing his knowledge of gastronomy by indicating the possible ways in which his model might be applied to the world of French cuisine, a task he did not undertake himself. However, it is important to note that Lévi-Strauss was not primarily concerned with culinary practices or table manners; his chief interest was in the combinatory logic governing structures and, underlying these, the universal invariants of "this uninvited guest which has been seated during this Conference beside us and which is *the human mind*" (Lévi-Strauss

1963, 71). As Jack Goody notes: "The aim of Lévi-Strauss's analysis is very different from the comprehensive (or 'thick') description of Richards's account of the Bemba. He does not attempt to provide 'an exhaustive knowledge of societies' but to derive constants which are found at various times from an empirical richness and diversity that will always transcend our efforts at observation and description" (Goody 1982, 22).

The debates sparked by Lévi-Strauss's structuralist perspective were centered on two themes: the theory of invariants, underpinned by the universally applicable model of the culinary triangle, and the connection between the deep and surface structures of social facts. With regard to the former point, the culinary triangle's basis on the vowel and consonant triangle of the Prague School's theory of structural phonology—which establishes a similarity between modes of vocalization supporting the function of language differentiation—disintegrated following the first developments implemented by Lévi-Strauss himself. Faced with the aberrant facts, he was rapidly led to envisage a transformation in his model, and replaced the triangle with a tetrahedron. We have shown how, although in a more complex and historicized form, Lévi-Strauss's model was able to take account of the culinary systems characterizing French gastronomic traditions, but lost its universal nature in the process (Poulain 1985a).

With regard to the second point, Luc de Heusch draws attention to the difference in the conception of structure between the functionalist and structuralist perspectives, indicating that the issue here relates to the level of the social fact and that it is advisable not to neglect the "surface" in favor of the "deep" (de Heusch 1971, 14). Less sensitive to questions of philosophy and of general epistemology, Mary Douglas pursued the structural analysis of food practices, considering that abandoning the perspective based on invariants—which remains at the heart of the "quarrel" over structuralism—by no means constitutes a challenge to its relevance or to its heuristic dimension. "Each meal is a structured social event which structures others in its own image" she states. Extending Lévi-Strauss's perspective, she argues that the significance of the structure of a meal is to be found in a network of recurring analogies, and continues: "We are left with the general question which must be raised whenever a correspondence is found between a given social structure and the structure of symbols by which it is expressed, that is, the question of consciousness" (Douglas 1971, 66, 69).

5 Sociological perspectives on food

It is possible to encounter aspects related to the act of eating in almost every sociological domain that emerges from the catalogue: rural sociology, the sociology of development, of work, of mobility, of urban living, of religion, of everyday life, of genres, of health and illness. In these contexts, however, food is merely a reference point for the study of social phenomena, and is included in more general themes such as identity, development, and the gendered division of social roles—this does not equate to an actual sociology of food. An inventory of all the areas of knowledge accumulated in the different domains of sociology could run to dozens of pages. Although this undertaking is not without interest, it soon creates an impression of division and fragmentation.

We will now identify various significant works on the subject of food and eating, although the following list is by no means exhaustive. It serves as a background theme in a large number of studies on rural sociology and the sociology of development.

Joseph Klatzmann is interested in food consumption and the transformations it has undergone, in order to research the balance between the evolution of human nutritional requirements and methods of manufacturing and processing foods (1978, 1991). The agricultural world now has to rise to the challenge of "feeding humanity". However, the technological, demographic and cultural landscape changes as a result of scientific discoveries and historical or political crises. Agronomists, economists, and sociologists are called on to study the problems presented by development (Malassis and Padilla 1987; Malassis 1994; Olivier de Sardan, 1995).

Although few food-related studies have been produced within the domain of the sociology of work, they are of a very high quality. Jacques Retel, a sociologist specializing in working-class life, took a seasonal restaurant job in a luxury hotel in Biarritz, where he joined a team of kitchen workers and waiters. The value system governing the French gastronomic tradition formed the basis of their professional relationships. *Les gens de l'hôtellerie* (Hotel Staff) remains a seminal work on the sector to this day (Retel 1965). The thesis by J.M. Vanhoutte (1984) should also be mentioned in this context. Fairly similar in its initial perspective, it is notable for its ambition to transcend the strict dividing lines traditionally separating different domains within the sociology of work. In order to understand the changes that have taken place in the professional duties of chefs and waiters, he studied transformations in the agrifood industry and their repercussions on the catering sector. This enabled him to produce a highly significant account of how food practices are influenced by production systems. In the same vein, Isabelle Terence (1996) focuses on the world of fine dining and Michelin-starred restaurants, and Sylvie-Anne Mériot (2000), on institutional catering. Restaurants and cafés are a vital part of our city spaces. Sociologists of urban life are therefore interested in how they are distributed within a city, in the forms of sociality that they generate, and the social imaginaries that they reflect (Membrado 1989; Clément and Megdich 1987; Vanhoutte 1989; Sansot 1990).

People circulate within the societies and countries of the world, bringing with them their food practices and table manners. The sociology of mobility approaches eating as a crucial element in the construction of identity, noting that distinctive dietary practices are among the last cultural markers to disappear (Calvo 1982; Hassoun 1997).

The sociology of everyday life, with its emphasis on the simple activities that make up our daily existence in its most tangible form, views eating practices as a means of indicating differences in social status and in forms of sociality (Strourdze-Plessis and Ströhl 1979; Maffesoli 1979, 1985; de Certeau et al. 1980). Its focus today is on the social uses for domestic objects and how these affect the lives of couples or families. One such example is the study by Marie-Christine Zelem (1999) on the uses of refrigerators, which continues the work of Jean-Claude Kaufmann (1992) and François De Singly (1996, 2000).

A wealth of knowledge relating to food practices has been accumulated in the sociological domain, through the study of other sociological subjects. However, it has not yet been possible to combine them in order to establish a sociology of food and eating.

7

Epistemological obstacles

1 "Grub": A second-rate subject?

There are subjects seen in intellectual circles as being of minor importance; these include food practices and cooking. As Jean-François Revel writes:

> Although a man of letters in the West, and particularly in France, is not looked down upon if he manifests an interest in gastronomy, it would nonetheless not be considered a serious endeavor were he to write treatises on cuisine. Alexandre Dumas's *Grand Dictionnaire de Cuisine* is an exception, but Dumas *père* is not exactly considered to be a representative of literature at its highest and purest. (Revel 1982, 108)

Culinary matters are not regarded as a serious area of study, a view not confined to the case of cookery manuals alone. Revel himself, a serious journalist and philosopher, does not escape the very problem he raises: "I hasten to add," he announces in the first page of the prologue to *Un festin en parole*, "that writing this book has been above all a diversion for me" (1982, 3).

Georges Vicaire, a nineteenth-century scholar and bibliophile, is almost apologetic in the foreword to his remarkable *Bibliographie gastronomique*, published in 1890, for writing on "such a subject." He even feels compelled to legitimize his endeavor with time-honored references: "A bibliography of cookery books might initially seem a somewhat frivolous enterprise, and yet is it not true to say that this *'science de gueule'* [science of the jaws] so dear to Montaigne and Rabelais has played a considerable role in people's lives since time immemorial?" (1890, VII).

If academic, literary culture is imprisoned within certain categories such as the body-mind and thought-deed distinctions, together with their attendant system of hierarchies, then so be it. It comes as more of a surprise that sociology should remain a prisoner of such preconceptions, without taking the trouble to challenge their conclusions. And yet all the sociologists and anthropologists who work, or have worked on food and eating practices have noted the paradoxical nature of this discipline. It marks a meeting point between the biological, the social, the natural, and the cultural . . . yet at the same time, it is treated as insignificant: a "Cinderella subject."

In 1910, in an introduction to an article devoted to the social aspects of eating, Georg Simmel (1997) writes:

> The indifference and the banality of the field with which these remarks are concerned should not deceive us. . . . The fact that we must eat is a fact of life situated so primitively and elementarily in the development of our life-values that it is unquestionably shared by each individual with every other one. This is precisely what makes gathering together for a shared meal possible in the first place, and the transcendence of the mere naturalism of eating develops out of the socialization mediated in this way. (Simmel 1997, 135)

Likewise assessing the difficulty of endowing food studies with intellectual credibility, Roland Barthes (1979) notes: "To the scholar, the subject of food connotes triviality or guilt." In a more recent article, Claude Grignon observes that the situation has hardly improved:

> The proposal to treat food practices as a serious sociological discipline encounters two sets of obstacles. The first is the picturesque nature of the subject, as evinced by the constant media interest it enjoys. . . . It seems that food as a "social reality" is still in danger of falling back into the category of a "minor" aspect of sociology. (Grignon 1995, 63)

In this way, the sociology of food seemed destined to be nothing more than a pseudo-subject, a second-rate form of sociology that served to enhance the prestige of the hard sciences with an interest in food or food practices (life sciences or human nutritional sciences). The recent food crises and the considerable social demand that they generated do not seem to have had a significant effect on the situation. Food sociologists have resources at their disposal and are the focus of much media attention, as an ever-increasing number of social, economic and political interests converge on their domain due to current food-related problems such as mad cow disease, dioxins, GMOs, and listeriosis. However, in the eyes of their "legitimate" colleagues, their role is merely to highlight the importance of other disciplines.

> Besides, everything related to the current and future development of food consumption represents very high stakes, both economically and politically. From this standpoint, the sociologist's position provides . . . the ideal pretext for organizing commissions and committees where practitioners rub shoulders with researchers, chefs and sociologists, food retailers, economists and so on. . . . The situation involves a form of sociology that

> provides simple information and validation, with limited requirements and ambitions, inclined to take trivial notions for concepts, one that is subject to competition from, or even worse, attraction to marketing, and is not particularly effective in distancing itself from the issues and theories inherent in the environments it is supposed to study. (Grignon 1995, 63, 64)

According to Grignon, the food sociologist should avoid becoming trapped in the role of a "purveyor of information", invited to "spout jargon in a more or less learned fashion", based on the received ideas (inherent theories) of the agrifood industry, the world of medicine, or of gastronomy. Yet surely all sociologists face this ever present risk? Sociologists of family life, of organizations, or of education are surely confronted with the same demands, and therefore the same pitfalls. This issue was clearly articulated in these different sociological domains, and no longer poses a problem.

The social environments they study present questions that are then translated by the sociologists into issues likely to generate research. The results produced by this process subsequently undergo a second translation, whereby they are presented in terms appropriate for their areas. In this way, they play a part in reshaping the perceptions of the various participants in the social domain that constitutes their field of specialization.

Yet, in the case of food practices, the problem lies elsewhere. The difficulty in this instance is that "grub" itself is not a serious topic: it lacks nobility. Moreover, as everyone eats and has very strong personal ideas on the subject resulting from their own experiences, people accordingly see themselves as experts (Lahlou 1996).

The old hierarchies of body and mind, applied and theoretical underlie this view of food as an unworthy subject. The expression "food research" (so often used in scientific research environments) refers to work motivated by allocated funding, rather than the discoveries promised by this field of study. In an ideal scenario, these resources could then be diverted in order to serve another purpose: that of serious, "vital" research. Why and how has scientific sociology remained so imprisoned by prevailing beliefs on this point? In order to understand this paradox, we must both revisit the circumstances that gave rise to sociology and anthropology, and seek to identify the place of food and eating within French culture.

2 The exclusive nature of the social fact and the dual tradition of Durkheim and Mauss

When, in the first chapter of *The Rules of the Sociological Method*, Émile Durkheim undertakes the task of defining a "social fact," he begins by noting the very frequent use of the qualifier "social." "It is commonly used to designate almost all the phenomena that occur within society. . . . Yet under this heading there is, so to speak, no human occurrence that cannot be called social."

He then endeavors to explain what constitutes a social fact through a negative definition, in other words, by indicating occurrences that cannot be described as such, and are therefore to be excluded from the category. Among other examples, he refers to food, considering eating and drinking to be biological acts. "Every individual drinks, sleeps, eats, or employs his reason, and society has every interest in seeing that these functions are regularly exercised. If therefore these facts were social ones, sociology would possess no subject matter peculiarly its own, and its domain would be confused with that of biology and psychology" (Durkheim 1982, 50–59).

The argument rests on the definition of the very purpose of sociology—a purpose to be accomplished by differentiating it from other, more epistemologically advanced sciences that have already been institutionalized, or are in the process of being so. This reflects the presence of tensions, underlying not only the conquest of a disciplinary field distinct from biology or psychology, but also the necessity of establishing the social domain as an epistemologically independent area of study. Two pages further on, abandoning the perspective of disciplinary territories, he now seeks to describe social facts through a positive definition, by explaining how they may be distinguished and characterized: "There are ways of acting, thinking and feeling which possess the remarkable property of existing outside the consciousness of the individual . . . they are endued with a compelling and coercive power by virtue of which, whether he wishes it or not, they impose themselves on him" (Durkheim 1982, 50–59).

On the basis of this strict definition, as Françoise Paul-Lévy (1997) has noted, certain aspects of the "food social space" very clearly pertain to social facts: "Table manners, food-related prohibitions and obligations, and culinary institutions, for example, may easily fall within the domain of sociology as defined by Durkheim."

The ambiguity of Durkheim's position becomes evident a few pages further on, when, in contrast to his initial approach of definition by exclusion, he provides examples. Eating and drinking now reappear, this time, however, they are categorized as social facts. As he explains:

Moreover, this definition of a social fact can be verified by an experience that is characteristic. It is sufficient to observe how children are brought up. . . . it is patently obvious that *all education consists of a continual effort to impose upon the child ways of seeing, thinking and acting which he himself would not have arrived at spontaneously.* From his earliest years we oblige him to eat, drink and sleep at regular hours, and to observe cleanliness, calm and obedience; later we force him to learn how to be mindful of others, to respect customs and conventions. (Durkheim 1982, 50–59)

Now excluded for being too close to the domain of biology, now included because it is imposed on the individual by society, the subject of food consumption has presented a paradox from the earliest beginnings of sociology.

Two series of questions have become crucial. The first relates to the consequences of these theoretical ambiguities regarding the status of food and eating within sociology. This is primarily a question of boundaries, of the frontiers between the social and the biological domains on the one hand, and the social and psychological on the other. What aspect of drinking and eating may be justifiably included in sociological studies, and what aspect is to be excluded? What is the assumed distribution of roles within the social sciences, among the domains of economics, human geography, ethnology and sociology? How, likewise, would roles be distributed among the fields of physiology, psychology and sociology, within the subjects conventionally known as food or nutritional sciences? Finally, a further problem is presented by the question of interaction and interdependence between the biological, social and psychological domains.

The second series of questions relates to the infrastructure of Durkheimian thought, its background and unconscious elements; these cannot be reduced to concerns regarding the system of territorial boundaries governing the newly established discipline of sociology. On what assumptions are they based? What blind spots do they determine? Lastly, and, perhaps still more crucially, on what nonexplicit paradigms was sociological science based when it was first founded? The ambiguous definition of the social fact, reflected in an almost caricatural fashion by this contradictory oscillation between inclusion and exclusion, gave rise to a dual tradition in the French social sciences. As Paul-Lévy observes, eating and drinking enable us "to establish one of the points of empirical disagreement between Durkheim and Mauss, between uncle and nephew" (1997, 189).

The first area relates to the argument for exclusion, and focuses its interest on the aspects of food consumption that appear to have the least connection with the corporal, biological and physiological domains. In other words, it deals with those areas most subject to social influence and to outside forces that are imposed on the eater, and are the easiest to sociologize. Any reference to taste is therefore excluded, as, despite the fact that this is largely shaped by cultural factors, it is deemed too psychophysiological in nature. Cooking, with its multiplicity of different techniques, is likewise excluded. Too closely connected with the biological dimension of food, it is viewed from this standpoint merely as a process of physicochemical transformation. Despite the fact that it is equally subject to outside influences, and therefore cannot simply be reduced to a technical procedure, the social aspect of cooking is totally obscured from this perspective. It was to be a considerable time before technology itself was regarded as relevant to the human sciences. The difficulties experienced by André-Georges Haudricourt in publishing his work on this subject attest to the impact of this sociological reductionism on French thought (Haudricourt 1987).[1] The processes of incorporation and the shaping of the body by social influences were also excluded from the strictly sociological perspective; much later, the sociology of the body was to focus its attention on the latter (Berthelot 1983; Drulhe 1996; Le Breton 1990).

The role played by food in constructing social identity was likewise excluded. This was a sociology that contained no reference either to the body or to technology, centering on the social fact alone, in all its purity and autonomy. The only aspects to escape this suppressive operation were the social links forged through eating, the normative structures that govern it and the process of interiorizing the rules accompanying and regulating food consumption. Meals and the forms they take are presented as an institution, with social functions that need to be identified. This provides us with a clearer understanding of how the sociology of consumption (which began, but also nearly ended with Maurice Halbwachs) enabled food to find a small niche in sociological thought. The social factors determining food consumption became a focus for analysis. In classical sociology, eating practices might at the very most be seen as a reflection of social organization.

The second perspective includes consumption in the domain of social science; interest here is focused on the shaping of the body by social influences. It gained greater authority within the ethnological tradition. This approach may be found in the work of Durkheim himself, in his reflections on magical thinking and the links between food consumption and the construction of social identities. However, the analysis remains confined to the religious domain (with the exception of Christianity) and only concerns "uncivilized" or "primitive" communities, as if "magical thinking" played no part in the food practices of modern developed societies.

Food and drink subsequently reappear in Marcel Mauss's *Techniques of the Body,* and are positioned at the crossroads between the biological, social and psychological domains.

What emerges very clearly from them [the techniques of the body] is the fact that we are everywhere faced with physio-psycho-sociological assemblages of series of actions. These actions are more or less habitual and more or less ancient in the life of the individual and the history of the society. Let us go further: one of the reasons why these series may more easily be assembled in the individual is precisely because they are assembled by and for social authority. (Mauss 1973, 70–88)

Clearly differentiating himself from Durkheim on this point, Mauss considers that progress in science takes place in those areas that mark an intersection between different disciplinary perspectives.

> When a natural science makes advances, it only ever does so in the direction of the concrete, and always in the direction of the unknown. Now the unknown is found at the frontiers of the sciences, where the professors are at each other's throats, as Goethe put it (though Goethe was not so polite). It is generally in these ill-demarcated domains that the urgent problems lie. (Mauss 1973, 70–88)

He positions himself clearly with regard to the roles of the different biological, psychological and sociological dimensions involved. Opposed to both the Comtian tradition and Durkheim's concept of the autonomous social fact, he sees these dimensions as clearly linked. The psychological aspect functions as a cog, establishing a connection between the social and the biological: ". . . here I see psychological facts as connecting cogs and not as causes, except in moments of creation or reform" (Mauss 1973, 70–88).

This original contradiction has had a profound effect on the status of food practices in French sociology. An initial group of studies was based on food as a reflection of social life and the changes it has undergone in developed societies. In this case, food is not a sociological subject as such, but is subordinated to other, broader sociological domains, for which it serves, at best, as a reference point. Since then, the objectification and positivization of the social dimensions of food have been only partially achieved, and reduced to the perspectives of the original issues. This lack of positivization still weighs heavily on the body of knowledge to this day. Studies in the second category have developed either within the domains of ethnology and anthropology, or in those disciplinary no-man's-lands situated on the margins of sociology, history, paleontology and the medical sciences. Once the fashion for the interdisciplinary approach has passed, these will remain areas without proper classification, badly organized from a scientific standpoint. Paul-Lévy (1986) has the distinction of having highlighted the importance of what she terms "primitivist ideology," in the distribution of roles between sociology and ethnology, when sociology was first established and institutionalized. She demonstrates the influence of the paradigmatic infrastructure based on oppositions: primitive—modern, body—mind, nature—culture.

"[it is] what I have called 'primitivist ideology,'" she writes:

in an endeavor to show its link with the evolutionist paradigm and the foundational role it played for both sociology and ethnology, as well as its role in allocating domains between the disciplines: everything under the heading "before" was assigned to ethnology: primitive peoples and their counterparts, the rural communities, traditions, etc., while everything under the heading "after" was assigned to sociology: modern societies and their counterparts, the city, innovations, etc. (Paul-Lévy 1997, 171)

In this context, food practices were cast into the domain of corporality and primitivism.

8

From sociological interest *in* food to sociologies *of* food

1 The sociology of food consumption

Interest in household food consumption originated in the late eighteenth century through the work of David Davies, an English clergyman. His aim was to understand the lives of the disadvantaged and to ascertain what they ate, in order to help them more effectively. To this end, he examined the budgets of over 100 poor families. In the same vein, Sir Frederick Morton Eden published *The State of the Poor*, which was likewise based on the study of a series of family budgets (Stigler 1954). Together with Nicolas Herpin and Daniel Verger (1991), we can identify three main causes for the emergence of a sociology of consumption. The first relates to that charitable attitude motivated by religion, which was embodied by Davies and replaced in the nineteenth century by socialist ideas. The second cause was the growing influence of the message spread by the hygiene movement and the domain of epidemiology, whose practitioners argued that morbidity rates were influenced by lifestyles (Lecuyer 1976). Last, the third cause is the dissemination of statistical tools, notably the theory of probabilities, and their application in the analysis of social facts. Mention should be made of the decisive influence of Belgian mathematician Adolphe Quetelet on Durkheim's thought, and the methods of applying statistical reasoning to social phenomena: "That which relates to the human species, considered en masse, is of the order of physical facts; the greater the number of individuals the more the individual will is effaced and leaves predominating the series of general facts which depend on the general causes, in accordance with which society exists and maintains itself" (Quetelet, quoted by Stigler 1954, 95–113, and Herpin and Verger 1991).

1.1 *The determinants of food consumption*

A student of Frédéric Le Play, who inspired him with an interest in studying living conditions, the German economist Ernst Engel[1] identified a law that still bears his name. Reworking a study by Edouard Ducpétiaux (1855) on the budgets of working-class Belgian families, he noted that the proportion of household expenditure allocated to food depended on changes in the family income. According to this law: "The poorer an individual, a family or a nation is, the greater is the percentage of their income that must be used to maintain themselves physically, the largest proportion of which is represented by food" (Engel 1857). In other words, when income and purchasing power increase, the food budget also increases in absolute value, although there is a decrease in the relative proportion (in percentages) of the overall budget that it represents. His successors completed this law with the addition of two other aspects, sometimes wrongly attributed to Engel himself:

- The proportion of expenditure on clothing and accommodation does not vary with income
- The proportion of expenditure on leisure activities and health increases with income

Using these tools as a starting point, the first generation of sociologists worked with the Durkheimian conceptual system. In 1912, Maurice Halbwachs defended a thesis entitled *La classe ouvrière et les niveaux de vie* (the working class and living standards), which carried the subtitle "Research on the hierarchies of needs in contemporary industrial society" (1912 [1970]). In accordance with the definition of the social fact, he isolates the social aspect of food consumption. First, he notes that the need for food appears as "the most natural" among all other needs, "because the preservation of the body depends on its being regularly satisfied," but that it is too complex, "it involves too many senses and organs, it evokes too many representations which, in turn, provoke it, not to have undergone considerable developments, and not to have become, to a large extent, *distorted*."[2]

"Distortion" here refers to its shaping by cultural factors; this is the social dimension of food, which it was necessary to bring to the fore and positivize, using the example of household budgets.

In accordance with Durkheim's method, Halbwachs seeks an explanation for the food-related social fact in other social facts. "In this way," he states, "we are led to investigate whether social causes account for the regularity and stability of the various expenditures on food."

Profession, family size and income are the variables used to explain consumption practices, objectivized through the focus on household budgets.

In order to do this, it is, therefore, necessary to objectivize the practices and study the statistical links that they maintain with individuals' social characteristics, presented as independent variables. Halbwachs studied, in turn, the problems posed by data collection, the representativeness of the resulting samples and the methods of statistical treatment applied. In order to extract the aspect of eating practices that fell within the definition of a social fact, thereby making it appropriate as a sociological subject, the first sociologists relied on the concept of institution. This is founded on the distinction between laws, mores and manners applied by Montesquieu in *The Spirit of the Laws*: "Laws are best suited to regulate the actions of the citizen, and mores the actions of the man . . . mores relate chiefly to interior conduct, manners to exterior."

For Durkheimians, the concept of institution refers to a set of rules—as distinct from laws—that structure society, or, more specifically, some of its governing bodies. According to the functionalist conception, an institution has a threefold purpose. It participates in the process of socialization, in other words, in the interiorization of rules of behavior. It allows for social control, with failure to observe a rule instigating sanctions on the part of the collectivity. Finally, it plays a role in regulating society; as institutionalized individuals are aware of the rules, their behavior is more or less predictable.

The family meal, with its highly precise normative system that calls for immediate sanctions in cases of transgression, is an institution central to society. It is through the meal that children interiorize the rules and values of cleanliness, respect for others, and sharing (the socializing dimension). It likewise plays a part in defining roles, not only within the immediate family, but also outside it, so that an individual's behavior in society is predictable (the regulatory dimension).

It may be said that eating practices truly acquired the status of a social fact with the work of Halbwachs. "The most important aspect of family life certainly appears to be the meal shared with one's wife and children . . . the working-class man is well aware that the organization of the meals, the habit of consuming certain foods and the value attributed to each of them are social institutions in themselves" (Halbwachs 1912 [1970], 420–22).

Halbwachs was unquestionably Durkheimian in outlook. However, as with other domains—such as urban sociology, for example—the author was to pave the way for new areas of study with heuristic potential that was not exploited until a much later date. After discussing the nutritional theories of his era, according to which dietary requirements were based strictly on physical activity, he explains that the mechanics of digestion are dependent on "mental dispositions," which "themselves result from the habits, from the imagination, the company one keeps, the beliefs and presumptions affecting the excellence or the good taste of food" (1912 [1970], 340, 341).

With this profoundly innovatory perspective, human food consumption was no longer strictly reduced to an example of adaptive behavior. It half opens the door to interaction between biology and sociology. Halbwachs was not to travel far down this path; his main results may be summarized as identifying the general rule whereby social class influenced the consumption of meat, bread, butter and vegetables. However, he indicated that it was possible to act much more effectively on eaters "by gradually modifying perceptions, suggesting diets that take great account of their customary opinions, rather than by confronting them purely and simply in the name of science."

The author was already motivated by the desire both to understand practices and to explain them; in this way, he clarifies the importance of being interested in "what the working-class man thinks about, when he is about to eat." And if this approach is adopted, it is understood that "much more than a given quantity of carbon, fat and albumen, the complex representation of a satisfaction (which includes, as we shall see, a number of social elements) is evoked by such dishes and foods" (1912 [1970], 343).

However, Halbwach's work provides evidence of the difficulties experienced by Durkheimian sociology in departing from an evolutionist perspective. "If we returned to a barbaric or primitive state, if rules and social customs were to disappear, they would doubtless take with them those artificial physical sensations; their predominance is therefore only to be attributed to social pressure" (1912 [1970], 413). In his eyes, the social dimension represents advancement, while nature is equated with the biological. Within the social structure, the working class is seen as closer to the domain of nature and, therefore, "the least socially evolved . . . In this way, as we move toward groups with a more intense, better organized and more complex social existence, we also see needs that are now devoid of all their 'primitive' content, so that natural, organic impressions and the satisfactions derived from them become blunted and almost vanish" (1912 [1970], 413).

Halbwachs clearly perceived the difficulties of his theoretical position and the contradictions between his intentions and the empirical data that his interpretive framework allowed him to see, but, as a positivist, he defers to what he perceives as reality. "Of course, we do not consider the working class as a group or a set of groups that are more primitive than other sections of society. But the more we have studied this class, the more we have recognized the uniformity and simplicity of its tendencies, to the point where group reactions are mechanical and limited" (1912 [1970], XIII).

From this perspective, as the working-class groups are more strictly subject to organic necessity, their food choices would be governed by biological determinants. The eating practices of the poorest social groups are therefore perceived as the being the closest to the biological domain. "Food is the first requirement *primum vivere* . . . if we place ourselves at the level of the working class, it must be said that there is no requirement that has a more pronounced physical, organic character than theirs, and where the actual social dimension recedes further into the background" (Halbwachs 1912).

The process of analyzing social and economic needs differentiates the so-called primary needs, such as food and clothing, which are linked to the maintenance of an individual's life, from secondary requirements, that is to say, not strictly vital needs, such as those associated with culture, leisure activities or health. From this perspective, the scarcer the available resources, the closer the expression of these needs should be to the domain of biology. Yet again, this interpretation finds itself imprisoned in primitivist ideology (Paul-Lévy 1986), as the definition of primary needs is not unproblematic. Indeed, it is possible to meet the so-called primary need for food in a number of ways, and these vary according to cultural space and era. A Vietnamese country dweller in the 1980s would consider a bowl of rice, a few vegetables and some *nuoc-mam* enough to nourish him and satisfy his need for food. Yet his French counterpart, living in the same era, would not share this view. What is an acceptable meal? What constitutes a sufficient quantity of food? These questions would only find their answer in a given cultural space.

The varying definitions of the supposedly primary need show that it is also a social construct. As Raymond Boudon and François Bourricaud have noted: "The definition of these primary needs is problematic. Food is certainly to be classed as a primary requirement. Yet there are many ways of eating, some approved and some condemned by health practitioners" (1982, 43, 44). The latter half of this observation immediately raises a second problem, as it establishes the biologist, or more specifically, the nutritionist, as a vital presence, being the purveyor of an ultimate, positive scientific truth; this constitutes a stumbling block for the concept of the social fact. Commenting on Halbwach's studies— in the wake of Engel's work—the authors of the *Dictionnaire critique de la sociologie* explain: "One could assert that the laborer, as an individual engaged in active physical work, needs to eat more meat, and drink more wine, than the office worker at her desk" (1982, 45). In fact, the need in question here is defined more by social perception than by nutritional science, with meat and wine viewed as energy-giving items according to French cultural tradition.

This concept, which has been demolished by modern nutritional biochemistry, was, nevertheless, central to scientific dietetics in its early days, highlighting the interconnection between social perceptions and "expertise" accumulated in the field of biology.

1.2 *Contemporary successors*

The sociology of consumption was to find a highly favorable domain for development within the Institut national de la statistique et des études économiques (INSEE). The first national household budget survey was conducted jointly by the INSEE and the Centre de recherche pour l'étude et l'observation des conditions de vie (CREDOC) in 1956 and again in 1963, with the backing of the European Economic Community (EEC). In the following year, the INSEE established two permanent surveys, the first on household budgets and the second on food consumption itself (Vangrevelinghe 1970). The latter, carried out annually on samples from 10,000 households, used self-administered questionnaires. "Each household is asked to note every food purchase made over a week: products, quantity, place of purchase, meals eaten (at home, in restaurants, in canteens and as snacks), exceptional purchases for guests, etc." (Vangrevelinghe 1970). The responses were counted using computer software, the data being received in the form of "over a million punch-cards." The data was processed by cross-referencing the information obtained with a small number of descriptive variables: place of residence, age of the head of the household, presence of children in the household and socioprofessional category. A dynamic analysis was then carried out by comparing developments from year to year.

However, the data collection method used (the self-administered questionnaire), presented some major disadvantages, as it demanded "a not inconsiderable amount of work for the people questioned." First, it gave rise to a nonresponse rate of over 15 percent, so that a selection process was in operation within the samples themselves. Second, it prevented the period of reference from being extended beyond one week, the timescale stipulated in the survey. And, as the project manager admitted, "some food purchases are not made on a weekly basis." Finally, it left out the question of self-produced food.

The results concerning food consumption that emerged from this major survey were therefore "marred by random variations," admitted Gabriel Vangrevelinghe, director of the Household Consumption Survey division (1970, 20). A further difficulty stemmed from the classification system operated by the INSEE, whereby products and services were grouped together according to the needs they were intended to fulfill. Divisions of this type invariably led to some questionable classifications. In this way, restaurant expenditure was allocated to the "commercial services" categories, as part of the sub-category "hotels, cafés, restaurants and canteens." Likewise, the food eaten by hospital patients was classed under expenditure on health. The marked social disparity evident in the case of restaurant expenditure would be enough in itself to justify a re-reading of Engel's first law. Despite such problems, however, this statistical series offers the unquestionable advantage of enabling dynamic comparisons to be made using data collected by the same method; this allows us to interpret transformations in French consumption practices.

At the same time, Léo Moulin was interested in the impact of the consumer society on eating practices in the context of affluence—a society in which products are seen "less for what they are, than for what they represent." He emphasized the benefits of conducting a detailed study of the consequences, at the household level, of the relative decline in the part played by food at the level of society in general, and the application of Engel's law to clarify cultural differences between countries and the dynamics of their changes. Moulin taught at the College of Europe, and his analyses encompassed this new political territory (Moulin 1974).

The decline in the consumption of "poor people's food" (farinaceous items, bread), and the rise in the consumption of foods associated with the rich (meat, fish), partially obliterated social contrasts in eating practices. A standard middle-class model (featuring meat at every meal, and menus comprising a starter, a meat dish, vegetables, cheese and dessert) now tended to dominate, homogenizing European dietary practices. Women's entry into the workplace, urbanization and pressures on daily schedules all transformed people's lifestyles. Institutional catering expanded in the professional and education sectors. Women, in charge of cooking for the household, turned increasingly to processed foods. Food became functional, in other words, easier to prepare.

In this way, cooking for one's family is gradually joining embroidery, watercolor painting and knitting, the painstaking work carried out by ladies of a bygone era, in being consigned to the category of nineteenth century activities. . . . The only defenders of traditional cooking, an all-consuming, exhausting and thankless task, are those women who feel they have no other means of proving their worth, that is to say, in most cases, those whose purpose and aptitude are limited exclusively to the role of housewife. (Moulin 1974, 169)

An increasingly large proportion of culinary activity is being taken over by professionals in the domain: the food industry and institutional catering. The dynamics of household budget allocations show that the amount spent on food has fallen in favor of expenditure on the car, the house and leisure activities (Figure 4). Eating practices are now associated with health. "Now, for the first time in history, the nagging fear of hunger, that old companion of the human race, has been replaced by an equally acute, but contrasting anxiety: cholesterol" (Moulin 1974, 166).

These tendencies persist to this day, despite the movement to downgrade everyday foods that occurred in the early 1990s, with the emergence of hard discount retailers, supermarket own-brand items, and so on, and the compensatory increase in the consumption of luxury products. The very marked developments that have been taking place since 1985 regarding preprepared products, such as ready meals or frozen fish and vegetables, confirm that domestic activities have effectively been transferred from kitchen to factory.

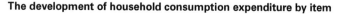

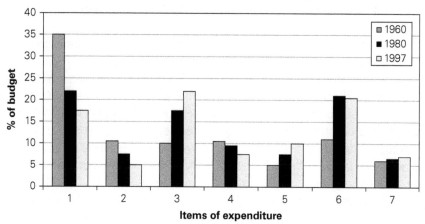

The development of household consumption expenditure by item

1   Food items, drinks and tobacco
2   Articles of clothing
3   Accomodation, heating, lighting
4   Furniture, household supplies, household articles and maintenance
5   Medical services
6   Transport and communication
7   Leisure, entertainment, education, culture

FIGURE 4 *The development of food purchases in household budgets.*
Source: INSEE, 1997.

Moulin notes that the growth rate of the "leisure and entertainment" and "expenditure made abroad by nationals" categories is "markedly higher than the growth rate of the gross national product" in the case of every European country. In this context, the cultural dimension of distinctive foods emerges as an emotionally enriching aspect.

Tourism plays an ever-increasing role in the leisure society defined by Joffre Dumazedier (1962).

> Traditionally characteristic foods are therefore required to change social status, to become a gateway to another culture and, in this way, to arouse an avid interest in visiting other lands . . . the man who lives in a large urban complex will therefore increasingly experience the pleasure of discovering different cuisines as an additional reason to travel. Yet that tired man, worn out by the life he leads in an artificial environment and by the standardized type of food that he is doomed to consume, will chiefly look to local, regional and national (foreign) cuisines, to provide him with a change of scene, a return to essentiality, to simplicity, to innocence and to authenticity. This raising of his sociocultural level will lead him to reject

the interchangeable flavors and stereotypical dishes that are all too often served to him in Europe's vast catering establishments. (Moulin 1974, 147)

This is a remarkable work of sociological foresight . . . but is it true to say that the contemporary eater always rejects stereotypical dishes?

Certain sociologists and socioeconomists have specialized in reprocessing data from food consumption surveys (d'Iribarne 1977; Combris 1980, 1995, 1996, 1998; Lambert 1987; Grignon 1988; Herpin 1980, 1984, 1988). We will begin by examining the very inspiring work carried out by Jean-Louis Lambert, who sought to reduce the blind spots in the INSEE's statistical surveys, by a detailed evaluation of the influence of self-completion. By cross-referencing the series completed in this way with sociological variables, he identifies food consumption models through dynamic comparisons, and outlines the tendencies characterizing their development. Social differences emerge as factors influencing the over or under-consumption of certain items. Higher social classes consume two and a half times more lamb than working-class groups, who consume more processed pork items, farinaceous foods and bread. Dynamic analysis shows that the 1960s and 1970s witnessed an increase in the consumption of meat and fresh dairy products, and a fall in the consumption of bread and farinaceous items. "The middle-class model is gradually imposing itself on the greater part of the population as the dominant model" (1987).

One question remains open to discussion, however. Are the structural transformations in French eating habits the result of changes in dietary practices affecting the whole of society? Or are they, more simply, the result of developments in the French demographic structure, which have seen a sharp numerical decline in working class and rural communities, and a corresponding rise in tertiary sector employees and executives? In other words, have the food sub-cultures of different French social groups become more similar, or have certain groups with a preference for particular types of food receded in favor of new groups who have adopted the famous middle-class model?

Lambert's work has been extended through connections between economic and nutritional approaches that have facilitated energy efficiency calculations (Lambert et al. 1987). In this way, for example, although the dietary practices of the 1960s and 1970s are characterized by a general fall in dietary energy consumption, it appears to be a socially diversified phenomenon. This drop is proportionately less marked in the case of lower social groups than in the more affluent classes. This data enabled the author to engage with nutritionists on a study of the development of obesity in the working classes.

In the same perspective, Pierre Combris revisited the work of J. C. Toutain, analyzing developments in dietary energy consumption in various countries over more than two centuries. He notes that a similar structural evolution occurred in most developed countries, albeit at varying rates. As he sees it, there were three phases in this process. In the initial phase, he notes a rise in the consumption of all types of food; the second sees changes in the structure of food rations, with the third and final phase being characterized by widespread differentiations in consumption practices (Combris and Volatier 1998). In France throughout the nineteenth century, for example, the calorie ration "rose steadily, thanks to an increase in all available categories of food." Then, around 1890, there was a fall in the consumption of grains, farinaceous foods, and dried pulses, while the consumption of products of animal origin, fruits, vegetables, and above all fats and sugars, continued to rise. With regard to nutrients, the protein content remained almost constant at between 12 and 15 percent of the total energy value, while that of carbohydrates and lipids showed contrasting movements; the energy content represented by the latter rose, to the detriment of the former. The two curves intersected in 1975.

However, this type of data presents a major drawback, expressed by Lambert in the following terms: "Although we know the contents of the shopping baskets and trolleys, we have no real idea of what is on the plates" (Lambert 1992).

The work carried out in preparation for the launch of a domestic survey, initiated by the INSEE in the late 1970s, is likewise of interest (Herpin, Chaudron 1983; Chaudron, Sluys, and Zaidman 1990, 1995). Although the project never saw the light of day, these different examples of preliminary research have contributed to the establishment of descriptors for food practices, and have enabled us to identify their various aspects. In this way, when investigating the theory of the destructuration of contemporary eating habits, Nicolas Herpin distinguishes five dimensions to the social institution of the family meal, thus decisively contributing to the objectivization of food intake (Herpin 1988). They are as follows: concentration, that is, the structuring of the instances of food intake into meals (breakfast, lunch and dinner), and "extra-prandial," less heavily institutionalized intakes (light bites, snacks, teatime snacks and coffee breaks); time-frame, which refers to the time rules that accompany instances of food consumption and punctuate the day (lunch at midday, dinner between 7:00 p.m. and 8:00 p.m., etc.); social synchronization, which designates the points during the day at which the various family members are able to meet together in order to share meals; locale, which concerns the location of meals eaten in the home (the kitchen or dining-room) or outside (the café, restaurant or canteen); and finally ritualization, which corresponds to the rules governing the alternation and interconnections between ordinary and festive meals.

This framework of reference is intended both to describe the institution of the meal and to assess the changes that affect it. It was put into practice by Herpin himself, in a survey on working-class families in the suburbs of Lille, and provided the material for a famous article intended to answer the question of the destructuration of modern eating practices[3] (Herpin 1988, reprised in Herpin and Verger 1991).

1.3 *The sociology of taste*

This aspect—taste—of the sociology of food consumption originated from the critique of Halbwachs's stance, the intention being to escape from a reductionist conception of the food-related social fact. As Claude and Christiane Grignon have emphasized:

> From this perspective, food cannot be established as a sociological subject, unless we eliminate its economic and biological material aspects and choose the most selective practices; this will lead us to favor the gastronomic over the everyday meal, instances of public, ceremonial food consumption over ordinary, daily eating practices, and the study of forms—meal rituals, table manners, etc.—rather than techniques. (1980, 565)

The sociology of taste began with Pierre Bourdieu. Indeed, his theory of "habitus" originated from the study of concrete, routine social practices, one of the foremost of these being the act of eating. Taking tastes and the differences that distinguish them as his starting point, he identifies their origin in the "habitus": "a structure that organizes perceptions, beneath which lie the objectively classifiable, material conditions of existence." In this way, he eradicated, or thought to eradicate, an entire aesthetic tradition. "What I like, and find to my taste, is actually what I normally consume, that is to say, the food eaten by my own social class."

In this way, gastronomy becomes part of an irrational process of distinction by which elite groups differentiate themselves from the aspiring middle classes. Bourdieu's stance emphasizes the autonomy of working-class tastes: "The art of eating and drinking remains one of the few areas in which the working classes explicitly challenge the legitimate art of living" (Bourdieu 1984).

In pursuit of more pragmatic objectives, Claude and Christiane Grignon, researchers at France's National Institute for Agricultural Research (INRA) were commissioned by the organization to examine the reasons governing food consumption practices from a sociological perspective. The project formed part of research programs linked to changes in the world of agriculture. They focused their attention on food products and the reasons behind consumption or self-sufficiency.

They rejected the idea of a French food consumption model trickling down from elite groups to the whole social body. This model dominates common perceptions, the sociology of Norbert Elias and, to a certain extent, the sociology of consumption from Moulin to Lambert. They sought to reveal an autonomous working-class food culture, distinct from middle-class food practices in both its forms and its dynamics (Grignon and Grignon 1980). As such, they emphasized the influence of socioeconomic determinants.

> A conversation about food with a working class family first and foremost involves budgets and pay-slips . . . price rises, problems with "making ends meet," in all, living standards rather than lifestyles, [so] it could be said that working class food practices are the result of a small number of harsh economic constraints, . . . the "tastes" themselves being a reflection of purchasing power. (1980, 548)

What emerges most strikingly from their studies is the permanence of the class system. In their view, changes in consumption practices occur at a superficial level, and have no effect on the deeply rooted social structure. In more recent publications, Claude Grignon (1995) adopts a critical distance from Bourdieu's position, which he deemed "too populist," yet which he shared in his first works on food and eating practices.

2 The "developmentalist" perspective

We owe the term "developmentalist," which is very rarely used in France,[4] to Stephen Mennell, Anne Murcott, and Anneke van Otterloo (1992). It refers to certain contemporary English-speaking authors, working in the tradition of Jack Goody, Mennell himself, and Marvin Harris. However, contrary to the cases of functionalism and structuralism, it is not possible to identify a truly coherent body of knowledge that would characterize these authors. Above all, these sociologists and anthropologists share a critical position with regard to the structuralist perspectives of Claude Lévi-Strauss and Mary Douglas, which they consider incapable of taking the dynamics of social changes into account. In their approach to change and, to a certain extent, to the relationships between the social, the psychological, and the corporal, more or less all developmentalists refer to the works of Norbert Elias (1939).

2.1 The influence of Norbert Elias

Elias presented the concept of the "civilizing process" as a result of his studies of treatises on good manners and works devoted to the subject of civility. He sought to explain how social norms shape the body and control the instincts. With regard to treatises on correct etiquette, he writes: "I suddenly found myself in possession of material that described the diversity of norms applied in ancient times, and which provided a reliable means of analyzing their development" (Elias 1990, 71).

What interested him in these types of document were the historical changes that they highlighted, and the fact that they offered us an opportunity to understand "current norms as the result of a process of becoming" (Elias 1990, 72).

"In order to comprehend the current situation . . . we must look back to history with a view to identifying the situation from which it originated. Civilization is a process, of which we are ourselves the subjects" (Elias 1974). He indicates the shifts in the "threshold of sensibility," which separates the clean from the unclean, and the presentable from that which should be concealed, and maintains our connection to animality, instinct, and desire. The "civilizing process" emerges as a mechanism of interiorization, shifting the violence of the social sphere toward the individual subject. "In a sense, the battlefield has been transposed into man's innermost being. It is there that he must grapple with some of the tensions and passions that were formerly exteriorized by hand-to-hand combat, where men were in direct confrontation with one another" (1975).

Elias's theories were not accepted immediately. Published in Basel in 1939, his book *Über den Prozess der Zivilisation* went completely unnoticed. In France, only Raymond Aron devoted a review to the work, which was then forgotten (Burguière et al. 1995, 213). The initiative to republish this work in the 1970s came from French sociologists. It was translated and published in two volumes as *La civilisation des mœurs* (1974), and *La dynamique de l'Occident* (1976), in a collection published by Jean Baechler, who would have been made aware of the work by Aron. It is thanks to this French edition that the work has become famous. However, for a long period of time French sociology was to remain curiously closed to Elias's thought[5]—with the exception of his probable influence on Bourdieu's *La distinction* (1979). Elias's work was to be received in France through the historians of the Annales School, specifically through the movement that was established in the 1960s under the designation historical anthropology, with François Furet, Emmanuel Leroy-Ladurie, Raymond Aron, Bartolomé Bennassar, André Burguière, and Georges Vigarello.

On the publication of *La civilisation des mœurs*, the historian François Furet devoted a very lengthy article to the work in the *Nouvel Observateur*,[6] ensuring that its renown would extend far beyond a readership composed of professional social scientists. It was indeed the case that these French historians, who were becoming increasingly well known at an international level, were able to promote Elias in this way, giving rise to English translations. These, however, came via the United States rather than England, although Elias had settled there, teaching at the London School of Economics.

In André Burguière's view, the success of Elias's thought in relation to "French new history" is based on his elaboration of what he terms a "sociogenesis" of the state and a "psychogenesis" of the individual. For these historians, who sought to escape from the socioeconomic paradigm that prevailed in the early days of the French new history, Elias's perspective represented a way to "reintroduce the political, or the state, and through the state, for Elias, the notion of power: and at the same time, with psychogenesis, they had found the philosopher's stone, that is to say, the way to relate the (let us say) structural evolution of context and the internal transformations of ways of thinking, of mentalities" (Burguière et al. 1998, 89–103).

The rediscovery of Elias by English sociologists therefore occurred via France. In his comparative study of English and French table traditions (1985), Stephen Mennell cites Elias and emphasizes the civilizing process at work in Western society as a whole over several centuries. One of the most notable effects of this is the interiorization of impulse control. He seeks to understand whether "long-term changes in the structure of societies which Norbert Elias argues . . . brought about changes in manners, in the expression of the emotions, and in personality structure were also reflected in the patterning and expression of so basic a drive as appetite" (Mennell 1985, 20).

In Mennell's view, a culture of taste will only emerge when one is certain to be able to eat one's fill. Gastronomic culture, with its specific norms that regulate the social display of hunger is therefore a "response to changing supply and social distribution of nourishment" (1985, 20). With reference to the civilizing process, Mennell proposes the expression "the civilizing of appetite," to describe the process of controlling the appetite in a society of plenty.

Although Jack Goody focused chiefly on material of an exotic nature, and drew on his knowledge of ethnic groups in Northern Ghana, his work was not solely confined to monographic ethnological studies, but extended to encompass the anthropological perspective. In order to understand the changes that have taken place in the eating practices of these ethnic groups, it is necessary not only to reconsider them in the context of colonization, which led them to eat in the English manner in formal situations, just as they would speak English on these occasions, but furthermore, to see these changes as the result of the increasing globalization of food production systems (1982). Well before the topic made front-page news, he highlighted the impact of industrial production processes and the development of food preservation techniques, such as canning and freezing, on everyday eating practices throughout the world.

2.2 *Cultural materialism*

Although he describes himself as a "cultural materialist," Marvin Harris is often associated with the developmentalist approach (Mennell, Murcott, and Van Otterloo 1992; Beardsworth and Keil 1997). It is probably in his radical critique of the structuralism of Lévi-Strauss that Harris's perspective is closest to that of Mennell and Goody. In his most complete work, *Good to Eat: Riddles of Food and Culture* (1986), he contradicts Lévi-Strauss's theory according to which, if a food is "good to think," it will therefore be "good to eat" (Lévi-Strauss 1966b). In his view, all food taboos and prohibitions may be justifiably analyzed in terms of ecological benefits. In this way, the assumed irrationality of different cultures recedes before the rational nature of processes of adaptation that escape the individual consciousness. The real reasons why the Jewish and Muslim religions prohibit the consumption of pork, and the Hindu religion that of beef, for example, would be traced to ecological or sanitary considerations, rather than religious or symbolic motives, which from this perspective are reduced to simple phenomena of rationalization in the psychoanalytical sense (Harris 1977). In all, Harris's approach is simply a more or less sophisticated development of Robert Merton's functionalism, and is founded on his distinction between "latent" and "manifest" functions (Merton 1965). One of the criticisms leveled at classical functionalism related to its difficulty in taking the motivations of social actors into account. As Roger Bastide noted, if a structure functions, it does so "according to models, to the values of ideas or ideals, which have a signification for the elements composing that structure" (Bastide 1960, 11). Merton succeeded in reinstating meaning into functional analysis, through establishing a difference between manifest and latent function. This was inspired by the distinction operated by Freudian psychoanalysis with regard to the analysis of dreams, between manifest content (as recounted by the dreamer on awakening), and latent content (what was actually dreamt, constituting the hidden meaning of the dream). The manifest function refers to the meaning that a specific social unit (an individual, group, or society) consciously confers on an institution, while the latent function refers to the objective but involuntary consequences which escape the individual's consciousness (Merton 1965, 135).

From the social actors' viewpoint, symbolic reasons explain and justify established conventions, providing reasons to respect taboos or prohibitions, or simply to implement practices. However, the reasons that endow these acts with their true effectiveness are material, ecological, or nutritional in nature. From this perspective, a specific cultural characteristic is therefore simply the hidden aspect of an adaptive benefit, although the individuals benefiting from it do not really understand it. In Harris's view, all dietary taboos and distinctive features may be treated in this way. Adaptive reasoning is always concealed behind the apparently arbitrary nature of cultures.

However, there are several examples to support the argument in favor of the relative autonomy of culture. They include those of the Massa, the Moussey, and the Toupouri peoples of North Cameroon, studied by Igor de Garine. Despite the fact that they live within the same biotope, have access to the same technology, and frequently intermarry, they make very different uses of the food resources available to them. In most cases, this is to the detriment of efficient nutrition (de Garine 1978, 1979; Fischler 1990). Other practices within food cultures appear frankly counter-productive. The most striking examples of these must surely be the wholesale slaughter of pigs and the ostentatious consumption characterizing the great traditional banquets of Melanesia (Lowie 1942), or the killing of water buffalo at burials carried out by certain Proto-Indochinese ethnic groups living on the borders of Thailand, Laos and Vietnam (Hassoun 1997). Such cases seem difficult to justify on the grounds of long-term nutritional benefits. To support his theory, Harris even draws on certain studies by ecological anthropologists (Katz 1979, 1982), although their works explicitly argue in favor of taking interactions between bio-socio-cultural aspects into account. At a strictly sociological level, the chief criticism that could be directed at Harris's theory is his disregard for the processes of social differentiation. What in fact unites these different authors is above all their criticism of the symbolic approach to cooking and table manners, which they consider too disconnected from their material dimensions. In their view, food practices cannot be understood without reference to nutritional, ecological and economic aspects. That interpretive framework prompts an assessment of the interrelations between the social and cognitive dimensions of eating practices on the one hand, and between production systems (Goody and Mennell) and connections to the environment (Harris) on the other hand. Equally, however, it tends to favor the influence of the environmental connection on the causal chain.

3 The H-omnivore or the sociology of the eater

The pluri, inter, or even in-disciplinary movement promoted by Edgar Morin in the 1970s—both in his research on the nature of man (1973) and in his approach to complexity (1977)—led to the emergence of the sociology of the eater.

> How is it not possible to see that what is most biological—sex, death—is at the same time the most permeated with symbols, with culture! Our

most fundamental biological activities, eating, drinking and defecating, are closely linked to norms, prohibitions, values, symbols, myths, rites—in other words, to what is most specifically cultural. And, in this way, it becomes clear that it is that unique, highly inter-communicative, unifying and integrated system, the human brain, which assimilates, in a unifying, or biological manner, cultural and spiritual elements (simultaneously complementary, competing and antagonistic, with markedly different degrees of integration according to individuals, cultures and eras) into a single bio-psycho-socio-cultural system. (Morin 1973, 146)

It was in Morin's wake that the first works of this type appeared in France. Issue number 31 of the journal *Communications*, edited by Fischler, unquestionably marked the launch of this movement in 1979. In the introduction, he clearly expresses the desire to work on the margins, at the interfaces between disciplines.

Here is a transdisciplinary theme in the truest sense of the word, a subject with multiple entry-points, and which should be considered from multiple standpoints: biological, economic, anthropological and ethnological, socio-logical and psycho-sociological, psychoanalytical, psychological, historical, archeological, geographical and geopolitical, and so forth. This being said, these specialist perspectives will not reveal the truth by juxtaposing their analyses, by fitting themselves together like the pieces of a puzzle: each of them is a purveyor, not of one aspect of the truth, but of an entire truth in itself. These truths, moreover, are complementary rather than competing, as they are interactive and mutually irreducible. In other words, the transdisciplinary approach, even if it is venturesome in nature, must prevail over mere pluridisciplinarity. (Fischler 1979, 1)

Faced with the ambiguity in Durkheim's definition of the social fact, the "sociology of the eater" is clearly positioned within the Maussian tradition, and aims to explore the connections between psychology, physiology, and sociology that operate with regard to food consumption.

What we have sought to do . . . is to break down the barriers between the *latifundia*, and to re-establish the domain of eating and food as an "open range," with free circulation among the various disciplines. Therefore, rather than revealing definitive results, this was more a matter of instigating questions and investigations, hypotheses or speculations, curiosity or discussions, and of suggesting approaches and themes for research, from case-studies, or, conversely, from general reviews. Of course, there is no question of presenting an exhaustive, complete panorama of all the disciplines, nor of reducing the questions posed by food consumption to a single issue. This is no invitation to a lavish banquet: at the most, it will be an opportunity to pick at a few appetizers together with a heuristic "apéritif." (1979, 3)

Being in tune with the interdisciplinary approach in vogue during the 1980s, the journal issue enjoyed resounding success, both with the disciplines mobilized for food research and with the general public, although not without sparking a few controversies (Herpin 1991; Gomez 1992; Grignon 1993).

Fischler's article "Gastro-nomie et Gastro-anomie" became a seminal text for the emerging movement, instigating a focus on the eater. It is to him that we owe the clarification of the issues involved in human food consumption. He emphasizes the fact that the act of eating is unique by its very nature, as items of food are absorbed and pass through the barrier formed by the body, thus becoming the eater himself. The consumption of food differs from other types of consumption because of this incorporation, whereby it crosses the frontier of the self. Consequently, food practices ceased to be seen as forms of expression and affirmations of social identities, as had been the case with the sociology of consumption or the sociology of taste; instead, they were viewed as being central to the process of constructing identity. The cognitive and imaginary dimensions of the act of eating subsequently became pivotal to the sociology of the eater.

Published in English in a simplified form (Fischler 1980), this text constituted the starting point of a series of collaborations between sociologists and psychologists (Chiva 1985, 1996; Rozin 1994; Lahlou 1996; Piattelli-Palmarini 1996), anthropologists (de Garine 1979; Barrau 1983; Cohen 1993), and historians (Flandrin and Montanari 1996; Nahoum-Grappe 1979; Levenstein 1993). It also instigated renewed perspectives to research within the sociological domain itself (Poulain 1985a; Lambert 1987; Beardsworth 1995; Falk 1996; Lupton 1996; Warde 1997; Pfirsch 1997). The first doctoral theses on this sociological subject were part of that movement. In 1985, our *Anthropo-sociologie de la cuisine et des manières de tables,* supervised by Edgar Morin, initiated this series. Combining the legacies of Lévi-Strauss's structuralism, the anthropology of the imagination (Durand 1960), and the sociology of the eater, it presents taste as the expression of the sociological, psychological, and biological elements of food consumption, then focuses on identifying the structures of the dietary and culinary conceptions that characterize French gastronomy (Poulain 1985a). This was partially reprised in a version of the work intended for the general public (Poulain and Neirinck 1988).

In 1990, after collating and summarizing the results of over ten years of research on the human eater, for whom he coined the term "*homnivore*," Fischler presented a doctoral thesis, also supervised by Morin. In it, he distinguishes an "eternal eater," governed by laws, from the invariants of dietary behavior[7]: classificatory thought, the principle of incorporation, and the *homnivore's* paradox. However, these general principles are actualized in various ways depending on the cultural contexts. In this way, Fischler is able to present a "modern eater," who lives in an industrialized society with an abundance, or even a superabundance of food. The symposium "Manger Magique," organized by Fischler in 1994, marks a second stage in the sociology of the eater. Magical thinking, long seen as one of the characteristics of the primitive mentality, emerges as a normal aspect of the functioning of dietary awareness, coexisting with rational thought within the mind of the modern eater (Fischler 1994; Rozin 1994; Chiva 1994).

3.1 *Classificatory thought*

The principal characteristic common to human eaters is the establishment of a classificatory system that determines what is edible and what is inedible. All cultures make selections from a considerably wide group of items with nutritional properties, adopting a greater or lesser number of these as their food. "There has been no known culture to date that is completely devoid of a system of categories and dietary regulations, that has not experienced any dictates or prohibitions concerning what must be eaten, and how one should eat" (Fischler 1990, 58).

Although some attempts have been made to limit it to materialist explanations that are more or less functionalist in approach (Harris 1985), the process that transforms a natural product containing nutrients into food, cannot be reduced to utilitarian reasoning or availability (Sahlins 1976), and forms part of a classification system (Douglas 1971). It is related to reasoning, to rationalities that are rooted in perceptions, in the collective imagination of the culture in question. The biological need to eat, therefore, becomes integrated into a value system. Whether they are based on the rationale of totemism (Lévi-Strauss 1962), of animal sacrifice, (Détienne and Vernant 1979), of rational hygienism,[8] of aesthetics,[9] or of a combination of one or several of these forms of reasoning, all cultures establish a classification system whereby animals and vegetables potentially representing food are placed into two categories: edible and nonedible.

3.2 *The incorporation principle*

Fischler (1990) presented the "incorporation principle" as the second invariant of human dietary behavior. His analyses constituted an extension of general anthropological research (Frazer 1911; Lévi-Strauss 1962), and of the anthropo-sociology of food and eating (Moulin 1974; Aron 1976; Poulain 1985a), and were supported by the studies conducted by Paul Rozin (1976), who adopted an experimental approach to the Kleinian concept of incorporation. This principle has a dual significance. From the psychological perspective, the eater becomes what he eats. To eat is to incorporate, to appropriate the qualities of a particular food. This is true from an objective standpoint, as in certain cases—notably that of amino acids—the nutrients are absorbed into the body of the eater himself, but it is also true at a psychological level. From the subjective viewpoint of imaginary realities, the eater believes, or fears, that he appropriates the symbolic characteristics of a food according to the principle that "we are what we eat," a perspective related to magical thinking.

A large number of anthropologists have drawn attention to this thought process. "The savage commonly believes," writes Sir James Frazer, "that by eating the flesh of an animal or man he acquires not only the physical, but even the moral and intellectual qualities which were characteristic of that animal or man" (Frazer 1911). In *The Savage Mind,* Lévi-Strauss examines food taboos from the totemist perspective. Reviewing a variety of anthropological studies, he provides a few examples: "Squirrels [are] forbidden to pregnant women among the Fang of the Gabon. Squirrels shelter in the holes of trees and a future mother who ate their flesh would run the risk of the foetus copying a squirrel and refusing to leave the uterus." Conversely, the Hopi Indians assert that pregnant women should eat the flesh of weasels and badgers: "They hold that the meat of these animals is favourable to child-bearing because of their habit of working their way through the ground and 'getting out' at some other place when they are chased into a hole. They therefore help the baby to 'come out quickly'" (Voth 1901, quoted by Lévi-Strauss 1966). Culturally closer to us, such diverse practices as the celebration of the Eucharist in the Catholic Mass, or the *appellation* system of postrevolutionary French gastronomy (Poulain 1985b), are likewise associated with this magical dimension of incorporation.

From a psychosociological perspective, in eating, man incorporates himself into a cultural space. Being culturally determined, food, cooking, and table manners integrate the eater into a social domain, a cultural system. The act of eating forms a basis for collective identity, as well as the principles of identification, differentiation, and "otherness." From Barthes (1961) to Bourdieu (1979), from Aron (1976) to Fischler (1990), a number of works based on differing theoretical approaches take account of this function of food consumption. Whether perceived as a signal, an emblem, or a symbol, the daily repetitions of the act of eating integrate and maintain the eater within a system of meanings. It is on daily eating practices, essential for the preservation of life, that the feeling of belonging or of social difference is constructed. It is through cooking and table manners that the most basic social training takes place, and through which a society transmits its values, enabling them to become internalized. And it is through eating that social links are forged and maintained.

3.3 *From the omnivore's paradox to the ambivalent natures of human food consumption*

For Fischler (1990) and Rozin (1976), the omnivore's paradox is regulated by the "culinary system," a subdivision of the cultural system comprising a series of rules defining what may be eaten, and the methods of preparation and consumption that should be applied.

In this way, new food is made acceptable as it is adapted to a particular culture by being stamped with a characteristic and familiar taste. The introduction of avocados into France is a good example of this. They are served either with mayonnaise or with a vinaigrette dressing, two taste markers of French cuisine (indeed, the latter is known in English as French dressing). The culinary system likewise establishes rules regarding food combinations, thereby enabling various dishes to be created from one basic item. For instance, classic nineteenth-century French cuisine features several hundred recipes for egg dishes, combined with a multitude of secondary accompaniments. Likewise, it is the culinary system that determines the combinations of dishes within a menu. Integrated within a culture, the eater, therefore, has very few decisions to make; his choices are dictated by the culinary system operating in his society. In this way, the system resolves the "double bind" that characterizes the (h)omnivore's situation. The anxieties accompanying modern food consumption are consequently interpreted as a breakdown in the regulatory function of culinary systems. The social constraints impacting upon the eater have weakened; this is linked on the one hand to the rise of individualism, and on the other hand to the industrialization of food production, processing, and marketing, which is severing the connections between man and his food. These circumstances have given rise to a situation of gastro-anomie, where food anxiety is dominant. "If we do not know what we are eating, we do not know what we will become, but neither do we know what we are" (Fischler 1990, 70).

3.4 *Revisiting incorporation*

The analyses that we have conducted on food safety risks[10] with the aid of recent works by Fischler, Rozin and Beardsworth, prompt a reconsideration of the process of incorporation, and a broadening of the narrow perspective based on the theme of "we are what we eat," to which it is sometimes reduced. In this context, the eater is presented as exclusively susceptible to the effect of the symbolic qualities of the object consumed. In other words, he is viewed as receptive, faced with food that might influence him at a symbolic level, for better or for worse. Revisiting the concept of incorporation, it is possible to create a matrix showing the connection between eater and food, according to whether the former is presented as receptive or nonreceptive, and the latter as symbolically dangerous or not dangerous. The various different forms of cannibalism,[11] and an examination of the structures of the imaginary governing the acts of swallowing and biting may serve as our guide (Poulain 1985a). With this approach, we are following in the wake of Gaston Bachelard, who, basing his work on the discoveries of psychoanalysis, identifies two phases in the preconscious oral stage of development: "swallowing" and "biting." "Jonah and the Whale" and the ogre in "Tom Thumb" may serve as images of these two phases.

Swallowing corresponds to sucking, the primitive phase within the oral stage, where the infants sucks at his mother's breast and enjoys the sensation of the warm milk flowing into his mouth. At this stage in psychological development, object relations have not yet been formed; the world, and individuals, only exist for the infant as "food or a source of food, to which, in his fantasies, he imagines himself united, through swallowing or incorporation" (Housser 1976). At a mythological level, the positive nature of the act of swallowing is associated with prelapsarian paradise, where man, not yet torn between the realms of good and evil, draws both his sense of personal unity, and of unity with the world, from his respect for the divine purpose. For swallowing does not destroy the item that is swallowed; on the contrary, in many cases it "increases its worth, or, better still, sanctifies it" (Durand 1960, 234). In the Christian tradition, the host, the body of Christ, is not bitten, but swallowed whole or left to melt in the mouth.

The experiences of the great mystics likewise establish the innocence and sacralization of the act of swallowing. Saint François de Sales wrote:

> Our Saviour, showing the most delightful breast of his divine love to the devout soul, draws her wholly to himself, gathers her up, and as it were folds all her powers in the bosom of his more than motherly sweetness, and then burning with love, he clasps the soul, joins, presses and glues her on his lips of sweetness, and to his delicious breast, kissing her with the sacred kiss of his mouth, and making her relish his breasts more sweet than wine.

The same images occur in the writings of Saint Teresa of Avila, who compares the soul to an infant at its mother's breast: "And the mother without the babe's effort to suckle puts the milk in its mouth in order to give it delight." In another passage, she likens souls to infants, suckling at the divine breast and experiencing supreme joy (examples quoted by Durand 1960, 295, 296). The act of sucking therefore appears as the archetypal model of innocent pleasure. Bachelard remarks that the signs of "primitive unconscious pleasures and return to the *sucking* phase" would be found by "an observer skilled in physiognomy . . . on the face of someone guzzling oysters" (Bachelard 2011, 113).[12]

The oral-sadistic period emerges after this initial phase in the oral stage, and occurs just as the teething process begins. During this period the infant takes pleasure in biting: this crunching stage is associated with fallen man, the eater of flesh. The desire to incorporate is still in evidence, but it becomes sadistic, in other words, destructive. According to Melanie Klein, in the imagination of a small child, the "introjected" object is attacked, mutilated and absorbed. He experiences the dilemma presented by the acts of sucking and biting; although he feels the desire to bite his mother as he feeds, if he actually does so, she will withdraw her breast. In this way, he enters the world of ambivalence—the ambivalent nature of his desire, which lies at the heart of a "split" in the object, and of his accession to the "objectal sphere," and the ambivalent nature of objects, which consequently become simultaneously "good" and "bad" (Klein 1959).

It is interesting to note that the fall from Eden to earth, and to suffering, occurs after Eve has bitten the apple. The act of biting marks the entry into the world of good and evil. The teething stage, which shortly precedes the weaning process, is the cause of an unavoidable trauma that is perhaps more distressing than the weaning itself. It is this trauma that reinforces the negative nature of biting, and the image of the ogre is rooted in this concept (Durand 1960, 13). The innocent pleasures of sucking and swallowing, and the pleasure of biting, which, although associated with guilt, nevertheless releases the individual from a powerful, aggressive impulse, are both expressions of the gastronomic imaginary.

> The will to swallow is very weak in comparison with the will to bite. Psychologists studying the will must integrate different coefficients in images that are so dynamically different. Gastronomy will be totally renewed by this, since it needs psychological preparations every bit as much as culinary ones. We can easily understand that a meal must be assessed in terms not just of nutritional content but also of how it satisfies the whole of unconscious being. A good meal must bring together conscious and unconscious values. Alongside substantial sacrifices made to the will to bite, it must include a tribute to that happy time when, with our eyes tightly shut, we swallowed everything. (Bachelard 2011, 113)

"Gastronomy will be totally renewed by this," declared Bachelard; it also cast new light on the subject of dietetics, doing away with a mechanical image of the eater, who had been reduced to a mere digesting machine.

In this way, two distinct systems may be discerned in the imaginary associated with incorporation (Table 12). In the case of swallowing, the eater allows the item swallowed to enter his body with its entire symbolic identity intact: "swallowing does not destroy the object that is swallowed"—on the contrary, in many cases, through this act, an object is *"enhanced, or better still, sanctified"* (Durand 1960, 234).

In the case of biting, the eater firstly reduces the item eaten to its constituent elements, decomposing and recomposing its symbolic meaning(s). Taking these two systems of incorporation, and the positive or negative conceptions of the foods in question as a starting point, four situations may be identified:

Positive influence: The eater allows himself to be penetrated, invaded, and influenced by the positive qualities of the food eaten. This perspective corresponds to the imaginary associated with endocannibalism, which offers deceased ancestors the bodies of living beings as their tombs. In this way, the qualities and wisdom of the deceased will be expressed through the

TABLE 12 The dimensions of food incorporation

Dominant system of incorporation	Eater	Food	Significations of incorporation
Penetration (Swallowing)	Receptive	Positive	Eating in order to be penetrated by the qualities of the object eaten. The eater allows himself to be "invaded" and influenced by the positive qualities of the food.
	Receptive	Negative	Refusal to eat, in order to avoid "invasion," leading to taboos, permanent or temporary prohibitions, fasting, etc.
Appropriation (Biting)	Nonreceptive	Positive	Eating in order to appropriate the constituent elements of the object eaten, and to strengthen the eater.
	Nonreceptive	Negative	Eating in order to destroy the object devoured.

personalities of the living. In this case, the object that is incorporated takes precedence over the eater. This belief is also apparent in the sacrament of the Eucharist.

Negative influence: The eater views the process of incorporation in terms of risk and danger, as the characteristics of the object eaten are likely to jeopardize his integrity and identity. There is an incompatibility between eater and eaten. This leads to a refusal to eat, in order to avoid invasion, which takes the form of taboos, prohibitions, fasting, and so on.

Positive appropriation: According to this perception, the eater is active and dominant in relation to the item eaten. Eating provides him with the opportunity to reinforce his own body by appropriating the constituent elements of the object. Exocannibalism, in which a victim—and a respected one[13]—is consumed so that the eater may imbibe his dead enemy's strength without compromising his own psychological make-up, is the ideal example of this.

Negative appropriation: In this case the eater, confident of his integrity, consumes foods that are negatively viewed, either in order to eliminate what they symbolically represent, or to sublimate them. Judicial cannibalism, which involves the killing and consumption of a deviant member of the group as a means of restoring him to order, is an example of this fourth category. It also corresponds to certain mystical practices carried out by Christian saints, who, as described by Jean-Pierre Albert, would consume items that were not regarded as food in their own cultures, or, worse still, the crusts or pus seeping from the wounds of the sick. These practices form part of a belief in sublimation; not only will the purity of the spirit remain untarnished by the negative character of the item incorporated, but it will achieve its fullest potential in this manner (Albert 1997). It is equally possible to include in this category the consumption, in small doses, of more or less dangerous or toxic items considered capable of correcting or reinforcing the characters of those who take them, based on the principle that "opposites cure opposites."

The Hippocratic dietetic strategy of the Renaissance period may be seen as an example of this perspective (Flandrin and Montanari 1996). This distinction enables us to identify two major families of food cultures according to the force of the prohibitions that they implement. Strong prohibitions are imposed in situations where a cultural space is oriented toward the invasive dimension of a food, and where a protective stance is, therefore, adopted through the enforcement of numerous prohibitions and taboos, and through precise instructions with regard to what may and/or must be eaten. This is the case with Jewish, Muslim, and Hindu eating practices. Cultures with few food prohibitions, such as for example the French or Chinese, consider a much broader range of items to be suitable for consumption. The Chinese proverb: "The Chinese eat everything that has two legs, and everything that has four legs except the table," shows that regulations tend to be applied to methods of consumption, rather than to foods themselves. Among the cultures prevailing within what are conventionally known as the Abrahamic religions (Judaisim, Christianity, and Islam), the food culture pertaining to Christianity belongs to this category: "Whatever goes into a man from outside cannot defile him. . . . What comes out of a man is what defiles a man." It is evident from this that a rupture occurred, with the Christian religion distancing itself from the highly specific Hebraic dietary laws of the Old Testament. The emphasis here will be on forms of food consumption.

All these systems are in operation when humans incorporate either food or medicines. This conceptual framework enables us to distinguish different methods of resolving dilemmas, and above all to dismantle the notion of the culinary system and to reapply the term in a different manner. Indeed, it seems to us that in his application of this concept, intended to take account of the methods of regulating the ambivalence of the human act of eating, Fischler alternates between a highly functional definition limited to the culinary dimension, and a second, much broader definition, closer to that of Lévi-Strauss, according to which the culinary system reflects both nature and culture. We propose to apply the concept of the "culinary system" to the former aspect alone, and to use the term "food social space" when examining the methods used to organize the bioanthropological connection between a human group and the biotope it inhabits (Poulain 1997e, 1999b).

4 The sociology of eaters:
An interactionist perspective

Writing in the USA in the 1940s, Kurt Lewin showed that the consumption of a product, and food choices in general, are not the results of individual decisions, but of a series of social interactions. In order for a food to be consumed by an individual, it is first necessary for it to reach him. In a famous study on the consumption of milk carried out for the US Department of Agriculture, he highlights the fact that the consumption or nonconsumption of milk is not the result of an individual choice made by "American man." Instead, it depends on a series of decisions made by his wife, who decides what is good for her husband, her children, and herself to eat. In this way, he puts forward the notion of an economic gatekeeper, whose function it is to open or close a series of channels through which foods must move before they reach the family dining table, passing through the whole system involved in the social organization of food consumption. The distinction between food consumers and food buyers is, therefore, established, launching the reign of the "housewife," so dear to marketing men and other social research organizations (Lewin 1943).

The theory of channeling is intended to answer certain questions: How and why do foods arrive at the table? Through what stages do they pass? Who controls these different stages, and how is this done? Lewin formulated his theories as a result of his research on the consumption of milk and offal in American society, and used the image of the channel, through which food must pass in order to reach the eater. The access to, and functioning of the channel is controlled by gatekeepers. These act according to a sociological and a techno-economic rationale subject to different representations. This conception is evident in the work of a number of contemporary authors such as Léo Moulin (1974) and Raymond Ledrut and his team (1979), and was to be systematically developed by Jean-Pierre Corbeau.[14]

4.1 Sociality, sociability, and social change

Corbeau makes a distinction between the notions of sociality and sociability. The former encompasses all the social and cultural determinants that affect the social actor, in this case the eater, whether he is conscious of this or not.

> We consider sociality to be the crystallized manifestation of the impact on the individual of dominant cultural models within a given conception of the world. It is this conception of the world within a given culture that determines what its members should acquire according to the position they occupy, within a given group, in a situation characterized by certain economic and social hierarchies, gender relations, access to knowledge and to modes of expertise. (Corbeau 1997a, 150)

In this way, sociality plays a part in the meaning that a social actor gives to his own practices at a very early stage. Corbeau explains that sociality may be described through a metaphor: "It is a kind of 'tattoo', a marker that is sometimes accepted, emphasized and exalted, at other times suppressed, hidden or denied, but which individuals can never discard." It corresponds to Peter Berger's and Thomas Luckmann's notion of "exteriorized objective reality" (1986).

Sociability refers to the way in which interacting individuals will portray rules imposed by society in a specific context. In other words, it corresponds to the original nature of the concrete actualization of their social determinants. "Sociability is established as an interactive process in which individuals choose the forms of communication and exchange that connect them to one another.

They can thus either decide to accept the social role of a simple element or product of sociality, or to develop creative dynamics through the interrelations they seek to bring about" (Corbeau 1997a, 151).

It emphasizes the individual's creative dimension, and it is the interstices that exist between sociality and sociability which form a starting point for the transformation and development of social practices. In Corbeau's view, eaters are therefore partly over-determined by their social origins, but at the same time they have access to a space, of varying breadth, which provides them with the freedom to adapt, modify and develop the forms of their eating practices.

4.2 *The plural eater*

According to the concept of the "plural" eater, eating practices are viewed as the result of the encounter between a socially identified *eater*, who may be defined according to traditional sociological categories (age, gender, profession and socioprofessional category, level of education, etc.), a *situation,* that is, a recognized social context (type of commensality: festive or ordinary meals, eaten inside or outside the home, in public or in private), and a particular *food,* which is imbued with the representations existing within a given sociocultural environment. These three elements constitute the points of an "eating triangle." This varies both within the social space and over time.

According to the individuals, the social contexts and the foods involved, sociability may be "totally dominated by sociality or even mistaken for it." Equally, the influence of sociality may be weakened, thus enabling sociability to "create new meanings" and new practices. Corbeau continues:

> The triangle varies according to social space, because we argue that the eater is a plural being, that attitudes and behaviors change according to individuals, and also according to the situations in which they find themselves involved—according to the nature of the food consumed, its appearance, and the imaginary associated with it. The triangle also varies over time, because each of these elements possesses a history: individual or collective in the case of the eater, and in the case of food, as a generator of symbolic meaning (through its arrival in our societies, its rarity, and the channel via which it reached the eater). These factors correlate with changes in the forms and rituals of dietary practices that affect the context of food consumption. (Corbeau 1997b, 155)

This leads Corbeau to establish the eater as a "plural individual," that is to say, capable of enacting behaviors that vary in rationale and meaning, depending on the social context and type of food involved. In this way, before practices are contextualized, the task of the sociology of food is to carry out a historical analysis of the social representations embodied in foods, to study changes in forms of sociability and their encoding in secular rituals and finally, to identify the influence of traditional sociological determinants (age, gender, socio-professional category). Once this has been achieved, it will then be possible to begin identifying the rationale behind the social actors' behavior and their interactions.

4.3 *The four types of ethos displayed by eaters*

To describe the plural nature of the behavior enacted by eaters, or more specifically, the reasons that underlie them, Corbeau applies Max Weber's concept of ethos. He uses it to describe the space marking the interconnection between the forms of social over-determination and personality dynamics contained within the margin of freedom provided by sociability. "The ethos results from the encounter between centrifugal forces—impulses, passions, the imaginary and invention resulting from interactions of the ego—and centripetal forces: civility, standardized images of the body, dietary, economic or commercial constraints, and so on."

It is a particular form, specific to individuals, which may be compared to a process of customization carried out by the subject on these different forces of nature. In this way, an individual gives meaning to his life, by "inventing trajectories that are original, but which the socio-analyst, engaged in a comprehensive approach, may assimilate and compare with others or superimpose on these; the ethos, always meaningful, therefore becomes transformed into a representative type" (Corbeau 1997b, 151). The concept of ethos, defined in this way, enables typologies to be constructed. In Corbeau's view, these escape both the unduly pronounced over-determination of Bourdieu's "habitus," and "the nominalism often associated with typologies or other forms of mapping proposed by marketing men, from the combination of a handful of factors deemed to be relevant social indicators."

In order to identify these different types of ethos associated with the eater, he refers to the studies conducted by Raymond Ledrut and his team[15] at the University of Toulouse-le Mirail. They identify three principal types of eater: "*les complexés du trop*" (subjects who are anxious to limit their food intake); "*les tenants du nourrissant léger*" (subjects characterized by a preoccupation with healthy foods) and "*les tenants du nourrissant consistant*" (traditional eaters favoring items perceived as energy-giving) (Ledrut et al. 1979a,b). Yet Corbeau does not view these models of food consumption as final categories, that is, as the results of the analyses that form part of the normal rationale governing sociological studies of food (the procedure adopted by Lambert, Grignon, and Lahlou, as well as Ledrut and his team). Instead, he integrates them into a comprehensive approach. Taking them as a starting point, he reconstructs the significations that social actors give to their own practices. What interests him above all is the meaning that eaters confer on what they do.

He adds a new category to the three groups of eaters defined by Ledrut, which he names *les gastrolastress*, distinguishing within the first category of "fearful eaters" (*les complexés du trop*), several possible trajectories that "lead to, verge on, or surround" this type of behavior.

- *Fearful eaters* share "an anxiety related to the absorption of food." They experience eating as a worrying activity, fraught with risk. This anxiety may be traced to multiple causes, and could also be the result of various processes of reasoning. These types of eaters are divided into four subcategories, defined as follows: *Eating disorders*, such as bulimia and anorexia: these occur when the anxiety becomes highly exacerbated. Their origins may be traced both to the subject's unconscious—in the psychoanalytical sense—and to certain social processes that "generate disorders," such as the "social vacuum," sometimes accompanied by significant economic constraints (Corbeau 1991, 367). *Social appearance anxiety*: the eater is heavily influenced by bodily aesthetics and the ideal of slenderness. *Health-related concerns*: eaters are attentive to the way food affects their health. *Attitudes based on religious beliefs or ideologies*: in this case, the meaning conferred on eating practices is constructed with reference to cultural prohibitions.

- *Subjects concerned with healthy eating* "are characterized by the careful attention they pay to dietary information and by a relatively balanced approach between enjoyment of food and concern with maintaining good health" (1991, 428). They are open to the influence of other cuisines and to exoticism, whether this is synchronic in nature (involving foreign cuisines), or diachronic (involving the revival of traditional local dishes and products). They overestimate the importance of fish and vegetables, and are the most keen to acquire information on nutrition and diet.

- *Traditional eaters* favor substantial meals. They enjoy *charcuterie* products and cannot envisage a meal without meat and farinaceous items. "This desire for meat and white bread reflects the dynamics of 'social revenge' on the part of those from humbler backgrounds still present within this model. For the most part, this category is made up of elderly subjects who can recall times of food shortage (working class taste, as studied by Christiane and Claude Grignon, 1980)." This category favors foods for their energy-giving properties.

- The *gastrolastress* category. This term was formed by combining the word *gastrolâtre*, created by Rabelais to describe eaters who "make a god of their belly," and the idea of stress, which encompasses both the burden of the constraints affecting modern life, and recuperative activities designed to reduce pressures and relieve tension (Corbeau 1991, 434). Eaters in this category alternate between dietary practices characterized by simplified, or even destructured meals, using fast foods due to pressure of time during the working week, and choices more motivated by gastronomic considerations in the evenings and at weekends, when they effectively turn into bona fide gourmets.

Corbeau views these various examples of ethos as "outlines of 'ideal types', which should not be confused with reality." He continues, with reference to Raymond Boudon:

As Simmel clearly suggests when he insists on making a distinction between the formal and the concrete, it is important to understand that explanatory systems such as those that have just been presented are not erroneous in themselves. On the contrary, they provide us with vital insights into social change. Difficulties only arise when these general outlines are interpreted in a literal manner, as descriptions of concrete mechanisms or distinctions, without the understanding that they must be refined and adapted before they can be applied to a particular subject. (Boudon 1984, 231, cited by Corbeau 1991)

4.4 *The eating sector*

Corbeau's most recent contribution is his reestablishment of eating practices within a wider area of social interaction. He initially referred to this domain as the "eating sector," recently rebaptizing it as the "eating diadrama," the secret of this pun being known to him alone. In the place of a linear and mechanical conception of the agrifood sector, composed solely of professionals ("from field to fork," as the saying goes), he has established his own food sector, which in addition to traditional participants includes three new categories. These are as follows: experts and researchers in the fields of agronomy, engineering, economics, social sciences, medicine, and so on, whose knowledge and explanatory discourses are, to varying degrees, mutually contradictory; the media, who dramatize both the discoveries and the opinions of researchers and experts; and finally, the decision makers, these being politicians, economists, or lawyers, operating at regional, national or international level.

These different groups of participants all interact and contribute to constructing the meaning that the eater confers on his practices. "A definition of this type deliberately distances us from an image of the eater as nothing more than a reflection of social reproduction, since the actors (decision-makers, food producers, processors, distributors, assistants, researchers and eaters), are constantly innovating, distorting and transgressing." Corbeau argues in favor of traditional, qualitative sociology:

> In other words, for an approach involving fieldwork, analysis and conceptualization, where tasks are not subject to division on a technical or a social basis. Researchers, whatever their status, should be involved in all the processes that lead to the development of an "ideal type." This will enable them to understand how the influence of the group affects the social actor and the meaning underlying the latter's response. (1997b, 161, 162)

These analyses led Corbeau to distance himself somewhat from the notion of a generalized concern "such as Fischler might propose" (1990, 433). Instead, through his concept of the plural eater, he envisages the potential for subjects to alternate between the forms of eating practices previously described.

9

The sociologies of food and attempts to forge connections

At the end of this journey, which has led us from an account of how the major sociological movements have approached the subject of food practices, to the different attempts that have been made to create a single sociology of food, it must be acknowledged that this has not yet been fully achieved: instead of one sociology, we still have sociologies. However, although we are still far from establishing a sociology of food, we can identify advances that have been made regarding a sociology toward food. These have taken place in the context of a system based on two opposing theories. The first of these pertains to the Mauss-Durkheim epistemological alternatives. It extends between two opposite poles: on the one hand, a research perspective that accepts the Durkheimian definition of the "social fact" and the principle of its autonomy, and on the other hand, a stance following the Maussian tradition, whereby the "total social fact" is the result of the combined interaction of sociological, psychological, and physiological factors.

Intermediary perspectives may exist between these two radical stances. In this way, Chombart de Lauwe, Herpin, and Bourdieu represent the tradition of the autonomous social fact, and on the opposite side, Richards, Elias, and Fischler embody the Maussian tradition. From this perspective, authors such as Ledrut, Hubert, Corbeau, and Mennell occupy an intermediary position.

The second movement corresponds to the way in which sociologists of food emphasize either change and transformation or, conversely, focus more on stability and permanence. The first approach highlights the developments that have occurred in food consumption models or representations. This is the case with Elias, Lambert, Mennell, and Warde. The second approach is represented by Lévi-Strauss and the quest for universal culinary structures, and also by Bourdieu and Grignon, who emphasize the permanent nature of social organization and the perpetuation of the class system underlying apparent changes. In this case too, it is possible for intermediary approaches to exist between these two opposing perspectives, examples being those of Fischler and Beardsworth, whose aim is to understand how the invariants of the behavior of the "eternal eater" manifest themselves in the "contemporary eater."

In this way, we can locate the main actors and movements involved in the sociology of food by means of a diagram with two axes. The first marks the opposition between the two epistemological stances, characterized on the one hand by the acceptance of and adherence to the principle of the autonomous social fact, and on the other hand, by adherence to the concept of the total social fact and a belief in the need to establish a dialogue with neighboring disciplines. The second axis links the opposing perspectives of a sociological focus on transformation, and an approach that highlights the invariants and mechanisms of social reproduction (Figure 5).

This representation likewise demonstrates how food and eating highlight opposing sociological perspectives, and extend beyond their boundaries. Léo Moulin founded the committee for research into the sociology and anthropology of food composed of members of the Association internationale des sociologues de langue française (AISLF). He revisits this epistemological question in *Les Liturgies de la table*:

> We might ask ourselves, however, if the sociological approach is the most suitable to apply to the analysis of Eating and Drinking. It is evident that in this domain, which is the most intimately linked to our personality, the role of sociologists is even more problematic than usual, and that one might justifiably suspect them, through professional bias, of emphasizing the sociocultural as a decisive variable, rather than the physiological and the psychological.

However, he goes on to state that in the case of eating, more than in that of any other domain: "The physiological dimension never stands entirely alone. In the case of man, the natural, ultimately biological phenomenon of hunger contains . . . an element of social influence, however minimal and inconspicuous it may be . . . the same is true, and even more so, of the psychological dimension. . . . I therefore feel justified in concluding that the sociocultural factor plays a decisive role in the domain of tastes and aversions, their evolution and recurrences" (Moulin 1988, 44, 45). The study of food practices requires sociology both to maintain a disciplinary focus and to initiate a dialogue between other academic territories involved in this subject.

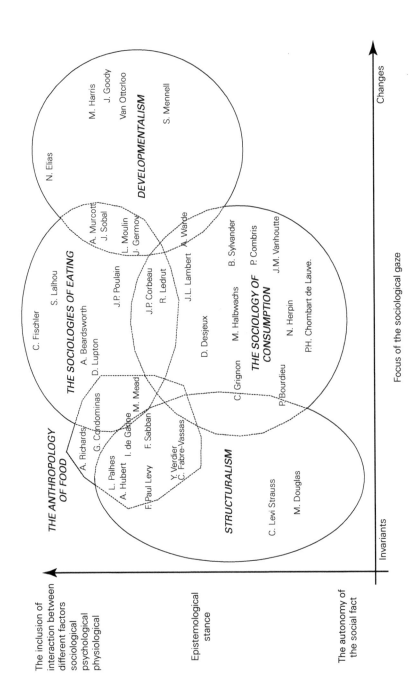

FIGURE 5 *The sociologies of food.*

Source: J.-P. Poulain.

1 Revisiting Durkheim

Faced with these diverse theoretical explanations for changes in contemporary eating practices presented by opposing movements, some authors have sought perspectives that could connect different viewpoints. This is the case with Alan Warde in England and Dominique Desjeux in France. Warde specializes in the sociology of genres and consumption, and it was through these subjects that he became interested in food and eating practices (1996). Strongly influenced by Fischler's studies, he sees food as a specific category within the domain of consumption, as it is destined to be incorporated and therefore generates a fundamental feeling of anxiety. In order to link the different tendencies that characterize the changes occurring in contemporary food consumption practices, he proposes revisiting Durkheim's theory of suicide. After noting the irony involved in the reuse of a theoretical framework constructed for the analysis of suicide as a social phenomenon in order to explain dietary behavior, he recalls the two dimensions of integration and regulation identified by Durkheim and the four categories of types resulting from these. *Egoistic suicide* is a consequence of low social integration, reflecting a personal rationale caused by the absence or weakness of the links connecting the individual to the social group. It therefore corresponds to excessive individualism. Conversely, *altruistic suicide* is the result of excessive personal investment in the group, leading to individual sacrifice in the name of collective interests. This is the consequence of a lack of personal autonomy. The third type, *fatalistic suicide*, is the result of unduly strong pressure exerted by group norms and values; in this case, the "spirit of discipline" is overdeveloped as a result of excessive social control. Finally, *anomic suicide* is characterized by a context of ineffective social control, resulting from a weakening of group norms and regulatory systems, in other words, from the absence of "the spirit of discipline."

When transposed into the domain of food consumption, this categorization enables us to distinguish four tendencies, or four directions of social change. These constitute social forces, which permeate and structure the domain of food and eating, and more broadly, that of consumption. At the same time, they are at work in the changes that occur in contemporary eating practices (Warde 1997).

The different theories applicable to the subject: gastro-anomie (Fischler 1979), the permanence of the class structure (Grignon 1980), the rise of individualism (Giddens 1991; Fischler 1979, 1990), and neotribalism (Maffesoli 1988), may appear to be in competition. This is because they emphasize one (sometimes two) of these trends, yet have not been able to assimilate the notion of their interdependence. Warde therefore distinguishes four tendencies in relation to change, which form two mutually contradictory pairs.

1.1 *Individualization*

This is associated with a lessening of the pressures to conform exerted by social categories. It reflects a weakening of the major, socially based determining factors, mainly the social classes that influence individuals and their dietary behavior. Numerous recent studies attest to this general tendency, which has become fairly dominant in the contemporary era (Beck 1992; Giddens 1991, and also Bauman 1990). With regard to eating, as Fischler notes, this development takes such varied forms as the extension of the food decision-making space, the trend toward individualized dishes, and the increasing tendency to create specific menus for individuals eating at the same table, such as family meals where children, husband, and wife eat different foods.

1.2 *Informalization or destructuration*

"Informalization" describes the tendency toward deregulation. It refers to the weakening of the spirit of discipline and corresponds to the dissolution of the structures governing food consumption, which vary in terms of their rigidity, their demand for conformity, and their emphasis on conventionality. The notion of informalization is founded on the distinction between formal and informal communication made in the fields of communication theory and the psychosociology of organizations. While formal communication is controlled by a system of official rules, informal communication is less constrained by conventions and is based instead on elective affinities. In the final analysis, Warde views the phenomenon of informalization in terms of the Durkheimian anomie, or gastro-anomie as described by Fischler, Corbeau or Rivière. These first two social forces are seen as the dominant movements, but each of them has corresponding countertendencies.

1.3 *Communitization (communification)*

Forms of attachment to social communities that have been reconstructed, to a greater or lesser degree, have emerged in parallel with the rise of individualism. These provide individuals with a sense of belonging. One such example is that of city dwellers who are interested in the community of their original provenance, in a regional culture and its manifestations (eating practices, language, and so on.) This trend is responsible for the development and appreciation of regional products, of items that emphasize geographical origin and a deeply rooted connection with a cultural context and a specific rural locality. It reflects the way in which communities differentiate themselves through tastes. The community in question may be national or ethnic, and structured around more or less nationalistic ideologies. In the greatest number of cases, it is regional and local in nature, and forms part of the global-local dialectic resulting from the globalization of production, distribution, and communication in the food sector (Warde 1997; Poulain 1997; Bessière 2000).

1.4 *Stylization*

This last tendency is related to the phenomenon of social fragmentation, and is referred to by some authors as "neotribalism." Warde, who explicitly bases his study on the works of Michel Maffesoli (1988) and Zygmunt Bauman (1990), views this trend as reintroducing "a kind of discipline or regulation over self-presentation through consumer practice." In comparison with communification, stylization implies a greater degree of discipline with respect to tastes and judgments. As aesthetic regulations are constitutive of the group and of its style, they are prominent and restrictive, and the sanctions resulting from failure to respect a norm or a value are more significant. Although these new social groups are much smaller than those formed by social classes, generations or religious faiths, they exhibit highly normified and regulated patterns of consumption (Warde 1997, 13, 185). It is through these shared tastes that groups within the neotribalist counter-tendency are bonded together.

Warde includes many diverse manifestations of this movement that are associated with food, such as animal rights groups, the promotion of vegetarianism, the boycott of certain products from ethically unsound countries, and the promotion of certain foods in connection with environmental protection. Examples of stylization in the catering sector are those legions of ethnically themed restaurants that spring up and vanish almost overnight, such as Tex-Mex establishments and Japanese sushi-bars. The advertising and marketing sectors, highly susceptible to the influence of neotribalist theories, make a significant contribution to the promotion and development of the phenomenon of stylization. In this way, these four tendencies form two mutually opposing pairs (Figure 6).

informalization ↑ stylization and individualization ↑ communitarization

By combining these different social forces we may identify and understand food market trends (Figure 7). The first of these is *individual diversification*.

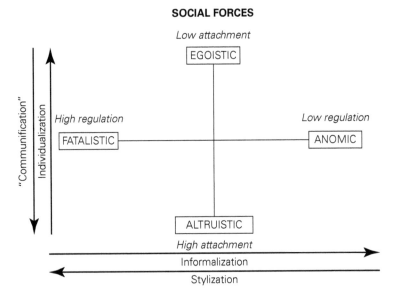

FIGURE 6 *Social forces according to Warde.*

Source: A. Warde (1997).

This results from tendencies toward individualization and informalization, and is therefore the product of a simultaneous lowering of Durkheim's two dimensions of integration: attachment and regulation. The second trend is the consequence of tendencies toward individualization and stylization, and occurs at the point of intersection between high regulation and low attachment. It leads to the *hyper segmentation* of the market into markedly homogenous subgroups, referred to by marketing specialists as "balkanization" or "niche marketing." The third trend is that of *massification*, which results from tendencies toward informalization and communification, which takes place at the intersection between low regulation and high attachment. Finally, *structural division* occurs at the juncture between high regulation and high attachment, resulting from tendencies toward communification and stylization. Warde uses this typology of forces that shape market trends in order to create a typology of eaters. *Individual diversification* is associated with the "switcher," who is swayed by gastronomic considerations; *hyper segmentation* corresponds to the *aestheticizing* eater, who experiences food consumption as a means of self-expression. *Massification* is associated with the eater who is easily *manipulated* by the food industry, while *structural division* corresponds to the *traditional* eater, subject to classic social over-determination.

Warde's analyses are of great interest; however, his perspective remains that of the sociology of consumption.

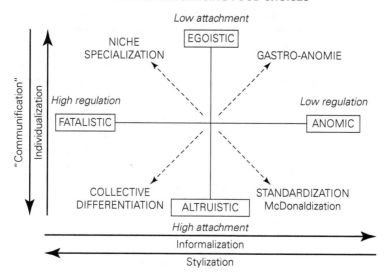

FIGURE 7 *Social forces influencing food choices.*
Source: A. Warde (1997).

2 Scale analysis

Although it is present in the definition given by Georges Gurvitch in 1958, the notion of scale analysis has been somewhat infrequently applied until the recent past. "Sociology," he writes, "is the qualitative and discontinuous typology based on the dialectic of the total social phenomena in all their astructural, structurable and structured manifestations. It studies all their depth levels, scales and the sectors directly with the aim of following their movement of structuration, destructuration . . . and rupture." He adds that the explanation for these phenomena is to be found through a collaboration with history (Gurvitch 1964). In recent times, scale analysis has been used as a pertinent basis of theoretical research (Desjeux 1998). In the domains of geography or architecture, scaling enables the same object to be examined in varying degrees of detail, yet allows certain aspects that are not in evidence from a particular perspective to escape; in the same way, sociological theories apprehend phenomena at different levels. Scale analysis simply involves applying discrete levels of observation, and each scale has its blind spot. By connecting the aspects of knowledge accumulated in relation to a social fact using different levels of analyses, that fact is understood in its entirety. In this way, Desjeux considers that the oppositions between different sociological theories are merely artificial (1998).

They correspond to levels of observation, to interpretations resulting from different scales of investigation. As social reality is "continuous, comprehensive and complex," while "observation is discontinuous," it is necessary to connect the different levels of observation (1999, 52).

In a recent collective work, published in England, on the current status of the sociology of food and nutrition, John Germov and Lauren Williams (1999), use the notion of scale analysis to organize the different tendencies that characterize the development of eating practices. They identify three levels of observation: the macrosociological level and the effects of McDonaldization on food behavior; the mesosociological level and the rationale of social differentiation; and finally, the microsociological level and forms of logic governing dietary practices. Dominique Desjeux proposes adding a fourth scale of observation to the traditional divisions into macro, meso and micro: the biological scale (1996b).

2.1 *The macrosocial level*

The macrosocial level is used with the aim of describing and explaining social differentiations on the aggregate statistical level. This is the perspective adopted by Durkheim in relation to suicide. "In this case actors, as subjects and individuals capable of making evaluations, are excluded in favor of the major categories of social classes, age, gender" (Desjeux 1996b). This is the approach applied in macrosociological, economic, and marketing analyses. The concepts of social class, lifestyle, or way of life find relevance here. It is not possible to examine individual desires or decision-making mechanisms at this level; instead, social phenomena are mainly explained by social conditioning. The works of Bourdieu (1979), Grignon (1980), Douglas (1981), Herpin (1984; Herpin and Verger 1991), Norbert Elias (1939), Goody (1982), Fischler, with regard to "Gastro-anomie" (1979), Rivière (1995), Combris and Volatier (1998) are representative of this level of analysis.

2.2 *The mesosocial level*

The mesosocial approach occupies the blind spot with regard to statistical studies, and focuses on the connections between social actors.

> The hypothesis on which this methodology is based is that decision making, and through it the will, play a part in the different dimensions of social reality that have been distinguished by various sociologists at the micro-social level to explain the social interactions that form the

bases of decision-making processes. Yet the will, the decision, and the action that contribute to this process are not observable as such. They are "black boxes." What is observable are the concrete indications of a move toward action, such as social networks or calculation, or the determinants operating before this transition, such as the imaginary, identity, intention, meaning or learning. (Desjeux 1996, 28, 29)

Dominant in contemporary sociology, the mesosocial approach encompasses five major interpretive categories, with which we can associate certain authors of works on the sociology of food, or, in some cases, specific examples of their work. The first of these corresponds to meaning, symbolism, intention, or affectivity; representative examples of this category include the works of Fischler on incorporation (1990), Desjeux and Taponier (1991) on purchasing decisions, and Beardsworth (1995) on the ambivalences of human eating practices. In the case of the second interpretive form, the emphasis is on vested interests and power relations. Corbeau's analysis of the eating sector (1995) and Poulain's work on the food decision systems operating in institutional catering establishments (1998) are examples of this perspective. The third category involves analysis in terms of the imaginary. This approach was applied by Maffesoli (1981, 1988), and Poulain for the analysis of the French food labeling system and the imaginary operating with regard to French gastronomy, or to the current interest in regional products (1985b, 1997a); it is likewise used by Warnier when examining the attraction toward supposedly authentic merchandize exhibited by modern consumers (1994). The fourth interpretive framework relates to identity construction, and is very extensively used by food sociologists Moulin (1967, 1974), Fischler (1990), Pfirsch (1997), and Poulain (1997a). Finally, analysis in terms of social networks has been applied by Corbeau to highlight the functioning of the eating sector (1997b), and to examine the tradition of French-style service (1985a).

2.3 The micro-individual level

Analyses carried out at this level focus on the individual and highlight another dimension of decision making, that of choice. The central interest here is in reasoning, in the decision process and in cognition. From this perspective, social facts are seen in terms of needs (biological or psychoanalytical) and of taste in the psychological sense. "In this case, the decision, manifested as choice, as the product of a cognitive process of selection between preferences, is relatively easily observable. However, choice is no longer in evidence if it is seen as resulting from the unconscious, just as it was no longer evident in the macrosocial level of observation in terms of habitus" (Desjeux 1996, 30).

Examples of this level of analysis in relation to food studies are works by Chiva (1985, 1996), Rozin, Hossenlopp and Aimez (1979), and Le Barzic and Pouillon (1998).

2.4 *The biological level*

From his experience with analyzing food practices and conducting research in cooperation with scientists in the medical field, Desjeux (1993), is aware of the need to integrate the interplay between biological and social dimensions into the examination of social facts, as a level of analysis in the study of certain

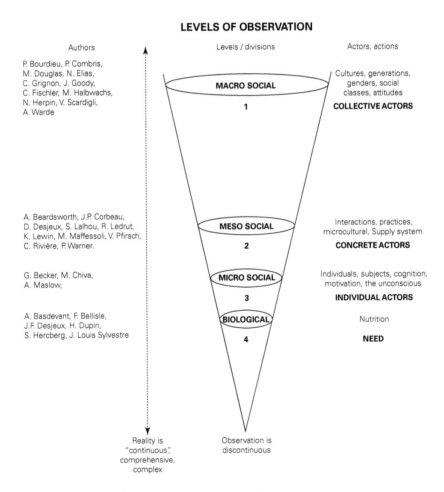

LEVELS OF OBSERVATION

Authors	Levels / divisions	Actors, actions
P. Bourdieu, P. Combris, M. Douglas, N. Elias, C. Grignon, J. Goody, C. Fischler, M. Halbwachs, N. Herpin, V. Scardigli, A. Warde	**MACRO SOCIAL** 1	Cultures, generations, genders, social classes, attitudes **COLLECTIVE ACTORS**
A. Beardsworth, J.P. Corbeau, D. Desjeux, S. Lalhou, R. Ledrut, K. Lewin, M. Maffessoli, V. Pfirsch, C. Rivière, P. Warner.	**MESO SOCIAL** 2	Interactions, practices, microcultural, Supply system **CONCRETE ACTORS**
G. Becker, M. Chiva, A. Maslow,	**MICRO SOCIAL** 3	Individuals, subjects, cognition, motivation, the unconscious **INDIVIDUAL ACTORS**
A. Basdevant, F. Bellisle, J.F. Desjeux, H. Dupin, S. Hercberg, J. Louis Sylvestre	**BIOLOGICAL** 4	Nutrition **NEED**

Reality is "continuous", comprehensive, complex

Observation is discontinuous

FIGURE 8 *Levels of observation according to Desjeux.*

Source: Jean-Pierre Poulain, from a diagram of levels of observation created by D. Desjeux.

social phenomena. This approach represents the fourth level of analysis. The object of study in this case is the impact of social phenomena on the biochemical and physiological elements involved in nutritional processes and food choices. Representing this level of analysis are works based on cognition such as those of Bellisle (1992, 1999), Louis-Sylvestre (1989, 1991, 1992, 1998), Fantino (1992), Stylianos Nicolaidis (1992), Mac Leod (1992), Faurion (1993), Vincent (1986), and Beck (2000), as well as the pluridisciplinary perspective adopted by Hubert, Lambert and Dupin (Figure 8).

Desjeux does not, in fact, adopt an approach consisting solely of scale analysis in the geographical sense; rather, he combines analysis in terms of level of interpretation with analysis in terms of paradigms. Each level has its favored methods, theoretical perspectives, and conceptual systems. Scale analysis originates from Gurvitch's concept of levels of social reality.

10

The sociology of French gastronomy

Before investigating how we might redefine the purpose of the sociology of food in order to analyze food consumption models, we should evaluate the specific difficulty presented by a new epistemological obstacle: French gastronomy. Given the status of food within French culture, the highly complex nature of gastronomy and its international influence (sometimes confused with the educative aims of French colonialists), this social phenomenon has been somewhat neglected by sociologists. First, a distinction must be made between eating and gastronomy. The latter involves an aestheticization of cooking and table manners. Gastronomic culture represents a hedonistic deviation from the biological purpose of eating. It is surrounded by a considerable number of social rules, which we are condemned to observe several times a day. Although all cultures have their own forms of aestheticized eating practices, few have taken them to the extremes of sophistication attained by French gastronomy. The French gastronomic tradition cannot simply be reduced to the cuisine and manners practiced by elite groups. It is a heritage, upheld with some pride by all who share French culture, whatever their social status. Gastronomy constitutes a social fact, vital to our understanding of the particular nature of French society and its organization. At the European level, why should it be that the most highly developed version of gastronomy is associated with France rather than with England, Germany, Spain, Portugal, or Italy? For, although there is general agreement that the countries mentioned (and the list is not exhaustive) offer interesting gastronomic experiences, there can be no shadow of a doubt that high gastronomy is certainly French.

Before we see what gastronomy can teach us about French society, a question must be asked. Is it not remarkably ironic that gastronomy was first highlighted as one of the unique features of French culture by foreign thinkers such as Georg Simmel (1910), Norbert Elias (1939), Léo Moulin (1967), Theodore Zeldin (1979), Jack Goody (1982), and Stephen Mennell (1985)? Renée Valéri, a researcher of Swedish origin, noted the curious fact that a country such as France, with its internationally renowned cuisine, had no serious, analytical body of written work on the subject of what, why, and when the French eat (Valéri 1971, 69).

1 The complexity of French gastronomy

A television presenter was interviewing the interpreter of the Emperor of Japan, who was on a visit to France. After having enquired about His Imperial Majesty's opinion of French cuisine, the presenter asked the following question: "Japan also has a highly prestigious food culture; could you tell us something about the tea ceremony?" The swift reply left the journalist lost for words: "I'm afraid I can't give you an answer. The subject is far too complex; one would need to have studied the matter for years in order to describe any aspect of it properly."

If a foreigner were to ask a French person a similar type of question, whether on the subject of wine, cuisine, or table manners, the latter would instantly launch into a reply, consisting in most cases of a series of clichés.

Is gastronomic culture seen as a common good in France and perhaps, like good sense, the most equally distributed of all things?

The French do not always fully appreciate the extreme complexity of the system of social rules that constitute their national gastronomy. The myopia caused by proximity, unthinking acceptance, and the influence of our own linguistic concepts, prevents us from perceiving the multiple dimensions of this phenomenon, and from fully understanding the complicated nature of the relevant factual and empirical data (Goody, 1982).

Moreover, gastronomy is a cultural characteristic, and, aside from the mechanisms of social differentiation in which it plays a part, it contributes to the construction of French identity through the way in which it is disseminated. In order to try and understand the level of sophistication that characterizes French gastronomy, we will focus on two features that distinguish it as a phenomenon: its degree of complexity and its ability to impose itself as a model on elite groups in other cultural spaces. Although the term "gastronomy" did not come into use until 1800,[1] with the publication of Joseph de Berchoux's *La gastronomie ou l'homme des champs à table*, it began to develop as a discipline, with some originality, from the latter half of the seventeenth century. It is characterized by a proliferation of recipes and the adoption of more complex table manners.

Of course, working-class cuisines also feature a variety of dishes. In our illusory quest to identify the ideal method of analysis among a profusion of different possibilities, we propose to adapt a methodological principle borrowed from Lévi-Strauss to the ethnoculinary perspective. This approach has proved to be effective in the study of myths: "A popular recipe is the sum of its variants" (Poulain 1996). Consequently, such variants cease to be interpreted as "deviations" and become "versions," whose function is purely that of markers, in an integration/separation dialectic of nuances relating to geography, society and the family. However, unlike working class cooking, which is based on the oral tradition, aesthetic cuisines are rigorously encoded in written works. The transition to the written word reduces this variability and establishes specific methods and their minute variations to form individual recipes.

Until the mid-sixteenth century, the sophisticated cuisines of Europe, such as those of Spain, Italy, Portugal, and France (which were almost indistinguishable during that era), featured between three hundred and four hundred original recipes. This already constituted a considerable amount. They were organized into major categories of dishes that gave rise to several series of recipes, of varying lengths. In France, their number increased gradually, starting with François Massialot's *Cuisinier Royal et bourgeois* (1691). Massialot's work contained 507 recipes and was presented in the form of a dictionary, a significant innovation. This change in format reflected a fundamental transformation in the nature of such works; now, instead of comprising simple lists of recipes acting as an *aide mémoire*, they served as tools that ensured the effective functioning of a code, already virtually establishing them as a genuine language, in the linguistic sense of the word. Massialot's book did not simply contain recipes for dishes, but also for secondary elements such as coulis, sauces, and garnishes. Above all, it included instructions for combining these in order to create new dishes. The culinary labeling system, which officially established not only recipes, but also their constituent elements, gave rise to a huge increase in the number of possible dishes (Poulain 1985b).

The first edition of Menon's *La cuisinière bourgeoise*, published in 1774, contained no fewer than 843 recipes. Marie-Antoine Carême's *L'art de la cuisine Française* boasted 1,347, while *La cuisine classique* by Urbain Dubois and Emile Bernard featured 3,544. The number rose to 5,531 with Joseph Favre's *Le dictionnaire universel de cuisine,* and to 4,568 with Auguste Escoffier's *Le guide culinaire,* culminating in the over 7,000 recipes featured in *Le répertoire de la cuisine* by Théodore Gringoire and Louis Saulnier, which was explicitly presented as "the practical dictionary of French gastronomy."

Although over 7,000 recipes are described in this work, it offers the possibility of creating many more, as it also serves as a vocabulary book and a grammar manual. It reveals a complex code that identifies basic products, techniques for cooking and combining ingredients, accompanying vegetable dishes, and sauces as a cooking medium and garnish. All these elements may be combined, following a system of extremely precise rules, to produce new dishes. Although these dishes are not described in the book, they are nevertheless contained within the code. From the eighteenth century onward, the French chef did not create a dish; he spoke a language. French gastronomy therefore distinguished itself, both from that of other European countries and from regional cuisines, by its level of complexity. It forms a genuine language, with several levels of differentiation. The transition from a list of dishes to a code, an open system capable of generating almost limitless possibilities, constitutes a paradigm shift unparalleled in Europe (Poulain 1985a,b).

Two gastronomic worlds, those of China and Vietnam, have moved in this direction. Although they have not reached the level of sophistication characterizing French cuisine, each is governed by a semi-developed code and features over a thousand different methods. (Sabban 1996; Poulain 1997b,d). Only Japanese gastronomy in its most sophisticated form, the *kaiseki-ryori* meal style, attains a comparable degree of complexity, but functions in different ways (Ishige Naomichi 1994).

Benefiting from the prestige of Versailles, French gastronomy extended its influence over Europe in the late seventeenth century. An essential element of French taste, and of the French art of living, it served as a model for elite groups in the Western world. Far from impeding this process, the French Revolution intensified it. Chefs who had been in the service of the aristocracy were now faced with two alternatives: following their masters into exile, or staying in France. Those who opted for the former solution accompanied their masters to London, Madrid, Geneva, Hamburg, or Berlin, where they rapidly became lionized ("you simply have to dine with the French"), and contributed to the development of French influence in Europe. Those chefs who decided to stay in France could choose either to serve the new incumbents, or to open their own restaurants (Aron 1976). It was therefore in the melting pot created by the French Revolution that the institution of the restaurant was established and rapidly exported throughout the world. Indeed, there are very few languages that have not adopted the French terms "restaurant" or "café" to designate a location offering a sophisticated cuisine.

When the turmoil of the Revolution had abated, and as empires were succeeded by republics and the restoration of monarchy, the era of the grand hotel industry emerged. These establishments first appeared in seaside or spa towns, which enjoyed unprecedented popularity. Europe now abounded in luxury hotels offering a nostalgic slice of upper-class life both to the aspiring bourgeoisie and to the aristocracy, now more or less in decline. In these grand nineteenth-century establishments, clients could hire the experience of living at court. There, French chefs were still at the helm, imposing their style of cuisine; this became the international style *par excellence*. French was the language spoken in these hotels, as well as in embassies and at the gaming tables in casinos; and of course, it was also the language of restaurant menus (Neirinck and Poulain 2000). In a somewhat hasty interpretation, the international influence of French gastronomy might be confused with the ethnocentrism of bourgeois colonialist culture.

2 Why is gastronomy French?

In order to understand how French gastronomy was able to attain greater complexity and began to assume this legitimizing role, we must first describe the social imaginary and the sociological landscape in which it emerged and developed. It is necessary to look beyond the social functions it has undertaken, and to examine its very structures, whether it reflects its native culture or those that imitate it. In this way, an investigation of gastronomy also involves reinterpreting French and European history from a sociological perspective.

2.1 *Science and gastronomy, the place of food in academic culture*

As a consequence of the Cartesian rupture, the study of culinary matters has been viewed as a minor genre of literature for centuries. Cartesian thought finalized the division between the world and man initiated by the Copernican revolution, establishing a distinction between object and subject. The truth is to be found in the former of these two terms, while error—which should be discarded with the aid of the method based on the ultimate criterion of rationality—resides in subjectivity. Cartesian thought banished the subject of food from academic culture. This ontological split between subject and object is founded on the divorce between body and soul, spirit and matter, which had already divided man into two distinct entities; the higher of these represented the principle of conscious thought, while the other was characterized by purely mechanical processes.

According to Bernard Valade, this represented a sign of *"the divorce between science and subjectivity"* (Valade 1996). It was later to give rise to scientific thought.

Food was consequently banished from the realm of thought and reduced to its strictly mechanical, organic dimension. And yet, through its symbolic dimensions, notably its underlying imaginary of incorporation, it reflects the originality of the "bio-anthropological connection" between a human group and its environment (Morin 1973; Fischler 1990). The symbolic scope of the *tabula rasa* extended beyond the domain of philosophy. Now too "fat" a subject, food made a bad impression at this table, which had been cleared purely in order to make way for the intellectual reconstruction of the world. In dismissing food and excluding it from the realm of philosophy, seventeenth-century thinkers broke with a long series of traditions, from the *Golden Verses* of Pythagoras, to Rabelais's *Gargantua*, by way of Plato's *Banquet*, works in which spiritual and earthly nourishment maintained harmonious relations, and where the thinker could ponder the subject of food without losing his status. This situation is specific to the Western world, as reflections on food form an obligatory aspect of the research conducted by Chinese philosophers.

Far from becoming impoverished by being cast into a clandestine cultural realm, culinary discourse experienced a period of remarkable development. Simultaneously scorned by philosophy and freed from its scrutiny, gastronomy was to establish itself as an autonomous discipline. This was achieved several centuries before the sciences, above all those known as the human sciences, were similarly established; it was not until the advent of the experimental method that they ventured to claim their independence from a domineering mother. Moreover, we have no hesitation in identifying Descartes as the involuntary father of gastronomy, however paradoxical this may seem. Given that the founder of the method that was to revolutionize Western thought was French, it comes as no surprise that the great art of cooking is likewise of French origin. The natural daughter of seventeenth-century philosophers, gastronomy was to remain in the cultural wilderness until the latter half of the twentieth century. During those four hundred years of exile it was occasionally visited by a few great literary figures, such as François-René de Chateaubriand, Charles Baudelaire, and Alexandre Dumas *père*. However, the works that resulted from these brief encounters remained minor distractions in the eyes of their contemporaries, interesting mainly for the illicit appeal of the "dangerous liaisons" responsible for creating them. As Roland Barthes noted, food is a trivialized subject in France, a dalliance conducted at the end of a career (Barthes 1967).

Moreover, being too associated with corporality, gastronomy has not completely attained the status of an artistic discipline. Simmel has shown the inherently different nature of the gastronomic aesthetic founded on incorporation: "The laid table should not appear as a complete work of art, whose perfect form must remain undisturbed. While the intrinsic beauty of a work of art lies in its integrity, which holds us at a distance, an elegantly presented table invites us to encroach upon its beauty" (Simmel 1910, 215).

And yet, like any artistic discipline, gastronomy is a space within which a culture constructs the elements that define its era (Borillo and Sauvageot

1996). What research could be more vital to an understanding of French society than a study intended to explore the perspectives, the imaginary and the mythology that gave rise to gastronomy and determine its internal dynamics? (Zeldin 1979; Moulin 1988; Maffesoli 1981)?

Due to its very specific position on the academic geographical map reorganized by seventeenth-century thinkers, gastronomy was viewed as a predominantly reductionist discourse of resistance, and the act of eating as a site for the resurgence of suppressed instincts—the figure of man present in the physical world. In this way, it fulfilled a cathartic function of maintaining balance in the social imaginary (Durand 1960 [1969]). Gastronomy is somewhat akin to a Freudian slip in French thought, and could well be the true pathway to its cultural unconscious. We will apply a series of interpretive frameworks in our approach to gastronomy: Norbert Elias's civilizing process, which is extended through the model of social distinction, alchemy as a basis of thought in relation to culinary creativity, and finally the relationship between gastronomy and Catholic religious morality.

2.2 *The model of social distinction*

The appearance of the term "civility" in the text by Erasmus of Rotterdam dating from 1530 and entitled *De civitate morum puerilium*, was seen by Norbert Elias as "the expression and the symbol of a transformation in social reality that was to form the backbone of Court society" (Elias 1939, 90). The concept of civility encompassed a set of instructions ensuring that "the behavior of men in society was directed above all, but not exclusively, toward *externum corporis decorum*"; that is to say, toward demeanor, the external appearance of the individual. The objective is "to distinguish the higher social strata from the lower" (Elias 1939, 92).

Manners were to be the focus of regulations intended to reflect social distinction. One of the most important categories of etiquette was that of table manners; at meal times the body was on display, and these principles defined the conditions in which food was incorporated. Historically, this phenomenon "involves and encompasses diverse nationalities which express themselves in a common language, initially Italian and later French, new languages that henceforth assumed the functions of Latin." These new languages, coupled with the new social reality, reflected a certain social cohesion that existed at European level during the Renaissance (Elias 1939).

In France, however, the expression of civility acquired a unique character. The establishment of the Court at Versailles in the late seventeenth century, heralded a period of decisive social changes. This continued the process of centralizing the state initiated during the reign of Henri IV, and attracted the provincial nobility to the capital, where they neglected their regional political duties. As a consequence of the local power vacuum, the increasingly affluent bourgeoisie determinedly aped the manners of the aristocracy, as lampooned by Molière in *Le Bourgeois Gentilhomme*. Imitated in this way, the nobility promptly commissioned the services of artists, officers of the King's kitchen, dressmakers, perfumers and wigmakers, adopting new social practices intended to emphasize their separate status. This effectively instigated the "civilizing process" highlighted by Elias (1939). Fashion in dress, perfume making, and gastronomy consequently established themselves as distinctive systems through which social differentiation was expressed and recognized. The art of living *à la française* was founded on these increasingly sophisticated practices, which emphasized the gap between the aspiring classes and the elites, and was rapidly adopted by the European aristocracy. The dynamics of fashion lay in this system of recognition and distinction, in the interstice between imitated and imitator.

Culinary literature was to contribute to the functioning of this social mechanism. Massialot's *Le Cuisinier royal et bourgeois*, which appeared in 1691, was the first cookery book to refer explicitly to the middle classes in its title. Indeed, from then on, culinary manuals were principally directed toward that social category. This established one of the main functions of gastronomic literature, which from Menon to Gault and Millau, via Alexandre-Balthazar Grimod de la Reynière and Jean Anthelme Brillat-Savarin, was intended to initiate the aspiring middle classes into the principles of good taste.

Far from halting this process, the French Revolution provided it with fresh impetus, offering the bourgeoisie the social status it had dreamed of for two centuries. Gastronomy was now marketed through the restaurants created by former chefs to the aristocracy who had lost their official posts, so that gourmet experiences were available to a greater percentage of the population. The gastronomic model operated according to the trickle-down effect, in a process that saw it transcend the function of social differentiation, as it contributed to the construction of French identity.

In his analysis of French society in the 1970s, Pierre Bourdieu created variations on the same theme. The theory of "habitus" emerged from the study of practical, specific daily routines, among the most important of which are food practices. Taking tastes and how they are differentiated as his starting point, he identifies their origin in the habitus: "A scheme of perception, behind which lie the objectively classifiable material conditions of existence." However, established within the critical tradition of sociology, he sees gastronomy and its underlying discourse as no more than an ideological construction associated with the irrational nature of the process of differentiation, and focuses on emphasizing the permanence of the class structure and the autonomous character of working-class tastes. "The art of eating and drinking remains one of the few areas in which the working classes explicitly challenge the legitimate art of living" (Bourdieu 1984, 179).

In the wake of Bourdieu's work, certain sociologists have sought to highlight the autonomy of working-class or rural eating practices. It is surprising to see that even some of the best studies of this type, and those that pay the closest attention to empirical data, fail to take evidence of this trickle-down effect into account. One such example is the appearance of the *bouchée à la reine* in the rural menus of South Western France during the 1970s, as noted in the survey conducted by Bages and Rieu (1988).

Bourdieu's stance confines him within a militant populism that prevents him from seeing gastronomy, and the social practices resulting from it, as anything other than the various manifestations and irrationality of social distinction. They are underpinned by other dynamics, which sociologists of the imaginary aim to identify. "There are many French sociologists," writes Corbeau,

> who "naively" confuse the language of the gourmet with the way in which it is expressed in an ethnocentric French bourgeois culture. They fail to perceive its poetic, multi-faceted, and indeed even universally applicable dimensions, which are apparent as soon as one escapes the encoded theory of social reproduction to embark upon the adventure of gastronomy, conceiving it purely as the "ritualization" of a sensory emotion. (Corbeau 1991, 12)

2.3 *Taste as an axis of development*

Spices played a central role as markers of social differentiation during the Medieval period and the Renaissance.[2] In the late sixteenth century, following the developments made in navigation and the discovery of the New World, they became both less expensive and less exotic, and were used by the middle classes as an item of conspicuous consumption. This caused them to be shunned by aristocratic cuisine. Having abandoned the use of spices as a sign of rarity, luxury, and detachment from need, French gastronomy was henceforth to demonstrate its sophistication through an emphasis on the taste of the foods themselves. In his seminal work entitled *Les délices de la campagne* (1654), Nicolas de Bonnefons presented a revolutionary principle: "A cabbage soup," he stated, "should smell of cabbage; if it is made of leeks or turnips, then it should smell of leeks or turnips, and so forth. . . . What I say of soups, I mean to be understood as applicable in every instance, and to serve as a general rule for everything that is eaten" (1654). This introduced the fundamental principle of French cuisine. There was a major shift from a culinary style based on masking (a characteristic of every sophisticated cuisine in Europe), with powerfully tasting secondary ingredients being superimposed onto the main elements of a dish, to a cuisine based on the taste of the main elements themselves. The quest now centered on creating associations and harmony according to rules very similar to those of musical harmony or the theory of pictorial complementarity. In this way, a new culinary category now emerged, the purpose of which was to enhance the flavors of food: stocks and sauces. Unlike Medieval versions, which were very similar to our mustard or to Vietnamese *nuoc-mam*, sauces now served as actual backgrounds to dishes, in the pictorial sense of the term, highlighting the various flavors of the main elements composing the dish, with all their specific characteristics. In this way, Massialot replaced the *coulis universel*, which was referenced by the unidentified L. S. R. and which served as the mother of all sauces, with no fewer than twenty-three different coulis. These were used in highly precise ways, each being characterized by a predominant flavor (1691).

In this way, from François Marin to Marie-Antoine Carême, from Antoine Beauvilliers to Auguste Escoffier, and from Jules Gouffé to Joël Robuchon, French cuisine developed and grew increasingly refined. Of course, Massialot's notion of taste differed from that of Robuchon, and when the former refers to the flavor of an item, it should be understood in relation to context, that is to say with reference to the preceding culinary style. Although to a contemporary palate, the taste of the main ingredients in Massialot 's style of cookery would appear to be utterly overpowered by a quantity of secondary elements, it was, in its turn, equally different from that of the Medieval era. This obsession with taste should be understood from a dynamic perspective.

The Medieval conception of cookery, which involved superimposing the taste of spices onto that of foods, evolved into a cuisine where the flavors of the various constituents of a dish were connected and combined in an increasingly subtle manner.

We have shown how the alchemistical approach—which views the relationship between man and the world as one of correspondence and symbolic interdependence—served as a theoretical model to eighteenth and nineteenth-century cooks, engaged in this quest for taste. Aware of the magic inherent in the notion of transforming an oven into an athanor, they set out to discover liquid gold. Sophisticated cookery books of that period adopted genuinely alchemical language to express the aim of improving stocks and sauces (Neirinck and Poulain 2000; Poulain 1994). Yet for the eighteenth-century cook, alchemical research was not limited to the quest for the most perfect sauce; in improving his cooking, he believed that he was also improving himself, and, going further still, that he was contributing to the progress of the human race as a whole. The art of cooking plays a direct role in "the development of the human mind." Such is the opinion of Menon: "Will it therefore be an exaggeration to state that modern culinary preparations should be included among the physical elements, which, in the midst of barbarism, cause us to recall the reign of courtesy, of the talents of the mind, the arts and the sciences?" (1749).

With even greater clarity, Joseph Favre, founder of the Académie Culinaire de France, illustrates the magical nature of the principle of incorporation highlighted by Fischler (1990): "In consuming these sublime sauces, this 'liquid gold', the human race transforms itself. It is thanks to them that France carries the torch of gastronomy. Sauces form the basis of good cuisine, and it is to their excellence that French cuisine owes its superiority over that of other nations" (Favre 1883).

Ultimately, by eating what is good, the French become better still: we do indeed become what we eat. It was therefore through taste that French cuisine acquired greater complexity, but in order to develop the sensual quality characteristic of French gastronomy, it was necessary to find a philosophical and spiritual context that would enhance the sensation of pleasure. This was to be provided by the Catholic religion.

2.4 Catholic morality and the spirit of gastronomy

The theory that we propose to defend runs in counterpoint to Max Weber's *The Protestant Ethic and the Spirit of Capitalism*, by which it is partly inspired and which is still debated today. The aestheticization of eating, and the emergence of a hedonistic approach to food, owes much to the moral stance of Catholicism. For the sake of brevity, one might say that the spirit of gastronomy could only have emerged, and above all developed, within the Catholic world of the Classical period. Is enjoyment sinful? This question has exercised Christianity from its earliest beginnings. Three principal opposing attitudes coexist with regard to food: a quasivegetarian asceticism, through which the dietary behavior of the believer appears to conform to the Creator's initial plan, as revealed at the very beginning of Genesis (Soler 1973); the observance of moderation, which finds its most precise expression in Augustinian temperance; and finally, a hedonistic attitude whereby the man engaged in the service of religion views the enjoyment of earthly pleasures as a means of glorifying the works of God.

From the sixteenth century onward, the response to the question formed part of the schism between the Reformed and Catholic religions. The former was characterized by an anxious asceticism; the body and its coarsest senses were regarded as base, as the individual reached out to the infinite in the hope of entering heaven. For the latter, however, the glorification of God was achieved by aestheticizing His presence in the world and in others.

This type of theory has been the subject of numerous explorations. In romanticized form, it lies at the heart of Karen von Blixen's *Babette's Feast*, which was made into a film directed by Gabriel Axel and surely ranks as one of the finest presentations of the aesthetics governing French gastronomy. The actors' remarkable performances, the gradual relaxation of their anxious faces and the conviviality—in its truest sense of living together—achieved through the effects of alcohol and food, are the most eloquent translations of the significance of taste in French culture.

In the sociological domain, Stephen Mennell refers to this theory when exploring reasons for the differences in the attitudes to food displayed by the English and French aristocracy. He begins by examining the notion that the 18th English gentry's supposed taste for plain food forms part of the Puritan ethos of mortifying the flesh. He rejects this argument, and makes the point that the "plainness" in question "can be exaggerated." He offers the possible explanation that the English "actually liked their food the way they ate it" (Mennell 1985, 107). The fact that the English liked to eat in the English manner is simply an artificial way of settling the question, as the word "like" reintroduces the issue of the representations that operate in value judgments and calls for a more precise analysis of the famous Puritan ethos. Mennell, therefore, discards this hypothesis to seek the reasons for the contrasts between French and English gastronomy in different forms of "curialization." He focuses particularly on what he sees as the major difference between the English and French aristocracy, this being the fact that the latter were permanently established in the capital or at Versailles, whereas the former moved to and fro between London and their country estates. We owe the most detailed analysis of this theory to the geographer Jean-Robert Pitte. He concluded his study by remarking: "The world of the Reformation thus did away with the possibility of sanctifying food, of moving a little closer to God by eating fine fare, an ancient animist belief more or less tacitly appropriated by Christianity" (Pitte 1991, 75).

In a study of Puritan conceptions of happiness and sexuality, Edmund Leites questions the idea that Puritanism advocated the renunciation of all things worldly, and shows that the ideal espoused by the seventeenth-century English theologians better known as the Cambridge Platonists, was that of sensual pleasures combined with spiritual joys (Leites 1986). Bernard Valade suggests that any difference between Catholics and Protestants is more likely to result from the break created by the Reformation in "the cycle of sin / confession/ penitence / absolution established by the Church" (Valade 1996, 75).

Our aim is to seek precisely what the gastronomic aesthetic owes to the Catholic view of morality, not only in the unique nature of its relationship with pleasure, but above all in the specific relationships maintained between food and the sacred in the Catholic world. In order to provide full support for our theory, it would have been necessary to include developments that somewhat exceed the framework of this chapter,[3] particularly with regard to reestablishing the Christian attitude toward food. However, we propose to outline the major aspects of this question, retaining three points, which form the infrastructure of the spiritual and the imaginary that organizes the relationship between Catholicism, food, and the pleasure generated by eating.

In the sacrament of the Eucharist, which is based on the physical act of eating, the Christian religion as a whole has created the perfect model of man's relationship to the divine. In doing so, it uses the imaginary of incorporation, with its dual elements: I become what I eat, therefore, what I eat transforms the substance of my own body, and in consuming an item valued by a social group, and sharing this act of consumption, I become integrated into this community. This imaginary is common to a great many cultural spaces, and was applied by a large number of the religious cultures that preceded Christianity.

However, although Christianity applied the principles of the imaginary of incorporation, it was to attach a great deal of importance to establishing a difference between the Eucharist and both animist and Judaic sacrificial practices. Through the transition from making sacrifices to a god, or gods, to commemorating the sacrifice of the Son of God made man, whereby all other sacrifices become redundant, Christianity created a fundamental break with regard to the concept of sacrifice.[4] The spiritual dimension of the Lord's Supper reduces its association with food. Marcel Détienne shows how the defenders of the Christian faith, who were led to study ancient Greek sacrifice, denied the corporal nature and food-related dimension of Eucharistic sacrifice:

> To avoid any confusion between the base rites of "peoples of nature" and the spiritual mystery of the Eucharist in the only true religion, a division was created within sacrifice, between instincts so perverted as to initiate the abject practice of devouring bloody flesh, and, in contrast, the noble impulses of a purely spiritual exchange, where forms of consumption play a negligible role, and whose associations with food are suppressed, as if denied. (1979, 31)

Within the Christian religion, the ritual of the Eucharist is one of the major points at issue between Catholicism and the churches of the Reformation. There is no doubt that, during the first millennium and in accordance with the evangelical messages ("this is my body, this is my blood" and "do this in memory of me") Holy Communion was mainly celebrated using the two elements of bread and wine. These correspond to Christ's body and blood respectively. The wine, representing blood, had to be red, and the bread, which was leavened, was based both on Christian symbolism—"I am the bread of life"—and on the opposition/distinction made between Christians and Jews, who ate unleavened bread in memory of the exodus from Egypt (Dupuy 1986).

Toward the end of the Middle Ages, the rituals of Communion underwent their first transformation, as the ceremony was divided into two types: one reserved for the clergy, the other for the laity, who took bread alone (Loret 1982). This established the system of hierarchies within the Catholic community and separated the faithful into those members of the congregation who were only permitted to take bread at Communion, and the ranks of the clergy, who took both bread and wine. Wycliffe, Huss, Luther, Calvin, and all the movements within the Reformation, called for the return of Communion involving bread and wine for all members of the Christian community, putting all believers on an equal footing before God.

The second major change was implemented as the Reformation took hold. It involved abandoning the use of leavened bread for the host, and replacing red wine with white (Poulain and Rouyer 1987; Albert 1991; Fabre-Vassas 1991).[5] This change from red to white wine has a far deeper significance than the functionalist and superficial explanations given by some members of the contemporary clergy, as reported by J. P. Albert: "White wine is generally preferred for reasons of convenience, as it is less likely to stain the altar-cloths." It reflects the establishment of a symbolic distance between blood and wine, a euphemism applied to the image of blood. Through the switch from leavened bread, a strongly distinctive sign for early Christians, marking their separation from the Jews, to the unleavened host, its association with "food" was effectively removed. Behind these seemingly anodyne changes to ritual, which constitute a distancing from the food-related dimension of the Eucharist, there lies a paradigmatic change in the relationship between the sacred and profane.

In order to understand the full significance of these changes, they should be reestablished within the context of transubstantiation. According to Catholic doctrine, which has been continually reaffirmed[6] and was once more reiterated, as recently as 1992, in the latest version of the *Catechism of the Catholic Church*, during the celebration of the Eucharist, "the fundamental substance of the bread and the wine is wholly converted into the body of the risen Christ." Therein lies the mystery of the Eucharist, as the essential nature of bread and wine is ontologically changed, so that they become the body and blood of the Son of God made man. This explains why the desecration of the sacred host could have been seen as one of the gravest mortal sins, much graver, for example, than murder or rape.

In the twelfth century, Berenger de Tours challenged this "sacramental materialism," which he saw as the basis of the theory of Christ's presence in the bread and wine of the Eucharist. He initiated a debate on the subject, which became increasingly significant until the Reformation, and which led to a radical schism within the Christian religion. The leaders of the Reformation denied the existence of this ontological change and maintained concepts that can be divided into two principal stances: on the one hand, Wycliffe and Luther proposed the notion of "consubstantiation," whereby "Christ's body is in, with and beneath the bread and wine, thus entailing the permanence of these natural substances," and on the other hand, Calvin repudiated both transubstantiation, which he saw as an annihilation of the bread and wine, and consubstantiation, which he considered too spiritual in concept. "He therefore conceives a presence that is spiritual, and yet real," where bread and wine have such symbolic significance that they are bound with truth. "The emphasis here is placed on faith, and on that alone; without it there is no presence, as there is no ontological link between Christ's body and blood on the one hand, and the bread and wine on the other: if one eats and drinks with faith, one likewise receives the spiritual gift" (Josua 1976; Daumas 1986).

With the discovery of the New World and of the cannibalism practiced by some of its inhabitants, the conflict over these theories intensified, creating a site of confrontation at the heart of the Christian religion. The Reformers accused the Catholics of "theophagism," or eating God, condemning "this God of flour" and "these butchering priests who dismember Christ's body" (Lestringant 1981, 1994). As a reaction to this criticism the ritual was altered, and the bread and red wine were replaced with the host and white wine. In order to preserve what they considered to be the essential aspect of Eucharistic celebration, in other words, the divine presence, the Catholics implemented a change that we have described as "desubstantiation." This involved establishing a division between the secular consumption of food and sacred incorporation (Poulain and Rouyer 1987). This desubstantiation is based on a threefold process of dematerializing the Eucharist; it involved a rejection of the alcoholic character of the wine and the intoxication it produces (Albert 1991), a change from red wine (too reminiscent of blood) to white, and the replacement of leavened bread (an actual food), with the host.

Catholic ritual consequently distanced itself from a process of incorporation that was too closely connected with magical thinking and, above all, too cannibalistic, as it indeed involved consuming the body and blood of a man, albeit the Son of God. Certain microrituals emphasized this distance: the host was not bitten, but left to melt in the mouth and swallowed whole. To chew it would be sacrilege, lowering it to the level of human food. In this way, a fundamental division was created between the sacred and the profane in the domain of food consumption. On the one hand, there was the Eucharist and its encounter with Christ, which effectively incorporated the communicant into the Christian community[7]; on the other hand, there was the daily practice of eating that involved real bread and wine, which characterized the human condition.

This separation between sacred and profane incorporation established the daily act of eating within a space that was free from the authority of the Church, a domain over which it had minimal control. Gluttony, however, was still a cardinal sin. It took an extraordinary mechanism of exculpation, involving confession, theories of repentance and purgatory, and even the granting of indulgences, to enable Catholics to value the concept of here and now and to venture to disobey the commandment that forbade greed and its aestheticization. In this way, gastronomy was able to become a celebration of all things worldly. And yet this was a perilous enterprise, as gluttony remained one of the seven deadly sins, hence the distinction between the vulgar, coarse *gourmand*, ruled by his senses, and the *gourmet*, with his appreciation of life's finer pleasures (Croze 1933). The imaginary of incorporation could accordingly be used in order to emphasize differences through gastronomic practices.

Gastronomy can be viewed as a central mechanism in the development of social dynamics in France; in addition to indicating differences, it contributed to the construction of the national identity. After the French Revolution, for instance, when some members of the aristocracy had been forced into exile and the King had just been guillotined, the middle classes appropriated the culinary domain, relishing such items as *Bouchée à la Reine*, *Poularde Royale*, *Fruits Condé*, and *Potage Conti*. In doing so, they were metaphorically cannibalizing the nobility in order to incorporate that quality of class, which was to endow them with the legitimacy that they had lacked for centuries. At the same time, in naming a dish after one of these new political incumbents, a chef effectively elevated and incorporated him into this aristocratic pantheon (Poulain 1985b).

2.5 The food critic: An intermediary between two worlds

The position of the bourgeoisie, both close to power and yet still seeking legitimacy, favored the emergence of a new authority for society: the food critic. It was he who defined the good and the beautiful. For the middle-class gourmet, lacking the correct criteria, could have no real concept of distinction. The profession was established by individuals who occupied the middle ground between the two worlds of the nobility and the bourgeoisie, such as Alexandre-Balthazar Grimod de la Reynière and Jean Anthelme Brillat-Savarin. The former had a particularly remarkable social career. His father was a farmer-general and his mother's family (the de Jarentes), was one of the most eminent in France. He was born into the highest aristocratic circles. His parents owned a mansion at the corner of the Rue Boissy d'Anglas and the Place de la Concorde, which now houses the United States Embassy. Grimod, however, was a turbulent child. Following a series of misdemeanors, his father obtained a *lettre de cachet* from Louis XVI, in order to have him confined in an abbey near Nancy. He was freed a few years later, with the proviso that he was not to set foot in the capital or the Court. In this way, he was banished from aristocratic circles. When the Revolution broke out, Grimod de la Reynière was, therefore, outside Paris and escaped the turmoil of the Reign of Terror.

Returning to the capital a few years later, he took stock of the emerging social phenomenon and published a book entitled *L'almanach des gourmands* (1802). This was explicitly intended to "guide the middle classes through the labyrinth of the new food shops, restaurants and catering enterprises," which had begun to emerge, and at the same time to instruct them in the principles of gastronomy. The work was a success, running to several editions from 1802 to 1812; it became a genuine guide book, classifying establishments in hierarchical order and awarding seals of approval. His *Manuel des amphitryons*, (*Manual for Hosts*) published a few years later, was intended to be "a type of catechism . . . in the art of fine living and entertaining." It was addressed to those "newly enriched by the Revolution," which, "by causing these riches to change hands, had placed them at the disposal of men who until now, had been strangers to the art of using them, and of enjoying them in a noble fashion" (Grimod de la Reynière 1808, 315). Thanks to the dual nature of his social position, being both born into the nobility and excluded from it, and being familiar with aristocratic codes of behavior without taking them too seriously, Grimod de la Reynière was to play the role of intermediary. He simultaneously invented gastronomic literature, food guides, and seals of quality. These systems of legitimization still serve as important criteria in the domains of modern gastronomy and food consumption (Poulain 1988; Poulain and Neirinck 2000).

The other key figure, who acted as a link between aristocratic and bourgeois food codes in the postrevolutionary world, was Jean Anthelme Brillat-Savarin, whose origins were much more modest. He was born into the liberal provincial aristocracy. A lawyer and a deputy in the National Constituent Assembly, he left France for the United States in 1793, following the vote condemning Louis XVI to death, in which he refused to take part. In his *Physiologie du goût* (*Physiology of Taste*) published in 1824, he adopted the same perspective as that of Grimod de la Reynière. If Brillat-Savarin, the progressive aristocrat, has remained by far the more prominent figure in the history of gastronomy, this is because he was more presentable, his image more in keeping with the ideals of the Republic and of morality. For Grimod de la Reynière was a shady individual, who personally transgressed the behavioral codes of the *Ancien Régime*. For instance, he opened a grocery shop in Lyon and set up home with an actress, and his private life did not bear scrutiny, as he was engaged in simultaneous amorous liaisons with his mistress from Lyon and his own aunt, his mother's sister.[8]

Food guides, reviews and gastronomic literature made a highly significant contribution to the culinary professions. By cataloguing gastronomic enterprises and indicating approval of their creations, these works conferred undreamed of fame on such establishments. Of particular interest here, however, is the social position of food critics, who were not chefs and certainly not *maîtres d'hôtel*, but occupied a position between these two worlds. They acted as mediators between a rising social group and the regimes that had previously held power, providing the former with the means to express their new social status through food. During the 1960s, with the emergence in France of the proprietor-chefs, who spanned the worlds of capitalist business and labor, deriving power from the former yet drawing the salary of the latter, Henri Gault and Christian Millau were to play a similar role, by helping them to gain recognition through their "nouvelle cuisine", (Poulain 1985; Aron 1986).

The advent of gastronomy in the seventeenth century and its development in France, is the consequence of a particular social situation. This has its origins in gastronomy's emancipation from academic thought, in the social dynamics of distinction, in the quest for taste as a vector of the development of culinary creativity, and finally in Catholic ethics. Although each element played an important role, these conditions were not sufficient in themselves to initiate the emergence of gastronomy. For this to happen, they needed to form themselves into a specific social configuration. We may now have an explanation as to why gastronomy is a French phenomenon: it was in France that these various elements came into conjunction.

11

The "food social space": A tool for the study of food patterns

Georges Condominas proposed the concept of the "social space" in reaction to the use of the term "culture"—with its varying definitions—and in order to escape the ambiguities characterizing the stance of American cultural anthropology. "The adoption of the term 'social space' was motivated by the need to take account of a series of facts that could not be encompassed by the concept of culture" (1980, 77).

He proposes the following definition: "the social space is a space determined by the entire system of relationships that characterizes the group being studied. It is an acceptance . . . that is based on the word "space" itself, in the broad sense of the term. In this way, we consider the habitat to be only one part of social space. . . . Let us add, moreover, that we do not forget that in French it originally referred to an interval of time, as did the Latin *spatium* from which it developed, and as such it is a dynamic notion" (1980, 14, 15).

He considers the expression to be Durkheimian in origin. The notion of social space—"the manner in which social phenomena are distributed on the map" (Lévi-Strauss 1958, 319)—is accepted and present in a limited fashion in the work of several sociologists, ethnologists and geographers; Condominas cites Sir Edward Evan Evans-Pritchard, Marcel Granet, André Leroi-Gourhan, and Henri Lefebvre. Based on the category of space or of time qualified as social, according to Condominas the idea conveys the aim of establishing the autonomy of the social fact; at the same time, however, by linking it to the Maussian concept of the "total social fact," he broadens the notion of social space, so that it becomes a site of connection between nature and culture. In this way, systems of interaction operating within an environment—and all its physical, climatological and biological elements—may be examined in conjunction with those that operate at the level of a culture, with all its linguistic, technological, and imaginary dimensions. It is within the social space that ethnoscientific knowledge develops. We should add that in the case of eating practices, the social space likewise enables connections to be made between the social, psychological, and physiological dimensions, a point that we will develop later (Poulain 1985; Paul-Lévy 1997).

In this way, the social space refers both to a physical space, comparable to the object of geographical studies, and a space governed by thought, the latter being closer in concept to what sociologists and anthropologists term systems of representation and the structures of the imaginary (Durand 1960).

The notion of a "food social space" has already been adopted by other sociologists specializing in food and eating, such as Claude Grignon (1980b), albeit in a somewhat different sense. When Factorial Correspondence Analysis (FCA) was first applied, it was used to take account of the way in which practices and explanatory sociological variables were distributed within the space defined by the structuring axes in graphical representation.

The notion of "social space," as defined by Condominas, is of interest for three reasons. First, it offers an escape from the artificial opposition between cultural and material determinism, whether these are based on geography (relating to climate or the resources within the biotope), technology (relating to production methods), or physiology (relating to the functioning of the digestive system). Second, it creates the conditions necessary to establish a system defining the relationships between man and nature. Third, considering the concept of space in the broad sense of the term, that is, including time, it facilitates the development of a dynamic perspective. We shall conclude by emphasizing that this definition of social space has the advantage of not being over-determined from the methodological standpoint, and is compatible with perspectives that are otherwise more or less contradictory.

1 The social space and the dual space of freedom open to human eaters

Human food consumption is subject to a dual series of constraints, which vary in their laxity. The first of these are biological in nature; linked to man's status as an omnivore, they are imposed on eaters by the biochemical mechanisms underlying the process of nutrition and the capacities of the digestive system. This leaves a liberated space that has become a largely cultural domain, contributing in this way to the socialization of the body and the construction of forms of social organization. The second constraints are ecological in character, and are imposed by the biotope in which the group of individuals has settled;

they likewise provide a liberated zone, relating to the management of the group's dependence on their natural environment.

Through their status as omnivores, human eaters are highly adaptable with regard to food, which has enabled them to live in extremely varied biotopes, and to inhabit almost every corner of the planet. To appreciate the significance of this liberated space, one only has to compare the eating practices of the Inuit, whose diet consists essentially of seal meat and fish, usually eaten raw, and those of the highland peoples of New Guinea, whose diet is based heavily on carbohydrates (de Garine 1991).

The human eater is subject to a few biological rules; although nutritional scientists are becoming increasingly knowledgeable with regard to these, the choice of items from which to obtain nutrients, the manner in which they are cooked and consumed, together with tastes and dislikes in general, are very largely determined by social factors. Drawing on over a hundred years of research, nutritional studies are beginning to identify the specific constraints imposed on the human eater. However, this is still a developing discipline and is mainly based on a deductive approach, which entails generalizing physiological information acquired in experimental conditions[1] that reduce the complexity of human food consumption.

Although human nutritional sciences are evolving on a daily basis, they are confronted with the problem of linking the physiological with the social. In their scientific version, they are Western in both origin and formation. For want of an epistemological foundation that only the anthropological perspective could provide,[2] they are often based on certain cultural prejudices that have affected, and continue to affect their development. The most characteristic and common of these combines an organicist reductionism with an ethnocentric perspective. An example of this are those studies which, having identified how mechanisms for regulating the appetite function within a given cultural environment, draw general, universal conclusions from that information. This approach has defined the history of nutritional sciences, and, despite its blatantly ethnocentric character, it still influences a large number of contemporary scientific studies. As Igor de Garine has stated, to recognize the margin of uncertainty in our knowledge of human nutrition, we have only to consider "the regular re-assessment of the calorie and protein needs established, and constantly revised downwards, by the committee of experts at the FAO and the WHO"—organizations as serious as they are prestigious (1991, 1449).

Despite the fact that nutritional science is a relatively new discipline, it is possible to establish a few fundamental principles that are linked to the biological inability of the human species to synthesize certain nutrients. Certain amino acids should be included, simultaneously, in our protein intake, and are therefore classed as essential. If the proportion of one of these amino acids is too low, it acts as a limiting factor, preventing the body from assimilating the others. Certain fatty acids should also feature with relative frequency in our daily diet. There are some vitamins, such as vitamin C, that cannot be stored in the body, and must be consumed on a very regular basis. For certain oligo-elements to be assimilated, they should be simultaneously present in specific proportions. To ensure a regular supply of nutrients, and as there is no single food item able to meet all these different requirements, human eaters must diversify their food intake. They are, therefore, biologically obliged to follow a diverse diet. At the same time, man can only consume, and above all incorporate, culturally identifiable and valued foods.

The function of the culinary system, understood by Fischler as the set of more or less conscious rules that structure the preparation and consumption of food, is to regulate the contradictions emerging from a dual imperative: to manage dietary diversification and, at the same time, to satisfy the cognitive need to consume culturally recognized foods (1990).

The second space that allows human eaters freedom is linked to the ways in which they connect with nature. This relationship is also of interest to geographers and anthropologists. As Jean Brunhes stated, man becomes part of a physical space through his need for food. To eat is to incorporate a territory:

> As for our food, it is composed of plant or animal products, all of which have initially occupied a place on the surface of the globe. Furthermore, the animals of this planet that feed man are themselves nourished by plants. . . . Almost all human foods should contain a modicum of the vegetation that covers the earth. The meals eaten by a human being therefore represent, either directly or indirectly, the "cuttings" from a more or less limited area of the earth's carpet of vegetation, whether natural or cultivated. (Brunhes 1942, 19)

In return, the foods favored by a human group, and the techniques it uses to procure or produce such foods, transform and shape the natural environment. "Every time human beings quench their thirst or feed their hunger, they effectively benefit from the surfaces they alter; and through the continual repetitions of their meals, they bring about continual geographical modifications" (Brunhes 1942, 19).

Theories relating to man's connection with nature are central to the study of human geography and developed within the discipline that was to become ecology. Three different approaches were formed. According to "determinist" theories, the forms and methods used to feed the human group depend on the environment and the constraints it imposes, such as the availability of resources, the influence of the seasons, the climate, and so on. Friedrich Razel, the German geographer and ethnographer who promoted a concept known as "anthropo-geography," is a representative example of this perspective.[3] Jacques Barrau gives a very concise definition of this theoretical stance: "A given civilization is determined by the conditions of its physical and natural surroundings" (Barrau 1991). In this case, feeding the group is perceived in terms of a series of adaptations to the environment. Man eats what nature places at his disposal according to his biological needs, which are themselves largely influenced by the climate.

The theories of "possibilism" are a reaction to the determinist stance. They "deny the mechanical action of natural factors on a purely receptive human race." Their most notable representative in France is Lucien Febvre, who, faithful to the ideas of Vidal de La Blache, the founder of the French school of humanist geography, developed the concept. "Necessity nowhere, possibilities everywhere; and man, the master of possibilities, decides how to use them!" (Febvre 1922). The history of plant cultivation is full of examples that show how nature has been shaped by human societies (Haudicourt and Hédin 1943).

The "environmentalist" theories, which were heralded by Sorre (1943), represent the third attitude. They endeavor to circumvent this opposition by positing a reciprocal interaction between nature and culture: humans mold their natural environment and in turn, they themselves are shaped by it. In the words of Pierre Gourou:

Neither "determinism" nor this type of "possibilism" provides the key to understanding geography. Man is not compelled by his physical environment to adopt a particular technique in order to use the earth's resources, or to organize his surroundings; he does not make a conscious choice among natural "possibilities." What is important in terms of geographical analysis, are the possibilities offered by the techniques available to the human group that is studied. The possibilities originate from man, not nature; *they are given to man by the civilization to which he belongs.* (Gourou 1953)[4]

A second liberated space emerges here, created by the different possibilities of using the natural environment, which culture—in the Maussian sense of the term—appropriates in its own manner. What is striking with regard to the choices made by a given culture from a variety of potentially edible natural products—that is to say, those with nutritional qualities—is the lack of a systematic utilization of the natural environment. The resources provided by the biotope are not optimized—far from it. Of course, there are ecological constraints preventing the cultivation of certain products: wheat and vines, for instance, cannot be grown in every biotope. Yet, due to the interest aroused by these products, they are cultivated over an infinitely more extensive geographical area than those of their origins, reaching the furthest limits of the terrains where they may be successfully grown.

The reason for using a plant or animal as a food is neither based solely on its availability, nor even on the existence of technological methods that may be applied to this end. In other words, the explanation is not purely utilitarian in nature; cultural factors are equally influential. Marshall Salhins (1976) has shown how the notion of need is socially defined, and, above all, how a technoeconomic organization is itself determined by how a human community defines "its" own needs:

> The productive relation of American society to its own and the world environment is organized by specific valuations of edibility and inedibility, themselves qualitative and in no way justifiable by biological, ecological or economic advantage. The functional consequences extend from agricultural "adaptation" to international trade and world political relations. The exploitation of the American environment, the mode of relation to the landscape, depends on the model of a meal that includes a central meat element with the peripheral support of carbohydrates and vegetables. (Sahlins 1976, 171)

In the same way, the irrigated paddy fields of Asia simultaneously reflect the popularity of rice, its symbolic status, the composition of Asian meals, and the mastery of irrigation techniques. Other cultural solutions, other modes of social organization based on the consumption of different foods, could naturally have been applied in this environment; yet the communities living in that part of the world founded a "civilization of rice." This choice was not only guided by reasons related to yield, since high levels of food productivity would also have been attained using other cereal crops and techniques; it is connected to a number of reasons, rooted in the interface between culture and environment. In the long term, changes may occur to transform the landscape and social structure. It is now acknowledged that taro was probably grown in South-East Asia before the cultivation of rice, which would have been considered a weed when it appeared in the taro fields (Condominas 1980, 198–221). "To broach the problem of the exploitation of the natural environment is obviously, first and foremost, to broach the subject of technology," explains Condominas, citing André-Georges Haudricourt's markedly Maussian definition of technology as:[5] "the study of a people's material activities, in other words, their way of hunting, fishing and growing crops, of clothing, housing and feeding themselves" (Haudricourt 1968, 731, cited by Condominas 1980, 34).

However, in most instances, the study of human food consumption remains limited to a focus on methods of gathering and preparation. Condominas himself sees this approach as common to contemporary ethnologists, constituting an initial stage that he defines as being more serviceable, "while waiting until the investigative methods necessary for the anthropological study of eating practices are perfected."

The second stage is therefore characterized by the availability of tools that will facilitate an understanding of how "diet constitutes a major element within the social space on account of the central position that it occupies in the production system, from which it dictates the technology and economics of a group" (1980, 32). An antithetic inversion operates here; diet is no longer presented as the consequence of the environment (as in the determinist theories of geography), or as reflection of cultural diversity (as in the possibilist theories of both geography and cultural anthropology). Instead, it appears as a structuring aspect of social organization, reconnecting in this way with one of the main contributions of Lévi-Straussian anthropology. For, as noted by Françoise Paul-Lévy and Marion Segaud in a work devoted to the anthropology of space, "we must turn once again to Lévi-Strauss . . . whatever the debates justified by his texts. . . . He has in effect provided us with the means of understanding that spatial configurations (one has simply to replace "spatial" with "dietary" or "culinary") are not only the products, but also the producers of social systems or, to clarify, they occupy not just the position of effect, but also that of cause" (Paul-Levy and Segaud 1983, 19).

In this way, Condominas created the conditions necessary to bring about a genuine paradigmatic shift, which was able to reinforce the epistemological foundations of the anthroposociology of food. At the same time, he placed the discipline in a pivotal position, where it played a crucial role by linking hitherto unconnected aspects of knowledge relating to the social and human sciences: human geography, ethnology, sociology, ethnobotany, ethnozoology, and so forth.

2 The various dimensions of the "food social space"

Mauss coined the term "total social fact" in order to describe certain categories of particularly complex social facts, that is, those "that have an impact on the whole of society and its institutions" (Mauss 1950). This clearly includes food consumption.

For his part, Georges Gurvitch showed that "total social phenomena are pluridimensional, formed as stages, layers, or levels of depth" (Gurvitch 1958; Corbeau 1991). We do not propose to engage with the levels described by Gurvitch in their entirety, as their generalized character occasionally presents problems regarding practical application; however, we will retain the notion that the "food social space" is composed of several interconnected dimensions. As a concept, it has a nested structure, with each of its numerous dimensions fitting inside the next, in the manner of Russian dolls. These will now be briefly presented. An attempt to provide a fully comprehensive account of these aspects would naturally be of interest. However, this would be more suitable material for an encyclopedia or a dictionary, as the immense scope of the subject would demand a significant collaborative endeavor. We will therefore limit ourselves to a programmatic perspective.

2.1 The "edible" space

The first dimension of the food social space corresponds to the set of choices applied by a human group in a natural environment in order to select, acquire—in the anthropological sense, that is, involving the series of actions from gathering to production—or to preserve its foods. It is always astonishing to note the decisions made by a human group when selecting items that it deems suitable for consumption from the extensive possibilities available in the biotope it inhabits. While a very large number of natural substances from the mineral, plant, and animal kingdoms could potentially be used as food, only a small number are selected. Even if this selection may be seen from a functionalist standpoint, whereby the ecological performance of the chosen solution is sometimes emphasized (Harris 1985), this cannot be the sole reason for the choices made. For these decisions are based on symbolic representations and play a part in the cultural differentiation of social groups sometimes inhabiting the same biotope. While they are unquestionably interesting as adaptive responses, in many cases they also deprive groups of a not inconsiderable contribution to their food supply, and prevent them from optimizing the resources in their natural environment (Fischler 1979; Kilani 1992).

The "edible" space is, therefore, the result of the selection made by a human community from the entire range of nourishing substances that are at its disposal in the natural environment, or that could be available if the decision were made to cultivate them there (Condominas 1980; Fischler 1990).

"In establishing the distinction between the edible and the non edible within the potential food supply, the social value invested creates the food in the cultural sense, organizing items into a hierarchy that transcends subjective individual tastes and affirms itself as the shared cultural value of the group as a whole" (Kilani 1992, 157). The "edible" space encompasses all the rules that contribute to the social definition of a food. It is the means by which a human community indicates its connection to nature. The construction of a society's food identity encompasses all the regulations that govern decisions concerning the acceptance of a given nutritious substance into the eating space.

The symbolic qualities of foods emerge within systems of classification that give them meaning and that are specific to each culture. These representations simultaneously define what may be eaten, the conditions in which the slaughter of animals may be carried out, and in which the preparation, consumption, sharing, and exchange of food takes place. In this way, they connect the natural with the cultural.

2.2 *The food system*

The second dimension of the food social space relates to the series of technological and social structures which, from the fields to the kitchen, via the various stages of production and processing, enable the food to reach the consumer and to be recognized as edible.

Lewin has shown that in order for a food to be eaten by a consumer, it must first make its way to him. In its progress from the natural world, where it was produced, to the table, where it is consumed, food travels within a society, undergoing a whole series of transformations. The "food social system" is the equivalent of what economists define by the term sector. It encompasses all the economic actors who, from production to consumption, contribute to the transformation, manufacture, and distribution of food products. The sociological perspective extends this notion of sector downward, including the domestic actors who acquire the items (usually through purchase, but also by activities such as gardening, gathering, and hunting), and who participate in their culinary transformation and in organizing the conditions in which consumption takes place.

The food system may be represented by a series of channels through which foods travel. When forming their decisions at each stage of the food system, causing foods to progress toward the consumer, and opening or closing the channels by which they reach the family dining table, the social actors responsible apply not only their technological knowledge, but also their representations.

We will now, in turn, extend this description of the food social system by distinguishing between the food consumption spaces and their supply channels (Figure 9). In the case of consumption, we have shown that the classic distinction made with regard to food-related expenditure, between eating at home and in restaurants, should be completed by adding places of work and transport. In this way, foods are consumed within the domestic space, where items are cooked, served, and eaten in the intimacy of the home; in the restaurant sector, either in institutional catering or commercial establishments, where culinary transformations are carried out by professionals and consumption takes place in public and in a more or less spectacularized manner, and finally, in the living environment, in places of work and in transit, where the foods consumed were made either in the domestic space or in catering establishments.

Foods may have traveled through multiple channels before reaching the eater. The primary channel is that of gathering, fishing, and hunting; these are the principal methods used by hunter-gatherer societies, yet whatever form social organization takes, they never entirely disappear. Even in industrial societies these activities persist, and may, indeed, become recreational pastimes (Larrère and de la Soudière, 1985).

The second means by which food reaches the eater is that of self-production. Here we should make a distinction between untreated foods, produced through plant cultivation, gardening, animal husbandry, and so on, and foods that have been transformed through culinary activity, in the form of preserved items made from foods that have been grown or bought.

The purchase of more or less transformed products from small-scale food suppliers or major supermarkets constitutes the third supply channel. These three initial supply channels lead to the domestic space, where the technical activities of selection, storage, and transformation will be carried out.

Professional catering enterprises constitute another food supply channel. In these establishments foods are normally consumed on site, but they are sometimes simply used for the purchase of products destined for the domestic sphere, as is the case with pizza delivery outlets or drive-in fast-food restaurants. Finally, the living environment, which includes places of work, entertainment, leisure, and transportation, is supplied by the traditional channels of purchase from food outlets or the restaurant sector, in addition to takeaway establishments and automatic distribution through vending machines.

The food within each channel passes through various technical stages regulated by physical and economic laws. However, in order to gain full insight into the sociological dimension of the food system, it should be borne in mind that the foods do not move through the channels in isolation. The way in which the channels function is controlled by individuals, whose actions are governed by professional or domestic considerations. Entrance into a supply channel and progress from one section to the next takes place through, thanks to and under the supervision of, individuals who interact with the eater and with each other. Consequently, their decisions are determined by their representations of the needs and desires of the other (the eater) and of their own social roles as both gatekeepers and eaters. It is this function, which is both technical and sociological, this strategic position within the concrete system of action that Kurt Lewin qualifies as "gatekeeping." For example, in order to understand which foods enter the purchase supply channel, and the reasons governing their use and consumption, it is first necessary to know whether the husband, wife, or a third party makes the choices and purchases for the household; second, it is necessary to know who cooks the food, and in what physical, temporal, and social conditions the products are consumed.

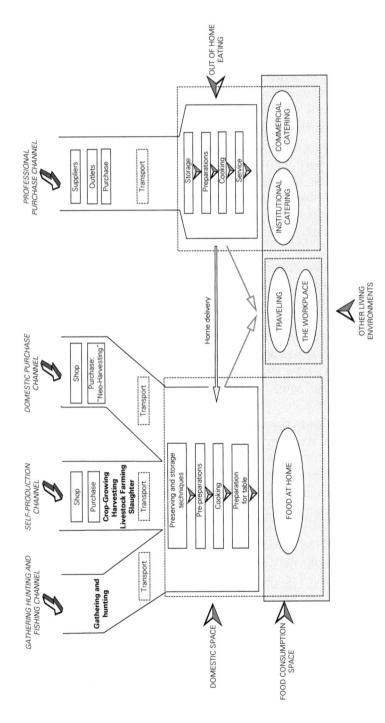

FIGURE 9 *The food system.*

Source: J.-P. Poulain.

2.3 The culinary space

Cooking constitutes a series of symbolic operations and rituals which, centering on the technical activities that play a part in constructing the identity of a natural food, render it suitable for consumption. The culinary space is the third dimension of the food social space. It is a space in the geographical sense of the term, relating to structural arrangement; this involves for example, the location of the kitchen, the space where culinary operations are carried out, either inside or outside the home. It is also a space in the social sense, which takes the gendered and social division of kitchen activities into account. Equally, however, it is a space in the logical sense of the term, the space of structural connections, Lévi-Strauss's "culinary triangle" being the most famous example of this (Lévi-Strauss 1968).

2.4 The space of food habits

The fourth dimension of the food social space, the space of food habits encompasses the series of rituals that surround food consumption in the strict sense of the word, that is to say, the act of incorporation. The structure of the "food day" (the number of instances of food consumption, the forms these take, their timing and social contexts), the definition of a meal, its structural composition, the ways in which it is consumed (using the hands, chopsticks, knife and fork, etc.), the locality of the instances of food intake, the rules regarding the positioning of the eaters—all vary from one culture to another and within the same culture, according to the social group.

One should rid oneself of the illusion—resulting from Western ethnocentrism—that meals constitute the only possible way to eat. In a study devoted to eating practices in the kingdom of Tonga (Western Polynesia), Marie-Claire Bataille-Benguigui explains: "The Tongans do not have meals as such. The time of day, the composition and the duration of instances of food consumption are all irregular, yet they appear to have met the biological needs of the human body for centuries" (1996, 257). It is more relevant here to speak of dietary regimes, in much the same way as geographers speak of a "river regime."

We should first distinguish between the instances of consumption defined as meals by the eaters themselves, and other types of food intake. In Vietnam, for example, the daily instances of food consumption comprise three organized, shared meals, which can be supplemented by more or less individualized instances subject to less constricting rituals. For South-East Asian peoples have two food spaces: one for organized meals, the other for intermittent snacks. The intermittent snacks involve specific preparation, and these types of foods are consumed throughout the day. The Vietnamese use the charming expression "*an choi*" ("to eat for fun") to describe this type of between-meal consumption (Krowolski 1993, 148), while the French use the more guilt-inducing term of "*grignotage*"—"grazing" or "nibbling."

In the case of China, Françoise Sabban has shown the importance of eating between meals:

> However, Chinese eating practices cannot be restricted to this meal system, which can seem fixed and constraining, although it is intended to contribute to food sufficiency. When economic and/or political conditions allow it, the time between meals is used for personalized consumption, which is not bound by rules. For centuries, the alleys and lanes have been lined with street food stalls and vendors offering specialty snacks that people eat whenever they like, quite informally, at any time of the day or night. (Aymard, Grignon, and Sabban 1993)

Older studies by Jacques Dournes on the eating practices of the Jorai of Central Vietnam[6] had already highlighted the existence of this dual system of established meals and the spontaneous food consumption that takes place throughout the day. He emphasizes the functions of these between-meal refreshments. Far from being desocialized in nature, these casual instances of food intake play a part in forging social bonds, as they occur when meeting friends, during breaks from working in the fields, or in celebration of the fortunate discovery of a fruit or some small game (Dournes 1981, 180).

2.5 *Eating and the rhythm of time*

Eating takes place within a series of socially determined temporal cycles. The first of these is the human life cycle, with the succession of foods consumed in infancy, childhood, adolescence, adulthood, and old age. Each stage corresponds to a particular style of food, with some items being authorized and others forbidden; the stages are further characterized by the occurrence of meals, the status of the eaters, roles, restrictions, obligations, and rights. These major phases are connected to one other by initiations and rites of passage: the first glass of wine, the first inebriation, the wedding breakfast, the first communion meal, and finally, the funeral reception. In some societies, deceased ancestors also play their part in everyday and festive meals. Second, there are the temporal cycles. In the case of farming communities, these are defined by the rhythm of the seasons and agricultural work, while for hunters they are marked by the migration of game. The start of the year brings the first foods, times of hunger alternate with periods of plenty, whether these occur naturally—during or between harvests—or are established by the community—periods when all foods are permitted and others marked by partial or total fasting. Finally, there is the daily temporal rhythm, with alternating periods of work and leisure time, various meals, instances of between-meal consumption and their respective places in the daily timetable.

2.6 The social differentiation space

Food defines the identities of social groups within the same culture, whether in terms of social class or regional provenance. A particular food favored by one group will be rejected by another. Eating marks the boundaries that distinguish the different identities of human groups from one culture to another, as well as those of the various subgroups that make up the same culture. This final dimension of the food social space is much more characteristic of Western sociology.

3 Food and its social construction

The Latin verb *alere* means "to feed"; an "aliment" is therefore something that nourishes, providing man with the elements that he loses in the course of daily life. As an eighteenth-century dictionary informs us: "Everything that has the capacity to remedy the loss of solid or liquid parts of our bodies merits the name of aliment" (Lemery 1702, cited by Trémolières 1970). Although the term *aliment* appeared in France as early as 1120, its current usage was not adopted until the sixteenth century, when it replaced the word *viande* (meat), which from then on was only used to designate the flesh of animals used for food. In old French, *viande* meant "everything that serves to uphold life," and therefore encompassed food as a whole, meat-based or otherwise. *Viande* derives from the Latin *vivenda (vivere)*: "that which helps maintain life." In this way, the title of the first French cookery book, which dates from the fourteenth century, was *Le Viandier*.

However, for an "aliment" to be recognized as such, that is to say, capable of maintaining life, it is not enough for it to possess nutritional properties alone, in the form of certain amounts of carbohydrates, lipids, proteins, and oligo-elements. It must also be accepted as a food by the eater and his social group.

Man needs food to be more than an object that simply provides him with nutrients; it must also give pleasure and have a prestige, a quality of reassurance. Indeed, nutrition and ethology studies have highlighted the role of sensory stimuli in the release of secretions and in gastrointestinal motility, and the symbolic "gestalt" aspect of the stimulus signal that is food. (Trémolières 1970)

A food must possess four fundamental qualities: nutritional, organoleptic, hygienic, and symbolic. It should primarily be capable of supplying the individual organism with its requirements: energy-giving nutrients (carbohydrates, lipids); energy-giving, body-building nutrients (proteins); minerals (macro and oligo-mineral elements); vitamins and water. These should all be present in reasonably balanced proportions. With regard to the first criteria, a very large number of natural (or not natural) objects could be used as food. Grasshoppers, cockroaches, snakes, foxes, dogs, and plane-tree leaves are all, from this standpoint, potential foods. Some do indeed form part of the diets of certain cultures, while arousing only disgust in our own. This, therefore, proves that nutritional properties are necessary but not sufficient in themselves to transform an item that contains them into a food.

Second, a food must be free from toxic substances. When consumed, it should not cause secondary digestive disorders, rendering it liable to be rejected through negative conditioning. Dietary toxicity can result from two main causes: microbiological and chemical. The latter may be either natural, or caused by the treatments to which a person subjects his or her intended foods. The second quality is equally necessary, but not sufficient in itself.

Third, a food should possess organoleptic qualities. In the course of contact between eater and food, from ingestion to defecation, the physical characteristics of food items arouse psychophysiological sensations. These are initially exteroceptive in nature: visual, olfactory, gustatory, tactile, thermic, and even auditory. Yet food also generates proprioceptive sensations, such as the perception of the degree of resistance it presents to the jaw muscles, or its presence in the stomach.

Finally, foods arouse general secondary sensations: the euphoric effects of alcohol, the feeling of calm induced by a full stomach, the excited sensation produced by coffee or tonics, the stimulating effects of meat. These different characteristics of various foods are experienced by the eater in terms of the simple division between pleasant and unpleasant. As a whole, these sensations constitute a system of attraction and selection so fundamental that a nutrient which has not acquired a quality of "emotive dynamism" is not a food. "The normal individual could not tolerate a diet comprising a combination of the amino-acids and nutrients the body needs, without vomiting" (Trémolières 1971, 12).

However, in addition to these three main categories of qualities required by a natural product in order to become a food, it must also lend itself to a process of projection carried out by the eater, who thereby endows it with meaning. It must be able to acquire significance, to become part of a network of communications in an imaginary constellation, a vision of the world. "Man probably consumes as many symbols as nutrients" (Trémolières 1971).

3.1 *The transition from plant status to food*

The Neolithic Revolution was characterized by the identification, selection, and cultivation of a small number of plant species. This proceeded according to a three-dimensional pattern identified by André Leroi-Gourhan: biological constraints (the ability of the plants in question to satisfy nutritional needs); technical innovations (both cultural and culinary, but primarily the latter, relating to their transformation into soups, gruels, galettes or breads) and symbolic representations. As observed by Adam Maurizio (1932): "It should be noted that the staple food ration, in the quantitative sense, is almost always farinaceous"—and very often a cereal. The production process, which followed the natural cycle of the seasons, gave rise to the "granary civilization" that transformed man's relationship with food; it was now viewed in a temporal context, and social organizations were established in order to protect the reserve supplies produced. Through the myths associated with foods of plant origin, they have their place in the logical space of representations of the world, and of the role that man is thought to fulfill there.

The myths connected with cereals, for example, are very often based on an analogy between the cultural process or the techno-culinary transformations undergone by cereal plants in order to become food, and the human journey through life. This is the case, for instance, with the image of "good bread" used to characterize Christians, the "leaven" symbolizing Christ, and the bread and the wine of the Christian Eucharist. In Asia, the various stages of transformation leading to the production of edible white rice are seen as symbolic of man's journey. It is interesting to note that in Vietnam this association between the destiny of man and that of rice may be found even in the secular discourse of Ho Chi Minh: "How the rice suffers under the pestle! Yet soon it will be as white as cotton. The same is true of our lives: humans emerge from their ordeals as bright as polished jade".

According to the founding myths of West Africa, the world originated from a grain of fonio. In Cherokee mythology, the origins of maize are closely connected to those of gender difference, woman having been created by the Great Spirit from an ear of corn. It also organizes the relationship between man, the creator and the animals with which he shares the world (Dibie 1998, 150). The range of plant species that may be eaten varies according to the culture and to the social management of the process of predation, being extensive in hunter-gatherer societies, and more restricted in the case of those based on agriculture.

3.2 *The transition from animal status to food*

In order to eat an animal, it must first be recognized as edible, in other words, it must occupy a particular position within a system that classifies the animal species and its relationship with human beings. The symbolism associated with the species and the reasons governing its proximity to man contribute to its inclusion in, or exclusion from, the category of animals deemed edible (Leach 1980). Yet in order to eat the flesh of an animal, it must first have been killed, and this cannot be carried out without symbolic precautions.

Sir Edmund Leach has shown how the connections established between animals and humans determine the capacity of animals to become food. Animals can be listed into four categories according to the distance separating them from man. Ranging from the most distant to the closest, these are: wild animals, game, domestic animals, and pets. The two middle categories comprise animals that are used as food. The consumption of animals in the first and last categories is subject to emphatic prohibition, the first being too distant from man and the last, too close. However, the boundaries between these different categories vary according to culture (Leach 1972). Cynophagy, or the consumption of dog meat, is an exemplary case in point. Why is dog eaten in some cultures and not in others? Dogs are man's best friends; our faithful companions. The proscription with regard to the consumption of dog flesh in Western society is therefore explained through this proximity. Nevertheless, it is possible to find numerous examples of cultures where pets are eaten in addition to other animals. This is the case, for instance, with the Australian Aborigines, who eat dingoes. Some anthropologists have sought to explain this phenomenon as part of a substructure of the "cannibalism practiced in those regions" (Helm 1896, cited by Millet 1995, 82).

Before examining the issues presented by cannibalism, however, the rationale governing proximity should be studied in greater depth. Clearly, one does not eat one's companion, which therefore includes pets, but this attribute is not necessarily consistent. And if the family pet loses this status, returning to that of a domestic animal, or to its wild state, it is reintegrated into the category of objects that may be consumed. The phenomenon of distancing an animal from a human community on the eve of its slaughter has been well documented in European ethnological studies into eating practices. This symbolic process lowers the status of the animal, with which familiar relationships might have been established, to the ranks of livestock. In French rural communities, pigs are frequently given human names, such as Arthur or Jules, and by personifying and identifying an animal in this amicable way, he becomes part of the family circle. He is fed, "attentively and affectionately cared for," and "soup" is made for him. When the time for slaughter approaches he becomes a focus of anger, being accused of misdeeds often associated with the theme of cleanliness: "he's dirty, like an old farm dog!" or of lack of self-control: "All he thinks about is food." Such accusations create an initial distance from the animal, concluding in its slaughter (Poulain 1984, 1996b).

Another system, encountered in central France, links the process of familiarization with that of distancing. In this case, the pig is the central figure in a semimocking game; he is nicknamed "*lou seignur*" ("the lord") and becomes the most important character on the farm. Some folklore specialists describe him as "dressed in silk, like the nobility." When the moment of slaughter draws near the representations are reversed, and the "lord" finds himself berated for having lived at the expense of the community, who have "fattened him up." The slaughter might even take the form of a mock revolution. In a recent article devoted to this subject, Jacqueline Millet gives several examples from different cultural domains, which, in the case of cynophagy, attest to the reversible nature of the status of a family pet (Millet 1995, 82–84).

We have shown that the status of the dog in Western agricultural societies, and notably in livestock-rearing communities, is midway between that of humans and domestic animals (this being higher than their place in hunting communities, which is only midway between that of man and wild animals). This may partly explain why using them for food is regarded as unacceptable in these cultural spaces (Poulain 1997b). However, the principle of proximity to man is not sufficient in itself to explain the harsh attitude shown by Westerners,[7] who regard societies where dogs are used for food as barbaric. Indeed, when the study of anthropology was in its infancy, and dominated by an evolutionary perspective, the practice of cynophagy might be seen as an indication of the degree of civilization attained by a community. For in the question of consuming dog flesh, the imaginaries operating within Western and Asian societies collide. The origins of the feeling of disgust, or even horror, that the practice arouses in the West may be traced to symbolic representations and to the association of this tradition with that of cannibalism. Frank Lestringant shows how, during the discovery of the New World, Christopher Columbus invented the term "cannibalism" by putting together the Arawak word "caniba" (bad, fierce), the Latin "canis" (a dog), and the proper noun Kan, the name of a Chinese sovereign he sought to meet. In an entry dated Sunday, November 4, 1492, from the journal of the voyage transcribed by Bartolomé de Las Casas, the Admiral, having arrived on the north coast of Cuba a few days previously, notes that he had heard from witnesses how "further on" (continuing eastward), "there were men with one single eye, and others with the muzzles of dogs [who] eat human beings." The word "cannibal" did not appear in the diaries until November 23. "By making an analogy between these contexts and the verbal communication of the 4th of November," writes Lestringant, "we may see how the word 'cannibal' constitutes the exact equivalent of the men with dogs' heads" (Lestringant 1994, 43, 44). The basis of this imaginary may be traced to Greek mythology, according to which savage peoples, who had dogs' heads and barked, could be found inhabiting India. Not having acquired the use of language, they are presented as a symbol of the primitive state. For a Westerner, eating dog flesh is the equivalent both of becoming a cannibal and of being primitive.

The anxiety, and even dread, aroused by cannibalism in Christian cultures has connections with the issues surrounding the Eucharist and the principle of transubstantiation. Several authors have examined how, as the Reformation gained ascendancy, the imaginary relating to cannibalism was exacerbated by the question of the real or symbolic presence of Christ's body and blood in the two substances of bread and wine taken during Communion (Lestringant 1981; Albert 1991; Fabre-Vassas 1991).

To kill an animal is not a commonplace act, for in doing so, man intervenes in the natural order. The slaughter of animals for food may be managed according to different methods. The place attributed to human beings in the classification and hierarchy of the animal species determines whether the consumption of meat is prohibited or authorized. Prohibition is justified by respect for life, whether or not this is supported by myth-based conceptions (Ossipow 1989, 1994). In the Hindu religion, for example, the refusal to kill animals associated with higher castes should be viewed in connection with the theory of metempsychosis (Mahias 1985).

In traditional societies, when the consumption of meat is authorized, the slaughter forms part of a heavily ritualized system of sacrifice. Two different concepts may be distinguished. In the first, eating meat is the consequence of a sacrificial act. In other words, the main motive of the group concerned is that of sacrifice and its religious functions. The consumption of meat then occurs only because it has become available to the group, once the sacrificial act has been performed. This is the case with the ancient Greeks (Détienne and Vernant 1979) and the Proto-Indochinese (Condominas 1954).

In the second case, the consumption of meat is the reason for the slaughter, but it is necessary to take precautions against the potentially negative consequences of man's intervention into the natural order of life. The slaughter is therefore ritualized by being placed under the supervision of spiritual and religious authorities, as is the case with the Jewish and Muslim religions. Whether the aim of the slaughter is to produce food, or whether sacrificial ritual is the primary motivation, the responsibility for this intrusion into life falls on the community. In the Christian world, the killing of animals for meat is not subject to spiritual supervision. Historically, sacrificial practices in this context relate back to the sacrifice of the "Son of God made man" and its commemoration through the Eucharist. This renders all other actual sacrifices redundant, and, at the same time, it replaces them. In this way, animal slaughter has been cast into the secular domain.

However, ethnological studies of French traditions have noted the survival of practices and beliefs that could be qualified as pagan in rural Christian communities. This is the case, for example, with the ceremony of killing the pig, which is surrounded by a set of specific rituals. The slaughter is carried out by the master of the house or by a professional slaughterman, known as *lou Sangnaïre*, or *lou Mazelier*, who travels from farm to farm. The occasion is marked by a certain number of rituals and is prolonged by a series of gifts given to relatives and friends, who reciprocate with counter-gifts when the time comes to slaughter their own pigs. In this way, social bonds are reforged and consolidated through this "sacrificial" death. In modern Western societies of Christian origin, slaughter has therefore become secularized. The killing of animals for food is managed by a dual process of evacuation and repression; this, together with the scientification of the act, could be described in general terms as medicalization.

Noëlie Vialles (1987) and Colette Méchin (1992) have shown how the Taylorized approach applied in abattoirs contributes to a objectification of the animals. In the same way, the banishment of abattoirs to the outskirts of cities is tantamount to masking the deaths taking place there. This is echoed by the suppression of the dead animals' bodies, as highlighted by Elias (1939), when the practice of serving the entire animal at table came to an end.

The sociology of food has not produced sufficient studies examining the presence and role of veterinary surgeons during the slaughtering process. Their attendance at the precise moment of slaughter cannot be explained in terms of hygiene monitoring alone; it also fulfills symbolic functions, as a way of "labeling" the slaughtered animal as edible, in the name of science. This reflects the Western system of values, with its emphasis on those of science and rationality; we have seen how the mad cow crisis may be analyzed in terms of the difficulties involved in managing the slaughter of animals for food.

3.3 *Milk and milk derivatives*

If milk has the status of a universal food for children, cheeses serve as significant identity markers for adults, indicating culturally–based dietary differences.

Milk, and above all cheeses, have a privileged status in French culture. France is often presented as the quintessential land of cheese. Roquefort cheese played a central role in the protests that took place during the World Trade Organization (WHO) summit in Seattle. In a shift of focus from the country to its inhabitants, the Sylvester Stallone character, representing the voice of the USA in the satirical French TV puppet show *Les Guignols*, uses the expression "stinking cheeses" to designate the French themselves.

There have long been attempts to explain the aversion for milk felt by certain Asian cultures as the result of genetic factors. A number of adults in Asia do indeed have an enzyme deficiency that blocks the digestion of lactose, a sugar present in milk. As adults, the peoples of East Asia do not consume milk and have a genuine dislike of this product, as they lack, or have lost, the biological capacity to digest it. However, if the enzyme deficit is a possible explanation for the aversion to milk, it cannot account for the nonconsumption of fermented cheeses, in which lactose is absent or transformed into lactic acid, making it perfectly digestible (Sabban 1986). The accepted explanation today, which we owe to anthropological studies, is that the continued ability to digest lactose is an adaptive benefit. In this way, the modification of the genotype results indirectly from the alimentary systems of pastoral societies (McCracken 1971; Fischler 1990). In the case of livestock farming societies, it is seen as an adaptation to dietary changes, and constitutes an example of the interaction between cultural and genetic factors. If certain Asian peoples do not have this digestive capacity, this is because it is not required in a cultural space where adults do not consume milk. The reasons for the consumption or nonconsumption of milk, and for the liking or distaste for milk and milk products in general, are therefore cultural in nature (Barrau 1983; Fischler 1990; Poulain 1997b).

It is, of course, impossible to create a fully comprehensive list of all the symbolic representations attached to milk in every civilization. However, we can highlight the huge variations in its status from culture to culture. While it is not considered suitable for consumption in China, North Vietnam or Cambodia, it is permitted, subject to certain restrictions, in the Jewish religion, highly valued in Western Christian societies, and has an almost sacred status in Hindu culture. Yet food historians have taught us that the status of milk also varies within the same culture over time. For example, milk and its by-products have not always belonged to the same categories in the Catholic distinction between "fat foods" and "lean foods" (Flandrin and Montanari 1996). In milk-consuming societies, milk and milk-based products form a particular family of foods. Products of animal origin that do not necessitate slaughter, they symbolize the continuity of life, and conjure up images of purity, innocence and vitality. Milk is seen as the drink of paradise in a large number of mythological systems.

4 A socio-anthropology of food: Aims and issues

A sociology, or to be more precise, a socio-anthropology of food, therefore focuses on the way in which cultures and societies inhabit and organize the liberated space left by the physiological functioning of the human digestive system, and by the methods used by man to exploit the resources provided by the natural environment, or those that can be produced within the biophysical and climatic conditions existing in the biotope. By entering that liberated zone, the social domain plays its part in constructing identities and in the socialization of the body. However, the socio-anthropology of food has an equal interest in the interactions that take place between the biological, ecological and social factors. For, through their ways of life and the techniques they implement, human communities shape both their own biological functioning and their natural environment. The purpose of the socio-anthropology of food is therefore to study the original nature of this "bio-anthropological" connection of a human group to its environment. Presented in these terms, the food social space and the representations of the imaginary on which it is based, is comparable not only to a "total social phenomenon" (Mauss), but to a "total human phenomenon," to quote Edgar Morin's happy turn of phrase (1973). From this perspective, dietary practices are no longer viewed as resulting from biological or ecological phenomena, and instead become one of the factors that form the basis of social organization. They are just as significant as sexuality or kinship, if not more so.

The socio-anthropology of food therefore fulfills a dual role. First, as its epistemological foundations have been established in the food social space, it is both a social science and, at the same time, it is open to an interdisciplinary perspective. This enables it to investigate connections between cultural and physiological factors on the one hand, and the natural environment on the other. Second, through the role it plays in structuring social organization, the food social space is situated at the intersection between the social and human sciences; in this way, it creates the conditions that facilitate the processing of socio-anthropological knowledge.

First, it presents a sociologically centered subject of study that has an autonomous dimension (the liberated space); in other words, it is compatible with a definition of the subject matter of sociology as autonomous. Second, as a concept, it lends itself to a perspective that takes account of disciplinary boundaries and of the interactions between biological and cultural factors. Finally, it highlights the multiple dimensions, the nested and layered character of the subject matter (Gurvitch), an approach particularly suitable for scale analysis.

As a conclusion: The call for constructivist positivism

The analysis of the movements occurring within the food social space (the delocalization and relocalization of foods, changes in eating practices, the development of obesity, the aggravated sense of crisis, and so on) highlights the fact that the biological need to eat and the expression of hunger are both shaped by society. It has freed us from simplistic debates reminiscent of "the chicken and the egg" question, in which biological factors are sometimes presented as superseding eating practices, while at other times cultural influence is seen as dominant.

Diet, including foods eaten in extreme circumstances such as illness or hospitalization, is always both socially constructed and biologically determined. Food consumption models have emerged as the result of a long series of interactions between social and biological factors, as a complex combination of various types of empirical knowledge. Consequently, an analysis of this subject is no longer justifiable solely in terms of a concern with preserving a heritage that reflects an era; it is motivated by a desire to understand the functioning and dynamics of a body of operational knowledge that enables human communities to establish themselves in their environment.

There are two possible sociological approaches to the subject of eating when it is presented as a "total human fact." The first respects the principle of the autonomous social fact, and focuses on its socially imposed dimensions. The second approach, faithful to the principle of the "total social fact," is open to dialogue with nutritional sciences and epidemiology. In this way, the theme of food challenges the epistemological division on which the discipline of sociology is based.

And yet, how might a dialogue with neighboring disciplines be achieved? Nutritional sciences are dominated by an etiological, empiricist, and positivist approach. From this perspective, theory is understood as the result of a series of laws obtained from the analysis of data that has been collected without an initial intellectual premise. The data is therefore seen as totally neutral and objective. The scientific work involved amounts to a particular manner of organizing this primary material obtained directly from real-life sources. Sociology originated from an epistemological context marked by positivism and the knowledge model deriving from the natural sciences, which presupposes the existence of a reality that researchers are responsible for discovering (Comte, Durkheim). From this perspective, the sociologist's primary task involves the objectification of social facts from which it is possible to develop general principles: laws that may be applied in a widespread context. Achieving a dialogue between the positivist fringe of sociology and epidemiology or nutritional sciences is a straightforward undertaking, as they share a number of founding premises; it falls within the tradition of social epidemiology, the seminal text of which is Durkheim's study of suicide.

Today, however, the discipline of sociology is largely dominated by a constructivist interpretation. According to this perspective, data collection involves not only the selection, but also the actual organization of real phenomena, processes largely over-determined by the theoretical framework within which the researcher operates. In its most radical versions, constructivism may lead to hyper relativism, in other words to a conception according to which reality itself dissolves in the methods used for its construction. In this case, the most important factor is no longer reality as such, but the methods used in order to examine, question, and construct it, and to give it meaning. As a result of its intercultural position, anthropology has played a very significant role in promoting this relativist perspective. The analysis of the methods used to construct descriptors partially calls into question the idea of neutral data. The development of a descriptor is always based on a theoretical perspective (even though this may well be implicit) and constitutes a type of forcible "takeover" of reality. For this reason, updating the processes involved in the construction of theoretical ideas based on data constitutes an essential axis of contemporary sociological research.

From a less radical perspective, despite the "constructed" dimension of descriptors, there is thought to be some resistance to reality. An empirical confrontation between research tools and the phenomena, which we should still term reality, often produces a few surprises. Indeed, there have been numerous discoveries to contradict the initial premises, which, however, were instrumental in separating subject matter and in developing the related issues and descriptors, thereby demonstrating that the object of study cannot be entirely reduced to the tools used in its construction.

The dialogue with nutritional sciences is governed by a dual perspective: the first accepts the positivist premise, and contributes to the objectification of food, while the second focuses on the different forms of knowledge acquired in relation to the subject of food—including sociological knowledge—in order to study the conditions in which they were constructed.

The study of the human eater requires clarifications from various disciplines: chemistry, biochemistry, microbiology, biology, physiology, psychology, psychoanalysis, sociology, ethnology, history, human geography, and economics. These specialist domains all have their own focus and methods, and operate according to a system that presents the functioning of contemporary science in a negative light. How can different disciplines be brought to communicate with each other when the researchers within these disciplines already have difficulty communicating among themselves? The increasingly complex nature of analytical research, hyperspecialization, and the divisions created between subjects are all contributing to the atomization of knowledge. Issues do indeed emerge within each discipline calling for input from the "owners of neighboring academic territories." However, the frameworks of reference in which these are presented rarely allow a response. Apart from the different conceptual tools that create the initial pitfalls, the various theoretical backgrounds of each discipline, which are often unalterable, cause seemingly shared notions to deviate in meaning, thereby hindering communication. One of the challenges facing the sociology of food consists of describing the social dimensions of dietary behavior in positive language. It is important that the sociology of food should contribute to the positivization of food-related subjects, all too often imperfectly analyzed because they have been imperfectly described. Description should be rehabilitated; it is a scientific endeavor, particularly with regard to a new domain—an attempt to organize reality. The objectification of practices constitutes the basis on which to initiate pluridisciplinary dialogue. Given its complexity, the task of objectifying the subject is of key importance, and of interest both within and outside the domain of sociology. From the disciplinary perspective, it is an essential stage in the confrontation and communication of different sociological paradigms that may be applied to eating practices. From the interdisciplinary perspective, it constitutes the initial basis for communication, not only with the so-called "hard" sciences, which are more accustomed to dealing with subjects on the basis of positive, or supposedly positive knowledge, but also with the other social and human sciences, such as economics, history or psychology.

However, the sociology of food also needs to develop an exterior perspective, focusing its attention on the scientific knowledge acquired in relation to food. Concepts only exist as elements of propositions; they are the heuristic instruments intended to clarify a concrete reality. It is, therefore, essential to highlight the socially constructed dimension of concepts used by science that "deal with" eating practices. In this way, the knowledge encompassed by these sciences and the manner in which it is acquired become the focus of a sociology of food sciences.

La Pampa—Toulouse, 1998—March 2001

New chapter: Food studies versus the socio-anthropology of the "food social fact"

The interest shown by the social and human sciences in the practices of food and eating developed almost simultaneously in the English- and French-speaking worlds. The early 2000s marked a turning point in the United States, where *food* and *eating* were introduced into the domain of cultural studies and became known as "food studies." At the same time, their relations with the social sciences were being consolidated in France, and, in a more nuanced fashion, in the United Kingdom. In this way, two scientific fields evolved in somewhat different manners.

The first proclaimed, with some enthusiasm, the birth of a "new" scientific territory (Macbeth and MacClancy 2004; Miller and Deutsch 2010; Koç, Sumner, and Winson 2012; Albala 2013), while the second developed its subject within the classic disciplinary structure, revisiting the fundamental epistemological frameworks (Poulain 2012; Warde 2016).

In order to analyze these two dynamics, we must first retrace the circumstances in which they emerged. This will involve examining the development of cultural studies; the works of Richard Hoggart and his successors, and their connections with French Theory in North American universities, played a significant role in this process. We will consider various scientific standpoints, forms of institutionalization and ways of connecting with social movements. Second, we will focus our attention on the development of food studies itself. We will conclude by endeavoring to identify its inner dynamics, and to single out the epistemological issues and practices that underlie these two competing viewpoints.

1 The emergence of cultural studies

A casual glance at the way in which a bookshop or a library is arranged clearly reveals that the English- and French-speaking worlds have taken different

approaches to the cultural disciplines. In France, while the sociology and
ethnology and anthropology sections are not the best stocked of all the social
and human science subjects, they still account for several linear meters of
shelving. In the majority of cases, they follow a dual system of organization,
being arranged first according to theme (the sociology of health, of education,
of the family, of work, of organizations, of social inequality, and so on), and the
second by author, with works by the leading lights in the domain lined up in
alphabetical order. According to this arrangement, the Studies are allocated a
few shelves in the middle of the themes section.

In the English-speaking world, works forming part of the Studies category
are spread out over a wide area, taking up several rows of shelving. They are
organized according to subject: Cultural Studies, American Studies, European
Studies, Gender Studies, Gay and Lesbian Studies, Postcolonial Studies,
Science Studies, Tourism Studies, Ethnic Studies, Food Studies and so forth.
The section devoted to sociology is more modest, however, and in some
instances it is even submerged in the social-science section, where it is not
unusual to find works on political science, or the biographies of politicians.

On closer inspection, a second difference emerges. While in France the
authors are almost invariably academics or members of research organizations,
across the Atlantic, books by authors with academic backgrounds stand side
by side with works by journalists and others who present themselves more
or less explicitly as activists. With the Study category, therefore, the English-
speaking academic world has established a scientific and editorial pattern
that facilitates the production and distribution of multidisciplinary knowledge,
linked to current developments and social issues.

A glance inside one of the books reveals another typical feature, as the
indexes of cultural studies publications are characterized by the strong
presence of French authors, philosophers, sociologists, and linguists, all
grouped under the heading "French Theory." They are all authors who, with the
clear exception of Michel Foucault, do not exert a particularly marked influence
on the social sciences in France today. Moreover, the alleged "theory" does
not relate to any specific aspect of the French academic system. How could
such a discrepancy have occurred?

1.1 The CCCS: A new look at popular cultures

An intellectual academic movement emerged in England during the 1960s,
and subsequently also developed in the United States. It gave rise to the
new domain of cultural studies, whose origins can be traced to the creation
of The Centre for Contemporary Cultural Studies (CCCS) in Birmingham in
1964. The movement was characterized both by a critical stance with regard

to the traditional perspectives of academic culture, and by an appreciation of popular cultures. *The Uses of Literacy: Aspects of Working Class Life, with Special References to Publications and Entertainments* by Richard Hoggart (1957), stands as a type of manifesto[1] for this approach, with its hybrid mix of content combining ethnology, sociology, and literature. The works of Raymond Williams (1958) and Stuart Hall (1964), are in the same vein. The aim was to study local cultures, discarding the principle of implicit hierarchies and the dominance of academic culture. This stance was characterized by its distance from both the canonical notion of culture and the Marxist conception, according to which it was simply an inverted reflection of the infrastructure of relations of production. The domain of cultural studies focuses less on the class conflict and more on the social and daily lives of communities. It is interested in subcultures, local, ethnic, and mass cultures, as well as those created and promoted by the media. In this way, it has initiated a debate on the very status of culture itself.

This pluridisciplinary approach experienced its first success in England, in the newly established polytechnics that had been created to absorb the demographic flux and the ensuing demands on higher education. For these vocational institutions, some of whose teaching staff were not connected with traditional disciplines, the new category of "studies" represented a way of achieving a certain academic legitimacy. This phenomenon became more marked with the establishment of the Open University, and with the emergence of new specialist publishers who promoted the movement (Mattelart and Neveu 1996).

1.2 *The United States and "French Theory"*

It was in the literature departments of American universities that the works produced by the CCCS received a positive reception. They were seen as a new addition to American cultures, characterized by a variety of migratory movements and the diversity of "native" cultures. In the late 1960s, the American literary milieu entertained close relations with successive groups of French intellectuals, among them philosophers, sociologists, and linguists, who were regularly invited to travel across the Atlantic in order to give lectures or to teach. They included Michel Foucault, Jean Baudrillard, Jacques Derrida, Louis Althusser, Gilles Deleuze, Roland Barthes, Jacques Lacan, Jean François Lyotard, Julia Kristeva, and Michel de Certeau, to name but a few. Some of their works were translated into English, and before long, that somewhat heterogeneous group representing the French perspective was categorized under the single heading: "French Theory." This became a central reference point within the movement. At this stage, literature departments played a major role in these developments, while the social sciences, rarely taking the initiative, jumped onto the bandwagon.

According to François Cusset (2003), the symposium held at John Hopkins University in the autumn of 1966 and entitled "The Language of Criticism and the Sciences of Man" was a pivotal event. Richard Macksey, then director of the Humanities Center, which oversaw the project, aimed to bring about a clearer understanding of the "structuralist" movement then at its height in Europe. However, the chief focus of this colloquium was on the potential offered by structuralism with regard to literary criticism. Around ten French intellectuals were invited to attend, among them Roland Barthes, Jean Pierre Vernant, René Girard, Jacques Lacan, Jean Hyppolyte, and Jacques Derrida. These authors, who did not know each other well, if indeed at all (as they moved in different French intellectual circles), subsequently produced discourses that reflected a critical distance from structuralism. This gave rise to the idea that academic thought was now oriented toward a "poststructuralist" perspective (Macksey 1970).

In order to analyze the reception of these authors in American academic circles, it is necessary to consider the context in which it occurred, and to examine the political and academic climate of the day.

The 1970s were characterized by a critical discourse concerning a counterculture that experienced its heyday in American universities during the Vietnam War and the hippy movement. The oil crisis and the economic recession blew the cold winds of pragmatism over American universities, causing the students' choices to become more utilitarian in nature and altering the power relationships between university departments.

Ronald Reagan's accession to the presidency in 1981 reinforced this phenomenon. In these circumstances, literature departments experienced a drop in applications. They were subsequently to find that the critical analysis of the major changes occurring in American society provided them with a strategic position enabling them to resist this competition. By preempting the study of topical issues in American society, they sought to propose an alternative to the pathways offered by the MBA and the Master's Degree in Law, which were more oriented toward the job market (Cusset 2002; Angermuller 2013).

From the American standpoint, the French intellectuals represented a subversive product. Foucault, Derrida, Barthes and other "poststructuralists" ignited their interest in "the ambivalent subject," in the focus on "the production of discourse" and in the critique of "logicentrism," ethnocentrism and "phallagocentrism." All these elements contributed to the restructuring of literary criticism. This collection of theories was to play a part in casting suspicion on the utilitarian and scientific ambitions of those in rival camps. These included the departments of human and social sciences, which found themselves somewhat distanced from developments. The set of arguments in question is based on two foundational principles. Suspicion of narrative: "it's only fiction, when all's said and done"; "it's all just based on a story," and suspicion relating to the "constructionist" perspective: "the meaning is fluid"; one could "deconstruct" a work or "reveal its construction process."

The connection between cultural studies and the world of French academia is partly based on a misunderstanding. The "poststructuralist" label, which is strongly evocative of Paris's fifth *arrondissement* is, in fact, simply an American invention. It is based both on the fame of Lévi-Straussian structuralism on the other side of the Atlantic, and on the promise of its being superseded.

In France, the output of those authors representing French Theory is far from constituting a coherent body of knowledge. Moreover, if some had attained a high level of renown in their native land before their works were exported to the United States, others owed a great deal of their recognition to renewed influence. Ultimately, with the exception of Foucault, their influence on academic circles in France, particularly with regard to the social and human sciences, was negligible after 1980. Many French universities kept their distance from cultural studies and from combinations of theories that were more or less suspected of maintaining a relativist stance. This critique is likewise evident in the United States; the Sokal affair provided a focal point for this view (Sokal and Bricmont 1998).

By comparing this context with that of France, we gain greater insight into the difference between the French and American schools of thought, which cannot be reduced to a question of a theoretical stance. The election to power of François Mitterrand and the political left brought very different winds of change to French university campuses. New posts were created. In 1985, contracted researchers were granted tenure, half of them being based at the National Center for Scientific Research (CNRS) and half at the universities. Significant demographic fluxes, combined with the challenges of finding employment and freedom of access to higher education, caused student numbers to rise. Many opted for disciplines with unrestricted intake, notably history, psychology, sociology, and geography, to the detriment of classics and humanities. The expanding disciplines of human and social science were in a position to call for a significant amount of new posts. And, despite invitations to embrace interdisciplinarity, the disciplines remained firmly within the boundaries of their own epistemological territories. Structuralism and interdisciplinarity became outmoded, and postmodernism, in the eyes of the vast majority of academics engaged in teaching and research, constituted an error of taste.

This study of the position on either side of the Atlantic highlights a phenomenon which might be described as an "epistemological continental drift." It shows how this more or less heterogeneous set of theories governing philosophical and sociological works was received and reorganized in order to serve the strategic stances of literature departments in the United States. It also shows how in France, the demographic flux and the government policy of supporting higher education contributed to strengthening the departments and disciplines of the social and human sciences. It explains how intellectual environments began to drift, how French philosophers became stars in the United States and disappeared from the radar in France, and how a disconnection occurred between cultural studies and the French social and human sciences. It likewise explains the critical distance maintained by a considerable proportion of the French academic milieu, which is rooted both in the academic criticism of the culturalist approach to anthropology, and in a universalist perspective with regard to the critique of multiculturalism. Finally, it explains the surprise of American readers, who no longer find that contemporary French works relate to the references listed as French Theory.

1.3 Cultural studies and its "Big Bang"

From the 1980s onward, the domain of cultural studies began to encompass the popular cultures of various regions of the world, with the emergence of European Studies, American Studies, Asian Studies, and so on, in addition to studies devoted to the reciprocal influences between East and West: "easternization" and "westernization" (Nair-Venugopal 2012). Phenomena that had hitherto remained in the shadow cast by academic cultures now became visible, and aspects of daily life took on particular significance. Michel de Certeau became a key author in this domain, with *L'Invention du quotidien* (*The Practice of Everyday Life*) (1980). Through that almost archeological act of highlighting "the simple things in life," food revealed itself as an omnipresent feature. However, it still remained a reference point related to weightier issues, such as identity and gender.

The "studies" expanded, following two principal routes: thematic and geographic. A transformation occurred in the epistemological status of the concept of identity, as essentialist interpretations disintegrated, resulting in a fragmented series of social and ethnic microidentities, social or gender-based categories, and so forth. In this way, the subject expanded into a number of different academic territories. With regard to gender issues, this gave impetus to the debate over feminine and masculine identities through the promotion of a constructionist stance in opposition to feminist essentialism (Butler 1990). This extended and refined the queer movement with the notion of "gender fluidity" and the concept of "performativity" borrowed from Jacques Derrida (Kosofsky Sedgwick 1991, 1995).

The discipline of postcolonial studies aims to unravel the cultural influences of the former colonial powers on the affirmations of identity expressed by the previously colonized populations. To achieve this end, it found in the works of Michel Foucault a means of analyzing the ambiguous dialectic of the relations between dominator and dominated. The influence of theoreticians of Creole identity in the Francophone Caribbean and on Reunion Island has been decisive with regard to this theme: Raphael Confiant, Aimé Césaire, Patrick Chamoiseau, Françoise Vergès, Albert Memmi, and Carpanin Marimoutou (Bernabé et al. 1989; Tibère 2016).

This theme of identity, presented in the plural, marks a break with different forms of essentialism and relates perfectly to the topical issues facing American society.

The growing importance of ecological issues as a framework of reference, coupled with the promotion of biodiversity, transformed the way in which regional cultures were viewed. Article 8 of the Convention on Biological Diversity, which opened for signature in Rio de Janeiro in 1992, states the need to "respect, preserve and maintain knowledge, innovations and practices of indigenous and local communities," and promotes the notion of "ethno-diversity." The globalization of the economy transformed perspectives and gave cultures a visibility and a new status that broke with the traditional vision of high culture, disconnected from economic and biological infrastructures.

Finally, the growing importance of cultural studies is also the result of the increasing emphasis on the production of cultural assets. "Whether in reference to a definition based on the idea of creativity (books, audiovisual products), on the transmission and application of knowledge (training, data processing) or on broader meanings (recreational activities, leisure, tourism), culture is playing an increasingly significant role in economic activity" (Mattelart and Neveu 1996).

The expansion of this academic territory initially took place in the English-speaking world, followed by Spanish and Portuguese-speaking countries. In the latter two cases, particularly in South America, where French culture enjoys a certain amount of influence, the connection with French Theory served as a selling point. At the same time, due to the hegemony of the English language and the power of the American universities, the French authors involved in this domain achieved international fame. Some of their work has become known thanks to English translations, or through collected texts ("readers"). However, it is unquestionably the success of Gender Studies that has done most to extend the movement, including, in this instance, to the French-speaking world.

Yet the most important characteristic of cultural studies as a movement is its connection with social trends, and the fact that it has created a space for the theorization and expression of radical approaches. In doing so, it has transformed the publishing world by establishing a domain for texts that stand halfway between academic works and investigative journalism. From the former category, these publications have retained a certain ambition as theoretical works, a referencing system and an on-campus presence, and from the latter, greater readability, educational content as appropriate, and access to the media.

2 From cultural studies to food studies

We will now examine the way in which food studies emerged and developed. It is always difficult to trace the earliest use of a term, but one of the first instances, if not the very first, seems to have been the collective work[2] edited by Elisabet Furst, Ritva Prättälä, Marianne Ekström, Lotte Holm, and Unni Kjaernes entitled *Palatable Worlds: Sociocultural Food Studies* (1991). The term was used on previous occasions, but in these cases it formed part of a very different perspective, being based on the study of *animal* diets (Roelofs 1954). This use of the term has now been replaced with the expression "animal nutrition."

The theme of food studies established itself in the English-speaking world during the decade from 2000 to 2010. It brought together various movements connected with food and diet that had emerged within the disciplines of social science and literature (Counihan and Siniscalchi 2014; Gardner 2013).

The progress made by food studies was also evident in the position it gained within the university system. This was initially achieved in the domain of teaching, through the creation of specialist qualifications at degree, postgraduate, and doctorate level, but also in the creation of minor diplomas offered in neighboring themes. It is likewise evident in the development of research groups, the establishment of university chairs, the creation of professional associations and academic societies, and the organization of seminars and congresses, in addition to the emergence of specialist scientific journals. Its success can be gauged by its media presence, through the publication of books for the academic world and the general public, TV programs, press articles, and social media (blogs and Facebook groups). Certain works, characterized by the unprecedented hybrid mix of a popularizing, journalistic approach, an activist perspective, and the objective of formulating the issues involved, became best-sellers (Pollan 2006, 2008; Schlosser 2001; Belasco 2006; Nestle 2002). There are many authors today in the United States, in both academic and nonacademic circles, who will recognize themselves in this description.

How does this movement connect to cultural studies? On what dynamics is it based?

2.1 *The progress of food studies*

The 1980s and 1990s were marked by a consolidation of the work related to food studies, culminating in a series of books and articles combining the historical, sociological, and anthropological perspectives (Fischler 1979, 1980, 1990; de Garine 1979, 1994; Goody 1982; Douglas 1984; Mennell 1985; Lambert 1987; Mennell, Murcott and Van Otterloo 1992; Harris and Ross 1987; Flandrin and Montanari 1996; Sobal 2000; Mintz and Du Bois 2002; Poulain 2002). The driving forces of the discipline originated from both the English- and French-speaking worlds, yet despite this, the theme had not yet gained strong academic legitimacy.

The development of food studies was concomitant with the social movements that converged on the subject of food in the late 1990s and early 2000s. These social movements were to create the conditions necessary in order to link the perspectives of the various domains concerned to the disciplinary matrix of cultural studies (Nestle and McIntosh 2012). Based more or less on the emergence of crises, most of these movements were established within a critique of the contemporary situation regarding the food supply, at the level of both production and commercialization. They were to play a part in changing the status of this issue, both within society and in the media. Academics then found that their analyses were the focus of public interest, campaigners consulted the available scientific journals, and journalists were spurred into action, turning now to the world of science, now to society.

While in France this situation reinforced disciplinary stances, and, to a lesser degree, interdisciplinary dialogue, in the United States and in parts of the English-speaking world, the disciplinary matrix of food studies increased in importance. The situation and standpoints in the United Kingdom are characterized by greater contrasts (Murcott, Belasco and Jackson 2013; Warde 2016).

Marion Nestle has listed no fewer than thirteen different food movements in the United States, including anti-GM crops, farm animal welfare, local food ("locavore"), pro-organic farming, anti-food distribution systems, anti-food marketing, pro-food labeling, and anti-fast food. Although they vary in their degree of organization and their radical stance, they have established power relations with decision makers in the economic and political world. The movements encompassing these issues, form "part of the long tradition of American grassroots democracy" (Nestle 2009). The climate of concern that prevails in developed societies and echoes these various "anti" movements is exacerbated by the issue of world hunger and the challenge of feeding a planet whose population is growing geometrically. The "Slow Food" organization is unique among these movements for its ethical, global, hedonistic, and ecologically responsible vision. Originating in Italy, it has established itself particularly successfully in certain countries, such as the United States,

Australia, and Brazil, and now numbers over 100,000 followers worldwide. Its fame in the United States is such that in 2008, *The Guardian* listed its founder, Carlo Petrini, as one of the fifty people who could save the planet. Likewise, converging on the theme of food studies are those movements that consider regional food cultures to form part of a heritage that should be preserved. Signs indicative of a more positive outlook are becoming equally apparent, such as the support shown for farmers' markets, and the chefs who devote themselves tirelessly to promoting a particular region, a way of viewing food, and of transmitting their vision.

The "dismantling" of a McDonald's restaurant by José Bové in France in 1999, played a key role in the reception of the sociology of food, and, more broadly, in the discourse of social science in relation to food. This reception has taken place in two ways: external, involving the worlds of politics, the media, and society, and internal, involving the academic world and entailing a transformation in the epistemological status of food and its increased academic legitimacy due to the studies produced on these questions.

The emergence of food studies, and its appropriation of disciplinary perspectives in the English-speaking world, was made possible by the contributions of cultural studies. These involved giving visibility to popular cultures and their food-related aspects, and transforming the epistemological status of the concept of identity, thanks to studies on gender and on the issue of postcolonialism. In this way, the interpretive framework of food studies connected with the disciplinary matrix.

2.2 *Institutional dynamics and domains of thematization*

In 2013, a seminar entitled "The Future of Food Studies: an Interdisciplinary Workshop" (FoFS), involving sixteen universities from the United States, the United Kingdom, Belgium and Italy, was held in Bloomington, Indiana (Hamada et al. 2015). It was revealed that food studies programs were characterized by "a great deal of heterogeneity in administrative structures, pedagogy and institutional context." Indeed, each program described represented something of a unique case. Overall, the workshop identified three main areas of study:

- Culture: literature, history, civilization
- Agronomy and nutrition, which in the American system are offered as subjects by "Land-Grant" universities that provide professional and technical qualifications
- The hotel, restaurant, and tourist sectors

TABLE 13 Master's degree programs in food studies and in the human and social sciences applied to the study of food

Host departments				
Sociology & anthropology	Agronomy & agriculture	History & geography	Hospitality & tourism	Nutrition
9	9	8	6	5

Language of instruction	
English	Not English
24	13

Geographical area			
Europe	North America	Asia-Pacific	South America
18	14	3	2

Title of master's degree	
Food studies	Other discipline
8	29

N = 37

By drawing up a systematic list of master's degree programs offering a pluridisciplinary approach to the study of food based mainly on the social and human sciences, we have been able to identify thirty-seven universities located in nineteen countries throughout the world (Table 13).[3]

In this way, we find that there are eight master's degree programs entitled "food studies," and some twenty-nine other programs with a different title. These involve a disciplinary or pluridisciplinary approach, rooted in the social sciences. With regard to geographical distribution, two main centers of activity may be identified: North America, with fourteen master's degree programs, and Europe with eighteen (Figure 10). In twenty-four of these cases, the language of instruction is English. This list confirms that the situation does indeed feature a "great deal of heterogeneity." It likewise shows that food studies coexists with other disciplinary domains, and that these are (still) largely dominant. But it is chiefly of interest as a basis on which to pursue the analysis initiated at the seminar in Bloomington.

In this way, after examining all the master's degree programs centered on the social sciences applied to food (which may or may not bear the title "Food Studies"), we can identify two main institutional approaches and five main forms of academic supervision.

The first approach involves departments with strong academic legitimacy, extending their range of food-related courses. In this way, the traditional academic departments offer degrees in new subject areas. Two core disciplinary frameworks have emerged: the departments of sociology, anthropology, and ethnology, and of history, geography, and literature, and civilization. These account for seventeen master's degree programs out of thirty-seven. The second approach involves food-related programs, established in departments with a pluridisciplinary stance, offering vocational degrees. These have appeared on the scene more recently, but none within departments that constitute the historic heart of the university. The emergence of these degree programs, which examine the social and cultural issues related to food, forms part of its enhanced legitimacy and academic recognition, through the links that have been forged with the human and social sciences. The departments involved are those of agriculture, hospitality, and tourism, in addition to nutrition studies; they account for twenty master's degree programs out of thirty-seven.

We will now review the five academic fields that have been identified. The departments involved are as follows:

1 Sociology-anthropology. This department offers nine master's degree courses. The academic legitimacy they enjoy today is due to the cumulative effects of the work carried out by three generations of researchers, and to the dynamics created by paradigmatic competition

(MacIntosh 1985). The application of two research methods, *quantitative* and *qualitative*, has enabled a dialogue to be established with the health sector (nutrition, public health, and epidemiology), disciplines that have long-standing links with sociology. Moreover, the tradition of rural sociology has associations with the world of agriculture and land management.

2   History and geography, sometimes in combination with civilization or linguistics. These departments offer eight master's degree programs in total. They benefit from the legitimacy of a time-honored discipline, and, in this case too, from a considerable body of important studies (Parasecoli and Scholliers 2012). They have a well-established dialogue with cultural industries such as the museum and heritage sectors.

3   Hospitality and catering, together with tourism, constitute the third domain in which food studies has developed, offering six master's degree programs. In this area, the subjects of gastronomy, food cultures, and interculturality are important from an operational standpoint. The influx of students into this sector is quite substantial in the case of the English-speaking world, as these university courses begin at first-year undergraduate level. In France, Switzerland, and Germany, however, they begin after the third year of the degree course. The existence of catering colleges, and in the case of Germany, the *Hochfachschule* should also be taken into account. In the English-speaking world, the hospitality sector is dominated at doctoral level by tourism studies, which developed very quickly in the wake of cultural studies. For a certain number of teachers, notably in the fields of gastronomy, the culinary arts, and restaurant management, the emergence of food studies constituted a pathway to recognition and to the development of research. A new field has also emerged as a result of the connection forged between tourism and food studies. This sector has a rising influx of students and links with professional circles.

4   Nutrition and public health offer five master's degree programs. The approach taken in this scientific sphere has for some time echoed that of the human and social sciences. However, the establishment of specialized master's degree courses in these departments is a recent phenomenon and reflects a certain change in frameworks of reference. Obesity has largely contributed to the development of this dialogue (Maurer and Sobal 1995; Poulain 2009; Saint Pol 2010). Although the human and social sciences now play a part in the interdisciplinary research conducted in this sector, the rationale governing professional integration is still influenced by thought patterns and practices characteristic of the public health domain.

5   Finally, the schools of agriculture and agronomy offer nine master's degree programs. These degrees are much more vocational in nature and have been established in areas governed by more positivist principles. They are often in the service of productivist agriculture, and focus on the global issues involved in production and questions of food security. These departments have long-standing connections with rural sociology and are engaged in examining the question of organizing production at different territorial levels, from regional development to the global system.

Global Food Studies: Language

Global Food Studies: "Food Studies" Mention

FIGURE 10 *Maps.*

In this way, we can identify five themes in relation to food studies, five academic domains within which connections with the subject are forged. Each of these constitutes an original portfolio of disciplines, of theoretical and social questions, of spheres of application and mediatization, and, finally, of forms of legitimization. The profiles of the academic staff that teach and carry out research within these programs, the origins of the students and their trajectories when they leave, are all somewhat different. Some courses are more oriented toward the world of academia, while others are geared toward work in the field and the professional environment. The quest is for academic recognition or for an audience. While this adds to an impression of heterogeneity, it also generates particular dynamics in each specific case.

3 The challenges of food studies

Research always involves investment at a dual level. It requires a profound knowledge of a discipline (sometimes several), with its paradigms, its theoretical frameworks and its methodologies; it then requires the acquisition of knowledge relating to specific subjects within that discipline, and on which the researcher plans to base their work. In the case of the social and human sciences, where there are a number of competing paradigms, these dual levels of specialization are contributing to the "babelization" of research, a phenomenon that makes communication challenging. Food studies has the advantage of providing a site for professional socialization and encounters between colleagues in different disciplines who share an engagement with the subject of food. This enables them to escape the isolated world of their research, where they sometimes have difficulty in finding interlocutors from their respective disciplines who are familiar with the empirical objects on which their activities are based. Moreover, the theme of food studies contributes to raising the collective profile of their territories. In this way, it acts as a banner offering a certain visibility to a fragmented domain within the university system.

The most obvious advantage presented by food studies is that it has redrawn epistemological divisions by creating a pluridisciplinary space that attracts researchers on either side of the "Great Wall of China" that separates the biological sciences from the human and social sciences. It lends itself to a multiplicity of combinations. These range from the most conventional, that is, associations with disciplines based on the human and social sciences such as economics, sociology, anthropology, psychosociology, and linguistics, to the most ambitious. The more ambitious categories encompass bold alliances made with nutrition studies, agronomy, genetics, and epidemiology on the one hand, and the sociology of food, political science, and anthropology on the other. The advances made in genetics and nutrition (nutrigenetics, nutrigenomics, and epigenetics) have opened new areas of cooperation liable to disturb the boundaries established by the Durkheimian perspective and the definition of the social fact as autonomous.

The domain of cultural studies occupies a unique epistemological position on the disciplinary chessboard. It constitutes a space where knowledge is produced, and also one in which the knowledge acquired outside its territory in the different disciplines relating to the social and human sciences is integrated. This particular situation, which encourages the adoption of pluridisciplinary perspectives, is liable to lead to two major stumbling blocks: the risk of encyclopedism and the risk of concepts originating from the classic disciplines of the human and social sciences being treated as mere instruments (or even as gadgets).

Indeed, in referring to the studies produced in several disciplinary domains within the human and social sciences, researchers are sometimes led to adopt almost encyclopedic theoretical frameworks. As the task of keeping up to date in such varied disciplinary fields is already highly challenging, their references do not always stay abreast of the advances made by specialists in a specific area. Moreover, reviews of related literature are all too often carried out on the basis of second-hand documents, or even text books. This type of work does have its uses, in that it presents the academic dimension of food studies to journalists, heads of companies or associations, and even to the educated public. However, it gives the various specialists in the human and social sciences curious impressions of extending over a continuum, ranging from the outdated charm of certain foundation courses in general culture, to the exotic experience of delivering a lecture on their "domain knowledge" to an audience of anthropologists. A food studies conference brings together researchers whose conceptual frameworks and methods are so dissimilar that they may sometimes be only laboring under the illusion that they understand each other. There is a considerable risk that the subjects in question will be treated in a purely superficial manner, and that a description of the diverse nature of cultural influence will be seen as a sufficiently suitable approach.

With the rise of food studies, the scientific community involved in this field faces the risk of a (partial) disconnection from the scientific issues relating to their disciplines. The multiparadigmatic character of the human and social sciences imposes considerable limitations on the export of concepts outside the epistemological contexts in which they were forged. This problem is further exacerbated when they are brought together within the more or less implicit framework of an approach to rationality in line with the rational choice theory which is largely dominant in the fields of marketing, management sciences, econometrics, and human nutrition. This has a certain compatibility with cognitive psychology, which provides insight into the way in which cognitive biases impact on rationality. However, linking it with sociological or anthropological concepts, forged in less related theoretical frameworks, has proved to be a much more hazardous enterprise—indeed, the operation is sometimes quite simply forced, or even illusory.

Cultural studies has found in the discipline of literary criticism a shared theoretical base, a space for epistemological integration. It is this type of space that food studies currently lacks. The subject is consequently in danger of floating between associations with a variety of other disciplines, and having no strong anchoring point. This could well explain why several departments have not taken this step, and prefer to base their work on specific disciplines.

An examination of the situation in France brings to light the long-standing coexistence of two opposing viewpoints. The French sociological tradition is characterized by a tension between a disciplinary perspective faithful to the Durkheimian definition of the social fact, and the Maussian conception of the total social fact. The former adheres more or less scrupulously to the notion of the social fact as autonomous, while the latter is established within the tradition inaugurated by Marcel Mauss, as part of the concept of the "techniques of the body," according to which the disciplinary boundaries between psychology and biology are characterized by a certain fluidity. From the Maussian perspective, therefore, it is necessary to establish a pluridisciplinary dialogue. The reflections on transdisciplinarity that took place during the 1970s and 1980s, inspired by the work of Edgar Morin (Morin, Piattelli-Palmarini et al. 1974), played a key role in developing the connections between the social sciences and the subject of food, with the appearance of some of the first theses on this theme (Poulain 2012b).

In this way, human eating practices may be presented as a "social fact" (Émile Durkheim), a "total social fact" (Marcel Mauss), and as a "total human fact" (Edgar Morin). These three definitions all share the same principle, this being that the act of eating amounts to much more than the biological infrastructure on which it is based. Moreover, each of the definitions, from the first to the third and with ever-increasing emphasis, highlights the vital importance of implementing an interdisciplinary dialogue. In the case of France, therefore, underlying claims that the discipline should be defined as the sociology of food, one finds approaches to the food social fact that center on sociology and socio-anthropology respectively. This entails a wide-ranging interdisciplinary dialogue.

The situation in the English-speaking world is also characterized by shades of difference. Although food studies has attained a respectable status in the United States, certain authors specializing in the subject of food have kept their distance from that label. This is the case with the leading figures in the area of cultural sociology (Inglis et al. 2008; Back et al. 2012). Moreover, there are rich veins to be mined within English sociology. Notable examples of these are the developmentalist movement, which extends the approach of Norbert Elias (Germov and Williams 1999) and connects with the anthropological perspective of Jack Goody, the sociology of consumption (Warde 1997; Holm 2012), and, finally, the sociology of the politics of food (Rayner and Lang 2012).

There is still work to be done in this domain with a view to establishing a set of theories, concepts, and methods; while these will not be common to all, they will enable more or less competing perspectives to be placed under the same classification. This task has been undertaken, as reflected in the recent publications in relation to methodology (Miller and Deutsch 2009; Murcott, Belasco, and Jackson 2013) and to theory (Poulain 2012; Albala 2013; Warde 2016). Fruitful encounters have also been established with gender studies (Fournier et al. 2015; Cairns and Johnston 2015), in addition to examples of the concrete implementation of interdisciplinary perspectives (MacClancy, Henry, and Macbeth 2009; Fischler 2013; Fournier and Poulain 2016).

This book is intended to make its own contribution, but it is doubtless too early to know whether it will be defined within the category of food studies, or as an example of the social sciences applied to food.

Kuala-Lumpur-Toulouse 2016

Notes

Introduction

1 See the successive research programs funded by the Ministry of Agriculture since 1990: *"Aliment 2000," "Aliment Demain," "Aliment-Qualité-Sécurité"* ("Food 2000," "Food Tomorrow," "Food-Quality-Safety"), within the framework of the fifth European Community Research and Development Programme. One of its main aims was defined as "focusing on and reinforcing the links between food and health."

Part 1 and Chapter 1

1 A term coined by Stella and Joël de Rosnay in the 1970s to describe excessively rich, over-processed food, and to promote healthy eating practices akin to vegetarianism, revisited by nutritional science studies.

2 The term "French paradox" refers to the fact that cardiovascular mortality stands at an astonishingly low rate in the country where the consumption of lipids, wine and alcohol in general is among the highest in the world (Renaud 1995).

3 See the preface to the book by Robert Habsch, 1992, *L'art de présenter les plats*, Lanore.

Chapter 2

1 John Turteltaub's film *Instinct*, based on the novel *Ishmael* by Daniel Quinn, is another exemplary account of the transformations that have occurred in the relationships between humans and animals.

2 See Chapter 4: "From Food Risks and Food Safety to Anxiety Management."

Chapter 3

1 Here Mermet reprises Herpin's interpretive model (1988).

2   We distinguished between the following with regard to the implementation
    of eating habits:Instances of food intake described as "meals"; these are
    highly institutionalized, that is to say, governed by fairly specific social rules
    concerning structure (as we have just examined) timing, location, social
    context, and ritualization.
        Food intake between meals; this is less highly institutionalized. "Food
    intake between meals" refers to "all ingestion of solid or liquid products
    capable of providing energy." This type of food consumption is subject to
    varying degrees of institutionalization, in other words, to the influence of
    social status and the rules of ritual that structure practices. In this case, the
    French language provides identifiers, such as *apéritif, goûter,* and *casse-
    croûte* (predinner drinks, teatime snack, light bite). They may equally be
    noninstitutionalized and fall within the general designation of grazing, for want
    of a more precise term. The consumption of cakes, fruit, fruit juice, or coffee
    with sugar, is counted as eating between meals, while the consumption
    of unsugared coffee or tea, and above all water, is not. The consumption of
    chewing gum and sweets was likewise excluded from the survey.

3   The composition of a meal tray was the result of a combination of four
    subgroups associated with the normal French meal: starter, main dish and
    accompaniments, cheese and dessert, and the frequency with which this
    was adopted. Over 127 different configurations of this format were identified
    in the sample studied. However, twenty-two of these accounted for 93.8
    percent of the trays. The criterion used was based on a meal composed of
    three elements, combining:

    • *an introduction*, comprising one or more starters,
    • *a central element*, comprising a main dish and/or accompaniments, and
    • *a concluding element*, comprising one or several desserts, or items
      serving as dessert, such as yogurt or cheese.

    Six types of meals could be distinguished from these results.

4   For the notion of balance in contemporary dietetic discourse now tends not
    to be confined to meals, but to encompass the combination of meals and
    between-meal intakes occurring throughout, or even beyond the day.

5   *Le Monde*, February 1999.

Chapter 4

1   In other words, this is the case in eight out of eighteen citizen
    conferences held in Denmark, and in nine out of nineteen conferences
    held elsewhere.

Chapter 5

1   The BMI, or Quételet index, from the name of the Belgian statistician and
    sociologist who first devised the system, corresponds to weight/height^2 (W/H^2).

In this index, weight is expressed in kg and height in meters squared. The WHO classification distinguishes the following categories:

Category	BMI value (kg/m2)
Underweight: level 3	<16.0
Underweight: level 2	16.0–16.9
Underweight: level 1	17.0–18.4
Underweight	<18.5
Normal weight	18.5–24.9
Overweight	>=25.0
Pre-obese	25.0–29.9
Obese: level 1	30.0–34.9
Obese: level 2	35.0–39.9
Obese: level 3	>=40

2 For a critical history of the method for calculating ideal weight, see Fischler 1990.

3 The proportion of proteins, lipids and carbohydrates in daily food intake.

4 This work links the development of gastronomy to sociocultural history, from the beginnings of prehistoric cooking.

Chapter 6

1 Léon Pales was Vice-Director of the Musée de l'Homme in 1950.

2 With the exception of Lévi-Strauss's analysis in the first chapters of *Elementary Structures of Kinship*, these works have been all but completely overlooked in France. Within the history of anthropology, Richards's best-remembered contribution is her work on matrilineal kinship, using the example of the Bemba peoples of former Rhodesia.

3 In 1996, on the initiative of the Ethnology Laboratory, the Musée de l'Homme organized an exhibition entitled "Histoires de Cuisines." Its structure was very largely based on the technical categories identified by Leroi-Gourhan. See the catalogue raisonné *Histoires de Cuisines*, Muséum National d'Histoire Naturelle, Paris, 1996.

4 Committee on Food Habits of the National Research Council, National Academy of Sciences.

5 On the history of the CFH, see: Guthe (1943) and Mead (1964) and the reedited French version of the *Manuel of Food Habits*, entitled *Écrits sur l'alimentation*, by Hubert and Poulain (2001).

6 This chapter was first published in the form of an article in 1945.

7 The French text, published in 1958, dates from 1956.

Chapter 7

1 In an introductory note to *La technologie science humaine*, Haudricourt relates the following anecdote: "Georges Friedmann asked me to produce a book on the subject of man and technology for a collection that he was editing for Gallimard. . . . it was rejected by Edgar Morin, who had succeeded Friedmann as editor of the series, for being insufficiently connected with sociology." The text subsequently found a place in the first volume of *Ethnologie générale*, entitled "La technologie," a series edited by Jean Poirier. This was also published by Gallimard (1968) as part of the *La Pléiade* collection.

Chapter 8

1 On the history of Engel's work, its links with empiricism and its various theoretical influences (Le Play, Ducpétiaux) see Herpin and Verger (1991).

2 Our emphasis.

3 See Part 1, Chapter 3, "The Evolution of Eating Practices."

4 In French, the term "*développementalisme*," together with "*créationnisme*," refers to a sub-division of evolutionism, which focuses on the origins of the human species and, above all, on the different stages of development through which the human race has to pass (Rivière 1978). The theoretical approach designated by the English term "developmentalist" does not refer to this "*développementalisme*," but is closer to Balandier's "dynamic sociology" (1971, 1988).

5 Until its recent rediscovery, sometimes labeled "the new sociology" (Corcuff 1995) or "constructivist sociology." This rediscovery began with the special issue of the review *Sociétés* entitled "Pour Elias" (1991–93). The second stage was marked by an issue of the *Cahiers internationaux de sociologie* (1995, vol. 99), which contained a lengthy round table discussion on "The work of Norbert Elias, its content, its reception," led by Wieviorka, with the participation of Burguière, Chartier, Farge and Vigarello, followed by a previously unpublished work by Elias himself, entitled *Sur le concept de vie quotidienne* (*On the concept of everyday life*. French translation by Javeau), in addition to some articles, notably one by Singly. Philippe Corcuff's "Les nouvelles sociologies" (1995) is likewise of interest. However, in the 1980s, the sociology of food, in the process of being established, made multiple references to Elias (Mennell 1985; Poulain 1985).

6 "La fourchette de Byzance" ("The Byzantine Fork"), November 26, 1973, reproduced in the new edition of *La civilisation des mœurs* in the Pluriel pocket edition collection, Hachette, 395–401.

7 It is this interest in the invariants of dietary behavior that would lead Mennell to categorize Fischler as a neostructuralist.

8 This is the epistemological stance of Western dietetics.

9 The perspective of gastronomy.

10 See Chapter 4, Part 1 of this work.

11 For a general presentation of cannibalism, see, for example, P. R. Sanday, 1986, *Divine Hunger: Cannibalism as a Cultural System*, Cambridge: Cambridge University Press, and for an account of the structures of the imaginary regulating cannibalism as a fundamental fantasy relating to consumption, see Pouillon (1972).

12 See the lithograph by Boilly (1761–1845), *Les Mangeurs d'Huîtres* [*The Oyster Eaters*] (1825), B. N. Paris.

13 Such as the cannibalism practised by the Tupinambá (Hans Staden 1979).

14 It should be remembered that Corbeau and Moulin were responsible for the creation of the first group of sociological research into food consumption, research committee, n°17, "*Sociologie et anthropologie de l'alimentation*" conducted by the Association Internationale des Sociologues de Langue Française in 1985.

15 Serge Clément, José Forne, Jean-Paul Gorge and Odile Saint-Raymond.

Chapter 10

1 According to Robert, the word first appeared in 1623. However, Courtine informs us that it alludes to the title of a lost work by the Ancient Greek Archestratus: "'Gastronomie' or 'Gastrologie,' the existence of which is known only from a quotation by the Greek poet Athenaeus in his 'Banquet of the Sophists'" (Courtine 1970).

2 For discussions on the role of spices in Medieval cooking, see Flandrin and Montanari (1996) and Poulain and Neirinck (2000).

3 The works by Soler (1973) and Daumas (1986) are recommended for those interested in further reading on the subject, as well as our own thesis (Poulain 1985), in particular the chapter entitled "Eléments pour une fantasmatique du culinaire."

4 The idea of a break made by Christian thought with preChristian conceptions of sacrifice was present in the emerging discipline of anthropology (Hubert and Mauss 1899). Yet at that time it formed part of an evolutionist ideology, which did not take account of the connections that remained.

5 This practice was not uniformly abandoned, and regional ethnological studies highlight cases of Communion still being celebrated with red wine and leavened bread, notably in Provence, see Topalov (1986).

6 It was to be the subject of five successive Councils.

7 In his epistle to the Corinthians, Saint Paul, addressing the newly formed church, states: "Now you are the body of Christ, and each one of you is a part of it."

8 For GDR's biography, see Rival (1983) and Poulain (1988).

Chapter 11

1 Most of these use animal subjects.

2 When the discipline was first founded, the need for an epistemological framework became evident, and it is to Trémolières and Claudian that we owe its presentation in anthropological terms (Trémolières 1977, 1989; Claudian and Trémolières 1978). Aron, in a highly allusory manner, engaged with the study of the historical representations that form the basis of nineteenth-century concepts of nutritional biology (J. P. Aron 1969).

3 On the theories behind sociobiological movements, see Forde, *Habitat, Economy, Society* (New York: Dutton and Co., 1963).

4 Our emphasis.

5 For further information concerning this concept of technology, see Haudricourt (1987).

6 Also known as the Jarai, this is a Proto-Indochinese ethnic minority. They belong to the Malayo-Polynesian group, and inhabit the provinces of Gia Lai, Kantum, and the Dac Lac region.

7 The fact that neither Hindus nor Muslims consume dog flesh shows that the rationale of proximity is not enough in itself to explain the prohibitions attached to this practice.

New chapter

1 The work was published in France in 1970 and edited by Pierre Bourdieu for the Editions de Minuit, with a preface by Jean Claude Passeron. See J. C. Passeron, 1993, "*Portrait de Richard Hoggart en sociologue,*" *Enquête.* [http://enquete.revues.org/175] Online as of May 12, 2006, consulted on July 16, 2015.

2 This work is the publication related to a scientific event entitled "Food, Symbols and Everyday Life" (1991) held during the First Nordic Symposium of Sociological Food Research, which took place in the Danish town of Gilleleje from September 10 to 12, 1990.

3 This is based on an overview of the situation in July 2015. Certain programs that had existed but were no longer active did not appear on the list. We are grateful to Kremlasen Naidoo, a research student registered in the MPhil Food Studies program at Taylor's Toulouse University Center, for his help in gathering information. The criterion for including a program on the list was that it should offer a pluridisciplinary course of study based on food and with

a strong focus on the human and social sciences. The research strategy consisted of a Google search using the keywords "food studies" and "master," then "food" and "social sciences." The search was then extended to the university websites of the authors who collaborated in producing the main food studies textbooks.

References

Adorno, T., 1938, "On the fetish-character in music and regression of listening," in A. Arato and E. Gebhart (Eds.), *The Essential Frankfurt School Reader*, Oxford, Blackwell, 1978, 270–99.

Aimez, P., 1979, "Psychopathologie de l'alimentation quotidienne," in *Communications*, Editions du Seuil, 31(1), 93–106.

Aimez, P., Guy-Grand, B., Le Barzic, M., and Bour, H., 1972, "Contrôle du comportement alimentaire. Rôle de l'environnement dans l'obésité humaine," *Revue du praticien*, 22(6), 805–21.

Albala, K., 2013, *Routledge International Handbook of Food Studies*, Abingdon, UK, Routledge.

Albert, J. P., 1991, "Le vin sans l'ivresse," in D. Fournier and S. D'Onofrio (Eds.), *Le Ferment Divin*, Paris, MSH.

Allon, N., 1981, "The Stigma of Overweight in Everyday Life," in B. Wolman (Ed.), *Psychological Aspects of Obesity: A Handbook*, New York, Van Nostrand Reihold, 130–74.

Amirou, R., 2000, *Imaginaire du tourisme culturel*, Paris, PUF.

Angermuller, J., 2013, *Analyse du discours poststructuraliste. Les voix du sujet dans le langage chez Lacan, Althusser, Foucault, Derrida et Sollers*, Limoges, France, Lambert Lucas.

Apfelbaum, M., 1994, "La diète prudente est-elle bien raisonnable?," in C. Fischler (Ed.), *Manger Magique: aliments sorciers, croyances comestibles*, Paris, Autrement – Série Mutations / Mangeurs no. 149, pp. 179–83.

Apfelbaum, M., Ed., 1998, *Risques et peurs alimentaires*, Paris, O. Jacob.

Apfelbaum, M. and Lepoutre, R., 1978, *Les mangeurs inégaux*, Paris, Stock.

Apfeldorfer, G., 2000, *Maigrir, c'est fou*, Paris, O. Jacob.

Arens, W., 1979, *The Man-Eating Myth: Anthropology and Anthropophagy*, United States and United Kingdom, Oxford University Press.

Ariès, P., 1997a, *La fin des mangeurs*, Paris, Desclée de Brouwer.

Ariès, P., 1997b, *Les fils de McDo, La McDonalisation du monde*, Paris, L'Harmattan.

Aron, J.-P., 1967, "Essai sur la sensibilité alimentaire à Paris, au 19ème siècle," *Cahiers des Annales*, n° 25, Paris, Colin.

Aron, J.-P., 1969, *Essais d'épistémologie biologique*, Paris, Bourgois.

Aron, J.-P., 1976, *Le mangeur du 19ème*, Paris, Laffont.

Aron, J.-P., 1984, *Les modernes*, Paris, Gallimard.

Aron, J.-P., 1987, "La tragédie de l'apparence à l'époque contemporaine," *Communications* n° 46, 306–13.

Aron, J.-P., 1997, "De la glaciation dans la culture en général et dans la cuisine en particulier," in *Cultures, Nourritures*, Internationale de l'imaginaire, Babel/Actes Sud, 13–37.

Arripe, M.-L., 1990, "Alimentation fin de siècle: permanences et stratégie, Monoprix," *Papiers du GRESE*, 7, PUM.

Attias-Donfut, C., Ed., 1995, *Les solidarités entre générations*, Paris, Nathan.

Aymard, M., 1997, "Les pratiques de l'alimentation carnée en France," *Le mangeur et l'animal, Autrement*, n°172, 87–102.

Aymard, M., Grignon, C., and Sabban, F., 1993, *Le temps de manger, Alimentation, emploi du temps et rythmes sociaux*, Paris, Éditions MSH-INRA.

Bachelard, G., 1950, "La formation de l'esprit scientifique," Paris, PUF. English translation 2002, *The Formation of the Scientific Mind: A Contribution to a Psychoanalysis of Objective Knowledge* by Mary McAllester Jones, Manchester, Clinamen.

Bachelard, G., 1957, *La poétique de l'espace*, Paris, PUF.

Bachelard, G., 2011, *Earth and Reveries of Repose: An Essay on Images of Interiority*, Mary McAllester Jones (trans.), Dallas, Dallas Institute Publications, The Dallas Institute of Humanities and Culture.

Back, L., Bennett, A., Desfor Edles, L., Gibson, M., Inglis, D., Jacobs, R., and Woodward, I., 2012, *Cultural Sociology: An Introduction*, Oxford, Wiley Blackwell.

Bages, R., 1995, "Permanences et innovations dans l'alimentation paysanne: du repas quotidien au menu de fête," in N. Eizner (Ed.), *Voyage en alimentation*, Paris, ARF éditions.

Bages, R. and Rieu, A., 1988, "Spécificité du mode d'approvisionnement alimentaire des agriculteurs," *Ethnologie française*, XVIII, 358–65.

Bahloul, J., 1983, *Le culte de la table dressée. Rites et traditions de la table juive algérienne*, Paris, Métaillé.

Baker, J., 1984, "The rehabilitation act of 1973: protection for victims of weight discrimination?," *UCLA Law Review*, 29, 947–71.

Balandier, G., 1971, *Sens et puissance*, Paris, PUF.

Balandier, G., Ed., 1983, "Sociologie des quotidiennetés," in *Cahiers Internationaux de Sociologie*, vol. LXXIV, Paris, PUF.

Balandier, G., 1988, *Le désordre*, Paris, Fayard.

Baré, J.-F., 1991, "Acculturation," in P. Bonte and M. Izard (Eds.), *Dictionnaire de l'ethnologie et de l'anthropologie*, Paris, PUF.

Barrau, J., 1974, "Écosystèmes, civilisations et sociétés humaines: le point de vue d'un naturaliste," *Information sur les sciences sociales*, 14(1), 21–34.

Barrau, J., 1983, *Les hommes et leurs aliments. Esquisse d'une histoire écologique et ethnologique de l'alimentation*, Paris, Temps actuels.

Barrau, J., 1991, "Les hommes dans la nature" et "L'homme et le végétal," in J. Poirier (Ed.), *Histoire des mœurs*, Paris, La Pléiade, Gallimard.

Barthes, R., 1957, *Mythologies*, Paris, Seuil.

Barthes, R., 1975, "Lecture de Brillat-Savarin," in J. A. Brillat-Savarin (Ed.), *La physiologie du goût*, Reprint, Herman.

Barthes, R., 1979, "Towards a Psychosociology of Contemporary Food Consumption," in R. Forster and O. Ranum (Eds.), *Food and Drink in History: Selections from the Annales*, E. Forster and P. M. Ranum, trans., Baltimore, Johns Hopkins University Press.

Basdevant, A., 1998, "Séméiologie et clinique de la restriction alimentaire," *Cahiers de Nutrition et de Diététique*, 33(4), 235–41.

Basdevant, A. and Benkimoun, P., 1999, "L'obésité, une maladie du mode de vie mal tolérée par la société," *Le Monde*, 20–21 June 1999.

Basdevant, A., Barzic le, M., and Guy-Grand, B., 1993, *Les obésités*, Paris, Ardix Médical.

Basdevant, A., Laville, M., and Ziegler, O., 1998, "Recommandations pour le diagnostic, la prévention et le traitement de l'obésité," *Cahiers de Nutrition et de Diététique*, 33(sup. 1), 1–148.

Bastide, R., 1958, "Problèmes de l'entrecroisement des civilisations et de leurs œuvres," in G. Gurvitch (Ed.), *Traité de sociologie*, Paris PUF.

Bastide, R., 1960, *Les religions africaines au Brésil*, Paris, PUF.

Bataille-Benguigui, M.-C., 1996, "L'ordinaire et l'exception dans l'alimentation au royaume Tonga. (Polynésie occidentale)," in M.-C. Bataille-Benguigui and F. Cousin (Eds.), *Cuisines, reflets des sociétés*, Sépia, Musée de l'homme.

Baudelot, C. and Establet, R., 1984, *Durkheim et le suicide*, Paris, PUF.

Bauman, Z., 1990, *Thinking Sociologically*, Oxford, Blackwell.

Beardsworth, A., 1990, "Trans-science and moral panics: understanding food scares," *British Food Journal*, 92(5), 11–16.

Beardsworth, A., 1995, "The management of food ambivalence: erosion or reconstruction?," in D. Maurer and J. Sobal (Eds.), *Eating Agendas: Food and Nutrition as Social Problems*, New York, Aldine de Gruyter.

Beardsworth, A. and Keil, E. T., 1992, "The vegetarian option: varieties, conversions, motives and careers," *The Sociological Review*, 40(2), 253–93.

Beardsworth, A. and Keil, E. T., 1997, *Sociology on the Menu: An invitation to the Study of Food and Society*, London, Routledge.

Beauvilliers, A., 1814, *L'art du cuisinier*, Reprint Morcrettes.

Beck, B., 2000, "Comportement alimentaire et facteurs nutritionnels précoces," in *Obésité dépistage et prévention chez l'enfant*, Paris, Les Editions INSERM, 131–63.

Beck, U., 1992, *Risk Society: Towards a New Modernity*, London, Sage, English translation by Risko Gesellschaft, Suhrkamp, 1986.

Becker, G. S., 1965, "A theory of the allocation of time," *Economic Journal*, 75, 493–517.

Belasco, W. J., 2006, *Meals to Come: A History of the Future of Food*, Berkeley, USA, University of California Press.

Bellisle, F., 1992, "Rôle et mécanismes de l'apprentissage dans les goûts et les conduites alimentaires," in I. Giachetti (Ed.), *Plaisir et préférences alimentaires*, Paris, Polytechnica.

Bellisle, F., 1999, *Le comportement alimentaire humain. Approche scientifique*, Monographie chaire Danone, Brussels, Danone.

Bellisle, F., McDevitt, R., and Prentice, A. M., 1977, "Meal frequency and energy balance," *British Journal of Nutrition*, 77(Sup. 1), 57–70.

Benedict, R., 1946, *Patterns of Culture*, New York, Mentor Books.

Bennassar, B. and Goy, J., 1975, "Contribution à l'histoire de la consommation alimentaire du XIVe au XIXe siècle," Annales, *E.S.C.*, 30(2), 402–30.

Benoit, J., 1991, "Anthropologie biologique," in P. Bonte and M. Izard (Eds.), *Dictionnaire de l'ethnologie et de l'anthropologie*, Paris, PUF.

Benson, P. L., Severs, D., Tatgenhorst, J., and Loddengaard, N., 1980, "The social costs of obesity: A non-reactive field study," *Social Behaviour and Personality*, 8(1), 91–96.

Berchoux, J., 1800, *La gastronomie ou l'homme des champs à table*, Paris, Giguet.

Berger, P. and Luckmann, T., 1966, *La construction sociale de la réalité*, French translation 1986, Paris, Méridien-Klincksieck.

Bernabé, J., Chamoiseau, P., and Confiant, R., 1989, *Éloge de la créolité*, Paris, Gallimard.

Berthelot, J.-M., 1982, "Une sociologie du corps a-t-elle un sens?," *Recherches Sociologiques*, XIII, n° 1 and 2, Louvain-La Neuve.

Berthelot, J.-M., 1983, "Corps et société," in *Cahiers Internationaux de Sociologie*, vol. LXXIV, Paris, PUF.

Berthelot, J.-M., 1990, *L'intelligence du social*, Paris, PUF.

Berthelot, J.-M., 1996, *Les vertus de l'incertitude*, Paris, PUF.

Berthelot, J.-M., 1997, "Le retour au(x) texte(s)," in C.-H. Cuin (Ed.), *Durkheim d'un siècle à l'autre. Lectures actuelles des Règles de la méthode scientifique*, Paris, PUF.

Berthelot, J.-M., 2000, *La sociologie française contemporaine*, Paris, PUF.

Besnard, 1987, *L'anomie, ses usages et ses fonctions dans la discipline sociologique depuis Durkheim*, Paris, PUF.

Bessière, J., 2000, *Valorisation du patrimoine gastronomique et dynamiques de développement territorial, Le haut plateau de l'Aubrac, le pays de Roquefort et le Périgord Noir*, Sociology thesis, Université de Toulouse Le Mirail.

Best, J., Ed., 1989, *Images of Issues: Typifying Contemporary Social Problems*, New York, Aldine de Gruyter.

Blixen-Finecke, von K., 1961, *Le Dîner de Babette*, Paris, Gallimard.

Bloch, F. and Buisson, M., 1991, "Du don à la dette: construction du lien social familial," *Revue du Mauss*, 11, 54–71.

Bloch, M., 1954, "L'alimentation de l'ancienne France," in L. Febvre (Ed.), *L'encyclopédie française*, vol. XIV, Paris, Société de l'Encyclopédie française.

Blumberg, P. and Mellis, L. P., 1985, "Medical students' attitudes towards the obese and morbidly obese," *International Journal of Eating Disorders*, 4(2), 169–75.

Bonnefons (de), N., 1654, *Les délices de la campagne*, Paris.

Bonnet, J. C., 1976, "Le réseau culinaire dans l'encyclopédie," *Annales ESC*, 31, n° 5.

Bonnet, J. C., 1978, "Présentation de . . . ," *Écrits gastronomiques de Grimod de la Reynière*, Paris, 10/18.

Bonnet, J. C., 1983, "Le vin des philosophes," in Max Milner and Martine Chatelain (Eds.), *L'imaginaire du vin: Colloque pluridisciplinaire*, Marseille, Jeanne Laffite.

Bonte, P. and Izard, M., 1991, *Dictionnaire de l'ethnologie et de l'anthropologie*, Paris, PUF.

Borie, C., Prado, V., Rios, M. et al., 1999, "Clonal diversity of Chilean isolates of enterohemorrhagic *Escherichia coli* from patients with hemolytic-uremic syndrome, asymptomatic subjects, animal reservoirs, and food products", *Journal of Clinical Microbiology*, 37, 778–81.

Borillo, M. and Sauvageot, A., 1996, *Les cinq sens de la création*, Paris, Champ Vallon.

Bott, E., 1971, *Family and Social Network*, London: Tavistock Press.

Boudon, R. *Dictionnaire de la sociologie*, Larousse.

Boudon, R. and Bourricaud, F., 1982, *Dictionnaire critique de la Sociologie*, Paris, PUF.

Bourdieu, P., 1979, *La Distinction: Critique sociale du jugement*, Paris, les Editions du Minuit.

Bourdieu, P., 1984, *Distinction: A Social Critique of the Judgement of Taste*, Richard Nice (trans.), Cambridge, MA, Harvard University Press.

Bourdieu, P. and de Saint-Martin, M., 1976, "Anatomie du goût," *Actes de la recherche en sciences sociales*, 2(5), October, 2–81.

Bourrec, J.-R., 1983, *La Gascogne gourmande*, Toulouse, Privat.

Boutaud, J.-J., Ed., 1997a, "Images du goût," *Champs visuels*, n° 5, L'Harmattan.

Boutaud, J.-J., 1997b, "Sémiotique de la représentation visuelle du goût," *Champs visuels*, L'Harmattan, 5, 52–63.

Bouvier, A., 2000, "La connaissance et la science," in J.-M. Berthelot (Ed.), *La sociologie française contemporaine*, Paris, PUF.

Boy, D., Donnet-Kamel, D., and Roqueplo, P., 1998, "France: Genetically Modified Foods", A Report on the "Citizens Conference" on Genetically Modified Foods, France, June 21–22, 1998, Amherst, MA, The Loka Institute.

Bras, M., 1992, *La cuisine de Michel Bras*, Editions du Rouergue.

Braudel, F., 1961, "Vie matérielle et comportements biologiques," *Annales ESC*, 196, 545–48.

Braudel, F., 1979, *Civilisation matérielle, économie et capitalisme*, 15–18ème siècle, Armand Colin.

Brillat Savarin, A., 1824, *La physiologie du goût*, Réédition Herman, 1975.

Brown, P. J. and Konner, M., 1987, "An anthropological perspective of obesity," *Annals of the New York Academy of Sciences*, 499, 29–46.

Brunel, S., 1997, *Ceux qui vont mourir de faim*, Paris, Seuil.

Brunel, S. and Léonard, Y., Eds., 1996, *Les problèmes alimentaires dans le monde*, Cahiers français, n° 278, La documentation française.

Brunhes, J., 1942, *La géographie humaine*, abridged version, PUF, Paris.

Burgat, F., 1997, *La protection de l'animal*, Paris, PUF.

Burgat, F. and Dantzer, R., 1997, "Une nouvelle préoccupation: le bien-être animal," in M. Paillat (Ed.), *Le Mangeur et l'animal. Mutations de l'élevage et de la consommation*, Paris, Autrement, 69–86, coll. Mutations/Mangeurs, no. 172.

Burguière, A., Chartier, R., Farge, A., Vigarello, G., and Wieviorka, M., 1998, "The Works of Norbert Elias: Its Content and its Reception," in Fuyuki Kurasawa (trans.), *Thesis Eleven*, No. 54, SAGE Publications and Thesis Eleven Pty Ltd.

Butler, J., 1990, *Gender Trouble: Feminism and the Subversion of Identity*, New York: Routledge.

Cahnman, W. J., 1968, "The stigma of obesity," *Sociological Quarterly*, 9(3), 283–99.

Cairns, K. and Johnston, J., 2015, *Food and Femininity. Contemporary Food Studies: Economy, Culture and Politics*. London: Bloomsbury.

Callon, M., 1998, "Des différentes formes de démocratie technique," *Annales des Mines, Responsabilité et environnement*, 9, 63–72.

Callon, M. and Latour, B., 1991, *La science telle qu'elle se fait: anthologie de la sociologie des sciences de langue anglaise*, Paris, Edition la découverte.

Calvo, M., 1980, "De la contribution actuelle des sciences sociales et humaines à la connaissance de l'alimentation," *Ethnologie Française*, X(3), 335–52.

Calvo, M., 1982, "Migration et Alimentation," *Information sur les Sciences Sociales*, 21(3), 383–446.

Canning, H. and Mayer, J., 1966, "Obesity- Its Possible Effect on College Acceptance," *New England Journal of Medicine*, 275, 1172–74.

Capatti, A., 1989, *Le goût du nouveau. Origines de la modernité alimentaire*, Paris, Albin Michel.

Carême, A., 1833, *L'art de la cuisine Française au XIXème siècle*, Paris, Imprimerie de Guiraudet.

Cazes-Valette, G., 1997, "La vache folle," *Culture Nourritures, Internationale de l'imaginaire* n° 7, Babel Actes Sud, 205–33.

Certeau, M. de., 1980, *L'Invention du quotidien, 1. : Arts de faire* and *2. : Habiter, cuisiner*, with Luce Giard, Paris, France, Gallimard.

Certeau, M. de, Giard, L., and Mayol, P., 1980, *L'invention du quotidien*, tome 2: *Habiter, cuisiner*, Paris, Gallimard, Folio, 1994.

Champagne, P., 2000, "L'affaire de la 'vache folle' (ESB): les nouveaux risques de santé publique et leur gestion," in A. Garrigou (Ed.), *La santé dans tous ses états*, Biarritz, Atlantica.

Chang, K. C., Ed., 1977, *Food in Chinese Culture: Anthropological and Historical Perspectives*, London, Yale University Press.

Charles, M. A., 2000, "Prévalence de l'obésité chez l'enfant," in *Obésité, dépistage et prévention chez l'enfant*, Expertise collective, Paris, INSERM, 17–27.

Charles, N. and Kerr, M., 1998, *Women, Food and Families*, Manchester, Manchester University Press.

Châteauraynaud, F. and Torny, D., 1999, *Les sombres précurseurs, une sociologie pragmatique de l'alerte et du risque*, Paris, Editions EHESS.

Chatelet, N., 1977, *Le corps à corps culinaire*, Paris, Seuil.

Chaudenson, R., 1979, *Les créoles français*, Paris, Nathan.

Chaudron, M., 1983, "Heur et malheur de la cuisinière," *Les temps modernes*, 1349–59.

Chaudron, M., Sluys, C., and Zaidman, C., 1990, "Activité professionnelle et cuisine au quotidien," GRES Working Paper n° 7, Université de Toulouse le Mirail.

Chaudron, M., Sluys, C., and Zaidman, C., 1995, "Pratiques culinaires et organisation domestique," in N. Eizner (Ed.), *Voyage en alimentation*, Paris, ARF éditions.

Chérubini, B., 1992, "Du métissage généralisé à la contre-culture: le cheminement de l'être antillo-guyanais," in J.-L. Alber, C. Bavoux, and M. Watin (Eds.), *Métissages, Linguistique et Anthropologie*, vol. 2, Paris, L'Harmattan, 277–94.

Chesnais, J.-C., 1986, *La transition démographique, étapes, formes, implications économiques: études des séries temporelles (1720-1984) relatives à 67 pays*, Paris, PUF/INED.

Chevassus-au-Louis, B., 2001, "Quatre attitudes face aux controverses," in *La Recherche*, special issue, *Le risque alimentaire*, 82–85.

Chippaux, C., 1990, "Des mutilations, déformations, tatouages rituels et intentionnels chez l'homme," in J. Poirier (Ed.), *Histoire des mœurs*, Paris, Gallimard.

Chiva, M., 1985, *Le doux et l'amer*, Paris, PUF.

Chiva, M., 1996, "Le mangeur et le mangé: la subtile complexité," in Giachetti Ismène (Ed.), *Identités des mangeurs, images des aliments*, Paris, Polytechnica, 11–30.

Chiva, M., 1997, "Cultural aspects of meals and meal frequency," *British Journal of Nutrition*, 77(sup.1), 21–28.

Chiva, M. and Roux, C., 1997, *Tendances comportementales et attitudes envers l'alimentation d'une population de consommateurs à bas revenus*, Ministry of l'Agriculture, "Food Tomorrow" program.

Chombart de Lauwe, P.-H., 1956, *La vie quotidienne des familles ouvrières*, Paris, CNRS.

Chombart de Lauwe, P.-H., 1969, *Pour une sociologie des aspirations*, Paris, Gonthier Denoël.

Chombart de Lauwe, P.-H., 1981, *Transformations sociales et dynamique culturelle*, Paris, CNRS.

Claudian, J., 1982, "Quelques réflexions sur les inquiétudes alimentaires de notre temps," *Cahiers de Nutrition et de Diététique*, 16(4), 165–66.

Claudian, J. and Trémolières, J., 1978, "Psychologie de l'alimentation," *Encyclopédie L'univers de la psychologie*, Paris, Lidis, vol. 5, 67–97.

Claudian, J., Serville, Y. and Trémolières, F., 1969, "Enquête sur les facteurs de choix des aliments," *Bulletin de l'INSERM*, 24(5), 1277–1390.

Clavel, J., Ed., 1989 (2nd ed. 1990), *Vins et cuisine de terroir en Languedoc*, Toulouse, Privat.

Clément, S., 1990, "Les restaurants à Toulouse," in J.-R. Pitte and A. Huetz de Lemps (Eds.), *Les restaurants dans le monde et à travers les âges*, Grenoble, Glénant.

Clément, S. and Megdich, C., 1987, "La distribution des restaurants dans le centre de Toulouse," *Revue géographique des Pyrénées et du Sud-Ouest*, n° 3, 58.

Cobbi, J., 1981, *La vie alimentaire des Japonais, son évolution récente*, doctoral thesis, Department of Ethnology, Université de Paris X.

Cochoy, F., 1999, *Une histoire du marketing*, Paris, La Découverte.

Cohen, P., 1993, *La réunion, une île entre nourriture et nourritures: Approche anthropologique et bio culturelle de l'alimentation*, thesis, Department of Anthropology, Université d'Aix-Marseille 3.

Cohen, P., 1998, "Un champ urbain de l'alimentaire: *La vente des produits liés au souci du corps et de la santé*," *Journal des anthropologues*, 74, 29–46.

Cohen, P., 2000, *Le cari partagé. Anthropologie de l'alimentation à l'île de la Réunion*, Paris, Karthala.

Combris, P., 1980, "Les grands traits de l'évolution de la consommation alimentaire en France 1956-1976," *Académie d'agriculture de France*, 12, 1273–84.

Combris, P., 1995, "La consommation alimentaire en France de 1949 à 1988: continuité et ruptures," in N. Eizner (Ed.), *Voyage en alimentation*, Paris: ARF éditions.

Combris, P., 1996, "Mangeurs et aliments: que nous apprend l'analyse économique?," in I. Giachetti, *Identités des mangeurs, images des aliments*, Paris, Polytechnica, 91–122.

Combris, P. and Volatier, J.-L., 1998, "Evolution des consommations et des comportements alimentaires," *Lettre Scientifique de l'Institut Français pour la Nutrition*, 56, 1–12.

Condominas, G., 1954, *Nous avons mangé la forêt*, Paris, Mercure de France.

Condominas, G., 1965, *L'exotique est quotidien*, Paris, Plon.

Condominas, G., 1972, "Marcel Mauss et l'homme de terrain," *L'Arc*, n° 48.

Condominas, G., 1980, *L'espace social à propos de l'Asie du Sud-Est*, Paris, Flammarion.

Condominas, G., 1994, "Sauvegarde et promotion du patrimoine culturel immatériel des groupes minoritaires du Viêt-Nam," *Les Études Vietnamiennes*, new series, n° 42 (112), Hanoi.

Condominas, G., 1997a, "Les pratiques alimentaires: un patrimoine culturel à sauvegarder," in *Pratiques alimentaires et identités culturelles, Les études vietnamiennes*, n° 125 et 126, Hanoi, 21–30.

Conrad, P., 1992, "Medicalization and Social Control," *Annual Review of Sociology*, 18, 209–32.

Conrad, P. and Schneider, J. W., 1992, *Deviance and Medicalization: from Badness to Sickness*, Philadelphia: Temple University Press.

Corbeau, J.-P., 1986, "L'avaleur n'attends pas le nombre des années, ou l'éducation alimentaire," *Les Cahiers de l'IFOREP*, n° 49.

Corbeau, J.-P., 1991, *Essai de reconstruction utopique des formes et des jeux du manger*, Doctoral Thesis in Sociology, supervised by J. Duvignaud, to be published as Le mangeur imaginaire, Métaillé.

Corbeau, J.-P., 1992, "Rituels alimentaires et mutations sociales," *Cahiers internationaux de sociologie*, vol. XCII, PUF.

Corbeau, J.-P., 1994a, "Le manger, lieu de socialité. Quelles formes de partage pour quels types d'aliments?," *Prévenir*, n° 26, 203–17.

Corbeau, J.-P., 1994b, "Goût des sages, sages dégoûts, métissage des goûts, in *Le métis culturel, International de l'imaginaire*, n° 1, Paris, Babel/Actes Sud, 164–82.

Corbeau, J.-P., 1995, "L'imaginaire du gras associé à divers types de consommation de gras et les perceptions de leurs qualités," in F. Nicolaïs et E. Valceschini (Eds.), *Agro-alimentaire: une économie de la qualité*, Paris, Éditions INRA-Economica.

Corbeau, J.-P., 1996, "De la présentation dramatisée des aliments à la représentation de leur consommateurs," in I. Giachetti (Ed.), *Identités des mangeurs, images des aliments*, Paris: Polytechnica, 174–98.

Corbeau, J.-P., 1997a, "Socialité, sociabilité et sauce toujours," in *Cultures, Nourritures*, Internationale de l'imaginaire, Babel-Actes Sud, 69–81.

Corbeau, J.-P., 1997b, "Pour une représentation sociologique du mangeur," *Économies et Sociétés*, Développement agro-alimentaire, 23, 147–62.

Corbeau, J.-P., 1997c, "L'exotisme au service de l'égotisme. Nourritures vietnamiennes et métissages des goûts français," in *Pratiques alimentaires et identités culturelles Les études vietnamiennes*, n° 125 and 126, Hanoi, 323–45.

Corbin, A., Ed., 1995, *L'Avènement des loisirs, 1850-1960*, Paris, Aubier.

Corcuff, P., 1995, *Les nouvelles sociologies*, Paris, Nathan.

Counihan, C. and Siniscalchi, V., 2014, *Food activism, Agency, Democracy and Economy*, London, UK, Bloomsbury.

Courtine, R. J., 1970, *La Gastronomie*, Paris, PUF.

Cousin, F., 1996, "catalogue résumé de l'exposition," *Histoires de Cuisines*, Muséum National d'Histoire Naturelle.

Cramer, P. and Steinwert, T., 1998, "Thin is good, fat is bad: *how early does it begin?*," *Journal of Applied Developmental Psychology*, 19, 429–51.

Croze Austin de, 1933, *La psychologie de la table*, Paris, Au sans pareil.

Csergo, J., 1996, "L'émergence des cuisines régionales," in J.-L. Flandrin and M. Montanari (Eds.), *Histoire de l'alimentation*, Paris, Fayard, 823–41.

Cuin, Ch., 1993, *Les sociologues et la mobilité sociale*, Paris, PUF.

Cuisenier, J., 1991, *Ethnologie de l'Europe*, Paris, PUF.

Cuisenier, J., 1995, *La tradition populaire*, Paris, PUF.

Cuisinier, J., 1948, *Les Muong*, Institut d'ethnologie, Musée de l'Homme.

Cuisenier, J. and Segalen, M., 1986, *Ethnologie de la France*, Paris, PUF.

Cusset, F., 2003, *French Theory, Foucault, Derrida, Deleuze & Cie et les mutations de la vie intellectuelle aux États-Unis*, Paris, France, La Découverte.

Daumas, J. M., 1986, "La cène dans la conception de l'église réformée," in Rencontres de l'École du Louvre, *La table et le partage,* Paris, La documentation Française.

Davis, D. M., 1795, *The Cases of Labourers in Husbandry*, Bath, cited by Stigler (1954).

De Spiegelaere, M., Dramaix, M., and Hennart, P., 1998a, "Social class and obesity in 12-year-old children in Brussels: influence of gender and ethnic origin," *European Journal of Pediatrics*, 157, 432–35.

De Spiegelaere, M., Dramaix, M., and Hennart, P., 1998b, "The influence of socio-economic status on the incidence and evolution of obesity during early adolescence," *International Journal of Obesity and Related Metabolic Disorders*, 22, 268–74.

De Spiegelaere, M., Dramaix, M., and Hennart, P., 1998c, "Socio-economic status and changes in body mass from 3 to 5 years," *Archives of Disease in Childhood*, 78, 477–78.

Debry, G., 1999, "A qui profite l'obésité?," *Cahiers de Nutrition et de Diététique*, 34(3), 129.

Déchaux, J.-H., 1994, "Les trois composantes de l'économie cachée de la parenté: l'exemple français," *Recherches sociologiques* 25, 3.

Descamps, P., 1930, *État social des peuples sauvages*, preface by Paul Rivet, Paris, Payot.

Desjeux, D., 1993, "La décision, entre stratégie consciente et force aveugle," *Sciences Humaines*, 2, special issue (May–June), 43–46.

Desjeux, D., 1996a, "L'ethnologie, une méthode pour comprendre les comportements alimentaires domestiques," in J.-F. Desjeux and S. Hercberg (Eds.), *La nutrition humaine, la recherche au service de la santé*, Paris, INSERM-Nathan.

Desjeux, D., 1996b, "Tiens bon le concept, j'enlève l'échelle . . . d'observation!," *Utinam*, n° 20, Paris, l'Harmattan, 15–44. Black boxes.

Desjeux, D., 1997, "L'ethnomarketing, une approche anthropologique de la consommation: entre fertilisation croisée et purification scientifique," *Utinam*, n° 21–22, Paris, l'Harmattan, 111–47.

Desjeux, D., 1998, "Les échelles d'observation de la consommation," in *Comprendre le consommateur*, Paris, Éditions Sciences Humaines.

Desjeux, D. and Taponier, S., 1991, *Le sens de l'autre*, Paris, L'Harmattan.

Desjeux, D., Taponier, S., and Le Van Duc, A. C, 1990, *Mise au point d'une méthode anthropologique d'analyse micro-individuelle des comportements alimentaires*, MRT, Université de Paris V-Sorbonne.

Desjeux, J.-F. and Hercberg, S., Eds., 1996, *La nutrition humaine, la recherche au service de la santé*, Paris, INSERM-Nathan.

Détienne, M. and Vernant, J.-P., 1979, *La cuisine du sacrifice au pays grec*, Paris, Gallimard.

Dibie, P., 1998, *La passion du regard*, Paris, Métailié.

Digard, J.-P., 1999, *Les français et leurs animaux*, Paris, Fayard.

Dirn, L., 1998, *La société française en tendances 1975–1995*, Paris, PUF.

Douglas, M., 1971, "Deciphering a meal," in C. Geertz (Ed.), *Myth, Symbol, and Culture*, New York: Columbia University Press.

Douglas, M., 1979, "Les structures du culinaire," *Communications*, 31, 145–69.

Douglas, M., 1981, *De la souillure*, Paris, Maspéro.

Douglas, M., 1984, *Food in the Social Order*, London: Routledge.

Douglas, M. and Wildavsky, A., 1982, *Risk and Culture: An Essay on the Selection of Technological and Environmental Dangers*, California, University of California Press.

Dournes, J., 1981, "L'espace d'un repas," in Kuper Jessica (Ed.), *La cuisine des ethnologues*, Paris, Berger-Levrault.

Drishel, J.-P., Poulain, J.-P., and Truchelut, J.-M., 1988, *Histoires et recettes de l'Alsace gourmande*, Toulouse, Privat.

Drouard, A., 1998, "Le régime alimentaire du Dr Carton et les régimes 'naturels'," *Cahiers de Nutrition et de Diététique*, 33(2), 297–300.

Drouard, A., 1999, "Naissance et évolution du petit déjeuner en France," *Cahiers de Nutrition et de Diététique*, 34(3), 167–71.

Drulhe, M., 1987, "L'incorporation," *Sociétés*, 15, 5–6.

Drulhe, M., 1996, *Santé et société. Le façonnement sociétal de la santé*, Paris, PUF.

Ducpétiaux, E., 1955, *Les budgets économiques des classes ouvrières en Belgique*, Bruxelles.

Duff, J., 1990, "Nutrition and public health: division of labour in the study of nutrition," *Community Health Studies*, 14, 162–70.

Dumazedier, J., 1962, *Vers une civilisation des loisirs?* Paris, Seuil.

Dupin, H., 1980, "Évolution des habitudes alimentaires et de la ration alimentaire des Français," *Ethnologie française*, 10(3), 319–24.

Dupuy, B., 1986, "L'eucharistie et le Seder pascal juif," in Rencontres de l'École du Louvre, *La table et le partage*, Paris, La Documentation Française.

Durand, G., 1960, *Les structures anthropologiques de l'imaginaire*, Paris, Bordas.

Durkheim, E., 1982, *The Rules of the Sociological Method*, W. D. Halls (trans.), New York, Free Press.

Durkheim, E., 1897, *Le suicide. Étude sociologique*, Paris, PUF, 1969.

Durkheim, E., 2008, *The Elementary Forms of the Religious Life*, Joseph Ward Swain (trans.), Mineola, NY: Dover Publications.

Duvignaud, J., Ed., 1979, *Sociologie de la connaissance*, Paris, Payot.

Duvignaud, J. and Corbeau, J.-P., 1981, *Les tabous des Français*, Paris, Hachette.

Echaudemaison, C.-D., 1996, *Dictionnaire d'économie et de sciences sociales*, Paris, Nathan.

Eden, F. M., 1797, *The State of the Poor*, London, cited by Herpin and Verger (1991).

Eizner, N., "L'alimentation entre diversité et normalisation," in *Alimentation et lien social, Pour*, n° 129, Paris, L'Harmattan, 61–67.

Elias, N., 1939a, *La civilisation des mœurs*, Paris, Calmann-Lévy, 1973.

Elias, N., 1939b, *La dynamique de l'Occident*, Paris, Calmann-Lévy, 1974.

Elias, N., 1990, *Norbert Elias par lui-même*, Paris, Fayard.

Engel, E., 1857, *Die Produktions und Consumtionverhaltnisse des Konigreichs Sachsen*, réedité in *Die Lebenskosten belgisher Arbeiter-Familien*, Dresden, 1895.

Escoffier, A., 1902, *Guide Culinaire*, Paris, Flammarion.

ESRC, 1999, *The Politics of GM Food: Risk, Science and Public Trust*. Global Environment Change Programme, Special briefing n° 5, University of Sussex, cited by Marris 1999.

Esterle-Hedibel, M., 2000, "Le corps en force ou le corps en forme," in A. Garrigou (Ed.), *La santé dans tous ses états*, Biarritz, Atlantica, 185–203.

Fabre-Vassas, C., 1991, "L'azyme des juifs et l'hostie des chrétiens," in D. Fournier and D'Onofrio Salvatore (Eds.), *Le Ferment divin*, Paris, MSH.

Fabre-Vassas, C., 1993, *La bête singulière*, Paris, Gallimard. English translation *The Singular Beast: Jews, Christians and the Pig*, 1997, translated by C. Volk, New York, Columbia University Press.

Falk, P., 1991, Homo culinarius: towards an historical anthropology of taste," *Social Science Information*, 30(4), 757–90.

Falk, P., 1994, *The Consuming Body*. Published in association with *Theory, Culture & Society*, London, Sage.

Falk, P., 1996, La magie des vitamines ou l'avenir exorcisé, in C. Fischler, 1996c, *Pensée magique et alimentation aujourd'hui*, Cahiers de l'OCHA, n° 5, 54–64.

Fantino, M., 1992, "État nutritionnel et perception affective de l'aliment," in I. Giachetti (Ed.), *Plaisir et préférences alimentaires*, Paris, Polytechnica.

FAO, 1986, *Plan indicatif mondial de développement agricole*, Rome, Food and Agriculture Organization of the United Nations.

Farb, P. and Armelagos, G., 1982, *Consuming Passions, the Anthropology of Eating*, Boston, Houghton Mifflin Compagny, French translation, *Anthropologie des coutumes alimentaires*, 1985, Paris, Denoël.

Favre, J., 1883, *Dictionnaire universel de la cuisine*, 1910, Paris.

Faurion, A., 1993, "Sémantique et physiologie du goût: la rupture épistémologique," *Lettre Scientifique de l'Institut Français pour la Nutrition*, 21, 1–6.

Febvre, L., 1922, *La Terre et l'évolution humaine: introduction géographique à l'histoire*, Paris, Albin Michel, 1970.

Febvre, L., 1938, "Répartition géographique des fonds de cuisine en France," in *Travaux du 1er congrès international de folklore*, Tours.

Fischler, C., 1979a, "Gastro-nomie et gastro-anomie, Sagesse du corps et crise bioculturelle de l'alimentation moderne," *Communications*, 31, 189–210.

Fischler, C., Ed., 1979b, "La nourriture. Pour une anthropologie bioculturelle de l'alimentation," *Communications*, 31, 1–3.

Fischler, C., 1980, "Food habits, social change and the nature/culture dilemma," *Social Science Information*, 19(6), 937–53.

Fischler, C., 1986, "Diététique savante et diététiques spontanées: la bonne nutrition enfantine selon des mères de famille française," *Culture technique*, 16, 50–59.

Fischler, C., 1987, "La symbolique du gros," *Communications*, 46(1), 255–78.

Fischler, C., 1989a, "Peut-on changer l'alimentation par décret?," *Cahiers de Nutrition et de Diététique*, 24(1), 59–61.

Fischler, C., 1989b, "Le dégoût: un phénomène bio-culturel," *Cahiers de Nutrition et de Diététique*, 24(5), 381–84.

Fischler, C., 1990, *L'Homnivore*, Paris, O. Jacob.

Fischler, C., 1993, *Le Bon et le Saint, évolution de la sensibilité alimentaire des français*, Cahiers de l'OCHA n° 1.

Fischler, C., 1994a, "Magie, Charme et aliments," *Autrement*, n° 149, 10–19.

Fischler, C., Ed., 1994b, *Manger Magique. Aliments sorciers, croyances comestibles*, Paris, Autrement, Coll. Mutations/Mangeurs, no. 149.

Fischler, C., 1996a, "Alimentation, morale et société," in Giachetti Ismène (Ed.), *Identités des mangeurs, images des aliments*, Paris, Polytechnica, 31–54.

Fischler, C., 1996b, "La 'Macdonalisation' des mœurs," in J.-L. Flandrin and M. Montanari (Eds.), *Histoire de l'alimentation*, Paris, Fayard, 859–79.

Fischler, C., 1996c, *Pensée magique et alimentation aujourd'hui*, Cahiers de l'OCHA, n° 5.

Fischler, C., 1997a, *Le repas familial vu par les 10–11 ans*, Cahiers de l'OCHA, n° 6.

Fischler, C., 1997b, "Le consommateur partagé," in *Le mangeur et l'animal, Autrement*, n° 172, 135–48.

Fischler, C., 1998a, "Raison et déraison dans les perception des risques alimentaires," *Cahiers de Nutrition et de Diététique*, 33(5), 297–301.

Fischler, C., 1998b, "La maladie de la vache folle," in M. Apfelbaum (Ed.), *Risques et peurs alimentaires*, Paris, O. Jacob.

Fischler, C., 2013, *Selective Eating: The Rise, Meaning and Sense of Personal Dietary Requirements*. Paris, Odile Jacob.

Flandrin, J.-L., 1987, "La distinction par le goût," in Ph. Ariès and G. Duby (Eds.), *Histoire de la vie privée*, Paris, Seuil, 267–309.

Flandrin, J.-L., 1993, "Les heures des repas en France avant le 19ème siècle," in M. Aymard, C. Grignon, and F. Sabban, *Le temps de manger, Alimentation, emploi du temps et rythmes sociaux*, Paris, Éditions MSH-INRA.

Flandrin, J.-L. and Cobbi, J., 1999, *Tables d'hier, Tables d'ailleurs*, Paris, O. Jacob.

Flandrin, J.-L. and Montanari, M., Eds., 1996, *Histoire de l'alimentation*, Paris, Fayard.

Foucault, M., 1963, *Naissance de la clinique*, Paris, PUF.

Fournier, T. and Poulain, J. P., 2016, "La génomique nutritionnelle: (re)penser les liens alimentation-santé à l'articulation des sciences sociales, biomédicales et de la vie," Natures, Sciences et sociétés. (To be published).

Fournier, T., Jarty, J., Lapeyre, N., and Touraille, P., 2015, "Alimentation, arme du genre," *Journal des Anthropologues*, 140–41, 19–49.

Frazer, J., *The Golden Bough: A Study in Comparative Religion*, (1890) 1911, *Le Rameau d'or*, Laffont, reprinted 1981.

Frelut, M.-L., 2000, "Conséquences de l'obésité chez l'enfant," in *Obésité, dépistage et prévention chez l'enfant*, Expertise collective, Paris, INSERM, 29–50.

Furet, F., 1973, "La fourchette de Byzance," Le Nouvel Observateur, November 26, 1973, reprinted in the new edition of N. Elias, "La civilisation des mœurs," Pluriel, Hachette, 395–401.

Fürst, E. L., Prättälä, R., Ekström, M., Holm, L., and Kjaernes, U., Eds., 1991, *Palatable Worlds: Sociocultural Food Studies*, Oslo, Solum (Papers from a symposium held in Gilleleje, Denmark, in September 1990).

Gachet, N., 1998, *Ethno-cinémato-graphie des cuisines d'un restaurant parisien*, ethno-cinematology thesis, Université de Paris X-Nanterre, Septentrion.

Galan, P. and Hercberg, S., 1994, "Méthodes de mesure de la consommation alimentaire et techniques des enquêtes alimentaires," *Cahiers de Nutrition et de Diététique*, 29(6), 380–84.

Garabuau Moussaoui, I., 2000, *La cuisine des jeunes. Pratiques et représentations culinaires comme révélateurs d'une étapes de vie*, Paris, Université René Descartes Paris V-Sorbonne.

Gardner, B., 2013, *Global Futures: Feeding the World in 2050*, New York, USA, Bloomsbury.

Garine (de), I., 1978, "Population, Production and Culture in the Plains Societies of Northern Cameroon and Chad: The Anthropologist in Development Projects," *Current Anthropology*, 19, 42–65.

Garine (de), I., 1979, "Culture et nutrition," *Communications*, n° 31, 70–91.

Garine (de), I., 1980, "Pour une anthropologie alimentaire," *Ethnologie française: Usages alimentaires des français*, n° 3 T. X.

Garine (de), I., 1991, "Les modes alimentaires: histoire de l'alimentation et des manières de table," in J. Poirier (Ed.), *Histoire des mœurs*, Paris, La Pléiade, Gallimard.

Garine (de), I., 1994a, "Massa et Moussey: la question de l'embonpoint," *Autrement* n° 91, 104–15.

Garine (de), I., 1994b, "The diet and nutrition of human populations," in T. Ingold (Ed.), *Companion Encyclopaedia of Anthropology, Part 1*, London, Routledge, 226–64.

Garine (de) I., Ed., 1996, *Bien manger et bien vivre*, Paris, ORSTOM et L'Harmattan.

Garn, S. M., Sullivan, T. V., and Hawthorne, V. M., 1989, "Educational level, fatness and fatness differences between husbands and wives," *American Journal of Clinical Nutrition*, 50, 740–45.

Gaudillière, J.-P., 2001, *"Échos d'une crise centenaire,"* in La Recherche, special issue *Le risque alimentaire*, 2001, 14–18.

Georges, P., *Géographie alimentaire*, Paris, PUF.

Germov, J. and Williams, L., 1996, "The epidemic of dieting women: The need for a sociological approach to food and nutrition," *Appetite*, 27, 97–108.

Germov, J. and Williams, L., Eds., 1999a, *A Sociology of Food and Nutrition: The Social Appetite*, 1st edn, Sydney, Oxford University Press.

Germov, J. and Williams, L., Eds., 1999b, *A Sociology of Food and Nutrition: The Social Appetite*, New York, Oxford University Press.

Giddens, A., 1991, *Modernity and Self-Identity*, Cambridge, Polity.

Giddens, A., 1993, *New Rules of Sociological Method: A Positive Critique of Interpretive Sociologies*, California, Stanford University Press.

Girard, A., 1977, "Le Triomphe de la Cuisinière bourgeoise. Livres culinaires, cuisine et société en France aux XVIIe et XVIII siècles," *Revue d'histoire moderne et* contemporaine, 24(October–December), 497–523.

Girard, A., 1979, "Le livre de la cuisine à la renaissance," in *Pratiques et discours alimentaires à la renaissance*, Maisonneuve et Larose.

Goffman, E., 1963, *Stigma: Notes on the Management of Spoiled Identity*, Prentice Hall, Englewood Cliffs. French translation *Stigmates, Les usages sociaux des handicaps*, Paris, Éditions de Minuit, 1975.

Goffman, E., 1974, *Les rites d'interaction*, Paris, Éditions de Minuit.

Gomez, F., 1992, "Gastro-anomie: apparence ou réalité?," *Cahiers internationaux de psychologie sociale*, 13(March–April–May), 60–64.

Goody, J., 1982, *Cooking, Cuisine and Class: A Study in Comparative Sociology*, Cambridge, Cambridge University Press, French translation *Cuisines, cuisine et classes*, collection *Alors*, Centre Georges Pompidou, 1984.

Gouffé, J., 1980, *Le livre de la cuisine*, 6th edition 1884, Reprint Baudoin.

Gourou, P., 1940, *La terre et l'homme en Extrême-Orient*, Paris, Colin.

Grignon, C., 1986, "Les modes gastronomiques à la Française," *L'Histoire*, 85, 128–34.

Grignon, C., 1987a, "L'évolution des habitudes alimentaires des Français," Symposium "Agroalimentaire"—Report of the meeting organized by the Fondation Universitaire des Sciences et Techniques du Vivant and INRA, Pensières-Veyrier-du-Lac, November 20, 1987.

Grignon, C., 1987b, *L'alimentation des étudiants*, Paris, INRA-CNOUS.

Grignon, C., 1989, "Les consommations alimentaires," in *Le grand atlas de la France rurale*, INRA and SCEES, Paris, De Monza, 320–21.

Grignon, C., 1993, "La règle, la mode et le travail," in M. Aymard, C. Grignon, and F. Sabban (Eds.), *Le temps de manger, Alimentation, emploi du temps et rythmes sociaux*, Paris, Éditions MSH-INRA.

Grignon, C., 1995, "L'alimentation populaire et la question du naturel," in N. Eizner (Ed.), *Voyage en alimentation*, Paris, ARF éditions.

Grignon, C., 1997, "Évolution de la consommation de viande en France depuis 30 ans," *Cahiers de l'OCHA*, n° 7.

Grignon, C., Ed., 2000, *Les conditions de vie des étudiants*, Paris, PUF.

Grignon, C. and Grignon, Ch., 1980a, "Styles d'alimentation et goûts populaires," *Revue française de sociologie*, XXI, 531–69.

Grignon, C. and Grignon, Ch., 1980b, "L'espace social des pratiques alimentaires," *Bulletin d'information du département d'économie et de sociologie rurales*, INRA, n° 6.

Grignon, C. and Grignon, Ch., 1981, "Alimentation et stratification sociale," *Cahiers de Nutrition et de Diététique*, 15, 4.

Grimod de la Reynière, A. B., 1803, "Almanach des gourmands," *Écrits gastronomiques*, Paris, 10/18.

Grimod de la Reynière, A. B., 1806–07, *Journal des gourmands et des belles, ou l'épicurien français*, Paris, Capelle et Renand.

Grimod de la Reynière, A. B., 1978, "Ecrits gastronomiques," Paris, UGE.

Gringoire, T. and Saulnier, L., 1914, *Le répertoire de la cuisine*, Dupont et Malgat, later Guériny, 37th edition 1980.

Guerard, M., 1976, *La Grande Cuisine Minceur*, Paris, Robert Laffont.

Guerard, M., 1977, *La Cuisine Gourmande*, Paris, Robert Laffont.

Guillemard, A., 1988, "La naissance du troisième age," in H. Mendras and M. Verret (Eds.), *Les champs de la sociologie française*, Paris, Colin.

Guptill, A. E., Copelton, D. A., and Lucal, B., 2013, *Food and Society, Principles and Paradoxes*, Cambridge, Polity.

Gurvitch, G., 1958, *La multiplicité des temps sociaux*, Paris, Centre de Documentation Universitaire.

Gurvitch, G., 1962, *Dialectique et sociologie*, Paris, Flammarion.

Gurvitch, G., Ed., 1964, *The Spectrum of Social Time*, Myrtle Korenbaum, assisted by Philip Bosserman (trans.), Dordrecht, Holland, D. Reidel.

Gurvitch, G., 1966, *Les cadres sociaux de la connaissance*, Paris, PUF.

Guthe, C. E., 1943, "History of the Committee on Food Habits," in *The Problem of Changing Food Habits*, Report of the Committee on Food Habits 1941–43, Bulletin of National Research Council, National Academy of Sciences, n° 108, October 1943.

Guy-Grand, B. and Gozlan, M., 1998, "8% des adultes français sont obèses," Interview with Bernard Guy-Grand conducted by M. Gozlan, *Le Quotidien du Médecin*, n° 6234, March 3, 1998.

Habsch, R., 1992, *L'Art de présenter les plats: garnir et décorer pour le plaisir des yeux*, Paris, Editions J. Lanore.

Haeusler, L., 1985, "Alimentation, aspirations des Français et réalités des comportements—L'enquête du CREDOC," *Économie & Consommation*, 167, 4–5.

Halbwachs, M., 1912, *La classe ouvrière et les niveaux de vie, Recherches sur la hiérarchie des besoins dans les sociétés industrielles contemporaines*, Paris, Alcan, reprint Gordon and Breach (1970).

Halbwachs, M., 1933, *L'évolution des besoins dans les classes ouvrières*, Paris, Alcan.

Halbwachs, M., 1938, *L'analyse des mobiles dominants*, reprint *Esquisse d'une psychologie des classes sociales*, Paris, Marcel Rivière, 1964.

Hall, S. and Whannell, P., 1964, *The Popular Arts*, London, Hutchinson Educational, 241.

Hamada, S., Wilk, R., Logan, A., Minard, S., and Trubek, A., 2015, "The Future of Food Studies," *Food, Culture and Society: An International Journal of Multidisciplinary Research*, 18, 167–86.

Harris, M., 1977, *Cannibals and Kings: The Origins of Cultures*, New York, Random House.

Harris, M., 1985, *Good to Eat, Riddles of Food and Culture*, New York, Simon & Schuster.

Harris, M. and Ross, E. B., Eds., 1987, *Food and Evolution: Towards a Theory of Human Food Habits*, Philadelphia, Temple University Press.

Hassoun, J.-P., 1997, *Hmong du Laos en France. Changement social, initiatives et adaptations*, Paris, PUF.

Haudricourt, A.-G., 1968, "La technologie culturelle, essai de méthodologie," in J. Poirier (Ed.), *Ethnologie générale*, Gallimard, 731–822, in collaboration with Igor de Garine.

Haudricourt, A.-G., 1987, *La technologie science humaine, recherches d'histoire et d'ethnologie des techniques*, Paris, MSH.

Haudricourt, A.-G. and Granai, G., 1955, "Linguistique et sociologie," *Cahiers internationaux de Sociologie*, 19, 114–29.

Haudricourt, A.-G. and Hédin, L., 1943, *L'homme et les plantes cultivées*, Paris, Gallimard.

Helm, R., 1896, *Anthropology: Report of the Elder Scientific Expedition*, 1891, Transaction of the Royal Society.

Hemardinquer, J.-J., Ed., 1970, *Pour une histoire de l'alimentation*, Paris, Colin.

Hercberg, S., 1991, "Les défis de l'approche épidémiologique dans le domaine de la nutrition dans les pays industrialisés," *Cahiers de nutrition et de diététique*, 26, 5.

Herman, J., 1983, *Les langages de la sociologie*, Paris, PUF.

Herpin, N., 1980, "Comportements alimentaires et contraintes sur les emplois du temps," *Revue française de sociologie*, XXIX, 599–621.

Herpin, N., 1984, "Alimentation et régionalisme," *Données sociales*, INSEE, 340–41.

Herpin, N., 1988, "Le repas comme institution, compte rendu d'une enquête exploratoire," *Revue française de sociologie*, XXIX, 503–21.

Herpin, N. and Verger, D., 1991, *La consommation des français*, Paris, La découverte.

Herzlich, C., 1984, "Médecine moderne et quête de sens," in M. Augé and C. Herzlich (Eds.), *Le sens du mal—Anthropologie, histoire, sociologie de la maladie*, Montreux, Éditions des archives contemporaines.

Herzlich, C., 1992, *Santé et maladie, analyse d'une représentation sociale*, Paris, EHESS.

Herzlich, C. and Pierret, J., 1989, *Malades d'hier, malades d'aujourd'hui*, Paris, Payot.

Heusch (de), L., 1971, *Pourquoi l'épouser? Et autres essais*, Paris, Gallimard.

Hill, J. O. and Peters, J. C., 1998, "Environmental contributions to the obesity epidemic," *Science*, 280, 1371–74.

Hinkle, L. E., Whitney, L. H., Lehman, E. W., Dunn, J., Benjamin, B., King, R., Plakun, A., and Flehinger, B., 1968, "Occupation, education, and coronary heart disease," *Science*, 161, 238–46.

Hoggart, R., 1957, *The Uses of Literacy: Aspects of Working-Class Life with Special References to Publications and Entertainments*, London, UK, Chatto and Windus. Published, 1970, in French as *La Culture du Pauvre*, Paris, France, Editions de Minuit.

Hollis, J. F., Carmody, T. P., Connor, S. L., Fey, S. G., and Matarazzo, J. D., 1986, "The nutrition attitude survey: associations with dietary habits, psychological and physical well-being and coronary risk factors," *Health Psychology*, 5, 359–74.

Hossenlopp, J., 1995, "Autre produit, autre goût," Autrement, série mutations/ mangeurs, n° 154.

Hossenlopp, J. and Jacquinot, M., 1979, *Calculs économiques dans la gestion de la production en industries alimentaires*, Massy, Ecole Nationale Supérieure des industries agricoles et alimentaires.

Housser, M., 1976, *Abrégé de psychopathologie*, Paris, Masson.

Hubert, A., 1985, *L'alimentation dans un village Yao de Thaïlande du Nord: de l'au-delà au cuisiné*, Paris, CNRS.

Hubert, A., 1990, "Applying anthropology to the epidemiology of cancer," *Anthropology Today*, 5, 62–78.

Hubert, A., 1995, "Anthropologie et recherche biomédicale," in J.-F. Barré (Ed.), *Les applications de l'anthropologie*, Paris, Karthala.

Hubert, A., 1997, "Adaptabilité humaine: biologie et culture. Du corps pesant au corps léger: approche anthropologique des formes," *Diététique et médecine*, 1997, 83–88.

Hubert, A., 1998, "Autour d'un concept: 'L'alimentation méditerranéenne'," *Techniques et culture*, 31–32, 153–60.

Hubert, A., 2000, "Alimentation et santé: la science et l'imaginaire," *Cahiers de Nutrition et de Diététique*, 35, 353–56.

Hubert, A. and Estager, M.-P., 1999, "Anthropologie de l'alimentation: quelle utilité pour la nutrition humaine?," *Cahiers de Nutrition et de Diététique*, 34(5), 283–86.

Igoin, L., 1979, *La boulimie et son infortune*, Paris, PUF.

Inglis, D., Debra Gimlin, D., and Chris Thorpe, C., 2008, *Critical Concepts in the Social Sciences*, London: Routledge.

INSEE, 1993, *Enquête Budget de famille*.

INSERM Collective expertise, 1999, *Carences nutritionnelles, étiologies et dépistage*, Paris, éditions de l'INSERM.

INSERM Collective expertise, 2000, *Obésité, dépistage et prévention chez l'enfant*, Paris, éditions de l'INSERM.

Iribarne, d'P., 1977, "Consommations alimentaires et comportements socio-économiques," *Consommation*, no. 2.

Joly, P.-B., 1999, "Besoin d'expertise et quête d'une légitimité nouvelle: quelles procédures pour réguler l'expertise scientifique?," *Revue Française des affaires politiques*, 42(2), 219–34.

Joly, P.-B., Marris, C., Assouline, G., and Lemarié, J., 1999, "Quand les candides évaluent les OGM: nouveau modèle de 'démocratie technique' ou mise en scène du débat public," *Annales des Mines, Responsabilité et environnement*, 9, 12–21.

Joly, P.-B., Assouline, G., Kréziak, D., Lemarié, J., Marris, C., and Roy, A., 2000, *L'innovation controversée: Le débat public sur les OGM en France*, Grenoble, CRIDE-INRA.

Josua, J.-P., 1976, "Eucharistie," Encyclopédia Universalis.

Kardiner, A., Linton, R., and coll., 1945, *The Psychological Frontiers of Society*, New York, Columbia University Press.

Karris, L., 1977, "Prejudice Against Obese Renters," *Journal of Social Psychology*, 101, 159–60.

Kaufmann, J.-C., 1992, *La trame conjugale*, Paris, Nathan.

Kaufmann, J.-C., 1993, *Sociologie du couple*, Paris, PUF.

Kent, S., 1989, "Cross-cultural perceptions of farmers as hunters and the value of meat," in S. Kent (Ed.), *Farmers as Hunters: the Implications of Sedentism*, Cambridge, Cambridge University Press, cited by Beardsworth (1995).

Kilani, M., 1992, *Introduction à l'anthropologie*, Payot, Lausanne.

Kilani, M., 1996, "La vache folle ou le déclin de la raison symbolique," *Allez savoir*, n° 6, Université de Lausanne, 46–48.

Kilani, M., 1999, "Le cannibale, le cochon et la vache folle ou l'identité culturelle en question," in *Le Goût*, Acts of the 3rd cross-border colloquium, Dijon, 1999, 567–74.

Klatzmann, J., 1978, *L'agriculture française*, Paris, Seuil.

Klatzmann, J., 1991, *Nourrir l'humanité: espoir et inquiétudes*, Paris, Economica-INRA.

Klein, M., 1952, "Some Theoretical Conclusions Regarding the Emotional Life of the Infant", in *Envy and Gratitude and Other Works, 1946-1963*, The Melanie Klein Trust (First published in Britain by The Hogarth Press Ltd, 1975).

Klein, M., 1959, *La psychanalyse des enfants*, Paris, PUF.

Koç, M., Sumner, J., and Winson, T. (Eds.), 2012, *Critical Perspectives in Food Studies*, Toronto, Oxford University Press.

Koch, S. L., 2013, *A Theory of Grocery Shopping: Food, Choice and Conflict*, New York, USA, Bloomsbury.

Kosofsky Sedgwick, E., 1990, *Epistemology of the Closet*, Berkeley, University of California Press.

Kosofsky Sedgwick, E., 1995, *Performativity and Performance*, New York, Routledge.

Krowolski, N., 1993, *Autour du riz: le repas chez quelques populations d'Asie du Sud -Est*, Paris, L'Harmattan.

L.S.R., 1691, *L'art de bien traiter*, Paris.

Laburthe-Tolra, P. and Warnier, J. P., 1993, *Ethnologie Anthropologie*, Paris, PUF.

Lacoste, Y., 1968, "Genre de vie," *Encyclopeadia Universalis*, Paris, Encyclopaedia Universalis S.A.

Lafay, L., Basdevant, A., Charles, M.-A., Vray, M., Balkau, B., and coll., 1997, "Determinants and nature of of dietary underreporting in a free-living population," *International Journal of Obesity*, 21, 567–73.

Lahlou, S., 1990, "Quand les Français se mettent à table," *Sciences et Avenir*, hors série, n° 94.

Lahlou, S., 1996, "Cuisinons la représentation sociale," in C. Fischler, 1996c, *Pensée magique et alimentation aujourd'hui*, Cahiers de l'OCHA, n° 5, 10–17.

Lahlou, S., 1998, *Penser manger*, Paris, PUF.

Lahlou, S., 1999, "Des aliments tu feras ta médecine: Hippocrate revisité," *Cahiers de Nutrition et de Diététique*, 34(2), 108–13.

Lambert, J.-L., 1987, *L'évolution des modèles de consommation alimentaires en France*, Paris, Lavoisier.

Lambert, J.-L., 1992, "A table! La cuisine du statisticien," in *La cité des chiffres*, Autrement, Sciences en société, 5, 77–85.

Lambert, J.-L., 1994, "Évolution de la consommation de produits allégés en France," *Cahiers de Nutrition et de Diététique*, 34(29), 147–50.

Lambert, J.-L., 1996, "Les mangeurs entre traditions et nouveautés: quelques spécificités du marketing alimentaire," in Giachetti Ismène (Ed.), *Identités des mangeurs, images des aliments*, Paris, Polytechnica, 151–73.

Lambert, J.-L., 1997, "Quelques déterminants socioculturels des consommations de viandes en Europe. La 'Vache folle' va-t-elle renforcer la tendance à la sarcophagie et au néo-végétarisme?," *Revue de Droit Rural*, 252, 240–43.

Lambert, J.-L., 2000, "La sensibilité à l'innovation et les déterminants de la consommation de nouveaux produits alimentaires," *NAFAS pratique*, 1, 7–13.

Lambert, J.-L. and Bassecoulard-Zitt, E., 1987, "La place de la restauration dans la consommation alimentaire en France," *Cahiers de Nutrition et de Diététique*, 22, 210–19.

Lambert, J.-L., Château, L., Rouaud, C., Dupin, H., and Berthier, A.-M., 1987, *Essais dévaluation des apports nutritionnels en France*, Nantes, INRA, 2 volumes.

Larrère, R. and de la Soudière, M., 1985, *Cueillir la montagne*, Lyon, La Manufacture.

Lascoumes, P., 1999a, "L'expertise peut elle être démocratique?," *Le monde des débats*, n° 8, November, 20–21.

Lascoumes, P., 1999b, *Corruptions*, Paris, Presses de Sciences-Po.

Le Barzic, M. and Pouillon, M., 1998, *La meilleure façon de manger, les désarrois du mangeur moderne*, Paris, O Jacob.

Le Breton, D., 1990, *Anthropologie du corps et modernité*, Paris, PUF.

Le Breton, D., 1991, *Passion du risque*, Paris Métialié.

Le Breton, D., 1995, *La sociologie du risque*, Paris, PUF.

Le Play, F., 1856, *Les ouvriers européens: études sur les travaux, la vie domestique et la condition morale des populations ouvrières de l'Europe. Précédée d'un exposée de la méthode d'observation*, Paris.

Le Play, F., 1879, *La méthode sociale*, Paris, Méridiens-Klincksieck, 1989.

Leach, E. R., 1980, *L'unité de l'homme et autres essais*, Paris, Gallimard.

Lecuyer, B., 1976, "Médecins et observateurs sociaux: Les Annales d'hygiène publique et de médecine légale (1820-1850)," in M. Volle (Ed.), *Pour une histoire de la statistique*, Paris, INSEE.

Ledrut, R., Ed., in coll. with Clément, S., Forne, J., and Saint Raymond, O., 1979a, *L'alimentation naturelle, les changements culturels dans le sentiment de l'existence et les relations avec le monde naturel*, Toulouse, CERS.

Ledrut, R., Ed., in coll. with Clément, S., Gorge, J.-P., and Saint Raymond, O., 1979b, *L'évolution des pratiques alimentaires sous leurs aspects qualitatifs*, Toulouse, CERS.

Lefebvre, H., 1974, *La production de l'espace*, Paris, Anthropos.

Leites, E., 1986, *The Puritan Conscience and Modern Sexuality*, London, Yale University Press. Translated into French as *La passion du bonheur. Conscience puritaine et sexualité moderne*, French translation, 1989, Paris, Éditions du Cerf.

Leroi-Gourhan, A., 1943, 1945, *Évolution et techniques*, volume 1, *L'homme et la matière*, and volume 2, *Milieu et techniques*, reprint 1973, Paris, Albin Michel.

Leroi-Gourhan, A., Poirier, J., Haudricourt, A.-G., and Condominas, G., 1953, *Ethnologie de l'Union Française*, Paris, PUF, 2 volumes.

Lesourd, B., 1998, "Santé et aliments: le cas des seniors," colloquium "Comment mieux connaître les consommateurs et communiquer dans la filière alimentaire?," Paris.

Lester, I. H., 1994, *Australia's Food and Nutrition*, Canberra, AGPS.

Lestringant, F., 1981, "Cannibalisme et guerre de religion," in *Pratiques et discours alimentaires à la Renaissance*, Maisonneuve et Larose.

Lestringant, F., 1994, *Le cannibale, grandeur et décadence*, Paris, Perrin.

Levenstein, H., 1980, "The new England kitchen and the origins of modern American eating habits," *American Quarterly*, 32(4), 369–86.

Levenstein, H., 1988, *Revolution at the Table: The Transformation of the American Diet*, New York, Oxford University Press.

Levenstein, H., 1993, *Paradox of Plenty: A Social History of Eating in Modern America*, New York, Oxford University Press.

Levenstein, H., 1996, "Diététique contre gastronomie: traditions culinaires, sainteté et santé dans les modèles de vie américains," in J.-L. Flandrin and M. Montanari (Eds.), *Histoire de l'alimentation*, Paris, Fayard, 843–58.

Lévi-Strauss, C., 1958, *Anthropologie Structurale*, Paris, Plon.

Lévi-Strauss, C., 1962, *Le Totémisme aujourd'hui*, Paris, PUF.

Lévi-Strauss, C., 1963, *Structural Anthropology*, Claire Jacobson and Brooke Grundfest Schoepf (trans.), New York, Basic Books.

Lévi-Strauss, C., 1964, *Le cru et le cuit*, Paris, Plon.

Lévi-Strauss, C., 1966a, *Du miel aux cendres*, Paris, Plon.

Lévi-Strauss, C., 1966b, *The Savage Mind*, George Weidenfeld and Nicolson Ltd. (trans.), Chicago, The University of Chicago Press.

Lévi-Strauss, C., 1968, *L'origine des manières de tables*, Paris, Plon.

Lévi-Strauss, C., 1969, *Elementary Structures of Kinship*, James Harle Bell, John Richard Von Sturmer, and Rodney Needham (trans.), Boston, Beacon Press.

Lévi-Strauss, C., 2008, "The Culinary Triangle," in Carole Counihan and Penny Van Esterik (Eds.), *Food and Culture: A Reader*, 2nd ed., Peter Brooks (trans.), New York, Routledge.

Lévy, P., 1956, "Le sacrifice du buffle et la prédiction du temps à Vientiane," *France -Asie, Présence du Royaume Lao*, XII, n° 118–20, 846–58.

Lewin, K., 1943, "Forces Behind Food Habits and Methods of Change," Report of the Committee on Food Habits. Washington, *Bulletin of the National Research Council*, CVIII, 35–65. reprinted in *Psychologie dynamique*, PUF.

Lewin, K., 1959, *Psychologie dynamique*, Paris, PUF.

Livi Bacci, M., 1987, *Popolazione e alimentazione. Saggio sulla storia demografica europea*, Bologna, translated into English as *Population and Nutrition: An Essay on European Demographic History*, New York, Oxford University Press.

Loret, P., 1982, *La messe. Du Christ à Jean-Paul II, histoire de la liturgie eucharistique*, Ottawa, Novalis Salvator.

Lowie, R. H., 1934, *An Introduction to Cultural Anthropology*, New York, Farrar and Rinehart, French translation *Manuel d'anthropologie culturelle*, 1936 by E. Métraux, Paris, Payot.

Lowie, R. H., 1942, "The transitions of civilizations in primitive society," *American Journal of Sociology*, 47, 527–43.

Lupton, D., 1996, *Food, the Body and the Self*, London, Sage.

Macbeth, H., Ed., 1997, *Food Preferences and Taste*, Oxford, Berghahn.

Macbeth, H. and MacClancy, J., 2004, *Researching Food Habits*, Oxford, Berghahn.

MacClancy, J., Henry, C. J., and Macbeth, H., 2009, *Consuming the Inedible: Neglected Dimensions of Food Choice*, Oxford, Berghahn.

MacIntosh, W. A., 1996, *Sociologies of Food and Nutrition*, New York, USA, Springer.

Macksey, R. A., 1970, *The Structuralist Controversy: The Languages of Criticism and the Sciences of Man*, London, UK, JHU Press.

Maddox, G. L., Back, K. W., and Liederman, V. R. 1968, "Overweight as Social Deviance and Disability," *Journal of Health and Social Behavior*, 9(4), 287–98.

Mattelart, A. and Neveu, E., 1996, "Cultural studies' stories. La domestication d'une pensée sauvage?" *Réseaux*, 14, n° 80, 11–58.

Maffesoli, M., 1979, *La conquête du présent, pour une sociologie de la vie quotidienne*, Paris, PUF.

Maffesoli, M., 1981, *L'ombre de Dionysos*, Paris, Méridiens.

Maffesoli, M., 1985, *La connaissance ordinaire*, Paris, Méridiens.

Maffesoli, M., 1988, *Le temps des tribus. Le déclin de l'individualisme dans les sociétés de masse*, Paris, Méridiens Klinsieck.

Mahias, M.-C., 1985, *Délivrance et convivialité: Le système culinaire Jaïna*, Paris, MSH.

Maho, J. and Pynson, P., 1989, "Cantines comment s'en débarrasser?," *Nourritures, Autrement*, n° 108.

Malassis, L., 1994, *Nourrir les hommes*, Paris, Flammarion.

Malassis, L. and Padilla, M., 1987, *Économie agro-alimentaire*, Paris, Cujas.

Malinowski, B., 1944, *A Scientific Theory of Culture and Other Essays*, Chapel Hill: The University of North Carolina Press.

Malvy, D., Djossou, F., and Le Bras, M., 1999, "Toxi-infections alimentaires collectives," *Cahiers de Nutrition et de Diététique*, 34, HS 1, 166–78.

Marin, 1739, *Les dons de Comus, ou les délices de la table*, Paris.

Marris, C., 1999, "OGM: comment analyser les risques?," *Biofutur*, déc. 99, 44–47.

Marris, C. and Joly, P.-B., 1999, "La gouvernance technocratique par consultation? interrogation sur la première conférence de citoyens en France," in "Risque et démocratie savoirs, pouvoir participation . . . vers un nouvel arbitrage?," *Les cahiers de la sécurité intérieure*, 38, 97–124.

Marris, C., Langford, I. H., and O'Riordan, T., 1998, "A quantitative test of the cultural theory of risk perceptions: comparison with the psychometric paradigm," *Risk Analysis*, 18, 5, 635–47.

Marx, K., 1857, "Fondements de la critique de l'économie politique," in *Oeuvres économiques*, Paris, Gallimard, La Pléiade, 1965.

Massaliot, 1691, *Le cuisinier royal et bourgeois*, Reprint Dessagnes, 1982.

Matusewich, E., 1983, "Employment discrimination against the overweight," *Personal Journal*, 62, 446–50.

Maurer, D. and Sobal, J., 1995, *Eating Agendas: Food and Nutrition As Social Problems*, New York, Aldine de Gruyter.

Maurizio, A., 1932, *Histoire de l'alimentation végétale depuis la préhistoire jusqu'à nos jours*, Paris, Payot.

Mauss, M., 1925, "Essai sur le don. Forme et raison de l'échange dans les sociétés archaïques," in M. Mauss (Ed.), *Sociologie et Anthropologie*, Paris, PUF, 1968.

Mauss, M., 1973, "Techniques of the Body" (Ben Brewster, trans.), *Economy and Society*, 2:1, repr. In J. Crary and S. Kwinter (Eds.), *Incorporations*, New York, Zone Books, 1992.

Mauss, M., and Hubert, H., 1899, "Essai sur la nature et la fonction du sacrifice", article originally published in the review *Année sociologique*, vol. II, 29–138.

McClean, R. A. and Moon, M., 1980, "Health, obesity and earning," *American Journal of Public Health*, 70(9), 1006–9.

McCracken, R. D., 1971, "Lactase deficiency: an example of dietary evolution," *Current Anthropology*, 12, 479–517.

McDonald, C., 1978, "Notes sur les modes de cuisson, les goûts et les odeurs dans le vocabulaire Palawan," *ASEMI*, IX, n° 3–4, 29–42.

McIntosh, A., 1996, *Sociology of Food and Nutrition*, New York, Plenum Press.

McKeown, T., 1976, *The Modern Rise of Population*, London, Edward Arnold.

McKeown, T., 1983, "Food, infection and population," *Journal of Interdisciplinary History*, 14(2), 227–47.

McKie, L. J., Wood, R. C., and Gregory, S., 1993, "Women defining health: food diet and body image," *Health Education Research*, 8, 35–41.

McLeod, Patrick, 1992, "Circuits nerveux de la préférence alimentaire et du plaisir," in I. Giachetti (Ed.), *Plaisir et préférences alimentaires*, Paris, Polytechnica.

Mead, M., 1928, 1935, *Coming of Age in Samoa*, translated into French as *Mœurs et sexualité en Océanie*, Paris, Terre humaine, Plon, 1963.

Mead, M., 1943, "The problem of changing food habits," in *The Problem of Changing Food Habits*, Report of the Committee on Food Habits 1941–43, Bulletin of The National Research Council, National Academy of Sciences, n° 108, October 1943.

Mead, M., 1964, *Food Habits Research: Problems of the 1960's*, publication 1225, The National Academy of Science, National Research Council, Washington.

Mead, M. and Guthe, C. E, 1945, *Manual for the Study of Food Habits,* Bulletin of The National Research Council, National Academy of Sciences, n° 111, French edition with an introduction by A. Hubert and J.-P. Poulain, éditions OCTARES in preparation.

Méchin, C., 1992, *Bêtes à manger*, Nancy, Presses universitaires de Nancy.

Méjean, L., 1998, "Panorama des enquêtes alimentaires françaises," *Cahiers de Nutrition et de Diététique*, 33(1), 25–28.

Méjean, L., Lluch, A., Kahn, J.-P., Ziegler, O., and Drouin, P., 1998, "L'utilisation des grilles psychométriques pour la mise en évidence d'états comportementaux différenciés chez le sujet normal et chez le sujet obèse," *Lettre Scientifique de l'Institut Français pour la Nutrition*, 53, 1–12.

Membrado, M., 1989, *Poétique des cafés*, Publisud.

Mendras, H., 1992, *Voyage au pays de l'utopie rustique*, Arles, Actes-Sud.

Mennell, S., 1985, *All Manners of Food: Eating and Taste in England and France from the Middle Ages to the Present*, Basil Blackwell, Oxford, translated into French as *Français et anglais à table, du moyen âge à nos jours*, Flammarion, 1985.

Mennell, S., 1993, "Sociogenetic connections between food and timing," translated into French as "Les connexions socio-génétiques entre alimentation et l'organisation du temps," in M. Aymard, C. Grignon, and F. Sabban, 1993, *Le temps de manger, Alimentation, emploi du temps et rythmes sociaux*, Paris, Éditions MSH-INRA.

Mennell, S., Murcott, A., and van Otterloo, A., 1992a, *The Sociology of Food: Eating, Diet and Culture*, London, Sage.

Mennell, S., Murcott, A., and van Otterloo, A., 1992b, "The sociology of food: eating, diet and culture," a special issue of the *Current Sociology* series, 40(2), London, Sage, 1–152.

Menon, 1749, *La science du maître d'hôtel cuisinier*, Paris.

Menon, 1774, *La cuisinière bourgeoise*, Bruxelles.

Merdji, M. and Dion, E., 2000, *"Le goût du lait, une approche anthropo-sociologique,"* Colloquium *Imaginaires alimentaires et identités des mangeurs? LESMA, ESC Nantes*.

Merdji, M., Mathieu, J.-P., and Lambert, J.-L., 1999, "Représentations et déterminants des goûts: vers un enrichissement du concept d'attitude en marketing alimentaire," in *Économie et marketing alimentaires*, Lavoisier Tec. Et Doc., 101–15.

Mermet, G., 1995, *Francoscopie*, Paris, Larousse.

Merton, R. K., 1949, *Social Theory and Social Structure*, translated into French as *Éléments de théorie et de méthode sociologique*, 1965, Paris, Plon.

Michaud, 1997, "L'enfant et la nutrition: croyances, connaissances et comportements," *Cahiers de Nutrition et de Diététique*, 32, 1.

Michel, F., 1995, *En route pour l'Asie, le rêve oriental chez les colonisateurs, les aventuriers et les touristes occidentaux*, Éditions "Histoire et Anthropologie,"

Miller, J. and Deutsch, J., 2009, *Food Studies: An Introduction to Research Methods*, London, Bloomsbury.

Millet, J., 1995, "Manger du chien? C'est bon pour les sauvages!," *L'homme* 136.

Mintz, S. W., 1995, *Sweetness and Power: The Place of Sugar in Modern History*, New York, USA, Viking.

Mintz, S. W. and Du Bois, C. M., 2002, "The anthropology of food and eating," *Annual Review of Anthropology*, 31, 99–119.

Montanari, M., 1995, *La faim et l'abondance*, Paris, Seuil.

Morin, E., 1962, *L'esprit du temps*, Paris, Grasset, 1975.

Morin, E., 1973, *Le paradigme perdu: la nature humaine*, Paris, Seuil.

Morin, E., 1975, *L'Esprit du temps*, vol. 1, *Névrose*, Paris, Grasset.

Morin, E., 1977, *La méthode*, vol. 1, vol. 2, 1980, vol. 3, 1986, Paris, Point Seuil.

Morin, E., 1996, "Rationalité et rationalisation," in C. Fischler (Ed.), *Pensée magique et alimentation aujourd'hui*, Cahiers de l'OCHA, n° 5, 109–10.

Morin, E. and Piattelli-Palmarini, M. (Eds.); André Bejin, Irène Chapellaubeau, and Constantin Jelinski (collab.), 1974, *L'unité de l'homme: invariants biologiques et universaux culturels*, Paris, Seuil.

Moulin, L., 1967, "L'Europe à table," *Les Annales ESC*.

Moulin, L., 1974, *L'Europe à table, introduction à une psychosociologie des pratiques alimentaires*, Paris, Elsevier Séquoia.

Moulin, L., 1978, *La vie quotidienne des religieux au Moyen Âge*, Paris, Hachette.

Moulin, L., 1988, *Les Liturgies de la table*, Paris, Albin Michel.

Murcott, A., 1988, "Sociological and social anthropological approaches to food and eating," *World Review of Nutrition and Dietetics*, 55, 1–40.

Murcott, A., Ed., 1998, *The Nation's Diet: The Social Science of Food Choice*, London, Addison Wesley Longman.

Murcott, A., Belasco, W., and Jackson, P., Eds., 2013, *The Handbook of Food Research*, New York, USA, Bloomsbury Academic, 324–37.

Myers, A. and Rosen, J. C., 1999, "Obesity stigmatization and coping: relation to mental health symptoms, body image, and self-esteem," *International Journal of Obesity*, 23, 221–30.

Nahoum-Grappe, V., 1979, "La belle femme, ou le stade du miroir en histoire," *Communications*, 31, 22–32.

Nair-Venugopal, S., 2012, *The Gaze of the West: Framings of the East*, London, Palgrave Macmillan.

Najman, J. M. and Munro, C., 1982, "Patient characteristics negatively stereotyped by doctors," *Social Sciences and Medicine*, 16, 1781–89.

Naomichi, I., 1994, "Nourriture, cuisine" and "Manières de table," in A. Berque, dir., *Dictionnaire de la civilisation japonaise,* Paris, Hazan.

Nefussi, J., 1989, *Les Industries agro-alimentaires*, Paris, PUF.

Nestle, M., 2002, *Food Politics: How the Food Industry Influences Nutrition and Health*, California, USA, University of California Press.

Nestle, M., 2009, "Reading the food social movement," *World Literature Today*, 83(1), 37–39.

Nestle, N. and McIntosh, W. A., 2010, "Writing the food studies movement," *Food, Culture & Society*, 13(2), 159–68. http://www.foodpolitics.com/wp-content/uploads/02-FCS13.2-Nestle.pdf

Ngoc Hùu, 1997, "Les repas végétariens bouddhiques," in *Pratiques alimentaires et identités culturelles, Les études vietnamiennes*, n° 125 et 126, Hanoi, 515–32.

Nguyen Tung, 1997, "Les cuisines régionales existent-elles au Vietnam?," in *Pratiques alimentaires et identités culturelles, Les études vietnamiennes*, n° 125 and 126, 515–32.

Nicolaidis, S., 1992, "Quelques mécanismes des préférences alimentaires," in Giachetti, I., *Plaisir et préférences alimentaires*, Paris, Polytechnica.

NIH (National Institutes of Health), 1985, *Health Implications of Obesity*, Bethesda, National Institutes of Health.

Olivier de Sardan, J.-P., 1995, *Anthropologie et développement*, Paris, Karthala.

Omran, A., 1971, "The epidemiological transition," *Milbank Memorial Fund Quarterly*, 49(1), 509–38.

Ossipow, L., 1989, *Le végétarisme: vers un autre art de vivre?*, Paris, Cerf.

Ossipow, L., 1994, "Aliments morts, aliments vivants," *Autrement*, 149, 127–35.

Ostermann, G., 1997, "Aspects psychologiques de la rondeur: grâce et disgrâce!," *Diététique et médecine*, 5–9.

Padilla, M., Delpeuch, F., Le Bihan, F., and Maire, B., Eds., 1995, *Les politiques alimentaires en Afrique du Nord*, Paris, Karthala.

Pales, L. and Tassin de Saint Pereuse, M., 1954, *L'alimentation en AOF*, Organization for Research on Alimentation and Nutrition in Africa (ORANA), Dakar.

Parasecoli, F., 2013, "Food, cultural studies, and popular culture," in K. Albala (Ed.), *Routledge International Handbook of Food Studies*, Abingdon, UK, Routledge, 274–81.

Parasecoli, F. and Scholliers, P. (Eds.), 2012, *A Cultural History of Food*, vols. 1–6, London, Oxford, Berg Publishers.

Pascal, G., 1997, "L'évaluation de la sécurité alimentaire," *Cahiers de Nutrition et de Diététique*, 32(1), 17–18.

Passeron, J. C., 1993, "Portrait de Richard Hoggart en sociologue," Enquête. http://enquete.revues.org/175, online as of May 12, 2006, consulted on July 16, 2015.

Paturet, J.-B., 1992, *L'imaginaire vin*, Paris, OIV.

Paugam, S., 1991, *La disqualification sociale. Essai sur la nouvelle pauvreté*, Paris, PUF.

Paugam, S., 1993, *La société française et ses pauvres. L'expérience du revenu minimum d'insertion*, Paris, PUF.

Paul-Lévy, F., 1986, "A la fondation de la sociologie: l'idéologie primitiviste," *L'Homme*, n° 97–98.

Paul-Lévy, F., 1997, "Toxiques, épistémologisons, épistémologisons, il en restera toujours quelque chose," in J.-P. Poulain (Ed.), *Pratiques alimentaires et identités culturelles*, Études vietnamiennes n° 3–4, 163–204.

Paul-Lévy, F. and Segaud, M., 1983, *Anthropologie de l'espace*, Paris, Centre de Création Industrielle, "Alors" collection.

Pavageau, J., 1997, "Imaginaire alimentaire, projet de voyage et pratiques touristiques," in *Pratiques alimentaires et identités culturelles, Les études vietnamiennes*, n° 125 and 126, Hanoi, 599–622.

Péquignot, G., 1985, "Consommation alimentaire des Français. Tendances et risques d'après les données épidémiologiques disponibles," INSERM, Paris.

Périssé, J., 1996, "Typologie des disponibilités alimentaires par pays en 1990 basée sur un critère énergétique," in J.-F. Desjeux and S. Hercberg (Eds.), *La nutrition humaine, la recherche au service de la santé*, Paris, INSERM-Nathan.

Perusse, L., Bouchard, C., Leblanc, C., and Tremblay, A., 1984, "Energy intake and physical fitness in children and adults of both sexes," *Nutrition Research*, 4, 363–70.

Pfirsch, J.-V., 1995, "Beurre ou ordinaire?: L'ambivalence rituelle," in N. Eizner (Ed.), *Voyage en alimentation*, Paris, ARF éditions.

Pfirsch, J.-V., 1997, *Français allemands à table*, Rennes, Presses Universitaires de Rennes.

Phan, M.-Ch. and Flandrin, J.-L., 1984, "Les métamorphoses de la beauté féminine," *L'Histoire*, 68, 48–57.

Piattelli-Palmarini, M., 1996, "Les illusions cognitives," in C. Fischler, 1996c, *Pensée magique et alimentation aujourd'hui*, Cahiers de l'OCHA, n° 5, 25–29.

Picheral, H., 1989, "Géographie de la transition épidémiologique," *Annales de géographie*, XCVIIIème année, n° 546.

Pitte, J.-R., 1991, *Gastronomie française, Histoire et géographie d'une passion*, Paris, Fayard.

Pitte, J.-R. and Huetz de Lemps, A., 1990, *Les restaurants dans le monde et à travers les âges*, Grenoble, Glénant.

Poirier, J., Ed., 1990 and 1991, *Histoire des mœurs*, Paris, La pléiade, Gallimard.

Poitrineau, A., 1962, "L'alimentation populaire en Auvergne au 18ème siècle," *Hémardinquer*, 1970, 146–53.

Pollan, M., 2006, *The Omnivore's Dilemma: A Natural History of Four Meals*, New York, USA, Penguin Press.

Pollan, M., 2008, *In Defense of Food: An Eater's Manifesto*, New York, USA, Penguin Press.

Pool, R., 1987, "Hot and cold as an explanatory model: The example of Bharuch district in Gurajat, India," *Social Science and Medecine*, 25(4), 389–99.

Pouillon, J., 1972, "Manières de table, manières de lit, manières de langage," in *Destin du cannibalisme, Nouvelle Revue de Psychanalyse*, Paris, Gallimard.

Poulain, J.-P., 1984, *Le Limousin gourmand*, Toulouse, Privat.

Poulain, J.-P., 1985a, *Anthroposociologie de la cuisine et des manières de table*, Université de Paris VII, published by the Center for the Reproduction of PhD Theses, University of Lille.

Poulain, J.-P., 1985b, "Sens et fonction des appellations culinaires au 19ème," *Sociétés*, n° 6, Masson.

Poulain, J.-P., 1988, "Les racines du bien manger en Languedoc," in J. Clavel (Ed.), *Vins et cuisine de terroir en Languedoc*, Toulouse, Privat.

Poulain, J.-P., 1994, "L'essence et la saveur," *Autrement*, n° 149, 140–47.

Poulain, J.-P., 1995b, "Les dérives de 'l'approche qualité' dans la restauration collective," *Acts of the colloquium La qualité dans la restauration*, APASP.

Poulain, J.-P., 1996a, "Pour une anthroposociologie de l'alimentation," *Tourismes* n° 4, Université de Toulouse II.

Poulain, J.-P., 1996b, "Le cassoulet, histoire d'un plat," *Inventaire du patrimoine culinaire de Midi-Pyrénées*, Paris, Albin Michel.

Poulain, J.-P., 1997a, "Le goût du terroir à l'heure de l'Europe," *Ethnologie française*, XXVII, 18–26.

Poulain, J.-P., 1997b, "La nourriture de l'autre: entre délices et dégoûts, Réflexions sur le relativisme de la sensibilité alimentaire," in *Cultures, Nourriture*, Internationale de l'imaginaire, n° 7, Paris, Babel Actes-Sud, 115–39.

Poulain, J.-P., 1997c, "Postface à un inédit de J.-P. Aron," in *Cultures, Nourriture*, Internationale de l'imaginaire, n° 7, Paris, Babel/Actes-Sud., 39–47.

Poulain, J.-P., 1997d, "Mutations et modes alimentaires," Autrement, *Le mangeur et l'animal*, 172, 103–20.

Poulain, J.-P., 1997e, "La cuisine, c'est plus que des recettes," in *Pratiques alimentaires et identités culturelles, Les études vietnamiennes*, n° 125 et 126, Hanoi, 31–126.

Poulain, J.-P., 1997f, "On mange aussi du sens," *Communautés éducatives: Figures de l'obésité et conduites alimentaires*, 99, 16–21.

Poulain, J.-P., 1998a, "La modernité alimentaire: pathologie ou mutations sociales?," *Cahiers de nutrition et de diététique*, 33(6), 351–58.

Poulain, J.-P., 1998b, *Les jeunes seniors et leur alimentation*, Paris, Cahiers de l'OCHA, n° 9.

Poulain, J.-P., 1999a, "Les mutations contemporaines des pratiques alimentaires," *Lettre Scientifique de l'Institut Français pour la Nutrition*, 64, 1–12.

Poulain, J.-P., 1999b, "L'espace social alimentaire," *Cahiers de nutrition et de diététique*, 34(5), 271–80.

Poulain, J.-P., 2000, "Les dimensions sociales de l'obésité," in *Obésité, dépistage et prévention chez l'enfant*, Collective expertise, Paris, INSERM, 59–96.

Poulain, J.-P., 2002, *Sociologies de l'alimentation: les mangeurs et l'espace social alimentaire*, Paris, PUF.

Poulain, J.-P., 2009, *Sociologie de l'obésité*, Paris, PUF.

Poulain, J.-P., 2012, *Dictionnaire des cultures alimentaires*, Paris, PUF.

Poulain, J.-P., 2015, "The affirmation of personal dietary requirements and changes in eating models," in Claude Fischler (Ed.), *Selective Eating: The Rise, Meaning and Sense of Personal Dietary Requirements*, Paris, Odile Jacob, 253–64.

Poulain, J.-P. and Larrose, G., 1995a, *Traité d'ingénierie Hôtelière, Conception et organisation des hôtels, restaurants et collectivités*, Paris, Lanore.

Poulain, J.-P. and Neirinck, E., 2000, *Histoire de la cuisine et des cuisiniers, techniques culinaires et manières de tables en France du moyen âge à nos jours*, Paris, Lanore, 1st edition 1988, repr. 1992, 1997, translated into Japanese, 1994 and 1997, Spanish and Portuguese, 2000.

Poulain, J.-P. and Rouyer, J.-L., 1987, *Histoires et recettes de la Provence et du Comté de Nice*, Toulouse, Privat.

Poulain, J.-P. and Tibère, L., 2000a, "Évolutions des représentations nutritionnelles des jeunes seniors: 1966/1998," *Cahiers de nutrition et de diététique*, 35(1), 40–46.

Poulain, J.-P. and Tibère, L., 2000b, "Mondialisation, métissage et créolisation alimentaire, de l'intérêt du 'laboratoire' réunionnais," *Bastidiana*, n° 31–32, 225–41.

Poulain, J.-P., Gineste, M., and Delorme, J. M., 2000, "Le comportement alimentaire hors foyer et hors repas, quelle réalité? Perspectives d'avenir?," *Revue de Nutrition Pratique*, 13, 12–17.

Poulain, J.-P., Ed., in coll. with Delorme, J.-M., Gineste, M., and Laporte, C., 1996, *Les nouvelles pratiques alimentaires; entre commensalisme et vagabondage*, Ministry of Agriculture, "Food Tomorrow" program.

Poulain, J.-P., Ed. in coll. with Gineste, M. and Delorme, J.-M., 1999, *Aujourd'hui manger c'est choisir*, Ministry of Agriculture, "Food Tomorrow" program.

Poulain, J.-P., Ed. in coll. with Gineste, M. and Jeanneau, S., 1999, *Le mangeur en milieu médicalisé*, APHP-Université de Toulouse 2.

Powdermaker, H., 1960, "An anthropological approach to the problem of obesity," *Bulletin of the New York Academy of Medicine*, 33, 286–95.

Price, J., Desmond, S., Krol, R., Snyder, F., and O'Connell, J. K., 1987, "Family Practice Physicians' Beliefs, Attitudes and Practices Regarding Obesity," *American Journal of Preventive Medicine*, 3, 339–45.

Pynson, P., 1987, *La France à Table, 1945-1980*, Paris, La découverte.

Racaud, T., Volatier, J.-L., Babayou, P., and Collerie de Borely, A., 1997, *Les comportements alimentaires des Français en 1977*, Paris, CREDOC.

Radcliffe-Brown, A. R., 1992, *The Andaman Islander*, Cambridge, Cambridge University Press.

Raybaut, P., 1977, *Guide d'étude d'anthropologie de l'alimentation*, document multigraphié, Université de Nice.

Raybaut, P., 1997, "Pratiques alimentaires, compréhension et connaissance de l'autre," *Pratiques alimentaires et identités culturelles, Les études vietnamiennes*, n° 125 and 126, Hanoi, 539–48.

Rayner, G. and Lang, T., 2012, *Ecological Public Health: Reshaping the Conditions for Good Health*, London, Routledge.

Razel, F., 1882, *Anthropogéographie*, Engelhorm, Stuttgart.

Razzell, P. E., 1974, "An interpretation of the modern rise of population in Europe. A critique," *Population Studies*, 28, 1.

Reclus, E., 1869, *La terre: description des phénomènes de la vie du globe*, Paris, Hachette.

Renaud, M., 1987, "De l'épidémiologie sociale à la sociologie de la prévention: 15 ans de recherche sur l'étiologie sociale de la maladie," *Revue d'épidémiologie et de santé publique*, 35, 1.

Renaud, M., 1991, "The future: Hygiena versus Panakeia?," *Population Health Program*, Canadian Institute for Advanced Research, October.

Renaud, S., 1995, *Le régime Santé*, Paris, O. Jacob.

Retel, J.-O., 1965, *Les gens de l'hôtellerie*, Paris, Editions Ouvrières.

Revel, J.-F., 1982, *Culture and Cuisine: A Journey Through the History of Food* (Helen R. Lane, trans.), New York, Doubleday & Co., Inc.

Reynaud, J.-D., 1995, *Les règles du jeux, l'action collective et la régulation sociale*, Paris, Colin.

Richards, A., 1932, *Hunger and Work in a Savage Tribe: A Functional Study of Nutrition Among the Southern Bantu*, London, Routledge.

Richards, A., 1937, *The Food and Nutrition of Africans Natives*, International Institute of African Languages and Culture, Mémoire n° 13, cited by Goody, 1982.

Richards, A., 1939, *Land, Labour and Diet in Northern Rhodesia: An Economic Study of the Bemba Tribe*, New York and London, Oxford University Press.

Ricoeur, P., 1963, "Entretiens avec Lévi-Strauss," *Esprit*, n° 11.

Ritzer, G., 1995, *The MacDonalization of Society*, California, Pine Forge Press.

Rival, N., 1983, *Grimod de la Reynière: le gourmand gentilhomme*, Paris, Le Pré aux Clercs.

Rivière, C., 1978, *L'analyse dynamique en sociologie*, Paris, PUF.

Rivière, C., 1995, *Les rites profanes*, Paris, PUF.

Rochefort, R., 1995, *La société des consommateurs*, Paris, O. Jacob.

Roelofs, E. W., 1954, Food studies of young sciaenid fishes, *Micropogonias* and *Leiostomus* from North Carolina. Copeia 1954: 151–53.

Rolland-Cachera, M.-F., 2000, "Définition de l'obésité chez l'enfant," in *Obésité, dépistage et prévention chez l'enfant*, Collective expertise, Paris, INSERM.

Rolland-Cachera, M.-F., and Bellisle, F., 1986, "No correlation between adiposity and food intake: why are working class children fatter?" *American Journal of Clinical Nutrition*, 44, 779–87.

Rolland-Cachera, M.-F., Deeheeger, M., and Bellisle, F., 1998, "Increasing Prevalence of Obesity among 18-Year-Old Males in Sweden: Evidence for Early Determinants," *Acta Paediatricia*, 88, May, 365–67.

Romon, M., 1998, "Évaluation de l'apport alimentaire chez le sujet en restriction cognitive," *Cahiers de nutrition et de diététique*, 33(4), 249–52.

Romon, M., 1999, "Le renard et le petit Prince," *Cahiers de nutrition et de diététique*, 34(5), 257.

Rosnay, (de) J. and S., 1979, *Le mal bouffe*, Paris, Orban.

Rowley, A., 1994, *A table! La fête gastronomique*, Paris, Gallimard.

Rozin, P., 1976, "The selection of food by rats, humans and other animals," in J. Rosenblatt, R. A., Hinde, C. Beer, and E. Shaw (Eds.), *Advances in the Study of Behavior*, vol. 6, New York, Academic Press, 21–76.

Rozin, P., 1994, "La magie sympathique," *Autrement*, 149, 22–37.

Rozin, P., 1998a, "Réflexions sur l'alimentation et ses risques," in M. Apfelbaum (Ed.), *Risques et peurs alimentaires*, Paris, O. Jacob.

Rozin, P. and Fallon, A., 1987, "A perspective on disgust," *Psychological Review*, 94(1), 23–41.

Rozin, P., Gruss, L., and Berk, A., 1979, "The reversal of innate aversions: Attempts to induce a preference for chili peppers in rats," *Journal of Comparative and Physiological Psychology*, 93(6), 1001–14.

Rozin, P., Fischler, C., Imada, S., Sarubin, A., and Vrzesniewski, A., 1999, "Attitudes to food and the role of food in life in the USA, Japan, Flemish Belgium and France: Possible implications for the diet-health debate," *Appetite*, 33(2), 163–80.

Sabban, F., 1993, "Suivre les temps du ciel: économie ménagère et gestion du temps dans la Chine du VIe siècle," in Aymard, M., Grignon, C., Sabban, F. (Eds.), *Le temps de manger. Alimentation, emploi du temps et rythmes sociaux*, Paris, Éditions MSH-INRA, 81–108.

Sabban, F., 1996, "Art et culture contre science et technique. Les enjeux culturels et identitaires de la gastronomie chinoise face à l'occident," *L'Homme*, 137.

Sahlins, M., 1972, *Stone Age Economics*, Chicago, Aldine Atherton, translated into French as *Âge de pierre, âge d'abondance, l'économie des sociétés primitives*, Paris, Gallimard (1976).

Sahlins, M., 1976, *Culture and Practical Reason*, Chicago, University of Chicago Press, translated into French as *Au cœur des Sociétés: Raison utilitaire et raison culturelle*, Paris, Gallimard (1980).

Saint Pol, T. de, 2010, *Le Corps désirable, Hommes et femmes face à leur poids*, Paris, PUF, coll. "Le lien social".

Sansot, Pierre, 1990, "Identités territoriales et modes de restauration," in J.-R. Pitte and A. Huetz de Lemps (Eds.), *Les restaurants dans le monde et à travers les âges*, Grenoble, Glénant, 115–25.

Sauvageot, F., 1980, *L'analyse sensorielle: outil scientifique?*, Laboratoire de biologie physico-chimique, ENSBANA, Dijon.

Scardigli, V., 1983, *La consommation culture au quotidien*, Paris, PUF.

Schlosser, E., 2001, *Fast Food Nation: What the All-American Meal is Doing to the World*, London, England, Penguin Books.

Schütz, A., 1987, *Le chercheur et le quotidien*, Paris, Méridiens Klincksieck.

Ségalen, M., 1996, *Sociologie de la famille*, Paris, Armand Colin.

Serres, de O., 1600, *Théâtre d'agriculture*, Paris.

Serville, Y. and Trémolières, C., 1967, "Recherches sur le symbolisme des aliments et la signification du repas familial," *Cahier de nutrition et de diététique*, 1, 49–58.

Sharp, H. S., 1988, "Dry meat and gender: the absence of Chipewyan rituals for the regulation of hunting and animal numbers," in T. Ingold, D. Riches, and J. Woodburn (Eds.), *Hunters and Gatherers 2: Property, Power and Ideology*, Oxford, Berg.

Sigaut, F., 1993, "Alimentation et rythmes sociaux: nature, culture et économie," in M. Aymard, C. Grignon, and F. Sabban (Eds.), *Le temps de manger, Alimentation, emploi du temps et rythmes sociaux*, Paris, Éditions MSH-INRA.

Simmel, G., 1997, "Sociology of the Meal," in D. Frisby and M. Featherstone (Eds.), *Simmel on Culture: Selected Writings*, M. Ritter and D. Frisby (trans.), London, Sage, published in association with *Theory, Culture and Society*, Nottingham Trent University.

Singly, (de) F., 1996, *Sociologie de la famille contemporaine*, Paris, Nathan.

Singly, (de) F., 2000, *Le soi, le couple et la famille*, Paris, Nathan, collection Essais et recherches.

Skrabanek, P., 1994, "L'alimentation entre enfer et salut," *Autrement*, 149, 169–78.

Slovic, P., 1987, "Perception of risk," *Science*, 236, 280–85.

Slovic, P., 1993, "Perceived risk, trust and democracy," *Risk Analysis*, 13(6), 675–82.

Smith, R., 1889, *The Religion of the Semites*, Edinburgh.

Sobal, J., 1984a, "Marriage, Obesity, and Dieting," *Marriage and Family Review*, 7, 115–39.

Sobal, J., 1984b, "Group dieting, the stigma of obesity, and overweight adolescents: The contributions of Natalie Allon to the sociology of obesity," *Marriage and Family Review*, 7, 9–20.

Sobal, J., 1991a, "Obesity and nutritional sociology: a model for coping with stigma of obesity," *Clinical Sociology Review*, 9, 21–32.

Sobal, J., 1991b, "Obesity and socio-economic status: a framework for examining relationships between physical and social variables," *Medical Anthropology*, 13, 231–47.

Sobal, J., 1995, "The Medicalization and Demedicalization of Obesity," in D. Maurer and J. Sobal (Eds.), *Eating Agendas: Food and Nutrition as Social Problems*, New York, Adeline de Gruyter.

Sobal, J., 2000, "Sociability and the Meal: Facilitation, Commensality, and Interaction," in *Dimensions of the Meal*, Gaithersburg, Maryland, USA, Aspen Publishers.

Sobal, J. and Stunkard, A. J., 1990, "Socio-economic status and obesity: A review of the literature," *Psychological Bulletin*, 105, 260–75.

Sokal, A. and Bricmont, J., 1998, *Fashionable Nonsense: Postmodern Intellectuals' Abuse of Science*, New York, Picador, USA.

Soler, J., 1973, "Sémiologie de la Nourriture dans la Bible," *Annales ESC*, 943–55.

Sorcinelli, P., 1996, "L'alimentation et la santé," in J.-L. Flandrin and M. Montanari (Eds.), *Histoire de l'alimentation*, Paris, Fayard.

Sorre, M., 1943, *Les fondements biologiques de la géographie humaine*, Paris, Armand Colin.

Stevens, J., Cai, J., Pamuk, E., Williamson, D. F., Thrun, M., and Wood J. L., 1998, "The effect of age on the association between body mass index and mortality," *New England Journal of Medicine*, 338, 1–7.

Stigler, G. J., 1954, "The early history of empirical studies of consumer behaviour," *Journal of Political Economy*, LXII-2, avril.

Stouff, L., 1970, *Ravitaillement et alimentation en Provence aux 14ème et 15ème siècles*, Paris, Mouton.

Straus, R., 1957, "The nature and the status of medical sociology," *American Sociological Review*, 22, 200–04.

Strourdze-Plessis, M.-N. and Ströhl, H., 1979, "La connaissance du mangeur," in J. Duvignaud (Ed.), *Sociologie de la connaissance*, Paris, Payot.

Sylvander, B., 1988, "L'alimentation service: résultats d'enquêtes," Toulouse INRA—Économie et sociologie rurales.

Sylvander, B., 1991, "Conventions de qualité et lien social sur les marchés agro-alimentaire," *Pour*, 129, 35–46.

Symons, M., 1994, "Simmel's gastronomic sociology: an overlooked essay," *Food and Foodways*, 5(4), 333, 351.

Terence, I., 1996, *Le monde de la grande restauration en France*, Paris, L'Harmattan.

Thouvenot, C., 1974, "Les habitudes alimentaires dans la France du Nord-Est, essai de géographie alimentaire et sociale," thèse d'état de géographie, Université de Paris I.

Thouvenot, C., 1977, *Le pain d'autrefois*, Lesson-Masson.

Thouvenot, C., 1996, "Terroirs, aliments et mangeurs au fil de l'histoire," in I. Giachetti (Ed.), *Identités des mangeurs, images des aliments*, Paris, Polytechnica, 55–89.

Tibère, L., 1997, "Contribution à une approche sociologique de la découverte de l'altérité alimentaire dans le voyage," in *Pratiques alimentaires et identités culturelles, Les études vietnamiennes*, n° 125 and 126, Hanoi, 569–98.

Tibère, L., 2000, "Métissage et créolisation alimentaires," XVI Congrès de l'AISLF, *Une société-monde*, Québec.

Tibère, L., 2016, "Food as a factor of collective identity: The case of creolisation," *French Cultural Studies*, 27(1), 85–95.

Topalov, A.-M., 1986, *La vie des paysans bas-alpins à travers leur cuisine, de 1850 à nos jours*, Aix en Provence, Edisud.

Torny, D., 1998, "Inquiétude, alerte et alimentation: vers une politique de la vigilance?," in M. Apfelbaum (Ed.), *Risques et peurs alimentaires*, Paris, O. Jacob.

Toutain, J. C., 1971, "La consommation alimentaire en France de 1789 à 1964," *Économie et sociétés*—Cahiers ISEA, 5, 11, 1909–2049.

Trémolières, J. and coll., 1968, *Manuel élémentaire d'alimentation humaine*, Paris, ESF.

Trémolières, J., 1969, *Biologie générale*, 4 volumes, Paris, Dunod.

Trémolières, J., 1970a, "Base pour l'étude de l'évolution des habitudes alimentaires," *Cahiers de nutrition et de diététique*, 5(3), 85–92.

Trémolières, J., 1970b, Article "Faim," in *Encyclopédia Universalis*.

Trémolières, J., 1971, "Pollutions et nuisances: un nouveau mythe," *Cahiers de Nutrition et Diététique*, 6(3), 25–28.

Trémolières, J., 1975, *Partager le pain*, Paris, Robert Laffont.

Trémolières, J., 1977, *Nutrition, Physiologie, comportement alimentaire*, Paris, Dunod, Bordas.

Trémolières, J. and Trémolières, C., 1989, *Diététique et art de vivre*, Paris, Hatier.

Turner, B. S., 1982, "The government of the body: Medical regimens and the rationalisation of diet," *British Journal of Sociology*, 33(2), 254–69.

Valade, B., 1996, *Introduction aux sciences sociales*, Paris, PUF.

Valéri, R., 1971, "The state of food habits research in France," in Ethnological Food Research in Europe and USA: Reports from the First International Symposium for Ethnological Food Research, Lund, 1970, Nils Arvis Bringeus and Günter Wiegelman, Eds., Otto Schwartz and co.

Van Itallie, T. B. and Simopoulos, A. P., 1982, "Obésité: état ou maladie," *Médecine digestive et nutrition*, 18, 14–21.

Vanel, L., 1992, *Saveurs et humeurs*, Toulouse, Daniel Briand.

Vangrevelinghe, M., 1970, "Les enquêtes I.N.S.E.E.," *Cahiers de nutrition et de diététique*, 5, 3.

Vanhoutte, J.-M., 1984, *La relation formation emploi dans la restauration travail salarié féminin, fin des chefs cuisiniers et nouvelles pratiques alimentaires*, Sociology thesis, supervised by H. Mendras, Paris X-Nanterre.

Vanhoutte, J.-M., 1989, "Le cuisinier, nouvel animateur de la vie urbaine?," *Autrement*, n° 108, 112–19.

Verdier, Y., 1966, "Le repas bas normand," *L'Homme*, 3, 92–111.

Verdier, Y., 1969, "Pour une ethnologie culinaire," *L'Homme*, 9(4), 125–35.

Verdier, Y., 1979, *Façons de dire, façons de faire. La laveuse, la couturière, la cuisinière*, Paris, Gallimard.

Vialles, N., 1987, *Le sang et la chair—Les abattoirs des pays de l'Adour*, Paris, Maison des Sciences de l'Homme.

Vicaire, G., 1890, *Bibliographie gastronomique*, Reprints Slatkine.

Vincent, J.-D., 1986, *Biologie des passions*, Paris, Odile Jacob.

Volatier, J.-L., 1998, "Évolution des comportements alimentaires des seniors et rôle des médecins généralistes," CREDOC.

Volatier, J.-L., 2000, *Enquête INCA sur les consommations alimentaires*, CREDOC-AFSSA, Paris, Tec et Doc.

Voth, H. R., 1901, "The Oraibi Soyal ceremony," Field Columbia Museum Publication, 55 *Anthropological Series*, 3, 1.

Warde, A., 1997, *Consumption, Food and Taste*, London, Sage.

Warde, A., 2016, *The Practice of Eating*, Oxford, Polity, John Wiley & Sons.

Warnier, J.-P., Ed., 1994, *Le paradoxe de la marchandise authentique. Imaginaire et consommation de masse*, Paris, L'Harmattan.

Weber, M., 1964, *L'éthique protestante et l'esprit du capitalisme*, Paris, Plon.

WHO (World Health Organization), 1998, *Obesity: Prevention and Managing the Global Epidemic*, Report of WHO Consultation on Obesity, (WHO/NUT/NCD/98.1), Geneva.

Williams, R., 2011, "Culture is ordinary," in I. Szeman and T. Kaposy (Eds.), *Cultural Theory: An Anthology*, Chichester, UK, Wiley-Blackwell, 53–59. (Original work published in 1958.)

Wilson, C. S., 1981, "Food in a medical system: Prescriptions and proscriptions in health and illness among Malays," in A. Fenton and T. M. Owen (Eds.), *Food in perspective: Proceedings of the Third International conference on ethnological food research*, Cardiff, Wales, 1977, Edinburgh, John Donald Publishers.

Wilson, E. O., 1987, *Sociobiologie. La nouvelle synthèse*, Monaco, Éditions du Rocher.

Wolinsky, F. D., 1980, *The Sociology of Health: Principles, Professions and Issues*, Boston, Little, Brown.

Zarca, B., 1990, "La division du travail domestique. Poids du passé et tensions au sein du couple," *Économie et statistique*, 228(1), 29–40.

Zeldin, T., 1977, 1973, *A History of French Passions 1848-1945*, Oxford, Clarendon Press. Translated into French as *Histoire des passions françaises*, 1979 Paris, Encre.

Zeldin, T., 1979, *Histoire des passions françaises*, Paris, Encre.

Zelem, M.-C., 1999, "L'évolution de la fonction froid, les modes d'utilisation et les attentes des utilisateurs," Le froid domestique, *Les Cahiers du CLIP*, 11, 9–15.

Ziegler, O., 2000a, "Le comportement alimentaire et ses désordres," *La Revue du Praticien*, 50, 521–25.

Ziegler, O., 2000b, "Aspects nutritionnels des obésités," in INSERM, *Obésité dépistage et prévention chez l'enfant*, 131–63.

Index

Lightning Source UK Ltd.
Milton Keynes UK
UKHW020231140721
387136UK00003B/77